Religions of immigrants from India and Pakistan

"For the originality and importance of the topic alone this book promises to be a benchmark in the field."
Mark Juergensmeyer, University of California, Berkeley

Landmark changes in the immigration law of 1965 admitted to the United States large numbers of immigrants from India and Pakistan. The religious groups formed by these new immigrants have exerted and will continue to exert significant influence upon the fabric of American religion and culture. This book is the first comprehensive study of the religious groups formed in the United States by Asian-Indian and Pakistani immigrants and of their patterns of adaptation and organization. Professor Williams provides an overview of the variety of religions practiced by these new immigrants, examining Hindu, Muslim, Christian, Sikh, Jain, Zoroastrian, and Jewish communities, and the size and character of the various groups formed. Through analysis of demographic statistics as well as information gathered in extensive interviews with religious group participants, Professor Williams examines the trajectories of adaptation charted by these groups through their involvement in a wide range of ecumenical, ethnic, sectarian, and national organizations.

Detailed descriptions of Swaminarayan Hindus and Nizari Ismaili Muslims, two diverse religious communities, illustrate the national growth of immigrant religious groups and the formative power of their adaptive strategies, while religious profiles of Asian-Indian and Pakistani religious groups in Chicago and Houston illustrate varying patterns of development on the local level. In addition to examining the historical development of these groups, Professor Williams assesses the current problems and prospects of Asian-Indian and Pakistani religious organizations and the influence of these groups on the shape of religion in America.

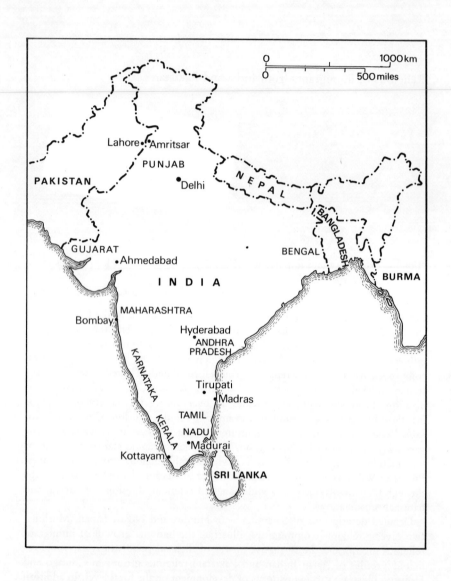

Religions of immigrants from India and Pakistan

New threads in the American tapestry

RAYMOND BRADY WILLIAMS
Wabash College

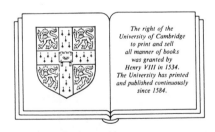

CAMBRIDGE UNIVERSITY PRESS
Cambridge
New York   New Rochelle   Melbourne   Sydney

For friends and colleagues
Eric Dean, Hall Peebles,
David B. Greene, and William C. Placher

Published by the Press Syndicate of the University of Cambridge
The Pitt Building, Trumpington Street, Cambridge CB2 1RP
32 East 57th Street, New York, NY 10022, USA
10 Stamford Road, Oakleigh, Melbourne 3166, Australia

© Cambridge University Press 1988

First published 1988

Printed in the United States of America

Library of Congress Cataloging-in-Publication Data
Williams, Raymond Brady.
Religions of immigrants from India and Pakistan.
Bibliography: p.
1. East Indians – United States –Religion.
2. Pakistanis – United States – Religion. 3. East Indian
Americans – Religion. 4. Pakistani Americans – Religion.
I. Title.
BL2525.W49 1988   291'.089914073   87–23895

British Library Cataloguing in Publication Data
Williams, Raymond Brady.
Religions of immigrants from India and
Pakistan: New threads in the American
tapestry.
1. South Asians – United States – Religion
2. United States – Emigration and
immigration
I. Title
291'.089914073   BL2520

ISBN 0 521 35156 1 hard covers
ISBN 0 521 35961 9 paperback

Contents

Preface

Many Americans celebrated the Fourth of July 1986 by rekindling the light of the Statue of Liberty – a symbol of immigration to a land of liberty, opportunity, and religious freedom. At the same time, recent immigrants were kindling sacred fires for the dedication of a temple for Rama and Sita in Chicago. Immigrants have always brought their religions and reshaped them in the United States. The first amendment to the Constitution provides the substance of religious freedom of which the Statue of Liberty is the symbol, and temples such as the one in Chicago are the embodiment. This work is about the exercise of that freedom by recent immigrants from India and Pakistan.

Research on Swaminarayan Hinduism (Williams, 1984) introduced me to the lives of these immigrants, to their rapidly growing religious organizations, and to the importance of religion in their cultural adaptation. The data in this study are based on questionnaires received from 369 of more than 700 Asian-Indian and Pakistani religious organizations and from personal correspondence and conversations with officers of those organizations. Between 1984 and 1986 I conducted several hundred interviews, especially in Chicago and Houston, and I attended scores of ceremonies, festivals, dedications, and social gatherings. Some of these people were naturally suspicious of a person asking questions about immigration, family, occupation, and organizational infrastructure; he may be an undercover agent for a governmental agency – the Immigration and Naturalization Service, the Internal Revenue Service, the Federal Bureau of Investigation, or the Central Intelligence Agency. I am grateful to those who overcame their suspicions and were able to share detailed personal information, and I hope the result of the research is worthy of their trust.

I urged each immigrant family I spoke with to preserve a detailed record of their experiences of immigration and of their efforts to establish themselves in the United States so they can pass that story on to their American children and grandchildren. The present work is, in part, an attempt by an outsider to preserve a record of early institutional development and the role of religion among these immigrants.

Many words from the Indian subcontinent have become regular parts of English vocabulary; others remain, at least for now, quite foreign. The result is that any decision about the use of italics and diacritical marks in the text seems arbitrary. The practice in this work is to italicize the first appearance of words about which some question may arise. Each of those words appears in the glossary with a brief definition or description. I have used the form of transliteration most often used for its words by each group in the United States.

Grants from the Rockefeller Foundation, the Eric Dean Fund, and the Faculty Development Fund of Wabash College supported this research. A McLain-McTurnan-Arnold Research Fellowship provided me with freedom from teaching and administrative responsibilities in the spring of 1986, enabling me to concentrate on writing.

My friends and colleagues, including Dr. David Maharry, Director of the Cragwall Computer Center, and Mr. Larry Frye, Head Librarian of Lilly Library, and their associates at Wabash College did everything they could to make the work of research and writing a pleasure. Dr. John Swan, Ms. Debbie Polley, and Ms. Ann Lebedeff expanded Lilly Library to research size by their skilled assistance. Professor Paul Mielke helped prepare my photographs for publication. Mr. Jim Nye and Mr. William Alspaugh of Regenstein Library at the University of Chicago also gave valuable assistance. Mr. Shams Vellani and the staff of the Institute of Ismaili Studies in London provided access to valuable resources and expertise. The Fellows of Fitzwilliam College and Westminster College, Cambridge, showed me many acts of kindness as a visiting scholar. Throughout my teaching career I have learned a great deal from Wabash College students, and Mr. Chris Coble and Mr. Keith Winton were excellent assistants during this work. No research is done in isolation, as bibliographical references make clear, and I am grateful to those whose work provided the context for this research.

Professors Eric Dean and William C. Placher commented on drafts of the entire manuscript, and other scholars, including Mr. Shams Vellani, Mr. Stephen Gelberg, Professor Mark Juergensmeyer, Professor Arif Ghayur, Dr. Ralph Strohl, Dr. Ahmad Sakr, Professor Basheer Khumawala, and leaders of several religious organizations, read relevant portions. I am grateful for their assistance because they saved me from errors of fact and interpretation.

Lois, my wife, was a regular companion on visits to homes of immigrants, at religious ceremonies, and at interviews with leaders; her insights, often derived from reflection on conversations with women, added depth of understanding in this study as in all things.

No person has better colleagues than those whose companionship I enjoy in the Religion Department of Wabash College. Their friendship and excellence as teachers and scholars are sources of great pride, and this work is dedicated, with gratitude for many years of pleasant association, to Eric Dean, Hall Peebles, David B. Greene, and William C. Placher.

Raymond Williams
Wabash College

Introduction

The "new threads" in the subtitle of this book represent immigrants from India and Pakistan; new ethnics who have entered the United States since the landmark change of the immigration law in 1965. Prior to that few Asian Indians – the designation had not even been formed – or Pakistanis became permanent residents, but now they are present in large numbers in every city and visible in most small towns. Their languages, arts, cuisines, and religions are threads of many colors and different textures newly interwoven in our common life. Their religious organizations, in which they gather in large numbers, and sacred buildings, which dot the urban landscape, are part of the regrouping and reformation of religious traditions that are changing both the image and the texture of American religion. To the "Protestant, Catholic, Jew" of the earlier immigrants must be added the Muslim, Hindu, Sikh, Jain, St. Thomas Christian, and Indian Jew of these new immigrants.

"Tapestry" conjures up a nonconfrontational image. The emphasis is upon the preservation of distinctive colors and textures of various groups in the process of adaptation, not on the melting into a new "global theology" or "civil religion." Indeed, the establishment of distinctiveness through the formation of ethnocentric groups provides a means of negotiating both personal and group identity in the new setting. Another area of emphasis is the integration of new, but distinct, elements in the evolving social fabric of religious life in the United States. Something could go frighteningly wrong, however; when new threads of colors and textures not used before are woven into a tapestry, the whole thing could become a travesty or be rent asunder. A more positive outcome, much to be desired, is the enrichment and strengthening of the whole. Knowledge of the various strands is essential if understanding and appreciation of the constantly changing tapestry is to result.

Although immigrants and refugees from many countries have entered the United States since 1965, the focus of this study is on immigrants, not refugees, from India and Pakistan admitted under the preference categories of the Immigration Law of 1965. The complex political and religious history of the Indian subcontinent and multiple emigrations from there to various parts of the world make it difficult to specify what is meant by "Asian Indian" and "Pakistani" in the United States. The ancestors of some of these immigrants had left the Indian subcontinent for East Africa, England, or Burma before the partition of India and Pakistan, certainly before the separation of Bangladesh. In this study, "Asian Indian" refers to those who designate themselves "of Indian origin" even though they may have emigrated from Uganda, Burma, or some other country. "Pakistani" is also used as a self-designation of origin and is not necessarily a designation of the nation-state from which a person entered the United States: It is the designation of a passport written on the heart.

Bangladeshis are not treated separately in this book because so few have emigrated and because they are generally hidden among Indian Muslims or Bengali Hindus; their national identity is not strong. Buddhists from Sri Lanka and Nepal are absent from this study for two reasons, even though South-Asian Buddhist groups exist in the United States: Their inclusion would require involvement with the large groups of recent refugees from Southeast-Asian Buddhist countries, an emigration pattern different from that of Asian Indians and Pakistanis[1]; it would also presuppose a treatment of the substantial Buddhist population among the earlier immigrants from East Asia.

Three propositions summarize the main conclusions reached in the research and presented in this study. These concern the creation of immigrant groups, the role of religion in personal and group formation, and variations in the function of religion among immigrants.

1.   Immigrant groups are created by specific legal decisions, economic opportunities, and social forces that bring them into existence and shape them at a certain place and time. The point is obvious, but its implications are often overlooked. Hinduism, for example, functions differently in the United States than in India because the religion is being reformulated as a minority religion in the new setting. Sikhism functions differently in Canada than does Sikhism in the United States because the patterns of emigration are different and the resulting religious groups face different problems of adaptation.

Canada and the United States share similar immigrant religious groups – Sikhs, Swaminarayan Hindus, Nizari Ismailis, St. Thomas Christians, and so forth – albeit in different proportions, but only religious organizations in the United States are the subject of this work. Canada's long association with the Indian subcontinent through the British Empire and in the Commonwealth provided a context for emigration, creating a unique immigrant community that has more in common with the Asian immigrants of Britain than with the Asian Indians of the United States. Britain and Canada share, for example, many Asian refugees from Uganda and persons from Kenya and Tanzania with Commonwealth travel papers. No one is an "Asian Indian" in Canada, Britain or India, only in the United States – and that is an important fact.

2. Religion is important for some immigrants in the formation and preservation of personal and group identity. Religious commitments and ties, including ties to families and religious leaders in India, provide for continuity with the past, which is essential to identity. A person without memory has no identity. Once in the United States, both group and personal identity is re-formed in a social process that involves concrete decisions on the part of the immigrants and members of the host society.[2] Religion is a powerful mechanism for establishing this identity because, in the United States, it is an accepted mode both of establishing distinct identity and of intercommunal negotiation; religion grounds personal and group identity in a transcendent sacred reality, and religion and religious groups thus provide a context for the socialization of children of immigrants and for complex negotiations between the generations. Strategies of adaptation and the role of religion in the formation of personal and group identity are central to the establishment of immigrant religious groups.

Many secular organizations also contribute to identity formation, and there are many Asian Indians and Pakistanis who do not participate in religious activities: Immigration provides freedom to break religious ties as well as to reformulate them. Few of the immigrants from India or Pakistan are vocally antireligion, however, even though some complain about the proliferation of religious organizations, ghettoization of the community by attempts to create "little Indias" in the United States, and the "waste" of money in costly construction of religious shrines when the community needs a financial base for building a secure future. In the 1981 census of India, only 24,086 persons identified themselves as atheists – over half of them in the state of Tamil Nadu – and it is difficult to identify those among the immigrants who could provide the counterpoint in a study of the role of religion. Thus this study covers only a part of the immigrant community: those who attend religious ceremonies, are members of religious organizations, and responded in the interviews and to the questionnaires used in this study.

3. The several religions covered here function differently for different immigrants because of individual variations in majority and minority status, social location, theological affirmations and commitments, history,

and especially national, ethnic, sectarian, or ecumenical commitments. Permission to emigrate was granted to individuals from a fairly narrow range of educational and professional scales, but no selection was either possible or attempted by government officials on the basis of religious affiliation. The immigrants thus represent all the major religious traditions present in India – Hindu, Muslim, Christian, Jain, Sikh, Parsi, and even Jewish. This study encompasses all of these in an attempt to illustrate the variations that have developed in adaptive strategies and how each religion functions differently in the formation and preservation of individual and group identity. The religious tapestry contains many colorful threads in different patterns contributed by these newcomers, and not all weavers work the same.

The goals of this study include providing clear and accurate information about the growth and development of the new religious organizations serving Asian-Indian and Pakistani immigrants across the United States and making a contribution to the study of the role of religion in identity formation and adaptation by immigrants in the United States.

Part One provides an overview of the people and their religions, showing that even though immigrants are selected from within a narrow range of the educated, professional elite, they nevertheless represent not only diverse religious traditions, but also various ethnic, regional, and linguistic groups. This great diversity existing alongside a basic class unity provides a good field for our study. Chapter One describes the immigrants from India and Pakistan through the analysis of demographic statistics and information from interviews to answer such questions as who they are, how they got to the United States, why they are so successful, and why the religious and cultural situation is so confused. Basically, the chapter reveals that what "Asian Indian" and "Pakistani" mean results from decisions made by the host society through immigration policy and decisions made by the immigrants as they shape new identities. The focus of the chapter is on the general role religion plays in the adaptation of the immigrants to the United States and on the relation of religious affiliation to ethnic identity.

Chapters Two and Three present an overview of each of the religions and religious organizations founded by and serving the new immigrants, first those that have their origin in the Indian subcontinent (Hinduism, Jainism, and Sikhism) and then those that migrated to the Indian subcontinent (Islam, Christianity, Zoroastrianism, and Judaism). Information about the development of these groups in every section of the country was provided by questionnaires and interviews with leaders. Attendance at meetings and visits to the homes of leaders in New York, Dallas, Indianapolis, St. Louis, Boston, and New Orleans provided primary material for these chapters, supplemented by the material on Chicago and Houston in Part Three.

Part Two focuses on case studies of adaptive strategies developed as immigrants relate to already established religious groups and as they develop their own national organizations with contrasting adaptive strategies. Although this study is of immigrant religion, Hindu, Muslim, and Sikh immigrants discovered "American cousins" in the United States in the International Society for Krishna Consciousness, the American Muslim Mission, and the Sikh Dharma Brotherhood, and they formed several types of relationships with these American cousins. Chapter Four deals with these three groups, not exhaustively, but only as they relate to the immigrant community. Separate studies are needed to trace the development, impact, and future of the hundreds of religious organizations with some ties to India and Pakistan that have attracted both white and black Americans; these serve different functions of group and identity formation that are outside the scope of this work.

Pictures taken from different angles and scale expose new aspects of any living organism, and so it is in the study of immigrant religion. A complete picture requires a treatment not only of the forms of major religions, but of types of local organizations and groupings, the complexity of the metropolitan centers that house them, and the development of the various denominational or sectarian forms. Groups develop longitudinally across the country, with national administrative structures, personal and organizational lines of communication, and a sense of close identification. Chapters Five and Six trace the development of two small but well-organized and rapidly growing groups that have developed national identities, the Swaminarayan Hindus and the Nizari Ismaili Muslims. These were chosen because their national character illustrates the general ways in which religious groups develop and spread throughout the country, and also because they represent distinct strategies of adaptation. The basic doctrines of the groups and the ways these developed in the past are important in shaping the direction of adaptation in America. Swaminarayan Hinduism is a powerful agent in the preservation of Gujarati ethnic identity and also preserves linguistic and regional ties with Hinduism in Gujarat. Leaders of Nizari Ismailis say that they preserve a Muslim tradition that is ecumenical in scope, with followers from several ethnic groups and many countries. Their strategy is to maintain religious unity through allegiance to the *Imam* without attempting to preserve any particular ethnic identity, a strategy they hope will allow both assimilation into American society and preservation of religious identity. Thus these two national groups illustrate both longitudinal growth and contrasting strategies of adaptation.

Part Three develops religious profiles of Asian-Indian and Pakistani immigrants in two metropolitan areas – Chicago in Chapter Seven and Houston in Chapter Eight – and provides a different angle and scale for picturing the growth and function of religious organizations. These metropolitan areas are sufficiently compact that a study could include material from personal contact with every organization. Although materials from contacts in larger metropolitan areas are included in other chapters, New York and Los Angeles are so spread out and so ethnically complex that it is not possible in the scope of this study to have personal contacts with and detailed information from every religious group in those metropolitan areas. Chicago and Houston, however, provide a good test of continuities and discontinuities of development because Chicago experienced an early and steady growth of Asian-Indian and Pakistani immigrants of diverse professional backgrounds, whereas Houston had a delayed and rapid growth related to the oil and space industries, followed by a deep recession. Thus these two chapters demonstrate two perspectives on growth of religious organizations in metropolitan areas, structurally through the growth of the major religious traditions in Chicago in Chapter Seven, and diachronically in Chapter Eight, which follows the rapid growth of the immigrant community and then its decline during hard times in Houston. The Conclusion traces trajectories in the dynamic of adaptation by religious groups and summarizes problems and prospects shared by immigrant religious groups as they make new homes under the aegis of the Statue of Liberty. These trajectories move from the most inclusive to the exclusive – ecumenical, national, ethnic, and sectarian – and affect the modes of adaptation and identity formation. Asian-Indian and Pakistani immigrants and the religious traditions they bring with them and reshape in the United States will certainly have a significant impact on American religion and culture. The wish of this author is that those who read this book will be able to place their new neighbors and acquaintances in appropriate religious contexts and that the book will contribute to interreligious and intercultural understanding and harmony.

PART I

The people and their religions

Immigrants from India and Pakistan have arrived in significant numbers since 1965 as part of the "new ethnics." Each immigrant comes as a private individual, selected by impersonal preference categories in the immigration laws and impelled by individual initiative. Soon, however, these individuals become identified by the groups through which they express their ethnicity and negotiate their relations with the host society. That is the point at which the variegated patterns of these new threads become apparent and begin to reshape the image of the whole tapestry.

Religion is an important aspect of the formation and preservation of personal and group identity, and recent immigrants from India and Pakistan provide a good study of its role. They have a great deal in common as part of the relatively young, well-educated, professional elite of the "brain drain" from the developing countries, at the same time representing most of the major communal groups of the Indian subcontinent.

The first three chapters identify these new immigrants and show how the various types of religious organizations they have established function to reshape and preserve their communal identities in the United States. Chapter One provides a social and economic profile of the immigrants. Chapters Two and Three introduce the variety of religions and religious organizations that serve them.

CHAPTER 1

A new pattern
Made in the U.S.A.

This study deals with the ways in which religious organizations shape and are shaped by the life of Asian-Indian and Pakistani immigrant communities in the United States. Even that short statement of the topic points to an odd fact: Asian Indians are "made in the U.S.A." This ethnic group does not exist as such in its country of origin and its members come to be transformed through a process of assimilation in American society. Rather, the category "Asian Indian" is a new creation in the United States, the shape and content of which is determined by members of the host society and by the new immigrants themselves. "Asian Indian" and "Pakistani" are official designations given by the census bureau, at the urging of the Association of Indians in America and some other groups, as special minority categories in the 1980 Census to take account of the rapidly growing population of immigrants with a heritage in the Indian subcontinent. Prior to the 1980 Census, immigrants from India were simply classified as Caucasian; now they are classified as an ethnic minority within the "Asian or Pacific Islander" classification. The designation as a minority group was a conscious decision of the U.S. government made possible, perhaps even necessary, by earlier governmental decisions. The determination of what the designation "Asian Indian" and "Pakistani" would mean required complex decisions by the immigrants and by other members of society. Religious organizations in the United States founded by and serving these immigrants have had a significant role in this decision-making process.

Emigrants from the Indian subcontinent have gone to other countries as temporary or permanent residents for well over a century, and in each place they have formed new minority groups, each with its own peculiar character due to the varying political and economic forces that led to that particular migration and social and cultural context. "Asian Indian" is now an accepted designation for immigrants to the United States from

9

India, although it and other such designations are not very precise. The designation in East African countries is "Asian," referring to a group with a different migratory pattern, longer residence in the area, different age distribution, and different occupational patterns. In Britain, the designations "Asian" or "Paki" refer to a social group created by migratory forces, immigration laws, and economic and professional opportunities quite different from those that have led to the presence of the Asian Indians of the United States. Michael Leonardo refers to the "metaphorical use of community," which labels thousands of individuals, unknown to one another, living often hundreds of miles apart, with different ideologies, and speaks of them in a folksy manner as if they were "village women meeting at the village well." He points out that labeling a collection of humans as a community or a social category confers upon it a hoped-for alliance of interest, solidarity, and tradition (Leonardo, 1984:134).

Minority communities of immigrants are of temporary character in the sense that the forces that call the community into existence and shape its character are transitory and specific to a particular locality and time. Immigrants and their descendants designated as an ethnic minority may persevere for decades and beyond, but the group originally came into existence through transitory decisions and forces, and thus the community is affected by revisions of these decisions. Variations among the communities of immigrants from India in East Africa, England, and the United States illustrate how quickly they change.

The major emigrations from India to East Africa took place in the first half of this century under the aegis of British colonial rule to provide laborers for the building of the railroad and other economic developments. Asians became well-established there until the trauma of independence of African nations and Africanization led to a great exodus. The emigration to Great Britain originating from East Africa and India began to be significant after World War II, when laborers entered a flourishing economy, and the number of Asian immigrants was greatly expanded by the flood of refugees in the late 1960s and early 1970s. Significant growth in the numbers of Indian immigrants to the United States took place in the 1970s and continues in the 1980s at an increased rate. More immigrants from India came in the single year of 1982 than came in all the years prior to 1960. Prior to 1965 a few Indian graduate students elected to remain in the United States, but they were a tiny and inconspicuous minority. The major immigration as part of what has been termed "the new ethnics" took place following the enactment of the immigration act of 1965. Because the communities in East Africa, Britain, and the United States result from different waves of migration, they differ significantly in size, age, length of residence, social standing, level of institutional organization, and manner of adaptation to the host society.

The immigrants in this study have established themselves in the United States within the short period of the past two decades. The social characteristics they share as occupants of a fairly narrow range of the social and economic class structure, regardless of ethnic group or religion, are balanced by the diversity of the group in regional–linguistic ethnicity and in religious affiliation. This diversity provides the material to study the effects of the various religious traditions on the process of adaptation to the new pluralistic cultural and religious situation.

Religions and identity

Immigrants are religious – by all counts more religious than they were before they left home – because religion is one of the important identity markers that helps them preserve individual self-awareness and cohesion in a group. It is common for the young professional to remark that although he was not very religious while at university in India or Pakistan, he now takes his family to the temple or mosque regularly. All of the major religions present in the Indian subcontinent are in evidence among the immigrants as shown by letters to editors of Asian-Indian and Pakistani newspapers, which complain that too many organizations – ethnic, caste, professional, and religious – request financial support from new immigrants. It is true that religious organizations make regular requests for support; furthermore, they are successful in gaining allegiance and contributions to support many programs, activities, and building projects.

All of the major religious traditions of the Indian subcontinent – Hindu, Muslim, Sikh, Jain, Christian, Parsi, Jewish, and many subsects and denominations – are in the process of adaptation to the new social setting. The context and relation of the religions vary in different parts of India, and change dramatically in the United States. Although adherents of various forms of Hinduism command a massive majority in parts of the Indian subcontinent and also among immigrants, they do not sustain that majority in other regions of the subcontinent; adherents of other religions, Christianity included, are dominant in some territories. Thus, the relation of religious affiliation to a particular ethnic tradition varies according to regions and undergoes changes in the new setting.

In the United States, religion is the social category with clearest meaning and acceptance in the host society, so the emphasis on religious affiliation and identity is one of the strategies that allows the immigrant to maintain self-identity while simultaneously acquiring community acceptance (Rutledge, 1982:96). That makes religion one of the most powerful of the value systems or ideologies of social groups. Apart from its spiritual dimension, religion is a major force in social participation; it develops and at the same time sacralizes one's self-identity, and thus the religious bond is one of the strongest social ties. Migration, however, forces reformulation of the religious identity.

Travel to places where one's traditional ways of believing and acting are not observed threatens anomie. The future is connected with the past by the slender thread of memory. For these reasons travel outside of the Indian subcontinent was traditionally circumscribed by threats of ritual impurity. The danger always exists that the plausibility structure of the religion and of the cultural symbols related to it will be destroyed. In the past that meant that certain forms of ritual purification had to be undertaken when returning home (Berger, 1969:50). Now the pattern is to try to establish ancillary supports for the structures of the religions that will enable continued faithfulness to the religious tradition. Religion sacralizes identity for the immigrant by associating the symbolic structures of meaning with the sacred past and transcendent realities in consort with a supporting group. Mol indicates that the mechanisms of sacralization of systems of meaning and definitions of reality can be observed in at least four elements of religion: objectification – the projection of order into a beyond where it is less vulnerable to contradictions, exception, and contingencies and where it can be preserved in the face of serious dislocations; commitment – the emotional anchorage of the various proliferating foci of identity; ritual – the repetitive actions, articulations, and movements that prevent the object of sacralization to be lost; and myth – the integration of the various strains in a coherent, short-hand, symbolic account (Mol, 1977:14–15).

Religious affiliations are not the same as ethnic structures; religious categories can harbor several nationalities and ethnic groups. Thus, a Punjabi may be either an Asian Indian or a Pakistani or, perhaps, a citizen of Kenya whose ancestors left the Indian subcontinent before partition. A Bengali may be Asian Indian or Bangladeshi or a citizen of Canada who left Bengal before Bangladesh separated from Pakistan. The Punjabi may be a Muslim, a Sikh, or perhaps a Christian. Her Gujarati neighbor in a Chicago suburb may be a Hindu, a Jain, or a Muslim born in Ahmedabad, Bombay, Mombasa, London, or Chicago. An immigrant can choose to emphasize one of several designations according to the context – American, Asian Indian, Gujarati, Hindu, or Swaminarayan – and designations by relatives and friends overlap in interesting and sometimes confusing configurations.

Although religious identity is often a significant aspect of ethnic culture, it is difficult to establish the exact relation between the two, whether the religious affiliation is essential to the ethnic community or if religious orientation is only ancillary to ethnic identity. Our sample from the Indian subcontinent clearly shows that the two are not identical. Indeed, immigrants use different aspects of their various religions to develop new patterns of adaptive strategies. Four patterns are in evidence among immigrants – ethnic, national, sectarian, and universal – but these are rarely found in pure form. Ethnic religious groups stress a union of religious devotion and regional–linguistic identity. Their common language, cuisine, dress, customs, and ties to their previous homeland are stressed in religious meetings and literature. For example, elements of Sikh rhetoric in the United States identify Sikh religion with Punjabi culture, whereas the Durga Puja incorporates many elements of Bengali culture and artistic tradition in the religious celebration. Such a union of religion and ethnic culture is attractive for members of the first generation of immigrants. National identity is a powerful force in modern India and Pakistan, and it is enhanced as a strategy of adaptation by the official census designation "Asian Indian" and "Pakistani." Some representatives of the Rashtriya Swatamsevak Sangh identify Indian nationalism with Hinduism, whereas officials of Pakistan speak of Islam as the national religion. The religious groups based on national identity that are formed in the United States may prove to be more effective for the second and third generations. The sectarian pattern of adaptation is characterized by allegiance to a particular religious hierarchy. Elements of the other patterns may be present, but these are mediated through a religious leader who, as the living symbol of the hierarchy, has the authority to adapt the tradition to its new context. The pattern of universality is stressed in those religions claiming to transcend the boundaries of language, religion, and nation. This pattern is tested in places of migration because in the native place virtually all members of a particular religion share the same ethnic culture and identity. This ethnic identity and religious pluralism exist in India, as in Kerala where all the Christians are Malayalee Christians, and in Pakistan, where all Muslims are Pakistanis; thus, universality becomes concrete only when the emigrant moves from an ethnic region to an area that is both ethnically and religiously pluralistic.

Religions have a different role among immigrant members of minority groups in the United States from that in India. Just as Asian Indians are made in the United States, so are Asian-Indian Hindus, Muslims, Sikhs, and so forth. These religious groups are new – they have different leadership and peculiar constituencies, and changed functions. The influence is reciprocal; new religious affiliations brought by immigrants to the United States affect the identity of the immigrant community and its surrounding society, while, at the same time, the move to the new setting transforms the religious tradition itself. It is the intensity of this reciprocal relationship that leads to the increased participation in religious affairs by many of the new immigrants. Religious affiliation, along with professional status and ethnic affiliation, both reflects the unity and diversity of the immigrant community and establishes lines of identity formation.

Unity: Doctors, nurses, engineers, scientists, and families

Prior to 1965 the few Indians who migrated to the United States were permitted to come in two small groups. Although the first immigrant came from India in 1820, it was not until the beginning of this century that more than 275 persons came from India in a single decade (INS, 1982:2–4). A pronounced movement from British Columbia into the states of Washington, Oregon, and California occurred in the latter months of 1907, following a serious antioriental riot in Vancouver on September 7 (Jacoby, 1979:161). The Sikh farmers, who faced many difficulties in the movement from Canada down through Washington and into California, formed a community that is still influential in Sikh affairs in the United States.[1]

Antagonism caused by the influx of numerous laborers from Asia led to the restrictive Immigration Act of 1917, which included India as part of the Asiatic Barred Zone and thereby made it virtually impossible for people from India to enter the country legally as permanent residents. Their opportunity for citizenship was further restricted in 1923 by a decision of the United States Supreme Court that ruled that Indian immigrants were not "free white persons" within the law and, therefore, were not eligible for citizenship. Many certificates of citizenship that had previously been issued were withdrawn. Not until 1946 did the Luce–Celler Bill remove India from the barred zone and make it possible for immigrants from India to become citizens. Even then only one hundred persons a year were allowed to enter (Wenzel, 1968:250–1).

The primary policies in effect until 1965 were established by the Immigration Act of 1924 and the Nationality Act of 1952 (McCarran–Walter Act), which assigned to each country an annual quota based on the national origin of the population of the United States in 1890. This perpetuated the pattern of the "old immigration," with approximately 90 percent of the quotas reserved for persons from northern and western Europe. The acts did permit students to enter for education, and thus the second group of Indian immigrants were mainly from among the large number of students who came to the United States for higher education, some of whom were persuaded to stay after they developed skills that were in great demand.[2] A few became very prominent in their fields – they are sometimes referred to as "the pioneers" – but the community was very small and relatively invisible. From 1820 to 1960 a total of only

13,607 persons emigrated from India, and an unrecorded number of these departed (INS, 1982:2–4).

The change since the act of 1965 is astounding. The 1980 Census of the United States recorded 387,223 Asian Indians and another 15,792 Pakistanis (USCen2:2).[3] People from the Indian subcontinent are now among the fastest growing immigrant groups in the United States, and some estimates place the current number between a conservative 525,000 and 800,000 permanent residents (Saran, 1985:26).[4] The changes in the Immigration Act of 1965 proposed by President Kennedy and signed by President Johnson at the Statue of Liberty (PL, 1965) are primarily two: in the countries of origin and in the education and professional status of immigrants. The act repealed the quotas based on the national diversity of the United States population in 1890 and replaced it with an annual limitation of 170,000 immigrants (now raised to 270,000) for countries outside the Western Hemisphere. For the first time since the 1920s, a person's right to enter the United States did not depend on the country of birth or, as immigrants rejoice in saying, on race. In the five years from 1965 to 1970, the volume of immigration increased about 30 percent and the geographic origins of the immigrants shifted so that the Eastern Hemisphere contributed a greater share; immigration from Europe and Canada fell sharply while migration from Asia increased. One change that had significant impact on the students from the Indian subcontinent was the provision that allowed persons who had entered the United States with a visitor's or student visa to change their status to that of resident alien. After 1978, however, a limit was set at 20,000 immigrants per year per country. In the decade between 1951–60 only 1,973 persons from India emigrated to the United States; by 1980 the number for one year was 22,607 and in 1982 it was 21,738 (INS, 1982:6). The change in the numbers is dramatic.[5]

Also dramatic have been the changes in the educational and professional background of the immigrants. The decisions reflected in the immigration laws led to the selection primarily of persons from the educated elite of their native countries. After 1965, the new immigrants came from educational and economic backgrounds quite different from those of the old immigrants. President Johnson signed the new act under Emma Lazarus's lines: "Give me your tired, your poor, / Your huddled masses, yearning to breathe free . . . / Send these, the homeless tempest-tossed, to me . . . ," but those who came are part of the "brain drain" from the Third World to the Western industrialized countries. They are the doctors, engineers, professors, and technicians, along with members of their families.

The Immigration Act of 1965 established an immigrant visa allocation system of preferences for the annual permitted number (which currently is a total of 270,000 for all countries). The preferences are:

First: Unmarried sons and daughters of U.S. citizens and their children: 20% or 54,000

Second: Spouses and unmarried sons and daughters of permanent resident aliens: 26% or 70,200

Third: Members of the professions of exceptional ability and their spouses and children: 10% or 27,000

Fourth: Married sons and daughters of U.S. citizens, their spouses and children: 10% or 27,000

Fifth: Brothers and sisters of U.S. citizens (at least 21 years of age) and their spouses and children: 24% or 64,800

Sixth: Workers in skilled or unskilled occupations in which laborers are in short supply in the United States, their spouses and children: 10% or 27,000

Nonpreference: Other qualified applicants. Any numbers not used above. (INS, 1982:viii)

Because few persons had previously emigrated from the Indian subcontinent, the first immigrants after 1965 came under the third and sixth preference categories in fields then designated by the Department of Labor as ones with shortages. Entry now requires a specific job offer and a labor certification, which are harder to obtain. A listing of the fields demonstrates the selection that was made: Accounting and Auditing, Architecture, Chemistry, Engineering (several branches), Mathematics, Nursing, Pharmacy, Physical Therapy, and Physics. A number of skilled occupations were included under the sixth preference: Chefs, Draftsmen, Machinists, Medical Technologists, Systems Engineers (data-processing), Technicians, Tool-and-Die Makers (IAMR, 1968:67–8). As a result of this selection process, the majority of persons who entered were of relatively high educational and professional status.[6]

Physicians were prominent among the new immigrants until 1977, and India became the world's largest exporter of doctors. Prakash Desai, a psychiatrist at the University of Illinois, reports that there are now around 20,000 Indian physicians and as many as 700 psychiatrists in the United States, more psychiatrists than in India itself (R. Singh, 1983:41). Several reasons are given for the increased importation of physicians. In the public sector, the basic change occurred in 1966 with the Social Security Amendments that established Medicare and Medicaid. Private health insurance plans were extended to many families. Because native physicians tended to establish practices in attractive, wealthy areas, a maldistribution of physicians in the health service system resulted. There were 4,000 to 6,000 unfilled positions per year in the inner-city hospitals (Ishi, 1982:42). Because physicians had priority as immigrants between 1966 and 1977, the number grew rapidly, reaching its peak in 1972 when 46 percent of all new physicians licensed in this country were foreigners who had been trained abroad. As a result of these developments between 1963 and 1973, 65 percent of the net increase in the ratio of physicians to population was attributable to the presence of physicians of foreign birth trained as undergraduates in other countries. Seventy-five thousand foreign trained physicians entered the United States in the decade from 1965 to 1975, and by 1974 about one-fifth of all physicians in the United States were graduates of foreign medical schools, as were one-third of all residents and interns in the hospitals (Smith, 1979:486–8). Many Indian physicians who came to the United States went on to provide significant leadership and financial support for Asian-Indian organizations.

It is common for Asian Indians to speak of their community as having two main occupational groups: doctors and engineers. That was certainly true of the immigrants in the decade after the change in the law. Of the 46,000 employed Indian immigrants in 1974, 16,000 were engineers, 4,000 were scientists, and 7,000 were physicians or surgeons, and the next year 93 percent of the Indians admitted were classified as either "professional/ technical workers" or "spouses and children of professional/technical workers" (I. Singh, 1979:41). The perceived shortage of physicians was temporary, however, even in inner-city hospitals, and by 1985, 78.4 percent of alien graduates of foreign medical schools who applied for residencies were not placed (CHE, 1986:4). It is no longer easy for physicians, engineers, and those in many of the other technical occupations to get labor certification and immigrant status.

During the early years after the change in the law, however, the consequence of the selection process was a group of highly educated and successful new immigrants. Nine out of ten were high school graduates, and two out of three were college graduates. Parmatma Saran's survey of several hundred Asian Indians in New York recorded that more than half had postgraduate degrees at the master's level or above, 26 percent for the married women and 79 percent for their husbands (1985:27). Only 16 percent of the overall population of the United States over the age of 25 is comprised of college graduates. Almost half of the immigrants over sixteen years of age born in India were employed in what are designated "professional specialty occupations." Many entered the United States for graduate study in one of the preferred occupations and changed their status to permanent resident after they were offered positions in this country: Nine out of ten in Saran's study of families in New York came as students, and later changed their immigration status (1985:92). Some of these had returned to India, but finding little opportunity to practice their profession at the level they had come to expect, or becoming frustrated with the bureaucratic malaise that restricted their advancement, they decided to return to the United States as immigrants.

The income of Indians living in the United States is very high; the median household income in 1979 ranked second highest among ethnic groups in the country at $25,644.[7] (The median household income for the entire country was $16,841.) The percentage of men in the work force was 89.4, which was predictable, but a surprising fact is that over half of the women were employed. Those from Pakistan had a slightly lower median income at $20,067, but that is probably due to the fact that a larger percentage of Pakistanis are more recent immigrants.

Such success should not obscure the difficulties that were faced and overcome by many of the young men. Many students arrived without any means of support and tell stories about real privation when they worked at several jobs in order to support themselves in school. Others tell about coming to New York with an Indian professional degree that was not immediately recognized. They lived at the YMCA or in cheap rooming houses and worked at odd jobs as dishwashers or janitors until they could complete the certification appropriate to the United States. Some underemployment still exists so that, even though they make more money than would be possible in India, some occupy positions inferior both to those their credentials might command and to those occupied by others with the same training. Illegal immigrants find it very difficult to practice a professional occupation unless they can arrange marriage to a citizen or permanent resident, which will permit them to change their status. In addition, the downturn of the United States economy in the early 1980s led to the layoff from high-paying jobs of many of these recent immigrants, so that many are unemployed and trying to enter new fields or open small shops and businesses. Even though the community as a whole is very successful and relatively wealthy, there are some among what one unemployed Asian Indian called "the educated poor" because their skills were not needed after the recent recession. Every researcher has interviewed at least some immigrants who are without jobs, and, for whatever reason, consider themselves to be failures. They do not earn enough to live in the United States, and they are too ashamed to return to India as failures in the eyes of those who sent them to the land of plenty. There were 3,176 families of those who emigrated from India between 1970 and 1980 whose income for 1979 was below the poverty level (USCen3:Table 255A).

Young families are quick to bring relatives for family reunification, which is encouraged by the current immigration laws, and which is changing the makeup of the Asian-Indian and Pakistani communities. The Immigration Act of 1965 established as its second preference category the spouses and unmarried children of permanent resident aliens, and as the fifth the sisters and brothers of adult U.S. citizens and their spouses and children. In the first instance the preference categories allow the immigrants to send for their wives – or, as in the case of Kerala nurses, their husbands – and their children to join them after they establish themselves in the new location. It also permits permanent residents who return to India or Pakistan for arranged marriages to bring the new spouse back to the United States. American citizens and those who hold permanent resident status are preferred marriage partners because marriage conveys legal rights to migrate under the family unification program, both to the marriage partner and to his or her siblings. Thus, the number of those eligible for entry under the family reunification preferences increases exponentially. The emigration of spouses, parents, siblings, and children continually renews the immigrant community, while establishing strong international familial relationships.

Most now arrive under the provisions for family reunification. In 1982, the most recent year for which data are available, 16,964 persons from India immigrated, only 2,208 of whom were admitted under the third and sixth preferences as professionals or skilled workers. The percentages for immigrants from Pakistan are roughly the same.[8] The rest entered under family reunification provisions, and these did not have to present educational or professional credentials to gain resident status. Indeed, few of these immigrants have the high level of attainment that marked the earlier arrivals, and some tensions exist within the Asian-Indian community as a result. The complaint is that many of these nonprofessionals are ill prepared to make a living in the United States and therefore become a burden to their relatives. The most recent immigrants face the frustration of wanting to succeed and to have the material benefits and status that characterize the earlier immigrants, but, having fewer skills, are relegated to the least-paid menial jobs. Just as the German Jews expressed dismay and animosity toward the East-European Jews who followed them to the United States, so the doctors and engineers from India express some resentment against the untrained new immigrants from India. Differences in social status, educational background, and goal expectations create tensions in some of the organizations of the Asian-Indian community.

A few of the couples have brought their parents to reside permanently with them. Family ties are very strong in Indian and Pakistani society, and it is the duty of children to take care of their parents. Even so, the number of persons over the age of sixty in 1982 amounted to only 1,748. The grandparent generation is almost absent from the Asian-Indian community, and that fact has important implications for the transmission of cultural traditions, especially the religious traditions, which in India are transmitted primarily by the grandparents. The immigrants tend to take their children back to India for visits and send them for holidays with their relatives while they are small. As the children reach the teenage years, it is more common for the grandparents to travel from India to the homes of their sons for extended stays. Generally, however, elderly parents and grandparents prefer to keep their residence in India, where they are known and where they feel comfortable with the daily routine and customs. To have to spend their days confined and isolated in a city apartment or in a house in the suburbs is foreign to the customs they practiced in India. Moreover, the parents' financial and social situation in India itself is frequently improved dramatically by the migration of some of their children to the United States.

New immigrants from the Indian subcontinent were able quickly to establish themselves in the professional class and move into affluent suburbs, so Asian Indians are not found in ghettos. Predictably, large numbers are found in the states of major metropolitan centers,[9] but even in the metropolitan areas of Chicago and Houston the Asian Indians do not live within narrow geographical limits, but rather are spread throughout the suburbs near other professional families (USCen2:8). Other Asian Indians are scattered in towns and cities across the country. In the census listing by place of residence of minority groups, out of 370 urbanized areas of 50,000 or more, only three did not have a number of Asian Indians, and of some 680 towns and cities of more than 50,000 only twenty did not include some Asian Indians (USCen4:Table 248). Many small towns have several Asian-Indian physicians. Thus, although some Indian shopping areas with Indian food stores, restaurants, and clothing and appliance stores are located in areas that become known as "Little Indias," the population itself is scattered throughout the metropolitan areas and across the country. Urban organizations and religious institutions serve a dispersed population of Asian Indians.

Students from India continue to come to the United States: In 1983–4 the number was 13,730, placing India in seventh place as regards the number of students in U.S. institutions (after Taiwan, Iran, Nigeria, Malaysia, Canada, and Korea; CHE, 1984:21). Indian students are scattered in institutions across the country. It is, however, much more difficult now for them to change their status to that of permanent residents.

The United States immigration policy to give priority to the best educated, the professionals, brought those who could make the most rapid adjustment to the new setting. In some senses these were marginal persons in their country of origin: They were among the elite who had been trained in scientific and technical fields imported from the Western countries; the first fruits of the attempt at universal education after independence. Most had both their early schooling and their university education in English, and except for some difficulties with accent were able to make the adjustment to the language and to the technical requirements of their new positions in the United States.

Even though we have noted some change in the background and training of many who are arriving under the family reunification provisions, the community as a whole is successful. Those who know them well consider Asian Indians well educated, technically trained, energetic, and relatively prosperous. They may well be the most talented and easily acculturated of all immigrants in the long history of American immigration. They left India under Prime Minister Indira Gandhi or Prime Minister Moraji Desai, politicians of the old India, and return to visit an India under Prime Minister Rajiv Gandhi, a person from the same class of technocrats as they.

They arrived in the United States at a time of emphasis on ethnicity and when governmental decisions were changing the role of government in racial and ethnic relations. These changes have encouraged the formation of distinct communal identities, such as Asian Indians, to promote a hoped-for alliance of interest, solidarity, and tradition. Soon after arrival these new immigrants had the skills and economic power to establish the networks and pressure necessary to have the Asian-Indian category added to the governmental lists of ethnic – not racial – minorities. This was possible because of a change in governmental policy that Milton Gordon describes as significant for the future of pluralism in the country (Gordon, 1981:182–3). He contrasts the liberal pluralism that characterized legal policy in the past with corporate pluralism, which seems to be the direction of current governmental policy. The issue is whether to treat persons as individuals before the law or as members of a categorically defined group. In liberal pluralism the government gives no formal recognition to categories based on race or ethnicity. Social and political reasons exist for persons to wish to be recognized in a designated minority group, but legal ones do not. In corporate pluralism, on the other hand, the racial and ethnic entities are given formal standing as groups both in the national polity and under the law. This places a positive value on corporate cultural diversity and encourages its perpetuation. Recent governmental decisions regarding affirmative action procedures in employment and stipulated public programs show a move in the direction of a corporate pluralistic future for the country.

A majority of today's immigrants can be identified as members of minority groups who satisfy the affirmative action requirements imposed on employers and schools. The designation of "Asian Indian" as a distinct minority group in the 1980 Census conferred special legal rights on the individuals as members of a designated group, and the highly skilled early immigrants and their families have now joined those favored by programs intended to assist groups who have been deprived. The decision of the Small Business Administration to grant minority status to the Asian Indians and to make them eligible for the Agency's program to promote minority entrepreneurship was a development that had great value for this already relatively prosperous community (FR, 1982).

The anomaly of a middle-class group with almost twice the national median income seeking minority status caused some within the community to oppose the move. The Indian League of America resisted the drive toward minority status for fear that the hostility of whites and other established minority groups might be directed against the Asian Indians (Fornaro, 1984:30). The feeling was that if Hispanics and Blacks suddenly found that they were competing against highly educated Asian Indians for the few jobs and small business loans they were eligible for under affirmative action, they would resent it and produce a backlash. However, the new group of immigrants from the Indian subcontinent that came under the family reunification plan makes the provisions of the affirmative action programs even more important for Asian Indians because this new group of immigrants does not have the educational or professional preparation of their predecessors. The whole community has gained benefits – social, cultural, legal, and economic – from their new designation as minority groups; now the difficult task is to shape decisions that will determine what that designation means.

Immigrant groups are shaped by reverse migration also, and some individuals do return to India and Pakistan, but the number is small considering the fact that most immigrants came with the intention of returning to the Indian subcontinent after completing their studies or after earning enough for a secure future. Saran reported that the overwhelming majority of Indians indicate that they wish eventually to return to India (Saran, 1985:108), but his data differs from this research; perhaps the variation is due to the adjustments in responding to a fellow immigrant or to a white representative of the majority population. Saran indicates, however, that very few make any definite plans to return, so their expressed desire exists in a vacuum. The considerable nostalgia immigrants feel for India may lead them to speak vaguely about returning to India for retirement.

The forces that join to cause the immigrants to stay are numerous. Those who are successful have attained a standard of living and professional satisfaction difficult to duplicate in India, whereas those who have not been successful are left without the necessary resources to return and establish themselves in family and career without considerable embarrassment. When they first come, they feel loyalty and responsibility toward their parents and other relatives in India, but these ties are weakened as they marry and become parents of American children. None of the members of the second generation who were interviewed wished to return to India for a career, with the single exception of a very religious young man contemplating monastic vows that would take him to India to serve his sect. It is impossible, of course, for immigrants to return to the same India they left. Those who left India in the 1960s and early 1970s are removed from the changes that have taken place in Indian society and politics, which include both secularization and modernization. In spite of regular visits to India, their memories of India do not reflect the India of today. With rare exceptions, therefore, those immigrants who gain permanent resident status will remain in the United States. A common joke among Indian immigrants who meet each other after a prolonged period is: "I see that you're still earning your passage back to India" (Badhwar, 1980:16).

The well-educated, professional, young men and women in technical fields whose skills were needed in the economy of the United States were able as a group to attain a status within a fairly narrow range of the upper-middle class in their new home. Thus the designation "Asian Indian" does not mean only the immigrants from India or the Indian subcontinent who occupy a designated social status; it refers also to the new shape or shapes of the Asian-Indian community they are creating in the new place. Ethnic groups are made, not born, despite the fact that race is involved. They are made by conscious choices in which people decide, because it suits their interests to do so, to emphasize certain differences rather than the similarities between peoples. Therefore the term "Asian Indian" is being defined by the immigrants themselves as they create their own organizations and cultural groups. An immigrant might well declare that he or she was not an Asian Indian until arrival in the United States.

Diversity: Gujarati, Malayalee, Sikh, Punjabi, and children

Individuals do bring their identities – they are not a tabula rasa upon which is stamped "Asian Indian" – yet identity can be differently perceived and variously named according to context. Charlotte Chapman caught this truth in her description of the Sicilian immigrant: In America he will be an Italian to all members of other nationalities, a Sicilian to all Italians; in Sicily, he will be Milocchese; in Milocca, he tends to remain a Piddizzuna who has moved (quoted in Tomasi, 1975:168). The immigrant from the Indian subcontinent is an Asian Indian in America; in India, he is a Gujarati; in Gujarat, he is a Patel; among Patels, he is known as Sunav Patel who moved. The clan, the village, the caste, the region, and even the country are thereby progressively transmuted, but never lost or forgotten in the process of adapting to the expectations of a pluralistic society and a new definition of identity.

Immigrants have come from many parts of India, and even though they generally fall into the class of the modern technological elite, they represent other divisions in India – divisions of language, region, caste, political group, and religion. Asian Indians do not come to the United States as a unified group, nor is "Asian Indian" even a primary ethnic designation they consider for themselves when they arrive. Pressures exist, however, to become known as Asian Indians. Seemingly, persons in the host society generally do not have enough knowledge of the Indian subcontinent to understand the other distinctions that could be made. "Patel" and "Singh" are regarded as last names. For the majority of U.S. citizens, the identification of a group requires elements of a fairly simple ethnic map based on national origin; thus, Asian Indian and Pakistani.

The real situation is not so simple. John Bodnar argues against the notion that any group of immigrants can be seen as a unity; rather, it has been badly fragmented into numerous enclaves arranged by internal status levels, ideology, and orientation. Group fragmentation is a most important aspect of the dynamics of immigrant adjustment. Thus, a whole range of competing ideologies, leaders, and models of life shape the ultimate pattern of immigrant adjustment (Bodnar, 1985:xvii). The multiple fragmentation found on the Indian subcontinent results in a great diversity when members of these groups become immigrants, creating difficulties for those who attempt to catalogue and interpret their experience. Even official governmental statistics are confusing.

Within this century what was once a unified political unity under British control was partitioned into two nations – India and Pakistan (East and West) – in 1947 and then experienced another division when the civil war in Pakistan led in 1971 to the separation of Bangladesh in the east from Pakistan in the west. Thus, Pakistani, Bangladeshi, and Indian are indications of nationality within the framework of the modern nation-state. When the Immigration and Nationalization Service calculates the nation of accountability for immigrants, it does so on the basis of the nation-state of citizenship. Thus, one can determine only the numbers of persons who enter the country from the various nations of the Indian subcontinent. That calculation proves to be different from that of nation of birth; for example, all persons from the subcontinent above the age of forty were born in an undivided India.

The history of migration from India has confused the picture further because the children of those persons who left an undivided India for East Africa, Britain, and other parts of the British empire earlier in this century became known as Asians in Africa and Asians or Pakis in Britain. As some of these now enter the United States from their parents' adopted country – the country of their birth – they are counted against the immigration quota of that country and become Asian Indians in the United States. Asian Indians from East Africa or Britain have a different experience of migration than do those from independent India or Pakistan.

They have already lived as minority groups away from India and as such have developed the professional, ethnic, social, and religious groups that molded their identities. No way exists in the official calculations of the United States government to distinguish, for example, between Asians and Africans among those who emigrate from Kenya, nor between those who came originally from territory that is now included in India and those from what is now Pakistan.

Within India and Pakistan the major ethnic distinctions are those between regional–linguistic groups. The regional–linguistic composition of the people of the Indian subcontinent is extremely complex, partly because of the diversity of peoples brought into the modern nation-states: Gujarati, Punjabi, Bengali, Tamil, Malayalee, and Sindhi are terms denoting ethnic affiliation, not ties to national boundaries. Within Pakistan alone there are five major languages: Urdu, Punjabi, Sindhi, Pashto (Pushtu), and Baluchi (Bruhi). Urdu, the official language, is a mixture of Hindi, Persian, Arabic, and Turkish, written in the Persian script. Among Pakistanis in the United States it is estimated that 80 percent speak either Punjabi (50%) or Urdu (30%) as their primary language. They represent the ethnic groups that are most highly educated and thus most likely to have the professional standing needed to gain entry (Ghayur, 1980:768). In India the ten Indo-European languages of the north and west and the four Dravidian languages of the south are the basis of divisions into cultural–linguistic regions, some of which have been recognized in state boundaries. The southern region includes four major subcultures in four states: Tamil Nadu, where Tamil is the principal language; Kerala, where the language is Malayalam; Mysore, where the language is Kannada; and Andhra Pradesh, where Telugu is spoken. The ten languages of the north and west are Hindi, Gujarati, Punjabi, Bengali, Rajasthani, Marathi, Kashmiri, Assamese, Bihari, and Oriya. These are not as distinct from one another as are the south Indian languages and they shade into each other. In addition, these ten linguistic regions share general characteristics that contrast with those of the south (Walpole et al., 1964:99). The official languages of India as established in the Indian constitution are Hindi and English; the presence of English as an "all-India language" is a result of the linguistic diversity of India and is very important for immigrants from the Indian subcontinent – virtually all of them, except for a few new brides and elderly parents, are fluent in English.

A person may be identified as a member of one of these regional–linguistic groups – Punjabi, Malayalee, Gujarati, and so forth – no matter what his place of residence. The designation refers not so much to his geographic residence as to the complex of language, culture, and social customs that provide the basis of his identity. In contemporary India, persons with these designations are scattered throughout the major cities; Gujaratis and Bengalis, for example, are prominent in Bombay and Delhi. A Punjabi may have his native place in Pakistan or India, and yet may be the heir of three generations of residence in East Africa. A Bengali may have his native place in India or Bangladesh. A Gujarati may be from a Marathi-speaking area of Bombay or from East Africa via London. Even with such extensive geographic distribution, the various groups are marked by distinct caste hierarchies, marriage customs, language, and food patterns, to say nothing of the religious diversity that is the focus of the next chapters.

"Asian Indian" and "Pakistani," self-designations by permanent residents and citizens in the United States, are generalized terms, and as such do not provide for careful distinction among various categories such as those we have just illustrated. "Asian Indian" is one of six Asian minority designations (Asian Indian, Chinese, Filipino, Japanese, Korean) listed on the census forms. Those who designate themselves as Pakistani or Bangladeshi, also recognized groups, must use a blank space marked "other." Of the 387,223 persons who chose the designation Asian Indian, including some who might have roots in the areas now known as Pakistan and Bangladesh, the vast majority are of Indian origin. Some 15,792 persons in the sample designated themselves as Pakistani and 4,989 as Bangladeshis in the 1980 Census. Statistics are not available for the various regional–linguistic groups, for the various castes, or for religious groups in the United States. The best estimates suggest that approximately 40 percent are Gujaratis and 20 percent are Punjabis (R. Singh, 1983:44), and that the rest are distributed among the other regional–linguistic groups, with Bengalis, Tamils, Telugu, and Malayalee in significant numbers. These figures comport with the careful analysis that John Fenton has made of the Asian-Indian population in Atlanta (1985:5).

The Asian-Indian population in the United States has a different constitution from that of other countries with significant numbers of immigrants. Ursula King gives the numbers for the various groups in Britain from research at the University of Leeds (King, 1983:3–4). Muslims from Pakistan, Bangladesh, and India number 353,610; Sikhs from the Punjab 304,950; Hindus from Gujarat and the Punjab 306,941; and Christians and other groups from India 68,809; for a total East-Indian population of 1,034,310. According to the official 1981 census of Canada, there are 196,395 people living in Canada who claim their origin in the Indian subcontinent. The Canadian census takes account of religious affiliation: The Sikh community in Canada numbers 61,875 and the non-Sikh Indians and Pakistanis number 134,610. Thus, Sikhs from the Punjab account for 31.5 percent of immigrants to Canada originating from the Indian subcontinent. The census revealed that 27.2 percent were Hindus, 21 percent

Muslims, 17.2 percent Christians, and that 3 percent had no religious preference. In Ontario Hindus outnumbered Sikhs nearly three to one, whereas in British Columbia Sikhs outnumbered Hindus nearly five to one.

Even though official statistics are not available for religious and regional–linguistic groups in the United States, it is clear that the relative strength of the groups is different. No such variations of Asian-Indian groups exist among the regions in the United States. The immigration patterns are different in Britain and Canada for many reasons: Immigration to those countries began in an earlier period, it represented a different process of occupational preferment, much of the migration to commonwealth countries was from Africa following the independence of African countries, and many of those who entered did so as refugees. The linguistic make-up, as well as the religious commitments, of the Asian-Indian community is unique to the United States.

Asian Indians have the potential to create their own identity based on a number of ethnic or minority designations, depending on which elements they decide to emphasize. Fredrik Barth has shown that immigrants may choose to emphasize one level of identity among several provided by their heritage. He indicates that tribe, caste, language group, region, or state all have features that make them a potentially adequate primary ethnic identity for group reference. (We should add religion to the list as one of the components.) He emphasizes the necessity of decision by the leaders of the community when he says that which level of identity is chosen will depend upon the "cold tactical facts" and the readiness with which others inside and outside the group can be led to embrace and recognize these identities (Barth, 1969:33–4). Of course, a person may seem to belong to several ethnic or cultural groups based on linguistic and cultural differences that become salient in different situations. Thus, to the majority of the population the new immigrant may be an Asian Indian, but to others from India he may be a Malayalee or a Sindhi. Other subgroups related to caste, religion, or political orientation may create significant boundaries and elements of identity to be activated in particular social situations.

The two ways of shaping the social identity are through intergenerational transmission from natal households, which will be largely idiosyncratic in selecting which elements of identity to maintain and which to drop, and through the existence of relatively bounded ethnic communities in which household networks of friends tend to support the same cultural values and customs (Brown & Mussell, 1984:71). The diversity of ethnic organizations that help shape the immigrant community is as socially complex as in India itself. Some groups are national in scope and reflect the continuation of modern nationalism that developed under the British and has been intensified in independent India. Both nationalism and regionalism rely on a pool of literary, religious, political, and social symbols, usually couched in linguistic terms. The process of adaptation to the new setting is selection, standardization, and transmission of symbols from the symbol pool, all of which result from interaction of complex forces.

A major venue for the selection of these symbols is the range of ethnic organizations that are formed among the new immigrants. Nationally based, "all-India" organizations are found in most major population centers and stress Indian culture and arts. They are officially secular, inviting the membership of all Asian Indians, but in practice they support the celebration of civil and religious events in a distinctly Hindu voice. That is noticed by non-Hindus, who often distance themselves from the local activities of these groups. The Pakistan Friendship Associations serve a similar function for the Pakistanis, and although they too profess to be national rather than religious, Muslims from India often associate with the Pakistani organizations instead of (or in addition to) the all-India organizations.

Many regional–linguistic organizations first form to provide films from India in the native language and fellowship around tables loaded with regional dishes. The advent of video cassette recorders has reduced the attraction of the film programs because families can now view Hindi or Tamil films at home. The associations have begun to sponsor musical programs, dances, food fairs, regional festivals, politicians, and sometimes religious leaders for programs for the community. These programs are conducted in the regional language, and the associations sponsor language classes for children and adults with varying degrees of success. The Gujarati community is relatively large, so the Gujarati Samaj is found in most major centers, but the Tamil Sangam and other regional–linguistic organizations also provide focal points for group association and individual identity.

Other types of ethnic organizations support certain elements of identity. Professional organizations are formed that reflect the occupations of a major portion of the population and give them benefits of status and finances; so there is an Association of Indian Physicians and the Association of Indian Engineers. Many of the Indian universities and institutes have alumni associations in the United States, and these and the professional associations support organizations and charitable work in India. Caste organizations exist but seem not to be particularly active or influential. In India, the role of caste organizations has changed dramatically, and their role in the United States is limited. Caste is still important in familial and marriage affairs, which are essential for maintenance of identity, but it seems, at least to an outside researcher, to have little impact on other social affairs within the United States. Asian-Indian political organizations of various types exist, some concerned with political affairs in India as branches of the Congress Party or the Akali Dal of the Punjab, others directed toward mobilizing Asian-Indian economic and political power for American politicians and for lobbying efforts. All these groups are flourishing as parts of a crazy quilt of ethnic organizations that are influencing the development of Asian-Indian identities.

Immigrants from the Indian subcontinent stress that they are more family oriented than established residents, and family is the primary agent for shaping social identity. Most of the immigrants in the 1960s and early 1970s came as male students or as young professionals without family. Those who were students went through a longer period in the liminal state, which is characteristic of the university setting, before they were able to establish themselves in a career and family. Foreign-student organizations and advisors took over some functions of family, and many report that the period as students, living with other students, was the time of closest personal contact with members of the host society and the time when they changed their patterns of conduct to conform to the majority mores; meat-eating, drinking of alcoholic beverages, and the neglect of religious duties are mentioned most often as examples. Marriage and the birth of children generally bring a return to some modes of behavior associated with their ethnic identity.

Families are created new and in new shapes in the United States. The immigrant usually has at most his nuclear family around him, and many support structures of the extended family are missing. Many of the young professionals work for a few months or years to be able to send for their wives and children; other young professionals and many students go back to India (or to the Indian community in other countries, such as East Africa or Britain) to arrange for brides. The quick trip to arrange the marriage and have the ceremony is a common experience. A significant gender variation exists in the experience of the female nurses and medical technicians who were recruited to come to the United States in the early 1970s. They gained entry because of their professional skills and then brought their husbands and children. The unmarried female nurses who were eligible to immigrate to the United States became preferred marriage partners. In some cases they were from castes and subgroups that had not previously been preferred marriage partners, and their immigration potential caused a significant change in status. The networks through which marriage arrangements are made in the Asian-Indian community are very complex – and worthy of more study – but the possession of citizenship or permanent resident status and the prospect of professional advancement in the United States have become significant elements in the marriage negotiations that often outweigh the more traditional elements of caste, subcaste (*gotra*), or village associations.

The family situation changes constantly for the new immigrants, from single individuals separated from their families, to couples, to nuclear families, to the beginnings of a revised extended family. The number of males and females is reaching parity, and most immigrants have reached the stage of living in nuclear families.[10] Religious and social gatherings are full of children because it is the custom that entire families attend the meetings. Thirty-two percent of Asian Indians are younger than twenty years old, and the older ones among these, most of whom came from the Indian subcontinent as small children, are just reaching college age (USCen4:Table 160).[11] Most of the single young men and women are siblings of earlier immigrants who have gained admission for family reunification or students who, unless they marry a permanent resident, will have to return because they are in the United States on temporary visas. The extended family as it exists in the Indian subcontinent is absent. The grandparent generation is virtually nonexistent, and even when brothers and sisters come with their families, when they establish the extended family residence and the joint economic arrangements common to the extended family in India, it is only temporarily.

As with every immigrant group, the Asian-Indian parents express concern and some anxiety regarding the appropriate socialization of the children. The persons who during the interviews expressed a desire to take their families back to the Indian subcontinent gave as the reason the wish to save their children from the influences of American youth culture. As children reach school age or the early teens the parents experience a major impetus to attend to those ethnic and religious institutions that are surrogates for the extended family. The development of these institutions is made possible by the prosperity and the political and social skills of the Asian Indians, but the regional–linguistic organizations and the temples, mosques, and *gurdwaras* spring up when the children began to find their contacts outside the home. The parents recognize that they enter a situation quite different from that in the Indian subcontinent of their youth, and that now the children will gain a much smaller proportion of their culture from specific traditions acquired through the family. The process is all the more delicate because the children are being socialized at the same time the parents are being resocialized in a new society.

Variations among the children are important, because the pressures for acculturation (acquisition of the larger society's characteristics), assimilation (social integration), and pluralism (preservation of traits of the ethnic community) differ among children according to age. It is well-known that the use of the native language of the ethnic group declines by generation, so that in the first generation 82 percent report a language other than English, in the second the percentage drops to 59 percent, and in the third to 7 percent (USCen1:1).

A more significant difference exists between the older children, who may have spent their childhood in India or Pakistan, and their younger brothers and sisters. A complaint of many parents is that although most of the children of the second generation understand uncomplicated communications in the ethnic language, the younger children refuse to respond in Hindi, Gujarati, or Urdu and even in India refuse to speak to relatives in their language. Greater pressure is exerted on the older children to speak the language, to return to India or Pakistan for vacations, to avoid dating, and to return to India or Pakistan for marriage. The pride and position of the family in the ethnic community is gauged to some degree by adherence to these norms, and the older children represent contacts with the traditional ways. Older children marginally follow traditions that their younger brothers and sisters seek to avoid, so the stages of child development and the differences between the oldest son and daughter and the younger are significant. Thus, regional–linguistic and religious organizations have to adjust to the temperament of two groups within the second generation itself. The third generation of Asian Indians and Pakistanis has not yet reached adolescence, but it will be the generation that will determine in truth what "Asian Indian" means. From the evidence so far, we can presume that it will mean several things, because generations will still vary in their commitment to an assortment of beliefs and practices and thus create different identities.

Migration is an enormous disruption of the social fabric. The idea that immigrants can recreate the behavior and traditions of their original villages and towns in the new setting is simply false (Leonardo, 1984:134). Migration itself prevents the reestablishment of the former familial and social structures, and the immigrant who says as he enters a temple or gurdwara, "It feels just like India," is simply engaging in nostalgia. R. K. Narayan writes: "Building imposing Indian temples in America, installing our gods therein and importing Indian priests to perform the pooja ritual and preside at festivals is only imitating Indian existence and can have only a limited value. Social and religious assemblies at temples in America might mitigate boredom, but only temporarily" (1985:169). The point is that emigration involves a crisis of epistemology that causes people to focus on their tradition or on narrative in the attempt to establish a known world. Perhaps that recurring return to a narrative and the restructuring of the religious story by immigrants is one reason that the United States as a nation of immigrants is relatively religious.

The change of the cultural environment requires at the same time a reorientation of the personality to a world of new symbols, values, and attitudes. Many of the professional immigrants began the reorientation during their university careers. Still, the greatest problem for those migrating from one social setting to another is the maintenance of their identity. The dilemma they face is to preserve their identity with the essential continuity of the self and at the same time accommodate that identity to the new setting with the necessary correspondence between them. The conscious feeling of having a personal identity, so important to immigrants, is described by Erik Erikson as having two simultaneous observations: the immediate perception of one's selfsameness and continuity in time; and the simultaneous perception of the fact that others recognize one's sameness and continuity (1980:22). Continuity and correspondence, the two essential elements for the immigrant's personal and social identity, are created through a complex negotiation of acculturation, assimilation, and pluralism and result in the creation of a new identity – personal and social – which did not exist before (see Kolm, 1980). The negotiation involves individual decisions, but it takes place in the social groups that create a collective identity of fairly stable commonly held beliefs, patterns, and values and that are the arena and agents for the negotiations internal to the community and between the community and the host society.

Ethnic groups and religions

Fredrik Barth shows that ethnic groups are categories of ascription and identification by the members of the group through which they organize interaction among themselves and with members of other groups, and he emphasizes the "generative viewpoint" in the attempt to explore the different processes that seem to be involved in generating and maintaining ethnic groups (Barth, 1969:10). The immigrants from the Indian subcontinent are in the process of generating the ethnic groups that will govern their internal relations and be the major institutions beyond the family to affect their relations with the host society. Three aspects of identity they share with other immigrants are effective in generating ethnic identity: the national, the regional–linguistic, and the religious. Thus, the legal minority group in the United States is based on national origin – in this case Asian Indian or Pakistani; the ethnic group is based on regional–linguistic criteria, and the religious aspect represents the various religions found on the Indian subcontinent.

The designations "Asian Indian" and "Pakistani" are related to the nationalism of this century, which attempts to mute the regional and linguistic divisions within India and Pakistan and use the new national identity to promote loyalty and emotional attachment to the nation. The national elite created out of the movements for independence from colonial rule helped shape the idea of each nation in all-inclusive terms coextensive with the territories. Centrifugal forces have continually threatened to destroy that unity, as the partition of India and Pakistan destroyed the hope for one India cherished by Mahatma Gandhi. The creation of the legal minority designations in the United States represents the community's attempt to maintain some unity in numbers sufficiently large to have political and economic effect. Many organizations are formed on an all-India basis, with major festivals that are all-India political or cultural events, and English as the language of communication. The point is often made that the children will not know or appreciate the regional language or culture, so the only hope for providing an ethnic identity for future generations is to emphasize the more universal identity and in that way to transmit the values and symbols appropriate to Asian-Indian or Pakistani identity – a new identity that will be determined through complex negotiation among the various regional–linguistic groups and the various religious groups that serve the community.

Ethnic groups are intermediate phenomena between kinship groups and the nation. An ethnic group is a minority population within a larger society, recognized as a distinct group by others in the society, whose members claim a common background, real or fictional, and who participate in shared activities, including speaking the same language, in which the common origin and culture are significant. The editors of the most comprehensive survey of ethnic groups in the United States give the following list of features characteristic of ethnic groups: common geographic origin, common migratory status, common race, common language or dialect, common religious faith or faiths; ties that transcend kinship, neighborhood, and community boundaries; shared traditions, values, and symbols; shared literature, folklore, and music; shared food preferences; settlement and employment patterns; special interests in regard to politics in the homeland and in the U.S.; institutions that specifically serve and maintain the group; an internal sense of distinctiveness; and an external perception of distinctiveness (HE, 1980:vi).

Among Asian Indians the primary ethnic groups are those based on the regional–linguistic divisions in India. The Gujaratis, Punjabis, Telugu, Bengalis, and Malayalee seem to be the more prominent, but other ethnic groups are in evidence in major population centers. Those in smaller cities and towns are linked through many communication media to the ethnic groups in the metropolitan centers. Milton Gordon outlines three functional characteristics of the ethnic groups. First, they serve psychologically as a source of group self-identification; second, they provide patterned networks of groups and institutions, which allows an individual to confine his or her primary relationships to the ethnic group through all the stages of the life cycle; and third, they refract the national cultural patterns of behavior and values through the prism of the more narrow regional cultural heritage (Gordon, 1964:38).

Ethnic identification has a significant role in the adjustment and integration of the immigrant. Richard Kolm shows that the immigrant has a great need for acceptance and for psychological security due to the lack of familiarity with the new social environment, and both of these lead to identification with the ethnic group (Kolm, 1980:171). The positive forces of attraction are based on the need for symbolic communication in familiar language and modes and the negative forces are a defense against anomie, rejection and anxieties about the loss of identity. These are powerful within the first generation, and they are intensified when the parents view their children growing up in the margins between the culture of the parents and that outside the home. Just as ethnic identity provided assistance in helping the immigrant maintain self-control and identity in the face of the threats to his or her sense of self, so the ethnic identity will provide some protection for the children from what are perceived to be the threats in American culture.

In the short time the immigrants from the Indian subcontinent have been in the United States changes have taken place in group formation. In the 1960s the group was relatively small even in major urban areas, and Asian Indians tended to form inclusive primary groups for all Indians that also included some Pakistanis. As the numbers became larger, the community could support many subgroups, so gatherings and organizations developed for the various regional–linguistic groups. Organizations such as the Gujarati Samaj merely reflect the refraction of the community into language-based subgroups for social and cultural affairs that allow the networks or systems of relationships tending to integrate the various subgroups within society. A change took place in the 1970s when the general designations "Asian Indian" and "Pakistani" became useful for administration and classification, but the regional ethnic designations became more important in sociological and psychological terms. Some leaders in the community think it is inevitable that future generations, who will have lost the ability to communicate in the regional language or to appreciate the regional customs and symbols, will return to the general designation "Asian Indian" as an ethnic as well as a legal minority designation, and they try to prepare their children for that future.

Herbert Gans warns, however, that ethnic identification, attitudes, and even identity depend not only on the desires and decisions of members of the group, but also on developments in the society generally. The "new ethnics," which include the Gujaratis, Punjabis, and others, enter the United States at a time when ethnicity is honored. The future shape of the community will be affected by how the host society comes to treat ethnics – what costs it will levy and what benefits it will award to them (Gans, 1979:15). Presently, various legal and social benefits accrue to the Asian Indians, in part because India has a rather high status recognition in American society. The current stress on ethnicity and on the values of a pluralistic society provide the basis for the development of regional–linguistic ethnic designations as well as nationality-based identity among immigrants from the Indian subcontinent. Gans may be correct, however, in his argument that there has not been a true revival of ethnicity as intense and frequent interaction among ethnic groups; indeed, he states that acculturation and assimilation have continued to take place at a rapid rate. What will develop in future generations is "symbolic ethnicity" or "ethnicity of the last resort," which does not require functioning groups or networks; instead, the feelings of identity are developed by allegiances to symbolic groups that do not meet, existing only for the handful of officers that keep them going. According to Gans, this type of symbolic ethnicity can persist for generations without much substance. At this time, however, the regional–linguistic ethnic groups still exist among immigrants from the Indian subcontinent as true ethnic groups, providing important networks and support for social cohesion. It is too early to determine what forms of symbolic ethnicity may develop.

These new immigrants are now well established in the United States, and they are forming strong religious and ethnic groups in the hope that these will aid in maintaining their distinct identity, assist in negotiation with other social groups, and be effective in transmitting their religious and cultural traditions to their children and grandchildren. Together these groups, representing all the major religions of India and Pakistan, will have a profound effect both on the recent immigrants and on American society in general.

CHAPTER 2

The religions

Hinduism, Jainism, and Sikhism

The immigrant engineer or physician from the Indian subcontinent who steps off the plane at Kennedy Airport may be Hindu, Muslim, Christian, Sikh, Jain, Buddhist, or "other." It is unlikely that he or she is thinking very much about religious affiliation at that moment. Entry procedures since 1957 no longer involve a record of religious affiliation. During the first hectic period of adjustment, religion may not be much in evidence, but soon for most immigrants the task of shaping a new identity that both preserves the memory of the past and brings continuity to the present circumstance leads to decisions that relate to the religious traditions thus far carried only inside, away from the view of immigration officials and neighbors. At this point they emerge to become public and visible. The religion of the family back home has been a major force in shaping identity, but personal and group identity and the role religion plays in their formation and preservation are not "givens," objects to be transmitted intact from the place of origin through mass migration. Rather, they are new social forms adapted to new cultural settings.

Due to regional variation, immigrants from the Indian subcontinent cannot be considered as each leaving the same place – political, cultural, or religious. Some of the religious variations are evident in statistics from the Census of India in 1981 for the states from which many immigrants come to the United States (see Table 2.1). Hindus make up a huge majority of the population in India overall (82.64%) and Sikhs account for only a small percentage (1.96%), but in the Punjab Sikhs are a majority (60.75%) and Hindus are in a distinct minority (36.93%). The situation is complicated further by the fact that most Sikhs, no matter where they live in India, consider themselves Punjabis. Pakistan is officially a Muslim country with a Muslim majority of 98.6 percent, many of whom migrated into Pakistan at the time of partition. A very large number of Muslims live in parts of

Table 2.1. *Religious variations in the population of India*

Area	Population	Hindu	Muslims	Christian	Sikhs	Buddhists	Jains
India [1]	665,287,849	82.64	11.35	2.43	1.96	0.71	0.48
Gujarat	34,085,799	89.5	8.56	0.39		0.07 0.02	1.37
Punjab	16,788,915	36.93	1.00	1.10	60.75	n	0.16
Tamil Nadu	48,408,077	88.86	5.21	5.78	0.01	n	0.10
Kerala	25,453,680	58.15	21.25	20.56	0.01	n	0.02
Pakistan [2]	84,253,000	1.5	96.7	1.5			
Ahmadis (no number given), Parsis 7,000, Sikhs 2,146, Buddhists 2,639							

[1]Adapted from the 1981 Religious Census of India.
[2]Adapted from the 1981 Census of Pakistan, *Main Findings of 1981 Population Census*, Population Census Organisation, Statistics Division. Government of Pakistan, Islamabad, 1983.

India and constitute 11.35 percent of that population. The variation among regions is great, however, so that Muslims are only a trace (1%) in the Punjab whereas in Kerala they are a fifth of the population (21.25%). A similar variation characterizes the Christian population across India. The relation that exists among the various religious groups, particularly in matters related to dominance and numerical superiority, depends on the area from which the immigrants come.

No reliable count or estimate of the religious affiliation of immigrants from the Indian subcontinent can be made now because of the legal prohibition of keeping governmental records on religious affiliation that has been in force since 1957. A couple of general conclusions can be advanced, however. First, for a variety of reasons, the percentages of immigrants from some areas of India – namely Gujarat, Punjab, and Kerala – are greater than from other parts. Gujaratis may make up as much as 40 percent of the immigrants, and Punjabis 20 percent. These numbers include those who migrated from East Africa – perhaps after their families had been there for generations – and from Britain. It is not possible to document accurately the data showing which Indian states send more people abroad, but the numbers of immigrants in some religious communities are affected. Second, persons who belong to the religious minorities, especially Sikhs, Jains, and Christians, are represented by a larger percentage among immigrants than among the total population of India. Emigration is one way to escape some restrictions of minority status.

What does it mean, then, that new immigrants establish themselves in the United States as Muslim, Hindu, Christian, or Sikh? It certainly means a dramatic change. A Gujarati Hindu from an area where nine out of ten people are Hindus is suddenly in a situation where Hindus are a tiny minority. Punjabi-speaking Christians from Pakistan or Malayalee Christians from Kerala, on the other hand, are suddenly part of a religious majority, one in which they must make a place for themselves, perhaps even as a new denomination. Muslims from India find much in common with Muslims from Pakistan as they worship in mosques with immigrants from many other countries. For all of these migration causes tremendous disruption of religious location that demands a reformulation and redefinition of what "Hindu," "Muslim," and other religious designations mean.

For some, of course, it means freedom from identification with any religious tradition. It is common for new immigrants to go through a period of reduced religious activity, and some go through what Mahatma Gandhi experienced in London as "the Sahara of atheism" – of course, he called it that only after he returned physically and spiritually to India. Single men especially enter the United States freed from the traditional mechanisms of social control, and they speak about the pressure exerted by university friends or professional colleagues who encourage them to break traditional rules to become "one of the boys," a powerful attraction for new immigrants. Many immigrants – there is no way of knowing how many – welcome the disruption caused by migration that permits them this freedom. These secularists complain in letters to editors of Indian newspapers against the "temple and mosque builders" and "communalists" who attempt to create "a little India" in the United States. Theirs is a strong but not dominant voice among immigrants. The question for the future is whether it will become louder, or be muted by more recent immigrants as they come for family reunification and reestablish religious ties.

Most of those who participate in the religious groups indicate that they are more religiously active and committed than before, with new identities formed in continuity with personal and group memory of the social and religious places they left, but requiring attention to new neighbors, new patterns of relationship, and adaptations of the beliefs and rituals to accommodate their new cultural situation. The decade from 1977 has been a period of community growth both in numbers and in the development of religious groups and organizations that reflect and create the new identity. In earlier periods immigrants from Europe created in the United States new forms of their ancient religions – American Catholicism, American Judaism – and now, nearly a century later, immigrants from the Indian subcontinent are creating new forms of other ancient religions – American Hinduism,[1] American Islam, American Sikhism, and, perhaps, new forms of American Christianity.

Hindus

The priest sitting in the temple with a family to perform a ceremony chants a portion of the ancient Sanskrit texts containing the names of the sacred rivers of India. He transposes, " . . . the Mississippi, the Ohio, the Rio Grande." The children, who understand little of the ceremony, rouse themselves at this startling introduction of the familiar. The scene is an illustration of the transformation of traditions that is taking place.

Hinduism is not a single thing; it is an amalgamation of sects, deities, sacred texts, temples, institutions, and cultural practices, some of which have very little in common with the others. It is hard to decide on one item of belief or practice that is common to all Hindus or on a belief or practice which, if accepted by an individual, would demonstrate that that person is not a Hindu. In India a person has to opt out of being a Hindu by claiming to be something else, such as a Muslim, a Jain, or a Christian.

A person is not, however, a "Hindu in general"; rather each person is a "Hindu in particular" in the sense that he or she is part of a tradition with a specific deity or deities, a group of sacred texts, a pattern of worship, an authorized body of religious leaders and teachers, and pre-scribed duties and obligations. One person is a Tamil Srivaishnava, an-other a Gujarati Vaishnava (Krishna devotee), a third is a member of the Arya Samaj, and yet another has recently become a follower of Sai Baba. The traditions overlap, and the common view among Hindus that it doesn't matter which religious path one follows means that people may participate in rituals of several traditions while not losing contact with their own. The result is that in a given location in India the situation is very complex, a complexity that increases when Hindus from several areas of India move to the same city in the United States.

It is possible to analyze what we call Hinduism both in India and in the United States according to several types of differentiation that are not exclusive, but are useful. One major distinction exists between Vaishnavas and Shaivas in the primary deities they worship and in the patterns of rituals (*agamas*) they follow. In India most temples can be identified as either Vaishnava or Shaiva according to the resident deities. Even within the major traditions, persons are devotees of various forms of the deities – Venkateswara, Yogeswara, Krishna, Rama, Durga. A typical shrine will contain a constellation of images related to one of the deities. Regional variations in religious forms relate to cultural differences, the most im-portant of which is language, but that also include cuisine, dress, and ritual patterns. Many all-India and regional sacred texts are in Sanskrit, but there are also many regional texts in the vernacular. Bengali devotees of Krishna receive inspiration from different sacred texts and sing different devotional songs than do Gujarati Vaishnavas even though they worship the same deity in the same devotional (*bhakti*) tradition. The reorganization of the Indian states on linguistic lines has reinforced cultural distinctions, and sectarian groups have formed to emphasize particular elements of the tradition. Some of these are related to regions as, for example, the Swaminarayan Hindus of Gujarat, whereas others cross regional and linguistic lines as, for example, the Arya Samaj. Many Hindus are followers of a particular religious teacher (*guru*) who directs their religious developments. The teacher may represent a sect, a regional form, or a particular deity. In any case, the attachment of the devotee to a religious teacher is very strong in many forms of Hinduism. Caste is an ever-present aspect of culture in India, and even though it is not as prominent in the United States, caste is important in some private and family religious functions. Srivaishnava Brahmins and Smarta Brahmins have specified rituals and religious duties to perform that are difficult to observe completely in the United States. That difficulty is the reason why in times past orthodox Brahmins were discouraged from traveling abroad. The role of Brahmins in the Hindu community is a matter of controversy both in India and in the United States. Even among non-Brahmins distinctions among caste groups in religious affairs can be noted. The Gujarati Vallabhacharya Vaishnavas generally come from caste groups that occupy a slightly higher rank than do the Swaminarayan Hindus. Members of Untouchable castes living in the San Francisco area recently established their own Ravidas temple near San Jose.

Sociologists of Indian religions point to the trend in the modern period, perhaps related to the independence movement and nationalism, toward all-Indian rituals and texts, producing what some scholars identify as neo-Hinduism. The movement is related to "Sanskritization" because lower castes adopt practices of the higher castes and it introduces into regional forms of Hinduism deities, texts, rituals, and duties from ancient Sanskrit tradition, relating local deities and rituals to them (Srinivas, 1962:42–62; Staal, 1963:261–75). Nationalism and increased communication across India is gradually causing an emphasis on these all-India Hindu celebrations and texts, which supplement and often compete with the regional forms and practices. However, in Gujarat a Hindu is still obviously a Gujarati Hindu, even though what that means may be changing slowly in contemporary India.

In the United States it is not so clear what it means to be a Gujarati Hindu, and a tension exists between forms of identification with regional–linguistic and sectarian forms and what is developing as an "ecumenical Hinduism." A recent organizational development among Indians abroad, ecumenical Hinduism builds on the traditional Hindu tolerance by including in one religious fellowship the followers of many different regions, language groups, and sects and by gathering in one temple or shrine the images and rituals of many sects. The regional or sectarian organizations select, standardize, and transmit one set of symbols from a single regional–linguistic area or sect, but in ecumenical Hinduism an attempt is made to include in one organization persons who represent many different organizations in India. The process of negotiation between regional forms of religion and the new ecumenical expression is similar to the negotiations among the European national Roman Catholic groups that resulted in the formation of the American Catholic Church. The leaders recognize that they are proposing organizational structures and relations different from those current in India and refer to "the pioneer work of union," urging Indians abroad to become examples for those back in India in the development of this ecumenical form of Hinduism.

The process of negotiation involves the establishment of boundaries through the selection of symbols from the storehouse of Hinduism that will establish and preserve personal and group identity. Fredrik Barth's influential essay on ethnic groups established the importance of ethnic and religious boundaries and boundary maintenance (Barth, 1969:9–38). He argued that an ethnic boundary defines the group, not the cultural stuff that it encloses. The identification of the individual in the group is based on those inclusive and exclusive features the members themselves regard as significant. The differentiation of fellow member and stranger involves the establishment of boundaries and boundary maintenance that persists over a time. These boundaries are institutional and social, not individual.

Immigrants are marginal people, however, and the process of marking out these boundaries is not one of maintaining the isolation of immigrants but of overcoming the separation to give immigrants an identity within the society. Religious expression and maintenance of boundaries is an accepted aspect of social intercourse in the United States, and it provides a base from which the Indian immigrant can negotiate the terms of assimilation. This negotiation among the immigrants involves the manipulation of religious and cultural symbols in the definition of religious groups – regional, sectarian, or ecumenical – that provide the bases for personal and group identity, and the formation, growth, and success and failure of the hundreds of Hindu groups in the United States is an ongoing part of that negotiation.

The situation of each location in the United States is different, and may be plotted on two related axes: size and length of residence. The size of the Hindu community in a city dictates to some extent the shape of the religious groups. Where only a few Hindus are present, they will generally meet together for Hindu worship and rituals in patterns identified with ecumenical Hinduism. The common language will be English and the religious texts and rituals will be those associated with the all-India Sanskrit tradition. When a larger community is gathered, the tendency is to splinter into regional and sectarian groups. The length of time the Hindu community has been present also determines some aspects of the negotiation. When the community is new to an area – and every Hindu community is relatively new – primary attention is given to the establishment of economic and social security for each family. Religious activity takes place within the family or among friends who meet in the homes. Once the family is established and children are present, attention turns to the provision of more structured and permanent forms of religious organization. The situation varies in each community: It is different in Omaha than in New York because of size, and in Houston because of length of residence.

The situation throughout the community is in rapid flux. Immigrants are by definition in a liminal state of transition. Moreover, new immigrants to the United States are highly mobile and may live in several cities with different jobs and social situations during the first few years. Geographic migration is accompanied by social migration and also by religious change. It is virtually impossible to keep track of the lay leaders of Hindu religious organizations in the United States. A religious group may appear to be fairly static, but the individuals within the group are always on the move – moving in or out, to greater or lesser commitment, or from one form of participation to another. None stay still for very long within a religious community. We will trace aspects of the transition of Hinduism in the United States by focusing on family religious activities, the organization of groups of various kinds, the building of temples, and the development of institutions of ecumenical Hinduism.

Home shrines and family religion

Hindus can participate fully in the ceremonies of their religion at home and rarely go to temples or official meetings because of the importance of the home shrines and family rituals. This family Hinduism is by far the most important carrier for the transmission of religious beliefs and practices, the earliest and most basic element of the religious observance of Hindu immigrants being the home shrine. Some are as elaborate as a separate room set apart for this purpose with a beautifully carved shrine cabinet from India; others are as simple as a few pictures of deities and religious teachers on a wall or placed in a china closet. The deities and religious objects in the family shrines are generally those of the regional or sectarian form of parental Hinduism. In some cases where the husband and wife come from different branches of Hinduism, the shrine objects will represent an amalgamation of both traditions. One leader of a Hindu worship society has a closet fitted out for the Hindu pantheon with the major deities on shelves on the top level and the sectarian images and pictures of religious teachers on the lower level. The array represents the relationship that he hopes will be incorporated in a planned temple; the major deities will be in the main shrine room with the others in small shrine rooms around the sides. The home shrine and the temple are both seen as residences of the gods, and rituals are performed in both places.

Few immigrants have the time to perform all the daily rituals prescribed for appropriate worship. Very few indeed have the specialized training to perform elaborate rituals because for the most part they received modern Western education and not training in the traditional Sanskrit schools. Many do not even perform any regular rituals at the home shrine. Somewhere between benign neglect and the full prescribed rituals, the families engage in morning or evening worship (*puja*), periods of meditation, reading of sacred texts, and prayer according to the level of their devotion. Some devout Hindus are very disciplined in observing morning and evening religious rituals; in these homes the food offered to the family and guests is first dedicated to god at the home shrine. The home shrine thus performs the function that the dinner table did for family prayers for some earlier immigrant families.

One of the disruptions of migration is the difficulty in arranging for the appropriate life-cycle rituals. Hinduism has an elaborate series of sixteen generally accepted life cycle rituals (*samskaras*), which begin before birth and continue after death with the cremation and the death anniversary observances.[2] Rarely, even in India, are all observed; those most often observed in the United States include prenatal rituals, birth and childhood ceremonies, the sacred thread for Brahmin boys, marriage, and cremation. It becomes necessary early for the immigrant community to make arrangements for the observance of some of these rituals. Death waits for no group to get organized, and the first necessity of each group, in spite of its relative youth, was to arrange for the appropriate rituals and cremation at the time of death. Some persons in the community mastered the legal requirements for cremation and disposal of the ashes here or in India; others learned the appropriate rituals and even prepared manuals of instruction for what should be done and said, including instructions for the son at the cremation and a list of appropriate religious texts to be read in English. Specified rituals for the children and marriage are often postponed so that they can be observed according to traditional patterns in India where grandparents and the extended family can participate. In the United States only the most important rituals are performed, and those in an attenuated form. One writer suggested that in the United States only certain necessary life-cycle rituals should be observed: Name giving, Sacred thread, Marriage, and Cremation (Dwivedi, 1985:9).

Occasional rituals are performed to mark auspicious events such as moving to a new home or establishing a new business. It is common in periods of transition to make vows regarding career choices, family security, and welfare and health that are fulfilled by performing certain religious rituals or sponsoring readings of sacred texts or cultural performances. Some of these rituals along with the life-cycle rituals are performed in local temples or in the large temples of major cities, which attract large numbers of tourist pilgrims. An individual may perform some of the rituals for his or her family, a privilege usually reserved for Brahmins. In many cases, however, the family calls upon the services of a Brahmin to perform the prescribed rituals.

Brahmins are available in most of the large cities to perform rituals for the families. Some are the resident priests (*pujaris*) in the established temples, and their service for the families is one of their responsibilities as priests in the temple. In smaller cities and in towns without established temples a Brahmin, although perhaps an engineer or industrialist by occupation, undertakes to perform the needed rituals. His authorization is through birth as a Brahmin; his training may be fairly extensive through the traditional apprenticeship of observing his father in India or it may be fairly minimal through reading the appropriate ritual manuals. Even in cities with established temples, several Brahmins may present themselves to the community as religious specialists for these life cycle and occasional ceremonies, some for each major regional community – Gujarati, Tamil, Hindi, Bengali. No single profile is adequate for these individuals. Some are employed as technocrat professionals and the position of ritual specialist provides status within the community. A few are parents of immigrants who have come from India to retire with their children, and, because retirement age in India is relatively young, they have considerable energy to begin a new career as Brahmin religious specialists. During the downturn in the United States economy that caused many recent immigrants to lose their jobs, some gave more time to the performance of religious rituals to help support the family. A few also are adept in astrology and prepare astrological charts and interpretations for clients for a fee – such astrological calculations are considered by many Asian Indians to be essential before establishing a marriage contract or the date for any major event. Others are trained in the traditional *ayurvedic* medicine of India and they dispense advice and some herbs, but they must be careful because they are not licensed to practice medicine in the United States.

A group of Brahmins in one city who advertised in a newspaper for Asian Indians listed the religious rituals which they were prepared to perform, including both life-cycle and occasional rituals: baby shower, marriage, Satya Narayan Puja, Havan, Vastu Puja, Laxmi Puja, Shanti

Path and Navagraha Puja, Gita Parayan, Bhagwan Kirtan, Ramayan Parayan, Shri Vishnu Sahatranam Archana, and cremation. They adapt some of the rituals to the new context, as in the prenatal rituals, which have become "baby showers," the name and many of the nonreligious aspects of the gathering taking on a distinctly American flavor.

Indian marriages are the rituals which attract many non-Indian friends and provide for them – and sometimes even for the bride and groom of the second generation – the first exposure to Sanskrit religious rituals. A mixture of strictly prescribed acts and informal conversation among the participants, the ritual provides many opportunities for adjustment and explanation. One wedding was held at a Holiday Inn, and a candle was used symbolically for the fire sacrifice because of fire regulations. At one wedding the Brahmin explained each portion of the ritual for the participants as he went along. He explained one portion of the text which said the woman is supposed to take care of the home and cooking and the man has the responsibility to provide the food. Then, looking at the two young professionals, he said, "But now we are in the United States and we will leave you to decide that." Everyone chuckled. A few marriages have been between men of Indian origin and American women, very few between American men and women of Indian families.

The Satya Narayan Puja is a very popular ritual that is performed in many homes on auspicious occasions. The family invites relatives and friends for the ceremony, which is followed by a dinner, so it is a significant social occasion. The Brahmins are scheduled for weeks in advance and may travel several hundred miles to perform rituals for Hindus in small towns. Generally the Brahmin must abbreviate the ritual and explain elements as he goes along to keep the interest of those who attend. Hindu groups often invite several Brahmins to participate together in some sacrificial rituals or in the chanting or reading of sacred texts, and these gatherings may attract two or three thousand persons.

It is the custom in India to give gifts to the Brahmins at the time of auspicious ceremonies and special rituals, but it is not possible to make a living from these voluntary contributions which vary in a range with few exceptions from $11 to $151. (The odd numbers are considered to be especially auspicious.) Some Brahmins complain that Brahmin activity has become commercialized in the United States, and there is a move to set standard fees for the rituals, a $51 minimum for a ritual, $151 for a wedding in the city, and $251 for a wedding that requires travel. Of course, the pattern is different in every location because the Brahmins who are not attached to established temples are independent religious specialists who come to the homes. An article in a Hindu journal in the United States has called for the creation of a professional order of Hindu priests, which would be called "Hindu Dharma Acharya," in order to establish some control over the training and qualifications of those performing the Hindu rituals (Dwivedi, 1985:9).

Homes are the first centers of extended religious activities in the towns and cities of Asian-Indian immigrants. A family may call a few friends and acquaintances to come to their home for a religious gathering, and soon a group of people meet in different homes once a month or each week for worship or study. On a Saturday or Sunday afternoon or evening a few people gather in the living room around worship centers prepared with the images from the home shrine or brought by leaders and placed on the couch with the appropriate adornments. The number and types of such home-based groups is very large, and each emphasizes an aspect from the Hindu tradition. Gita study groups read and discuss portions of the *Bhagavad Gita* and other religious texts; *bhajan* groups gather to sing devotional hymns; meditation groups based on the teachings of Shankara and other teachers study and practice forms of meditation. Some groups are ecumenical, including persons from several regions and language groups of India and worshiping deities of the several traditions represented by persons in the group. In larger towns and cities these home groups are formed on regional–linguistic bases because they provide the opportunity to enjoy the vernacular language and culture. Sectarian groups in many cities are started as meetings in homes of persons invited to learn about the teachings and practices of a sectarian form of Hinduism. In any major metropolitan center with large numbers of Asian Indians, scores of these home groups meet regularly for worship and study. Most of the larger religious and cultural organizations have grown out of these home gatherings.

The main reason given for these activities is to provide religious training for the children so they will have an identity as Asian Indians and as Hindus. Some groups provide for informal religious classes for the small children during the group meetings. Another development in the United States are Hindu summer camp programs. The purpose of most of these summer camps is both religious and cultural, and the advertisements for the camps offer assistance to parents in conveying their Hindu heritage to their children and in preserving, protecting, and propagating "the spiritual heritage of Mother India." The programs of the summer camps focus on religious and cultural aspects of Hindu heritage. Very successful camps are run by the Sri Rajarajeshwari Peethan of the Shankaracharya order in the Pocono Mountains of Pennsylvania and the Chinmaya West Mission of Chinmayananda. The former is run by an American woman convert to Hinduism who is particularly well-equipped to help these American children of Hindu parents make the transition between East and West. Many other Hindu groups and local temples have established summer camps and programs. Parents, some of whom do not participate in any religious activities themselves, pay for and send their children to these camps for total immersion in Hinduism otherwise not available outside India.

The family, however, remains the primary agent of transmission of religious tradition and the formation of personal religious identity. In the United States Hindu families are faced with this task without the supports available in Indian society, where Hindus are in the majority. And it is hard, as one mother remarked, "Here I have to be priest and preacher, and it doesn't work." Many immigrants are more religious in the United States than they were in India. Some say it is because they are no longer students and have become mature householders in the stage of life more concerned with religious matters. Others say it is because here they have to work as untrained lay persons to create and maintain institutions that in India are preserved by religious professionals. Although the primary reason for the growth of religious activities is to provide for the religious training of the children, when speaking of themselves the members of the first generation describe the manifest function of participation in religious groups as being "to gain peace," "to show devotion to God," and "to gain God's blessing." When members of the first generation speak of the function of religion for the second generation, however, the latent function comes to the fore: "so they will know who they are," "so they will not get lost in American society," "so my son will have the best of both cultures."

Organized religious groups

The past decade has seen a boom in the formation and incorporation of Hindu religious organizations in the United States. Any person can establish any type of religious organization he or she desires. Current research has discovered over 500 Hindu organizations, and many more exist in locations not covered by the research. The smallest of these had only three members and was more of a tax-dodge for persons living in apartments registered under the group's name, whereas the largest maintained a mailing list of over 15,000 in support of a well-established and well-endowed temple complex with a full range of programs. The groups represent virtually every branch of Hinduism and type of organization and change rapidly in location and leadership. A rough typology of the groups may be developed as follows: cultural; regional–linguistic religious; sectarian; yoga institutes and ashrams.

Indian cultural organizations in the United States are of two kinds. All-India cultural groups, under such names as the India Cultural Society, are the cultural counterpart of ecumenical Hinduism and sponsor programs from all parts of India, especially on the all-India traditional and national holidays. Regional groups such as the Gujarat Samaj and the Tamil Sangam promote regional festivals and arts. Persons from the different language areas, such as Gujarat, Punjab, Bengal, and Tamil Nadu, share some festivals but have different calendars of religious and cultural celebrations. The cultural groups are not explicitly religious, but they do reflect the union of the cultural and religious in India. Many of the traditional festivals and the arts are associated with Hindu tradition and mythology, so that the ethos of the groups tends to be Hindu and to push to the periphery members of religious minorities. An analogy would be the celebration of Christmas by the American community in Madras simply by the singing of Christmas carols and the celebration of a midnight mass. The Gujarat Samaj in some cities regularly sponsors explicitly religious meetings for the reading and interpretation of religious texts in Gujarati or for lectures by famous religious teachers that are attended by two or three thousand people. A parallel to this would be for the American community in Bombay to invite Billy Graham to preach there. If the India Cultural Society or the Gujarati Samaj and other regional groups are sufficiently large and prosperous enough to have a building as a cultural center, religious groups rent the buildings for their meetings – a regular calendar of religious meetings fills the schedule of many of the cultural centers.

Regional–linguistic religious organizations are not exclusive; they do not forbid others to attend and participate, but they do create boundaries through the use of the vernacular language, the celebration of regional festivals, the worship of forms of deities common to a region, and the use of regional dress, cuisine, and arts. One observer remarked, "If there is a language, there will be a group." They meet in homes or in rented churches or halls, with attendance at regular weekly or monthly meetings generally under a hundred for groups visited in the course of this research. Several smaller groups of the same linguistic identification may be active in a given city, so that for major celebrations or festivals several hundred people may gather. A typical response about size on the questionnaire is that weekly attendance is about fifty to seventy-five, perhaps a hundred have paid dues, some 300 to 500 names are on the mailing list, and 1,000 to 1,500 attend the major festivals. In practice, several groups join together for such festivals, and all take credit for the attendance. The regional identification of the group or its particular emphasis may not be obvious from the name; it is necessary to learn what language is used in the meetings, what images of gods or religious teachers are in the place of honor, and what pattern of worship is followed.

For seven years a Gita Forum has met in Dallas with about fifty active families. Thirty to forty people, mainly Gujaratis, attend the meetings in homes in north Dallas. The program of systematic study of the *Bhagavad*

Gita is a favorite among many regional groups. The period of meditation, chanting verses from the text, interpretation by a lay leader, and prayers is followed by a period of social fellowship and a meal. A Sat Kala Mandir meets on one Saturday of the month in a temple in Chicago to sing hymns (bhajans), and between thirty to fifty Tamilians are usually present. Parents in these groups are interested in providing instruction for their children in the regional languages, so they sponsor Sunday Schools or other occasions for language instruction and for classes on religious myths, texts, and rituals. The success in instruction in the Indian languages has been minimal, and in many cases it means nothing more than teaching the children songs through transliteration from the Indian language into English letters. A different kind of group, the Bengali Durga Puja Societies exist only to sponsor the major festival of Bengal once a year. They do not sponsor regular meetings throughout the year, but the Durga Puja celebration attracts several hundred people in the larger cities.

All Hindu groups in India are regional–linguistic because each is embedded in the languages and cultures where they exist. Thus, a Srivaishnava and a Smarta Brahmin in Tamil Nadu are both Tamilian Hindus, even though they may not think of themselves as such. The regional–linguistic identification is important among immigrants because the religious symbols are powerful aids in the formation and preservation of personal and group identity. Hindus who are Gujarati or Punjabi exist in India, but the designation of groups of Gujarati Hindus or Bengali Hindus is a new creation in the new land.

Sectarian groups

Sectarian groups overlap the regional–linguistic ones because many sectarian groups are related to specific regions of India. Swaminarayan Hinduism, which developed in Gujarat and is growing rapidly among Gujaratis in Britain and the United States, is a good example of a sectarian form; it uses the Gujarati language exclusively in meetings, primarily attracts Gujaratis, and meetings are accompanied by regional cuisine and arts (see Chapter Five). The Arya Samaj is primarily North-Indian Hindi and Punjabi in its constituency, but it is a sectarian group that follows a distinctive pattern of rituals following the teachings of Swami Dayananda Sarasvati (1824–83). Its programs and rituals are not restricted to a single regional–linguistic group, however. The Arya Samaj teaches a path that involves the rejection of the worship of images, a return to Vedic purity and the ritual of fire sacrifice. Small groups of the Arya Samaj meet in most of the metropolitan areas. Many other sectarian groups gather around a religious teacher, living or dead, whose teachings and person provide the focus for devotional activities within the group. It is common in meetings of these groups to gather around a worship center that contains the picture of the teacher along with a television set attached to a video cassette recorder playing tapes of lectures or chanting by the teacher. Many of these sectarian groups are in the devotional (bhakti) tradition because the path of devotion does not require a detailed knowledge of Sanskrit, use of vernacular rituals, or the presence of professional religious specialists.

Sectarian groups provide a focus of emotional unity and identity even when they attract persons from several ethnic groups. The unity of the group is preserved by the charisma of the teacher, and each individual has membership in the group by virtue of personal attachment to the religious leader. Some of these sectarian devotional groups have been successful in attracting non-Indian followers. The Chinmaya West Mission has regular programs based on the Advaita philosophy as taught by Swami Chinmayananda, which might be considered a philosophy and not a sectarian form of religion. Nevertheless, the branches of the Chinmaya Mission seek to preserve the "purity" of the religious teaching and practice as presented by their teacher. An official communication in the newsletter for December 1983 indicated that groups should use the study scheme prepared by Swami Chinmayanada, that other books should not be added or substituted, and that all funds collected must be used for mission-approved programs. Moreover, the headquarters should be consulted before inviting nonmission speakers to address formal programs, and only books, tapes and other items distributed by Chinmaya Mission are to be sold at official functions. Such sectarian groups are organized across the country and have national boards of directors, official publications, effective fund-raising programs, and extensive building projects in the United States and in India, all under the guidance of a respected religious teacher.

The devotional path is attractive to new immigrants because they can immediately become part of an identity-forming group without the necessity of emphasizing a regional ethnic identity or familiarity with classical Hindu scriptures. Indeed, in some groups studied it seemed that members come from very marginal immigrant Indians – for example, people of Indian origin who came to the United States after a period in central Africa or Fiji – and from other ethnic groups, such as Filipinos or American blacks.

The Sai Baba group is one which attracts many non-Indians. In fact, in the recent past none of the regional directors were of Indian origin, and in some parts of the country very few Asian Indians participate. In some cities, however, Asian Indians form groups of Sai Baba devotees. Most are attracted to Sai Baba after they arrive in the United States; no members interviewed for this study indicated that they were followers of Sai Baba in India. This movement centers on the figure of Satya Sai Baba, who was born in 1926 and claims to be the reincarnation of the Sai Baba of Shirdi who died in 1918. Sai Baba is well known for his "afro" hairstyle, and his followers consider him to be the divine manifestation of this age and praise him for his miraculous powers. Sai Baba has not visited this country, but trips by followers to visit his ashram in Andhra Pradesh often lead to passionate commitment to propagate the teachings of and devotion to Sai Baba. Followers occasionally make the disclaimer that such devotion is not "Hindu," but universal, and that some Christians and Jews are devotees, but the structure and practices of the group are clearly Hindu.

Some of the sectarian groups develop and transmit symbols that reinforce regional ethnic identity. Other sects shape a symbolic structure that supports a religious identity based on devotion to a teacher or set of teachings that transcend regional ethnic identity, but that do not express the universalism within the Hindu traditions of those forms of Indian religion called ecumenical Hinduism.

Yoga institutes and ashrams

Institutions exist for the teaching of yoga, some run by immigrants from India and others by American adepts, but it is not clear that they should now be included in a typology of religious groups that serve the Asian-Indian community. Most were begun by individual entrepreneurs prior to the immigration of large numbers of Asian Indians, and they attract Americans mostly for exercise classes and programs of "holistic health" where the religious aspects of classical yoga are ignored or muted. Many officers of these organizations responded to questionnaires with the comment that theirs is not a religious organization and should be excluded from the study. A few are businesses, like health spas, that profit from tax exempt status as educational or religious nonprofit organizations. Most Asian Indians are not attracted to yogic practices and discipline, so few of the organizations have many Asian-Indian members or clients. The relationship between these marginal forms of "American Hinduism" and the religions of the immigrants is complex (see Chapter Four), and it is difficult to determine the relationship that will exist among these groups in the future.

Ecumenical Hindu organizations

Ecumenical Hinduism is a recent organizational development among Indians abroad as an attempt to prevent the fragmentation of the Hindu community, which is such a small minority in the United States. It builds on traditional Hindu tolerance by including in one religious fellowship followers from different regions, language groups, and sects by including the deities and rituals of many sects. At one time the few Indian immigrants in a city found it necessary to gather across sectarian lines to observe festivals and perform rituals; now it has become a conscious strategy to develop a new form of Hinduism among immigrants. It represents an ecumenical approach to the formation and preservation of individual and group identity through the transmission of cultural patterns.

Ecumenical Hinduism has no single administrative headquarters in the United States or in India, nor are there all-Indian Hindu leaders who would be natural religious specialists for Hindus abroad. Indeed, it may well be that those attributes and abilities that would qualify a person to be an outstanding religious specialist in a region of India – oratorical skill in a regional language, intense devotion to a specific deity, administrative skills in the Indian setting – may not be the same attributes that are required for the upwardly mobile technocrats in the United States. Such specialists may develop on foreign soil, but they are not yet in evidence. As a result, the organizations of ecumenical Hinduism sponsor visits from India by religious specialists of different types and from different sects, mirroring the variety of deities and the variety of languages. Ecumenical Hinduism is congregational in the classic sense and calls its own leaders for temporary service to the whole Asian-Indian Hindu community.

The Gita Mandal in Indianapolis is an example of ecumenical Hinduism on the local level. The group started meeting in homes ten years ago as a group of three or four families, and now it meets once a month in the newly constructed India Community Center. Members of different sects and language groups participate in the meetings, bringing attendance to about two hundred. When leaders of Hindu sects visit followers in Indianapolis, the whole community is invited to meet them, and the occasion becomes a community celebration. Regional festivals are also occasions for community-wide celebrations. Even in larger cities where sectarian or regional groups are well-organized, members of these groups expect the support of the members of other Hindu groups and they in turn participate in the programs of other groups.

The symbols in the meetings are those that encourage the unity of Hindus. English, not one of the regional languages, is the language of the meetings and the social fellowship that follows. All members of the immigrant generation know English, and few members of the second generation are fluent in the Indian languages, so the use of English unites the immigrants from various parts of India as well as uniting members of the first and second generations. Some of the hymns have even been translated into English and the music transposed so that it can be played on a piano. As one leader remarked, "God understands English very well." Sanskrit is the only Indian language used for chanting the traditional verses, and those chants are learned by members of both generations from transliterations. Other modifications are made in parts of the service so that the rituals (puja) conform to the shortened period for the meeting. Brahmins are not required for the performance of the rituals, and the leaders are careful to avoid any caste discrimination. Just as the fellowship meals that usually accompany the meetings are a combination of regional cuisines, so an attempt is made in the organizations of ecumenical Hinduism to bring all Hindus together and avoid fragmentation of the community.

The Vishwa Hindu Parishad represents an attempt to develop a national and international organizational structure of ecumenical Hinduism. A world conference of international organizations held in Copenhagen in the summer of 1985 addressed the two major challenges faced by such groups: Identity (How can Hindus outside of India maintain their identity without enclosing themselves in ghettos?) and Mission (Now that the opportunity is open for Hindus to tell those in Western countries directly about their religion, how can they best present it?). The programs of the Vishwa Hindu Parishad in the United States are carried out through a national governing council that works through twenty-eight state units. Local chapters with varying levels of activity are located in about seventy-five cities and have about 3,000 members. Some local units have regular meetings for study and worship and sponsor summer camps that serve approximately 500 young people between eight and eighteen years old.

The primary function of this organization is to be an umbrella group that on the national and local levels maintains informal associations among Hindu groups, temples, and religious leaders to advance the concept of ecumenical Hinduism. It includes other religions of Indian origin – Jains, Sikhs, Buddhists. The annual national Hindu conferences that it organizes bring together lay leaders of many Hindu temples and organizations and some of the leading religious teachers and preachers from India to address the problems faced by Hindu individuals, families, and organizations in the United States. Its constitution refers to "the purpose of propagating dynamic Hindu Dharma representing the fundamental values of life comprehended by various sects and denominations including Buddhists, Jains, Sikhs, Lingayats, etc." A resolution passed at the Tenth Hindu Conference in Madison Square Garden in New York in 1984 "urges all the Hindus of the world – back home and abroad – to act in a broad and nationalistic manner rising above their personal beliefs and creeds, parochial languages, and provincial and sectarian considerations such as Gujarati, Punjabi, Tamilian, Telugu, Bengali, Jains, Sikhs, etc. etc. (sic)."

The Vishwa Hindu Parishad defines "Hindu" as "a person, natural or legal, or one believing in, following or respecting the values of life, ethical and spiritual, which have been developed in Bharat [India] and includes a person calling himself a Hindu." Leaders recognize that they are proposing organizational structures and relations different from those current in India and urge that Indians abroad make themselves examples to those in India in the development of an ecumenical form of Hinduism. The strength and growth of sectarian and regional forms of Hinduism and the secularization of the Asian-Indian community are threats from opposite sides to this new ecumenical group identity. What results from the tension will be a redefinition of what "Hindu" means in the United States and the redefinition of boundaries through the manipulation of symbols and the expansion of their cultural contextualization so as to include as many Asian Indians as possible under a single religious identity.

Swamis on the move

Swami Vivekananda is a model of success from an earlier generation, representing the Indian religious teacher who aspires to come to the United States to proclaim Hinduism. He came for the Conference on World Religions in conjunction with the Chicago World's Fair in 1893, creating a considerable stir and attracting many converts to his teaching of classical Advaitan philosophy for Westerners. The Vedanta Societies in major cities across the country are the results of his success. Swami Bhaktivedanta was equally successful in the 1960s in attracting followers to his form of Krishna devotion (bhakti), and the International Society for Krishna Consciousness has become a prosperous international organization. Sri Rajneesh's more recent arrival and activities were more spectacular, but the impact was transitory and an embarrassment to immigrant Hindus. These teachers have in common a mission to attract Westerners to Hindu philosophy, devotion or way of life. The groups they founded have trained Western men and women to become religious teachers and leaders, and, with the exception of the International Society for Krishna Consciousness, they focus their attention on Western converts (see Chapter Four). The converts have taken Hindu names and titles, and some of them have founded independent organizations. J. Gordon Melton has described some of these groups founded by both Indian and American Hindus (Melton, 1978:II,358–86).

Those Indian religious leaders who have adapted their message to attract Western followers have not been very influential among Asian Indians. On the contrary, those who are most influential among Asian Indians are generally not known outside the community and do not attract Westerners in significant numbers. In commercial terms, the two markets are different. That may change as the immigrants assimilate more in American society and as their children become more Americanized, but up until now the distinction is striking. No Hindu leader will say that his teaching is only for Asian Indians; rather, the claim is that it is universal truth. Most will even claim some Western followers, but the numbers are very small.

About twenty Indian teacher-monk-priests (*swamis*) have become permanent residents in the United States. One group are monks related to established orders in India who move to monasteries in the United States. Swami Bhashyananda of the Vedanta Society in Chicago represents this group, and he is well-received when he delivers lectures for Asian-Indian groups across the country. Another group are individuals who establish themselves in their own ashrams or institutions according to the idiosyncracies of their doctrine and practice. Some teach yoga or other forms of religious discipline. The ashram may be as small as a house with two or three live-in disciples or as extensive as several properties in more than one state. A typical pattern for these swamis is to spend nine or ten months in the United States and then a period visiting followers or religious institutions in India. Most of these groups are fairly small; few have more than fifty followers in the United States. A third group of swamis are those who are heads of temples. Some have started temples that have become centers of religious activity where they remain as resident teacher and priest; others have been called from India to become the resident teacher–priest of an established temple.

Every spring and summer large numbers of religious leaders come from India for tours across the United States to visit followers and acquaintances. They are part of a larger cultural movement that includes dancers, instrumentalists, singers, film stars, and other performers who find audiences in the Asian-Indian community. The Festival of India in 1985 brought programs of Indian culture to the attention of uninitiated Westerners, but they were also widely enjoyed by Asian Indians. Smaller "festivals of India" are held every spring and summer across the United States in schools, auditoriums, and Indian cultural centers as Indian artists and specialists of all kinds present programs for the Asian-Indian community. The traveling swamis are an important part of that larger cultural movement.

Over 90 percent of the Hindu organizations in the United States are founded and led by lay persons who have little training and, in many instances, limited knowledge of Hinduism. Leaders and members of Hindu groups in the United States are attached through family or sect ties to religious specialists in India, and the laymen rely on direction, encouragement, and instruction from those "professionals" in India. The networks through which these leaders are called over from India are many. Some sectarian groups, such as the Swaminarayan Hindus, sponsor regular, almost annual tours by the *acharyas* and *sadhus* to visit the homes and meetings of the sect across the country (see Chapter Five). Famous preachers from India arrange tours that take them to visit the major cities to lecture in programs sponsored by regional groups. At any time during the summer at least ten such preachers are touring the United States, and the most famous draw crowds of two or three thousand Asian Indians to their religious discourses. Tours are also arranged by individual families for their family guru or religious teacher from India by arranging a hall for lectures and inviting their friends. On occasion they will advertise by personal contact with acquaintances or in the newspapers for Asian Indians to ask for support in arranging for programs in other cities. Many of the local groups have been founded because the visitors themselves instructed and inspired a few followers to undertake the task. The major feature that distinguishes the breadth of the appeal of these visitors is whether they lecture in English or in one of the regional languages. It enhances the status of religious leaders in India if it is known that they have had a successful tour to "proclaim Hinduism in America," and some leaders of organizations in the United States complain about the swamis who come merely to impress their followers in India, suggesting that some controls should be exercised over the number and quality of visitors. The relationship between members of the immigrant community and the various types of religious specialists from India will determine to a large extent the shape of Hinduism in the United States.

Temples

Asian-Indian immigrants are temple builders. In every location with more than a hundred families of Hindus there is discussion of a plan for, or the actual construction of a Hindu temple. One informed estimate is that Asian-Indian immigrants have donated more than a hundred million dollars for such constructions. A recent issue of *Hinduism Today* lists forty Hindu temples in the United States (HT, 1986:8). The list is not complete – perhaps no complete list exists because no central temple organization has been formed, although one has been proposed. Moreover, new buildings are being constructed at a rapid pace, and no clear definition exists as to what constitutes a Hindu temple. Formal definitions of architecture, types of deities, ritual patterns, and officials that are applicable in India do not fit the situation in the United States. A handbook has been prepared to assist newly formed groups in the process of building a temple (Kannappan, 1984). As with other group activities, Hindu temples in the United States are not exclusive, and Hindus freely worship in temples across regional and sect lines. Nevertheless, temples in the United States can be distinguished by looking at architecture, deities, ritual patterns, language use, and place of origin of officials and board members and

Dedication ritual at Sri Venkateswara Temple in Pittsburgh

arranging them into categories – South Indian, North Indian, ecumenical, and sectarian.

South Indian temple architecture is spectacular. Built according to strict regulations from the ancient texts by craftsmen skilled in traditional construction, the exteriors of the temples have elaborately carved domes and towers. The gateways are sculptured works that reach into the sky, and the interior shrines are placed according to the requirements of the ritual texts (agama). Once the appropriate deities have been installed, the rituals must be performed by Brahmins with the appropriate status and training according to appropriate patterns. The most impressive of these South-Indian–style temples are the Shri Venkateswara Temple in Pittsburgh (dedicated 1976), the Ganesh Temple in Flushing, New York (dedicated 1977), the Meenakshi Temple in Houston (dedicated 1982), the Shri Venkateswara Temple in Los Angeles (dedicated 1984), the Shri Viswanatha Temple in Flint, Michigan (dedicated 1982), the Rama Temple in Chicago (dedicated 1986), the Shri Venkateswara Temple in Chicago (dedicated 1986), and the Shiva-Vishnu Temple in San Francisco (dedicated 1986). More are planned or under construction.

The planning and building of each of these temples has been a successful milestone for the groups and individuals involved. The Hindu Temple Society of North America was formed in New York on January 26, 1970, by a group meeting in the apartment of Mr. C. V. Narasimhan, an Under Secretary at the United Nations. The group gained the support of the Hindu community to build a temple to Vinayaka (Ganesh) on a residential street in Flushing two blocks from the Swaminarayan Temple in the middle of a large Asian-Indian population. The images of Ganesh, Shiva, Murugan, Lakshmi, Krishna, Rama, and Sita were installed in the temple on July 4, 1977, with dedication rituals timed to coincide with Independence Day celebrations. Now a full program of rituals is performed by a resident staff of priests (pujari). The foundation-laying ceremony for a Center of Indian Culture and Service adjacent to the temple was performed by Mr. N. T. Rama Rao, the Chief Minister of Andhra Pradesh, on June 9, 1984. The cultural center houses many cultural programs, classes, and meetings that previously were held in the basement of the temple building. The temple keeps contact with the community through a mailing list of 2,000 families in the adjacent tri-state area.

At about the same time, the largest, wealthiest, and most successful Hindu temple in the United States was planned and built in the Penn Hills area of Pittsburgh. Fred Clothey gives the details of the development of the temple and of the symbols and rituals of its dedication (Clothey, 1983:164–200). Plans for a temple began in discussion in December 1971 among a group that had been meeting in homes for the singing of hymns (bhajan). They were seeking ways they could provide for instruction for their children in Indian religion and culture, and they rented a basement as a temporary meeting place where Hindu rituals were performed on Sundays by the lay people. After canvassing the Hindu community, they talked with the leaders in New York who were planning the Ganesh Temple, and in March 1973 they incorporated the Hindu Temple Society of North America as an affiliate of the New York organization. In April 1973 they purchased a Baptist church building in Monroeville that served for a time as a temple for Hindus and Jains and as a gurdwara for Sikhs. The Pittsburgh group joined with the New York group in requesting the assistance of the Shri Venkateswara Temple at Tirupati in Andhra Pradesh.

The Shri Venkateswara Temple at Tirupati is the wealthiest temple in India, and it is visited by hundreds of thousands of pilgrims from throughout India and abroad. The Tirumala Tirupati Devasthanam (TTD) have offices throughout the world to arrange for pilgrims to visit the temple. The TTD and the Andhra Pradesh state government through its Commissioner of Endowments developed a scheme to give assistance to the New York and Pittsburgh temples and also to other temples built in the United States. The most recent form of the scheme (APSG, 1984) empowers the board "to spend its surplus funds for charitable or religious purposes with the prior approval of the Government, and with a view to propagate Hindu Dharma in Foreign countries and . . . to evolve a scheme for giving financial aid to temple committees in foreign countries" for the construction, completion, and renovation of Hindu temples. No more than approximately $150,000 is available for any project, and this is used for making available the services of temple architects, masons, and craftsmen for the construction of the building and for supplying the images, temple stones, and implements for worship. The value of these constitute a loan which is to be repaid without interest within five years after the completion of the temple in the form of medical or scientific equipment, books, or cash. A part of the agreement is that TTD will approve the plans for the temple and place representatives on the governing board of the temple. This TTD scheme has been very significant in the construction of South Indian temples in the United States. The visit of Mr. N. T. Rama Rao, the Chief Minister of Andhra Pradesh, took the form of a victorious religious pilgrimage as he dedicated temple and cultural center construction in four locations (New York, Lemont and Aurora in Illinois, and San Francisco). The commissioner of temples in Andhra Pradesh took early retirement to come to the United States as consultant and advisor to temples. In addition to the TTD, leaders established the Bharat International Trust in Madras in 1978 to assist in arranging for skilled assistance and artistic creations for the temples.

Ground-breaking ceremonies for the Pittsburgh temple were held in Penn Hills on April 17, 1975, with rituals performed according to the Pancharatragamic tradition of Vaishnavism, but tensions developed among the members concerning the regional identification of the proposed temple. In July a general meeting passed a resolution that "the Hindu Temple of Pittsburgh is and shall remain nonsectarian and broad-based, so as to meet the religious, spiritual, cultural, humanitarian, educational and social needs of all its members." The resolution called for the inclusion of images of other deities in addition to those proposed and for the right of groups to worship in the shrine area according to their own traditions. The TTD sent a letter in September 1975 to indicate that the revisions proposed in the resolution were not acceptable and support was withdrawn (Clothey, 1983:180–1). A split developed between the North Indians, who remained in Monroeville, and the South Indians, who purchased property in Penn Hills and continued with their plans to build the Shri Venkateswara Temple with the assistance of the TTD. The temple was dedicated in June 1977, and construction of additions to the building and grounds continues into the present.

The temple in Pittsburgh replicates the Shri Venkateswara Temple at Tirupati, and it quickly became the major pilgrimage temple for Hindus on the East Coast and the mid-West. Over two-thirds of the pilgrims to

Penn Hills are from the four South Indian states – Tamil Nadu (32.4%), Andhra Pradesh (23.3%), Karnataka (18.3%), and Kerala (3.7%) (Bhardwaj and Rao, 1983). The temple has a staff of three priests (pujari) who perform the full range of daily, annual, life cycle, and occasional rituals as performed in South India. Even here innovations are made that would be unlikely in a traditional Indian context: the use of bricks and mortar rather than stone in the construction, the willingness to erect the sanctuary above other parts of the building, including rest rooms within the temple precincts, openness of the shrine area not only to non-Brahmins but also to non-Hindus, and the preparation of food in the temple by non-Brahmins (Clothey, 1983:199). Secular activities include an active series of cultural programs that brings excellent musicians and dancers to Pittsburgh. During one period an astrologer was associated with the temple to cast and read horoscopes for fees ranging from ten to fifty dollars. Sunday School classes are held each week for language instruction in Tamil, Telugu, and Kannada and in the Hindu religion. A summer camp is held each summer in cooperation with the Chinmaya Mission West for over one hundred children.

The temple is wealthy; its annual income approaches a million dollars.[3] In 1984 more than 10,000 persons from across the country made contributions to the temple, so many that their names are no longer included in the quarterly publication. The temple provides university scholarships for needy students, support for a program of studies of Hinduism at the University of Pittsburgh, and support for a project to translate the *Pancharatragama* into English. Relief funds are solicited: the Ethiopian Relief Fund, the Prime Minister's Relief Fund, and the Bhopal Relief Fund. The temple also sponsored a Conference of Hindu Religious Organizations in North America in August 1984 to discuss the problems associated with the construction and support of temples, and it has given small loans to help other temple societies in Pennsylvania and Ohio. Its great success is one other Hindu societies across the country envy and hope to emulate. One of the arguments given by leaders for constructing temples in their own cities was, "We should not have to go as far as Penn Hills for our rituals."

The Hindu Temple in Monroeville originated as a split in the group in Pittsburgh and is known as the temple for North Indians. It now has a new temple building with facilities for many deities related to many groups from North India. The Jain group in Pittsburgh also has their services in the building. The Hindus called Swami Narayan Muni to be the chief priest of the temple and to perform the rituals; he also travels to other temples as guest lecturer. Fred Clothey concludes that this temple embodies "a world which stresses a more selective Hinduism, a neo-Hinduism that emphasizes eclecticism, diversity, and the Westernization of Indian values" (Clothey, 1983:198). Both temples in Pittsburgh seem to be prospering.

A few miles from the Ganesh Temple in New York, the Gita Temple Ashram is a North Indian temple in Elmhurst. It has an interesting history because it was started as an individual effort by a swami who came to the United States in 1969 on a preaching tour and stayed. The success of the temple indicates the value of starting early and being broad in scope. The swami opened a small temple a few blocks from its present location in 1972, and the numbers in attendance grew so large that a new temple building was dedicated in October 1983. The meeting hall, 80' × 100', was the largest Hindu temple in North America until the construction of a larger temple complex in Chicago in 1986. The display of images in the front of the hall is in North-Indian style and includes Radha and Krishna, Ambalji, Durga, Vishnu and Lakshmi, Rama and Sita, Shiva and Parvati, Hanuman, and Ganesh. Images of other deities are in shrines at the back. The temple is open from 8 A.M. until 9:30 P.M. every day with a regular program of rituals. All the major festivals are celebrated in the temple, and people come to the temple for the life-cycle rituals. The founder–priest runs the programs, and his estimate is that attendance at the Sunday programs averages two hundred, and that during a given weekend about 2,000 people visit the temple. Most are Hindi speakers, and many are Gujaratis. Visiting religious leaders from India give lectures in the temple, and Morari Bapu, a famous Gujarati preacher "like Billy Graham," attracted a crowd of some 5,000 to the temple in June 1984. The priest tried to begin language instruction in Hindi, Gujarati, and Sindhi without success. He also opened a satellite center in Pennsylvania that did not meet with success. Nevertheless, the Gita Temple Ashram is an example of a very successful temple that attracts large numbers of North Indians.

Most Hindu temples in the United States are ecumenical to some degree because images of several deities are found in each temple. Even in South-Indian temples images of deities are found together that would not normally be so closely associated in India. As one leader of the Ganesh Temple explained, "After all, we are at the seat of the United Nations." The Dallas/Fort Worth Hindu Temple Society, which plans construction of a Ganesh shrine for a Shree Mahalaxmi Temple in 1986, is an example of a group attempting to be independent and broadly ecumenical. Their motto is "Unity is Strength" and the hope is that they will be able to maintain the support of all elements of the Hindu, Jain, Sikh, and Buddhist communities in the metroplex area and avoid the proliferation of temples. One leader explained: "In ten years the children will not think of themselves as Gujarati, Tamil, or Hindi, but as Indian and they will need a unified group." The published objective of the Hindu Temple

Society is "to construct a temple and cultural center for the practice and promotion of religions that originated in India." They try to maintain their independence from temples in India so they can be more moderate and progressive in providing the programs that their children need. The board of trustees includes persons from all areas of India and from all the sectarian groups. In coordination with these groups they have sponsored various lecturers, festivals, children's camps, and language instruction in rented park district halls and university auditoriums.

The Asian-Indian community in Dallas/Fort Worth is widely dispersed, with many in North Dallas. After the group decided in 1982 to build a temple, they purchased 7.4 acres of land in Plano, one mile from the South Fork Ranch of the television program "Dallas," at a cost of $115,000. The total building project in three phases is estimated at $1.5 million. In September 1985 they raised $300,000 in a series of fund raising dinners, and they hope to raise at least $750,000 by the time of the groundbreaking for the first phase in 1986. The difficulties in maintaining the unity, interest, and enthusiasm of the various regional and sectarian groups are great; devotion to a particular deity, enjoyment of hymns and discourses in the native language, and attachment to a revered religious teacher all seem more powerful than attachment to Hinduism as a religion, which in India is an abstraction from individual and group experiences and not the lived reality. The relative success or failure of the attempts at building ecumenical Hindu temples and organizations will shape the form of Hinduism practiced by the next generations.

Different groups invest in the future in different ways

Organizations with close ties to sectarian groups in India chose to construct sectarian temples where the images of deities in the temple and the rituals performed are those associated with the sect. Usually a famous teacher, or even a manifestation of god, is worshipped as the founder and his or her teachings are treated as sacred scripture along with the traditional Sanskrit texts. Religious specialists of the sect come from India to direct the work of the lay leaders in the United States. Swaminarayan Hinduism has been among the most successful in establishing groups and building temples in the United States (see Chapter Five). The International Society for Krishna Consciousness developed as a unique sectarian form of Hinduism in the United States (see Chapter Four). The temples of these organizations compete with other Hindu temples for the allegiance, support, and attendance of their members and the larger Hindu community.

In India, every religious group is a minority. The Vaishnavas of Gujarat, Srivaishnavas of Tamil Nadu, Arya Samaj in the north, Shaivites of Bengal are all minorities within a larger whole. The relationships of the various groups have evolved over the centuries, especially in the modern period of increased mobility and communication, so that each individual and group has its identity within the whole. The situation is analogous to "Christian America," where each religious group has its place in an evolving kaleidoscope, although the evolution of relationships is slow moving and constant in India; in the United States all the pieces are placed in new configurations in a very short period. The process of fitting each piece into the picture is an intricate one currently being carried out through a series of decisions by individuals and groups about the shape of Hinduism in the various cities of the United States. The result will be an American Hinduism that will have some continuity with religious traditions in India but that will be a new form of Hinduism.

Jains

"Live and Let Live" is the motto on the letterhead of the Jain Center of North America in New York, a most appropriate one for this branch of Indian religion. Jains have lived as a small minority in India even though they claim a heritage as ancient as that of Hindus. By maintaining a strong emphasis on nonviolence (*ahimsa*) and self-reliance in things religious and secular, Jains have been able to live among Hindus in a symbiotic relationship that has affected both. Over the centuries some Jains have adopted concepts and rituals from Hinduism so that many Hindus consider Jainism to be a sect of Hinduism. The Vishwa Hindu Parishad in the United States includes Jains, Sikhs, and Buddhists as part of the Hindu tradition. Although most Jains consider themselves a separate group, Jainism has had a long and significant influence on Hinduism: The Jain teaching of nonviolence has been influential in Indian culture since the reign of the Buddhist King Ashoka (c. 265–238 B.C.), whose grandfather, Chandragupta, is described in Digambara Jain traditions as a convert to Jainism, culminating in its most important modern manifestation in the work of Mahatma Gandhi, a Hindu.

The Jains have been influential far out of proportion to their numbers in India. They make up only 0.48 percent of the population, and even in the states of highest concentration are only 1.5 percent of the population. The great majority, 77.24 percent, of Jains live in four western and north central Indian states; the rest are spread out in all the other states (see Table 2.2). A very large Gujarati Jain community is established in Bombay in Maharashtra, so the Gujarati Jain population is larger than shown on the state census. Another anomaly of the statistics is that the Jain population of Gujarat itself shows very small growth between 1970 and 1980, much smaller than for any other portion of the population or

Table 2.2. *Distribution of the Jain population in India*

Area	Population	% of pop.	% growth 1970–80
India	3,206,038	0.48	23.69
Gujarat	467,768	1.37	3.59
Madhya Pradesh	444,960	0.85	37.04
Maharashtra	939,392	1.50	33.50
Rajasthan	624,317	1.82	21.57
Karnataka	297,974	0.80	36.15
Uttar Pradesh	141,549	0.13	13.49
Tamil Nadu	49,564	0.10	20.60

Adapted from the *1981 Religious Census of India*, Varma 1984:vii.

than for Jains in other locations. One reason for this may be the emigration of Gujarati Jains to Bombay or Delhi, or abroad to Britain and the United States.

The only estimates of Jain population in the United States come from the mailing lists of Jain organizations, the best estimate being that 5,000 Jain families constitute a population approaching 20,000 persons. A statistical profile of the Jain community given in the 1986 directory of Jains shows that the majority of the respondents were either engineers (38.1%) or in the medical field (19.8%); even though Jains are known as businessmen in India, a small percentage (12.4%) are self-employed in the United States.[4] Jains live in most areas of the country, but 80 percent of the Jains in North America live in nine states and one Canadian province. These are (in order of population density) New York, California, New Jersey, Ontario, Michigan, Texas, Illinois, Ohio, Maryland, and Massachusetts.[5] Two of every five Jains are from Gujarat and another two are from Maharashtra. Some of those from Maharashtra are Gujaratis whose families actually had settled in Bombay.[6] Perhaps as many as 70 percent of those who are active in Jain affairs are Gujaratis. Most Jains came directly from India, with a small number arriving from East Africa or Britain.

The Jain Center of North America began in New York with meetings in homes for worship by two or three families in 1967–8. They continued to meet in homes and in rented halls for festivals until the group was large enough to purchase a building for a temple in 1981. The building was a three unit apartment building in Elmhurst near the center of the Jain population of Queens and Long Island. The four rooms of the first floor were opened to make a prayer hall that seats two hundred "Indian style." The shrine for rituals is in an alcove. A retired Jain from South

Africa looks after the daily requirements of the temple. Numbers have grown since they obtained a regular meeting place, with two hundred families now members and six hundred addresses on the mailing list. The temple is open for prayers and hymns (bhajan) on Friday evenings (about forty or fifty people attend) and on the first Sunday of the month a family sponsors a ritual (puja) to celebrate the birth of Mahavira (about a hundred people attend). It appears that a larger percentage of men attend the rituals in the United States than in India, perhaps because they have to provide transportation for the women in American cities. Jains in New York still must rent an assembly hall for special festivals, when 750 to 1000 people may attend. The prayer book and service are in Gujarati, but on occasion Hindi is used for families from Rajasthan. Three or four white Americans occasionally attend. In 1983 a Jain Youth Center was established to provide social occasions for their young people. Each independent Jain center stresses some aspect from the Jain tradition, and a New York leader indicated, "Here we stress the ritual; in Boston they stress the philosophy."

Jains in Boston began to meet in homes in the early 1970s, and from these meetings the Jain Center of Greater Boston was founded in 1973 with about twelve active families. They continued to meet in homes, university halls and town halls, and now about a hundred Jain families live in the Boston suburbs. The Boston group has had a significant influence through the distribution of a "Jain Study Circular," which began publication in 1979 and is distributed to Jains across the country. The mailing list for the circular was the only record of the Jains in the United States for many years. The circular contains serious articles on Jain philosophy and religion and "Jain School" lessons for children. Many articles deal with vegetarianism, nonviolence, the relation of science and religion, the relation of Jainism and Hinduism, and explanations of Jain rituals and festivals. As a supplement to the "Jain Study Circular" the book *Essentials of Jainism* (Jain, 1984) was distributed to people on the mailing list. These publications provide resources for the lay leaders of the Jain groups and for the education of their children born in the United States. Since 1985 the circular has included a newsletter of announcements about activities of Jain associations in other locations. In 1981 the Jain Center of Greater Boston purchased a church building in Norwood that seats two hundred. There was some controversy about having a temple because the installation of images (*murti*) requires daily worship, but adjustments were made in the ritual requirements. Attendance at the Sunday meetings ranges from twenty-five to a hundred. The meetings are conducted in English, but the prayers are in Gujarati or Hindi.

The Jain group in Dallas was more recently formed as a result of the recent growth of the Asian-Indian population in Dallas/Fort Worth, and they do not yet have a regular meeting place. Leaders estimate that a hundred Jain families reside in the Dallas area, mostly Gujaratis but including some Punjabis and Rajasthanis. They started to have regular meetings once a month in 1983, which some fifty people attend. Classes for children are held on the daily rituals and chants of Jainism and there is open discussion for adults. More attend for the major festivals and for lectures by Jain scholars. The possibility exists that the new temple planned by the Hindu Society will contain a separate Jain hall with a shrine so the Jains will have their own place of worship. If so, they will join other Jain groups who have separate shrines or meet regularly in Hindu temples.

Jains are so scattered in the metropolitan areas and across the country that the major festivals are the only times when Jains get together and Jain identity is asserted. The festivals of the Jain calendar that are most important in the United States are: the celebration of the birth of Mahavira (Mahavira jayanti in April/May), the commemoration of the liberation of Mahavira (vira-nirvana in October/November), and the annual rite of fasting and confession (Paryusanaparva, for eight or ten days in September).[7]

Jains are divided into several subgroups in India, but in the United States the numbers are so small that members of the various groups meet together. The ancient division between Digambaras and Svetambaras is manifested in various ways. The Digambaras follow a slightly different calendar, have a separate caste of Brahmins to perform the rituals, and have simple, unadorned images in their shrines. In general the Svetambaras have been more influenced by Hindu iconography and rituals. Svetambara images are given staring glass eyes, are adorned with golden ornaments and jewels, and are clothed. The majority of the Jains in the United States are Svetambaras, but in the temple in Boston both Digambara and Svetambara images are in the shrine. Strictly speaking, Jain philosophy does not include the worship of God; the images are of "ideal human beings." A more modern division is between the Jains who use images (murti) in their worship and those who do not. Two Svetambara groups represented among Jains in the United States do not use images: The Sthanakavasi group rejects image worship, as do the Therapanthi, who are followers of Acharya Tulsi of Rajasthan. Some groups in the United States use images and some do not, but they are willing to adapt their religious practices to one another so they can maintain their unity; otherwise they would be too small to maintain viable groups.

A Federation of Jain Associations in North America (JAINA) has been formed to try to maintain that unity and to coordinate the activities of the associations. Each of the twenty local associations is independent; three have their own buildings (New York, Boston, New Jersey), several have shrines in united Hindu temples (e.g., Monroeville, Pennsylvania), and the rest meet in homes or rented halls. The Federation has conducted biennial meetings in Los Angeles (1981), New York (1983), and Detroit (1985), and several projects have been undertaken. The Federation sponsors Jain scholars from India who visit the centers on lecture tours. Previously each center invited lecturers independently or provided hospitality for guests who came uninvited. The registry of scholars will impose some control over such visits, establishing regulations such as that lecturers must be able to speak good English so as to be understood by the young people. A youth directory is to be prepared to facilitate youth activities. A Jain Heritage Tour of sacred places in India for young people to be led by a Jain scholar was planned for 1983 but cancelled because of poor response. The Federation will publish a quarterly news booklet for associations to supplement the "Jain Study Circular." Plans are also underway to publish Jain literature in good American English for use in the United States.

The venerable tradition in India is that Jain monks (*munis*) do not travel except on foot and do not go abroad. Jain discipline for monks requires a gradual restraining of bodily activities and functions, and such restraint is generally thought to be antithetical to travel abroad (Jaina, 1979:241–71). Traditionally, a major threat to Hindus abroad is the loss of caste; the threat to Jains is the loss of proper restraint. However, two "progressive" monks emigrated to the United States and have given significant leadership to the development of the Jain community and at the same time attracted some white Americans to Jainism. Chitrabhanu Muni was the first to come, in 1971, for a series of lectures at Harvard University. He lectured widely on Jain philosophy, meditation, and vegetarianism and began to gather followers in a Meditation International Center in New York. Most of his followers are white Americans, but he has been active in lecturing to Jain groups across the country and at federation conventions. He was a Svetambara monk when he came, but he married and now has a family.

Sushil Kumar Muni is a Sthanakavasi Svetambara monk from Delhi who came to the United States in 1975. He attracted attention at religious gatherings because he wore the Jain mask over his mouth to keep from inhaling insects and carried a brush to sweep insects from his path. He established an ashram in a large house on Staten Island and gathered a group of followers. In 1981 they began negotiations to purchase a Jewish campground in the Pocono Mountains near Blairstown, New Jersey, which they finally purchased in 1983 and named "Sidhachalam." The camp has a large hall, kitchen, cabins, and other buildings on 103 acres. It is now the headquarters for Sushil Muni even though he maintains other properties on Staten Island and in Los Angeles. A group of white

American householder disciples live at the ashram in New Jersey. Two Indian monks who are disciples of Sushil Muni now visit Jain groups. A summer camp is held for Jain young people, and retreats are held for families. Some leaders of the Jain federation and of the International Mahavira Jain Association have plans to build one major Jain temple in the United States on the campground – "a marble temple in the hills just like India."

Sushil Muni was active in the establishment of the Third International Jain Conference, which was held in New Delhi in February 1985 for the purpose of uniting Jains from all over the world in one forum. The conference provided a showcase for Jain teachings about nonviolence and vegetarianism and about the relevance of these teachings to modern problems of nuclear war and personal tensions and conflicts.

It is estimated that now some 100,000 Jains live outside India. The two Jain monks have taken the significant step of traveling outside India in an attempt to meet the needs of Jains who live abroad, and as one leader explained, "to face the modern situation with Jain values." Some more orthodox Jains are critical of this breaking of the traditional rules and argue that the life of a Jain monk cannot be lived outside of India. That is the major issue for the lay people as well as the monks.

Two Jain men discussed their religious background in biographical interviews for this study. One came to the United States in 1969 for graduate work in business. In his Indian village the family went to one of several Jain temples every morning for prayers and study. From the fourth grade on he was a scholarship student in a boarding house of a Jain college, so he is well versed in Jain philosophy and rituals. When he first came to the United States, he did not know of any Jain groups, but after his wife came over, they started to attend home meetings. Now that he has children, he leads some of the rituals, but says that he is not as religious as when he was in India. The other man came as a civil engineer in 1970 and finds that he is more religious in the United States and visits the temple more often. He explained that here he has to "search for [his] identity," which was simply presented to him as a Jain in India. Moreover, he has two children, and he has to be active in the Jain group and in the Gujarati Samaj, he says, in order to help them know who they are.

The problem of identity is quite real for this small minority as it seeks to establish itself between the Hindu community of fellow immigrants and American secular society. A set of problems similar to those of other Asian-Indian immigrants dominates discussions about the future. Religious education for children and young people is difficult because the parents are very busy establishing themselves in careers and few religious specialists are available to assist with religious education. Too few resources are available to help lay leaders perform the rituals or to teach the children. A Jain monastery in Karnataka began publication of a journal in English, *Gommatavani*, for Jains abroad. A great emphasis is placed on education for the young people. Jain immigrants are well educated and generally successful, and parents place pressure on the children to excel in academic work. Vegetarianism is the outward symbol of Jain nonviolence, and parents have difficulty in maintaining this discipline in families. The mores of American teenagers, which include dating and the use of drugs and alcohol, are viewed as threats to Jain children and to the integrity of the families. Jainism does not have a "sacred language" but rather has always used the language of the region where its followers live. Thus the use of Indian languages in the United States is increasingly problematic. The young people do not read and write Gujarati, Hindi, or Punjabi – even those who have minimal ability to speak the languages in the home. When they return to India for visits, they cannot understand their relatives or religious leaders. Finally, a large question looms: What will happen to the girls? It is difficult to arrange marriages in a small community. Many boys go back to India and bring brides to the United States, but the girls neither wish to return to India nor to marry boys socialized there. It will become a major problem for the community, and it is one of the main reasons for moves to organize social activities for the young people, lest they marry outside the Jain community. It will be interesting to see what type of symbiotic relationship will develop between the Jains and the Hindus in the United States and between the Jains and the larger society.

Sikhs

The Sikhs have been more in the news than any other Asian-Indian group because of the conflict in the Punjab which has spilled over into the United States.[8] Scenes of the attack on the Golden Temple in Amritsar and of the events surrounding the assassination of Prime Minister Indira Gandhi are fresh in the minds of the American public and they leave a seared scar on the hearts of the Sikhs. The Sikh community, a part of which has the longest history of any Asian Indians in the United States, is angered, torn, and made apprehensive and heartsick by the events in the Punjab.

The history of the Sikhs has been fraught with conflict and tension, in part because from the beginning as a distinct religious group they have deliberately occupied a tenuous place in the Punjab among the Hindus and the Muslims. In thought and practice they combine monotheism and reverence for a sacred book, the *Adi Granth* – similar to aspects of Islam – with a tradition of ten religious leaders (gurus) and some rituals similar to Hindu devotion (bhakti). Physically and culturally they occupy a location in the Punjab as a slight majority among Hindus on the border of Muslim Pakistan. The Punjabi language can be written in either *Devanagari* (the North Indian script preferred by Hindus), Persian (that widely used for Urdu by Muslims) or *Gurumukhi* (the script of the *Adi Granth* and other Sikh writings). The Sikhs prefer to use Gurumukhi, and language is a powerful symbol of Sikh identity and the place Sikhism occupies between Hindus and Muslims.

The story Sikh leaders tell about their history recounts a quietistic beginning as a devotional movement under Guru Nanak that became militant late in the Mughal period (1526–c1750) when Sikhs had to protect themselves and Hindus in conflicts with Muslim rulers. (See McLeod, 1976:1–19, for comments on the evolution of the Sikh community). Gobind Singh, the tenth guru, passed the power of religious leadership to the sacred *Adi Granth* and to the community, called "Khalsa," which he established for those who would undergo an initiation rite, take the names "Singh" for men and "Kaur" for women, and preserve the five symbols (often called the five Ks because the Punjabi word for each begins with that letter): (1) unshorn hair and beard; (2) a wooden or ivory comb for care of the beard; (3) a special type of underwear; (4) a short sword, and (5) a steel bracelet. The common headdress worn by Sikh men is a turban, so the turban and beard have become the commonly understood marks of the Sikh male. The Sikhs became a powerful military force, so they say, to defend the rights of Hindus who were threatened by the Mughals, and established an empire in the northwest under the famous warrior Ranjit Singh that opposed the British in the nineteenth century. Religion and politics were fused, so the Sikh self-image includes a view of themselves as good soldiers and courageous defenders of Sikh, Punjabi, and Indian interests.

In this century, within the living memory of many Sikh families in the United States, Sikhs were uprooted in 1947 when the Sikh "homeland" in the Punjab was partitioned between Pakistan and India; three million Sikhs left their homes in the midst of communal rioting and moved to India. Sikhs had been active in the independence movement and claim the roles of patriots in opposition to the British and as protectors of Hindu lives during the partition. Sikhs claim that, in return for their loyalty to the new India, promises were made that their rights would be protected. Much of the emotion and rhetoric in subsequent conflicts involves understandings of regional or national patriotism and certain rights claimed by the Sikhs. In 1966 the government of India created the state of Punjab with a Punjabi-speaking majority by separating the Hindi-speaking areas into the new state of Harayana. Chandigarh, a city claimed by both states, was made the common capital even though it is in Punjab.

Table 2.3. *Distribution of Sikh population in India*

Area	Sikh population	%	Incr.	Hindu population	%
India	13,078,146	1.96	26.15		
Punjab	10,199,141	60.75	24.99	6,200,195	36.93
Chandigarh	95,370	21.11	45.67	451,610	75.55
Harayana	802,230	6.21	27.13	11,547,676	89.50
Delhi	393,921	6.33	35.31		

Adapted from the *1981 Religious Census of India*, Varma 1984:vii,xii,xiv.

Language and religion are powerful symbols of group identity and the two have played a confusing role in political, religious, and social developments in the Punjab (Brass, 1974). A separate state has been created for Sikhs in the Punjab where most Sikhs live, and the only place where they are a majority (see Table 2.3). Outside of the Punjab large numbers of Sikhs live in Delhi, Bombay, and Calcutta, but nowhere in the rest of the country are they more than 2.5 percent of the population. It is estimated that over a million Sikhs reside outside of India, but they remain Punjabis everywhere, their religious and regional–social identities firmly united. This fusion of religion and regional political power violates the principle of the secular state supposedly governing India. Sikhs both in India and abroad think of themselves as a Punjabi religious minority and make both religious and political demands on the government, but the secular government of India deals with them as a linguistic minority of Punjabis.

The Ghadar syndrome

During the time that the Indian independence movement was growing, Sikhs were the first Asian-Indian religious group to establish themselves in the United States. In the early part of this century a movement of Sikhs of the agriculture caste (Jat) emigrated to Canada to work in construction and on the railroads. After the Vancouver riots on September 7, 1907, many of these Sikhs moved into California and took up their hereditary occupation of farming. Between 1907 and 1920 approximately 6,400 Asian Indians, mostly Sikh agriculturalists, entered the United States, and a small number of illegal aliens entered through Mexico. A group of male Sikh agricultural workers began to establish themselves in California.

The first Sikh organization and the oldest gurdwara (Sikh temple) in the United States is in Stockton, California. Two Sikhs began to have programs of devotional hymns (*kirtan*) at their farm in 1904 and built a small wooden structure for a prayer hall in 1906. In 1912 they founded the Pacific Khalsa Diwan Society, and built a larger building in 1916. It became the recognized center for Asian Indians, and especially for Sikh activities, in the United States. Sikhs moved into the present building in 1929 and have continued their regular program of religious and social activities since that time.

They faced overt discrimination along with other immigrants from Asia. The Immigration Act of 1917 included India in the Asiatic Barred Zone, which meant that no new immigrants from India were permitted. The most important result of that legislation was that Sikh men could not send back to the Punjab for brides according to traditional caste marriage practices. There were only six Sikh women in the country from 1904 to 1947 (LaBrack, 1979:134, note 20). Many of the men married Mexican-American brides. The Sikhs argued that they are racially Caucasian and should be legally considered as such for immigration and citizenship purposes. The issue was decided in the case of *United States vs. Bhagat Singh Thind* (261, U.S. 204) by the United States Supreme Court on February 19, 1923. Justice Sutherland declared that a "Hindu" was not a "free white person" within the meaning of the law and hence not eligible for American citizenship. The lack of citizenship in that time meant that they could not own land, which forced some to marry non-Sikh brides so they could purchase land in their wives' names. By 1950 the number of Asian Indians in the United States had dropped to 2,649, including members of other religious communities (Jacoby, 1979:164).

The result of immigration and citizenship laws was a type of assimilation for Sikh males that Yusuf Dadabhay has called "circuitous assimilation" (Dadabhay, 1954:138–41). The men married outside the Sikh community because no Sikh brides were available, and the second generation was raised with little knowledge of Punjabi or of Sikh religion. Many men gave up wearing the beard and turban, and few of the children were initiated into full membership in the Khalsa. Even though their personal identity remained that of Punjabi Sikhs of the agricultural caste, they were treated by the host society as Hindus. Bruce LaBrack remarks, however, that this was not so much circuitous assimilation as "cultural genocide" (1979:134, note 20).

During this period of discrimination a revolutionary movement known as the Ghadar movement developed among the Sikhs. From a headquarters in San Francisco the leaders published literature and a newspaper begun in 1913, raised funds, and enlisted "freedom fighters" to oppose the British in India in an uprising planned in the Punjab in 1915. The movement continued in the United States after it was effectively banned in India, and the Ghadar members in the United States were more militant than most of the nationalists in India. Mark Juergensmeyer notes that this was not simply a nationalist struggle, but rather the struggles against oppression in both America and India were fused into one (Juergens-meyer, 1979: 173–90). He describes the "Ghadar syndrome" as "a militant nationalist movement created abroad by expatriates, for whom the move-ment is also an outlet for their economic and social frustrations, and a vehicle for their ethnic identities." Thus the awareness of identity was formed and preserved in the United States through a nationalist movement that allowed for the expression of the emotions caused by discrimination, which was a threat to the continuation of Sikh and Punjabi identity. The Ghadar movement was repressed during World War I, but it continued to publish a paper and agitate until India gained independence and the repressive laws of the United States were changed. The headquarters of the Ghadar party in San Francisco was given to the Government of India, and the government donated a Ghadar Party Memorial Building on the site in 1974.

At about the time of Indian independence the legal situation in the United States was changed by the passage of the Luce–Celler Bill in 1946. The bill permitted Sikhs to become citizens and allowed a hundred im-migrants a year from India. The Sikh community in California prospered in the agricultural areas of the Imperial Valley, in Stockton, and in the Yuba City–Marysville area. Many Sikhs became prosperous owners of their own farms, and one, who is identified as "the most powerful Sikh in the United States" (Dye, 1984:1), has amassed a farm of 10,000 acres. Several thousand Sikhs – 5,000 by some estimates – live in the Yuba City–Marysville area, which makes it now the largest localized Sikh settlement in the United States. A second Sikh gurdwara, of the Imperial Valley Khalsa Diwan (Free Divine Communion Society), was built in El Centro in 1948. Until the new immigration and the explosion of building of gurdwaras in the 1970s, Stockton and El Centro were the only two gurdwaras in the United States.

The new immigrants

The older settlers in California and their descendants preserved Sikh religion in the United States, but they abandoned some traditions they considered to be encumbrances. Most were cleanshaven without turbans and had developed a fairly relaxed view of Sikh identity. When the newer immigrants arrived from India, the earlier immigrants were faced with more conservative Sikhs recently from the Punjab, members of different castes and with different educational backgrounds. Some of the new im-migrants are *keshdhari* (initiates of the Khalsa who wear the symbols of the Sikhs) who look down on the *sahajdhari* (those who are not initiates or who do not wear the five Ks). Some Sikhs look upon the renewed emphasis on such outward symbols as an importation of "village India" that has little relevance to circumstances in the United States. Whereas the Sikhs who were here before 1965 are predominantly agriculturalists residing in the rural areas of California, the new Sikh immigrants are highly educated professionals or students who are widely dispersed in the urban areas. Even before the recent crisis in the Punjab, the arrival of the new immigrants resulted not only in a dramatic increase in the Sikh population, but also in new tensions between generations of immigrants, different castes and social groups, and between individuals about what constitutes the Sikh identity and how best to preserve both Sikh and Punjabi identity.

The decade of the 1970s was a period for growth of Sikh institutions across the country as the new professional immigrants founded Sikh societies in most major cities. Typically the Sikhs began to meet once a month in homes for the singing of devotional hymns (kirtan) and, as the numbers grew, rented halls and churches for festivals. Some groups purchased houses or churches and converted them into gurdwaras, while others dedicated new buildings as prayer halls and community centers. The most recent directory of Sikhs in the United States, published in 1983, contains a partial list of fifty Sikh societies, including thirteen in California. Of the fifty, eighteen have their own buildings, and ten more have purchased land for a gurdwara.[9] Estimates published in newspapers of the number of Sikhs now in the United States vary widely from 100,000 to 500,000, but these seem excessively high. Leaders of the Sikh organizations do not have accurate figures, but the best estimate seems to be around 50,000.[10]

The first and now the largest Sikh group outside of California is the Sikh Cultural Society in New York. The first meetings took place with consular officials and students in 1954, but regular monthly meetings in homes were not begun until 1963, when about ten families were active. After formal incorporation in 1968, the Sikh Cultural Society purchased an old Methodist church building in a residential area of Richmond Hill, Queens, and converted it into a gurdwara in 1972. During the period of the new immigration the gurdwara has grown from the twenty families who were active in 1965 to a formal membership of five hundred families as one of four gurdwaras in the New York-New Jersey area. Some five hundred people meet in the congregation on Sundays, and nearly 7,000 attend the largest festivals. The Richmond Hill gurdwara has had a significant influence on the formation of other gurdwaras and Sikh institutions; because it was one of the first established; because it is near the airports, which are points of entry for immigrants and visitors; and because of its size and prosperity. It has been a source of financial and other assistance for other gurdwaras on the east coast.

The sanctuary of the Methodist church was converted into a prayer hall with the shrine for the *Granth Sahib* (a copy of the sacred scriptures that is treated as the guru) in the place of the pulpit. The stained glass windows and the organ pipes are still in place, but the pews were removed to permit seating on the carpet. A full range of services is conducted. Morning and evening prayers are held every day. On Friday evening and Sundays the regular congregational services are held on the same pattern as in other gurdwaras. The service is fairly simple. The copy of the sacred scriptures is placed on a stand with a canopy over it as the central object of worship. The worshipper enters the prayer hall and bows before the *Granth Sahib*, says a prayer and leaves a gift of money or flowers. The men take seats on the left and the women on the right as viewed from the front. The first part of the service is the singing of devotional songs (kirtan), usually by a soloist, in Punjabi. Excellent singing is highly valued by Sikhs, and the attendance is often determined by the reputation of the professional or amateur singer scheduled for that day. The reading of the sacred text (*Gurbani*) is an important part of the service, followed by a lecture by the religious specialist (*Granthi*) of the gurdwara or some visiting scholar. At the conclusion of the service, before people leave the prayer hall, a sweet sacramental food is distributed to all. After the service a common meal (*langar*) is served from the gurdwara kitchen to all regardless of caste or creed.

An occasional ritual sponsored by families is an uninterrupted reading of the *Adi Granth* for a period of three days. The major festival is the birthday of Guru Nanak, when thousands attend. The most important ritual for the individual is initiation into the Khalsa (*Amrit Parchar*), which is a reenactment of the drinking of sweetened water by which Guru Gobind Singh established the Khalsa. It involves the vow to preserve the traditions, to wear the symbols of the Sikh faith, and to take the name "Singh" (for men) or "Kaur" (for women). Some families wait until they are in the Punjab to have the ritual performed, and many families fail to have it performed, so it is not common. The first such ritual held in the southwestern United States was performed in 1982.

The Sikh religion does not have an elaborate hierarchy of religious leaders or institutions. Each gurdwara is independent and is administered by a committee elected every year. These annual elections often bring to the surface personal and political tensions within the community. Any good Sikh can serve as the leader at the services, and the designation as Granthi (priest) does not require formal or sacramental certification. The head Granthi of the Richmond Hill gurdwara in New York came in 1976 after serving in gurdwaras in Delhi, Kenya, and Southhall, England. He is married and lives in an apartment in the gurdwara building, as does his assistant. The administration of the gurdwara affairs is the responsibility of the elected committee. The gurdwara has rooms for Sunday School in which the children learn some Punjabi, the devotional songs, Sikh history, and Punjabi folk music and dance. A library of 2,000 volumes in Punjabi and English is available for loan. A couple of rooms in the basement house a medical clinic, which was begun in 1982 to provide examinations for Sikhs who do not have insurance. A few rooms are set aside to house visitors, some visiting singers, or lecturers who come to provide programs for the gurdwaras in the United States. A Sikh Youth Camp is held each summer – such camps are popular and are organized by many gurdwaras including those in Pittsburgh, Houston, Detroit, San Francisco, Los Angeles, Chicago, and Albany.

Other gurdwaras have similar programs even though they may not have full-time professional Granthis. The Sikh Society in Dallas, which is not listed in the directory of Sikhs, purchased a house in a residential area of north Dallas in 1975 to be a gurdwara. Approximately seventy-five families are members, and 250 are on the mailing list. Approximately a hundred people are present on Sundays with a quarter of the men in beards and turbans. They have purchased two acres of land in Garland and plan to build a new gurdwara, but construction has been delayed because of tensions over the situation in the Punjab. Sikhs in Atlanta began to meet monthly in homes in 1973 and were chartered in 1980. They do not have professional singers or priests, but the women lead in the singing of the devotional hymns, and one of the men delivers a discourse on Sikh history and belief. The forty-five families have purchased ten acres of land with a house which they are using as a gurdwara until they can build a new one. About a third of the men wear beards and turbans. Other groups large and small around the country are in the process of group formation and construction of facilities for worship.

During this period of growth a central organization was formed to coordinate communication and assistance among the Sikh societies. The Sikh Cultural Society of New York sponsored a convention at the Richmond Hill gurdwara on April 22, 1978, at which twenty Sikh societies in the United States were represented. The Sikh Council of North America was established with the plan to have annual meetings of elected representatives of the gurdwaras. The goals are to obtain recognition of the Sikh religion, to organize the visits of singers and scholars from India, and to pool resources for the establishment of gurdwaras. Annual meetings have been held in New York (1979), El Sobrante, California (1980), Silver Springs, Maryland (1981), Houston (1982), Chicago (1983), Los Angeles (1984), and Pittsburgh (1985). The programs of the conferences in the early years dealt almost equally with the adjustments of the Sikh community in the United States (psycho-social development, religious education of children, Punjabi language instruction, and prospects of

Sikhs in America) and with the political and religious situation in the Punjab. The programs have dealt increasingly with the problems of Sikhs in India.

Prior to the tensions of the early 1980s the boundaries between the Sikhs and Hindus were not firmly fixed, and Sikhs actively participated in Indian cultural organizations – some Sikhs even served as officers. The Vishwa Hindu Parishad and other Hindu organizations included pictures of the Sikh gurus in prominent places and encouraged the participation and support of Sikhs in the construction of temples and cultural centers. The disputed Article 25 (B) of the Constitution of India identifies Sikhism with Hinduism, "the reference to Hindus shall be construed as including a reference to persons professing the Sikh, Jaina, or Buddhist religion, and the reference to Hindu religious institutions shall be construed accordingly." Some Sikhs stress the historical harmony and unity between Sikhs and Hindus, but other Sikhs stress that Sikhism is a separate religion and should be recognized as such.

The Sindhis, a merchant caste that emigrated to India in 1947 from the area of Sind (now in Pakistan), have been active supporters of Sikh gurdwaras and activities in the United States and exist on the boundary between Sikhs and Hindus. A few are full Sikhs, but most are Hindus who have a special relationship with the Sikhs because Sindhis respect and follow the teachings of the first guru, Guru Nanak. They are distinct from Punjabi Sikhs because they speak Sindhi – a language India shares with Pakistan – they perform rituals before the picture of Guru Nanak, and also revere Hindu deities and worship in Hindu temples. They preserve the Sindhi calendar with Hindu calculation of festivals separate from those of the Punjabi Sikhs, for example, New Year's celebrations. In India after emigration, the increased emphasis on Guru Nanak may have been an affirmation of the unity and distinctiveness of Sindhis, and some separate Sindhi gurdwaras are found in India. The Sindhis in the United States have been active participants in gurdwara activities, and some even became presidents of gurdwaras. More recently, the Sindhis have been caught in the middle of the tensions among Sikhs in the United States and of the formation of boundaries brought about by the conflict in India.

The Khalistan syndrome

One leader described the situation of the Sikhs in the 1980s as "a tremendous crisis in the Sikh psyche." Many Sikhs believe that the very existence of the Sikh community is threatened on every side. They speak of the "genocide against the Sikh people," which they claim is perpetrated by the government of India, and they cry out for a separate country of Khalistan as a homeland for the Sikhs or for a semi-autonomous Sikh state within a revised Indian federation of states. The greatest blow to Sikh pride and identity was "Operation Blue Star" on June 5, 1984, when the Indian Army occupied the Golden Temple in Amritsar, which is the most sacred shrine and cultural center of Sikh life – "the Vatican of Sikhism." The reaction of the well-educated, prosperous community of Sikh professionals in the United States has been one of anger, frustration, and fear both for the safety and well-being of their friends and relatives in the Punjab and for the future of Sikhism.

The feeling that Sikhism is under threat in India is compounded by the awareness of the Sikh immigrants that in spite of their efforts, and even success, in forming gurdwaras and Sikh organizations, Sikh and Punjabi identity is being seriously threatened by the secularism and modernism of American society. The threats on all sides produce a "Khalistan syndrome" similar to the "Ghadar syndrome" earlier in this century, in that the emotionalism and militancy of the response to attacks on Sikhs and on their shrines in India are outlets for fears about the threat of secularization among recent immigrants, and thus vehicles for a restatement and renewal of Sikh identity. It is impossible to understand what is happening to the Sikh community in the United States without some knowledge of events in India that have had only brief exposure in the news media, but it would also be a false interpretation to think that the fervor of the response is separate from the struggle of immigrant Sikhs to maintain their own identity and to transmit that identity to their children.

The sources of the conflict in the Punjab go all the way back to negotiations at the time of independence (1947) and at the establishment of the State of Punjab (1966) and involve both Sikh religious demands and Punjabi economic and cultural matters. The Golden Temple in Amritsar is the religious center of Sikhism, and the Shiromani Gurdwara Parbandhak Committee (SGPC) is the organization legally empowered to run the affairs of the gurdwaras in the Punjab from the Akal Takht, the administrative headquarters in the Golden Temple precincts. The Akali Dal is the political party that, under different leaders and sometimes divided, has negotiated with the government of India regarding Sikh and Punjabi demands. The most important among the economic and cultural demands made by the Akali Dal in the 1980s were: the return of Chandigarh as the capital solely of Punjab and the merger of Punjabi-speaking areas into Punjab; that control of rivers and waters be vested in the State of Punjab; and that no discrimination be made against qualified Sikhs in Indian government services, especially in the Army, of which Sikhs constituted 12 percent. The religious demands included: installation of a radio station at the Golden Temple to relay Sikh devotional hymns (kirtan)[11]; permission for Sikhs to carry their ceremonial short swords on airplanes; enactment of an All-India Gurdwara Act that would give the SGPC

Table 2.4. *Main events in the history of civil conflict in the Punjab*

24 Apr	1980	Assassination of Baba Gurbachan, the spiritual head of the Nirankari religious sect
Sept	1981	A list of 45 demands of the Akali Dal received by the central government
29 Sept	1981	Indian Airlines plane hijacked to Lahore by Sikhs
19 July	1982	Jarnail Singh Brindranwale moved into precincts of the Golden Temple
Aug	1982	Two more Indian Airlines planes hijacked
6 Oct	1983	State of Punjab brought under central government rule
15 Dec	1983	Brindranwale moved into Akal Takht, the central headquarters
26 Jan	1984	Akali Dal announced a new agitation against Article 25 of the Constitution of India; copies burned
5 June	1984	Indian army entered the precincts of the Golden Temple; Brindranwale killed in the action
31 Oct	1984	Prime Minister Indira Gandhi assassinated by Sikh bodyguards
Nov	1984	Riots against Sikhs in Delhi and other cities; many Sikhs were killed
June	1985	Rajiv Gandhi's visit to the United States; protests
24 July	1985	Punjab accord signed by Prime Minister Gandhi and Sant Harchand Singh Longowal, a moderate Sikh leader
20 Aug	1985	Assassination of Sant Harchand Singh Longowal
26 Jan	1986	Date set by accords for transfer of Chandigarh passed without action because of turmoil in Punjab
10 Aug	1986	Assassination of retired General A. S. Vaidya, who was in charge of Operation Blue Star
2 Oct	1986	Attempted assassination of Prime Minister Rajiv Gandhi by a Sikh

control of gurdwaras outside the Punjab; the granting of holy city status to Amritsar; and the removal of tobacco and liquor shops from within the walled city of Amritsar. As the negotiations continued, the Sikhs demanded a revision of Article 25 of the Indian Constitution to give Sikhs legal standing separate from Hindus. Some Sikhs in India and abroad began to agitate for a separate Sikh homeland, which they called "Khalistan."

The history of the negotiations and civil conflict in the Punjab is too complex to detail here, but the main events may provide a background for understanding the anger and frustration of Sikhs in the United States (see Table 2.4). The opposition to the government of India was led by

Jarnail Singh Brindranwale, who established himself and his supporters in the precincts of the Golden Temple. The rhetoric of his opposition to the government involved primarily calls to preserve Sikh identity (Juergensmeyer 1986). Several hundred people were killed in the Punjab during the period of civil unrest, and even after the central government took over direct administration of the state under the president's rule, the conflict continued. Prime Minister Indira Gandhi ordered the army to restore order in Punjab and to remove the armed supporters of Brindranwale from the Golden Temple. Fierce fighting ensued in the temple precincts in which several hundred more (the government and Sikh leaders disagree over the number) were killed, including Brindranwale, and the army moved throughout the Punjab to quell armed resistance. Sikh leaders refer to these maneuvers as "military occupation of the Sikh homeland." Operation Blue Star and the Sikh armed response in India as well as public protests in the United States brought the situation to the attention of the American public so that the rest of the story is familiar. Prime Minister Indira Gandhi was later assassinated by three Sikh bodyguards, an act that provoked further riots in which Sikhs were killed in Delhi and other cities.

If the invasion of the Golden Temple and the reprisal of the death of Mrs. Gandhi marked the nadir of the tragedy, some hope was engendered among Sikhs in America by the negotiations of Prime Minister Rajiv Gandhi with Sant Harchand Singh Longowal, a moderate Sikh leader who had been with Brindranwale in the Golden Temple but who surrendered before the final assault. The negotiations resulted in an accord that gave promise of returning order to the Punjab. Shortly thereafter, Sant Longowal himself was assassinated by opponents who now control a radical wing of the Akali Dal and the Golden Temple. Prime Minister Rajiv Gandhi said of Longowal, "Sant Longowal has joined the long line of martyrs from Sikhs and Punjab who have given their lives for unity and integrity of the country." Many Sikhs who hoped for some relief from tensions are depressed by the failure of the government to make any of the concessions in the accord by the promised date of January 26, 1986. Turmoil continues in the Punjab, and anxiety increases among Sikhs in the United States.

Sikhs in the United States have remained close to the events in India, and thus they represent an immigrant group whose adaptation to the United States has been dramatically affected by events in their home country. It is hard to estimate the impact of these events on the Sikhs and their frustration that the majority of the American people do not understand or care about what has happened. Some express guilt because they left the Sikh homeland prior to the conflict, but few have returned to take part. Others make explicit reference to what we have called "the

Khalistan syndrome" by claiming that the threats to Sikhs in the Punjab and the threat of secularism in the United States are two sides of the same modern threat to the continued existence of the Sikh Khalsa. Emotions in the Sikh community run very high.

Sikhs in the United States have been fractured by the conflict. In virtually every gurdwara and society a division exists between the moderates, who favor negotiation with the government with hopes for a peaceful resolution of the Sikh problem within a unified India, and the radicals, who support armed resistance and the establishment of Khalistan as a Sikh nation. Gurdwaras that were once filled with devotional hymns and songs and religious discourses have been caught up in arguments about types of support for various leaders and political programs in Punjab. A furor was caused during the singing of hymns on Guru Nanak's birthday in the Chicago gurdwara when songs other than Nanak's, thought by some to be too political, were sung. Previous leaders of the Richmond Hill gurdwara are criticized because they welcomed and showed respect to Prime Minister Indira Gandhi when she visited the gurdwara in 1982. Other Sikhs are called "stooges of the government." A youth speaker at one of the conventions of the Sikh Council of North America described the situation: "The gurdwara has become more than a place of worship. It has become a place of power struggles, a place of furthering one's own cause, even a place of violent dispute between Sikhs. In some instances, this has gone so far that the police have had to intervene." Some Sikhs want the gurdwara to be "a place of prayer" and attempt to exclude political speeches. Others see the gurdwara as the only gathering place where Sikhs can "cry on their shoulders" and try to do something about the threat to Sikhs. The annual elections provide an occasion for debate and even open conflict, and it seems that the more radical Sikhs have gained control of many of the gurdwaras. In some instances local societies have split, and new societies have been formed.

One response to the crisis and to the army action at the Golden Temple has been the creation of several more national and international Sikh organizations to mobilize support within the community and sympathy from others for the Sikh demands. A branch of the Akali Dal was formed in the United States late in 1981, and its first president was the person who had been the first president of the Sikh Council of North America. Immediately after the Amritsar incident the World Sikh Organization was founded, with a first meeting hastily called for July 28, 1984, in Madison Square Garden. The Sikh Students Association in the Punjab has been fairly radical, and an American affiliate was formed in June 1984 as a political group that grew out of discontent with other, more moderate, Sikh organizations that, the students claimed, "are not willing to take a firm stand on the current issues of Sikhs in India." A Sikh Association of America was formed in Washington on October 20, 1984, that would provide leadership and support to opposition in the United States to the Indian government. Each of these organizations has its own leaders, constituency, publications, and program for Sikhs in India and in the United States. Division among the groups reflects the uncertainty among Sikhs about the most appropriate and effective strategy for the future.

The intensity of feeling in the gurdwaras is overwhelming. Sikhs come to the gurdwaras for news about what is happening to relatives and friends in India. Attendance has increased as Sikhs who were once lax about Sikh rituals now express solidarity with other Sikhs and Punjabis by their presence at the meetings. Turbans are reestablished as outward symbols of Sikh identity, with orange-colored turbans as symbols of opposition to the government. Some Sikhs who had been clean shaven have grown beards and have begun to wear turbans, and agitations have been instituted for beards and turbans to be allowed for members of the United States military. Leaders report an increase of families who refrain from cutting their sons' hair and who have the formal initiation rituals performed for both sons and daughters. The call to support the Sikhs in the Punjab is also interpreted as a call to be faithful Sikhs in the United States and to transmit the tradition to their children. Hence, the gurdwaras continue to prosper in spite of the conflict.

At the other side of the intensity is the creation of boundaries and distinctions that have led to an isolation of the Sikhs. In the 1970s the Sikhs created their own institutions, but many were also participating fully in other Asian-Indian social and political organizations; in the 1980s they have become isolated from the other immigrants. In the United States, the conflict has been interpreted as a religious clash between Sikhs and Hindus, not as a regional and political dispute between Punjabis and the central government. Hindus in the United States have tended to support the Indian government, and, although to date there have been no incidents between Hindu and Sikh immigrants, tensions do exist. Individual friendships have survived and some overtures for reconciliation have been made since the signing of the accord, but the two communities remain far apart. One result of the tension is that most Sindhis have stopped going to the gurdwaras for worship; instead, pictures of Guru Nanak have been installed in some Hindu temples, and some Sindhis go there for prayers. The Sikhs feel abandoned on all sides. They complain that the other religious minorities in India, the Muslims and Christians, have been silent. Even worse, the Sikhs feel isolated from the American public. They have lost the public relations battle, in part because of the unbridled anger and fiery rhetoric unleashed in June and November of 1984, and they realize that many Americans have come to look upon Sikhs as terrorists to be equated with the Palestinian Liberation Orga-

Sikh protest during Prime Minister Rajiv Gandhi's visit to Houston

nization. Leaders complain that this is unfair, but they also recogniz(
that it will be a long time before Sikhs regain the positive public positioı
they enjoyed prior to 1980. They have approached members of the Uniteu
States Congress and other governmental officials, but they have not been
adept in using their political power or access to the media. No person
speaks effectively for the Sikhs. The turmoil and the isolation create
further problems for immigrants who are trying to put down roots and
to negotiate the terms of their adjustment to the new cultural setting.

The process of establishing Sikh societies and building gurdwaras that
was so successful in the 1970s has been disrupted. In the place of the Sikh
Council of North America, which was a unified, representative body for
the Sikh societies, there are now many Sikh organizations representing
varying ideological positions. The moderate leaders of the period of
growth have been replaced by others whose primary focus is not on
welfare of the Sikh community in the United States but on political gains
in India. Many Sikhs have raised their level of participation in the gurdwaras, but their energy has been redirected. The funds that previously
went to the purchase of land and the building of gurdwaras are now used

for relief of victims of riots in India and for support of opposition to government policy.

The "Khalistan syndrome" involves a two-edged sword. One side must repel the perceived universal threat to the Sikh community posed by the government's response to the Punjabi Sikh demands; the other side must fight the threat to Sikh identity posed by the secularism and materialism of American society. Thus far, the sword has been wielded only against foes thousands of miles away. It is too soon to say how the battle will go in the Punjab, and it is impossible to predict the full nature of the battle or its results when the other edge of the sword faces a threat such as secularism: "Will the Sikhs lose their identity in the new land?" Now, in the middle of the 1980s, Sikhs in the United States are vibrant, tormented, angry, frustrated, but whistling in the dark. They are torn between the towns and villages of the Punjab and the cities of the United States, a proud people struggling in the middle.

CHAPTER 3

The religions

Islam, Christianity, Zoroastrianism, and Judaism

Islam, Christianity, Zoroastrianism, and Judaism have their origins outside the Indian subcontinent, but, at varying times and in various locations, they each reached the subcontinent and became established. Together these groups contribute to the religious pluralism found there. "Communalism," a term primarily used for Muslim presence in India (because Muslims make up the largest minority), refers to the multiplicity of religious traditions. Persons of these religious traditions are found among the recent immigrants to the United States. Their religious commitments make their adaptation to the new society different from those discussed in Chapter Two because they already have a history of adaptation as minority communities. Even those Muslims now from Pakistan, where Islam is the dominant majority, have a memory of minority status in India. When members of these groups arrived in the United States, their minority status was further reaffirmed as they became religious minorities within a larger fellowship of their own religion. Created either by joining with other "new immigrants" from other countries, as in the case of Muslims and Parsis, or by associating with religious groups long established in the United States, as in the case of Christians and Jews, these new organizations face problems of adaptation and the preservation of identity quite different from those of the Hindus, who were in the majority in their native country.

Muslims

The sacred pilgrimage to Mecca (*Hajj*) is the time when Muslims from many countries and cultures of the world meet in an expression of the unity of Islam. On his pilgrimage to Mecca in 1964, Malcolm X was both surprised and enlightened by the cultural diversity of Muslims: "Packed in the plane were white, black, brown, red, and yellow people, blue eyes and blond hair, and my kinky red hair – all together, brothers" (Haley, 1966:323). At about the same time, a different sort of pilgrimage was taking place, one that brought similar diversity of Muslims to the United States as "beggars at the Western altar of knowledge," to use Ismail Faruqi's phrase. These were students who came to this country in the 1960s, many staying on to be joined later by other immigrants to create the Muslim community (*umma*), which has a diversity of nationalities and cultures not duplicated except in Mecca during the Hajj.

Muslims from sixty countries have come, and within each nationality the subdivisions are such that A. Ghayur estimates that there are over 100 subgroups in the United States (1981a:154–5). Muslims constitute one of the fastest-growing religious groups in the country; Ghayur's most recent preliminary estimates show that 598,266 Muslims entered the United States as immigrants between 1950 and 1983, and that as of 1986 there were 2.7 million in the country.[1] Afro-Americans, Albanians, Arabs, Central Americans, Cubans, Egyptians, Indians, Iranians, Lebanese, Pakistanis, Palestinians, South Americans, Syrians, Turks, Yugoslavs, and Indians from Fiji have established Muslim cultural and religious centers (Lovell, 1983:103). These centers may follow any of several schools of Muslim law depending on their country of origin and their subgroup, with each school related to the culture of which it is a part in matters of personal behavior, estates, marriage, and divorce. The Muslim ideal is unity; the reality is a constellation of many national and cultural groups moving slowly toward unity. The voluntary segregation Malcolm X witnessed on the Hajj, where "Africans were with Africans... Pakistanis were with Pakistanis" (quoted in Haley, 1966:344) is a common experience in the larger cities; the Shi'ite Muslims, for example, maintain separate centers for the different immigrant groups. Even so, the major difficulty in the study of Asian-Indian and Pakistani Muslims within the United States is in distinguishing them from others within the house of Islam.

The earliest Muslim immigrants to establish centers were Arabs from the Middle Eastern countries; the first mosque was built in Cedar Rapids, Iowa, in 1934. Over twenty years later, a major event for Muslims took place: the construction of the impressive Islamic Center in Washington, D.C. A Muslim businessman and the Egyptian ambassador initiated plans for a mosque in 1944, and the cornerstone was laid in 1949. Contributions came from governments of fifteen Muslim countries for the building, which was completed in 1957. The religious leaders for the mosque, as well as their support, came from Al-Azhar University in Cairo and from the Egyptian government. Although the mosque primarily serves the diplomatic community, it also emphasizes missionary and educational activity. It is an example of the importance of financial assistance from oil-rich Muslim countries in the establishment of Muslim institutions in the United States, although the early financial support has declined due to the recent decrease in oil revenues, which has caused a curtailment of plans for the growth of many institutions. The first national organization, the Federation of Islamic Associations, was formed in Cedar Rapids in June 1952 to encourage the building of mosques and cooperation among Muslim organizations. In June 1980 the federation moved into new national headquarters, funded in part by King Khaled, in the Detroit area (Lovell, 1983:104–5).

Arabs (459,000) and Iranians (215,000) are the largest Muslim immigrant groups. Among the "new immigrants," those who have entered the country since 1965, the Pakistanis (40,000) are second in size and the Indians (25,000) are third.[2] Professor Ghayur reports an estimate of the number of Pakistanis in the United States in 1980 as 60,000 (1981b:4) and for 1984 he gives the figure of 96,537 based on his own research (1984:114), including in the latter number those who left India at about the time of the creation of Pakistan and who identify themselves as Pakistani, not Indian.[3] It is common to hear the various Muslim groups categorized as "Arab," "Asian," and "Black" (the Muslims of Iran are members of a Shi'ite group, and so are not included with the Sunnis).

The Muslim immigrants from the Indian subcontinent, who coalesce as "Asians," have three tasks associated with the process of forming and preserving their identity in the United States. The first is to establish associations with fellow Muslims from Pakistan or India. One group comes from a majority population, the other from a rival country where Muslims are a minority, a situation that causes religion and nationalism to be in tension; the two countries have fought three wars since independence, but no group wishes to be identified as schismatic. The second task is to establish relationships with Muslims from other countries that will transcend, if not remove, cultural differences. One immigrant said, "The Pakistanis return to their curries and the Arabs to their kebabs after prayer," which shows the tenacity of cultural identity bound up with Muslim identity (Abu-Laban, 1983:87). The third task is to establish relations with the larger American society, where minority identity in a society of seemingly tolerant pluralism may pose almost as great a threat to identity as in an intolerant state.

The Muslim culture in the Indian subcontinent was unified until the time of the partition that divided the largest Muslim community in the world, one that shares the Urdu language as "the Muslim language of the Indian subcontinent," even though other regional languages are spoken. Even after partition, India still has the third largest national group after Indonesia and Pakistan–Bangladesh. According to the 1981 census, there are over 75 million Muslims in India, with almost three-quarters

Table 3.1. *Muslims as percent of population*

Area	Number	Percentage
Pakistan	84,253,000	96.7
India	75,512,439	11.35
Andhra Pradesh	4,533,700	8.47
Bihar	9,874,993	14.13
Gujarat	2,907,744	8.53
Jammu & Kashmir	3,843,451	64.19
Karnataka	4,104,616	11.05
Kerala	5,409,687	21.25
Maharashtra	5,805,785	9.25
Rajasthan	2,492,145	7.28
Uttar Pradesh	17,657,735	15.93
West Bengal	11,743,259	21.51

Adapted from the *1981 Census of India* and the *Main findings of 1981 population census (Pakistan)*.

living in six states (see Table 3.1). A large number of the Muslim immigrants from India are from Hyderabad in Andhra Pradesh, which was a Muslim princely state until the time of independence. Bangladesh has a large population of Muslims, but these do not constitute a significant number of Muslims in the United States.

The Muslims from India and Pakistan are the most highly educated and professionally qualified among the subgroups of Muslims. Many Pakistani men came to the United States as students in the late 1950s and early 1960s at a time when the governmental relationships between Pakistan and the United States were the most favorable, and many cultural and educational exchange programs were initiated as a part of Pakistan's cooperation in the South Asia Treaty Organization. Many of these Pakistani students then adjusted their status to permanent residents when the immigration laws were liberalized. Now fewer exchange and scholarship programs exist; students who come from Pakistan are supported by families and not by the governments. Of the Muslim immigrants who came from India, it appears that fewer arrived as students; rather, they came a little later as immigrants directly into the professions. The number of Muslims who come from India and later return to their native place is much less than for other Muslims, and Indians tend to bring over family members in greater numbers. One reason for this may be the minority status of Muslims, particularly in Hyderabad. The social status of Muslims from the Indian subcontinent varies from that of the Hindus; they do not follow the caste system, but they are identified on the basis of descent, from either early Islamic nobility (*sayyid* from the Prophet, *shaykh* from the Prophet's tribe) or from Muslim conquerors (Mughal from Turkestan, Pathan from Afghanistan), or as upper-caste Hindu converts (the Rajputs) (Qureshi & Qureshi, 1983:133).

During their period of extremely rapid growth in the United States, Muslims have maintained a relatively low profile, and, as Gordon Melton indicates, "There is probably no group whose presence in American history has been as well hidden as that of the Muslims" (1978:II,337). Leaders of Muslim organizations complain that less than 20 percent of the Muslim immigrants participate regularly, so the religious identification of the majority is only through personal discipline and family rituals. Among those most active in supporting the establishment of institutions have been the immigrants from the Indian subcontinent; during the period from 1983 to 1985 five of the six presidents of organizations associated with the Islamic Society of North America were immigrants from the Indian subcontinent. Even so, they have been fairly quiescent and withdrawn from public view. The leaders of many of these organizations are wary of the motives and affiliations of visitors and researchers and, hence, are reticent to give detailed information about Muslim activities. The reasons for this may relate to both internal and external tensions that require leaders to be careful about what they say publicly.

During the establishment of the diverse Muslim community, the energies of the leaders have gone into negotiating among various groups the basis for practical unity that is the ideal of Islam. The cultural differences in language, dress, cuisine, and practice of the religious tradition themselves are brought into the one room of the prayer hall, and each center and organization representing a different constellation of groups has to work out a common program that will attract the allegiance of as many Muslims as possible. Discord and tensions among varying traditions are inevitable, but within the Islamic community these are heightened by strife between the countries whose citizens are represented among the immigrants. The pilgrimage to Mecca itself has become a venue of conflict in the past few years, reflecting the political, military, and cultural conflicts. One leader said, "Muslims in the United States are everywhere like a little United Nations, and the conflicts are as real and the challenges to unity as great." Negotiation of these differences in the creation of a new Muslim minority – immigrants in the United States – has been the major priority of leaders, both local and national.

A further complication is that Muslims in the United States have been placed on the defensive by major world events that have caused the government or American individuals to be at odds with Islamic governments and groups. As Muslims, these immigrants have been insecure as to social standing and American opinion at the same time that, as doctors and engineers, they have achieved a relatively secure economic and professional position. For example, Muslims were arriving in large numbers at the time of the 1973 oil embargo that caused many anti-Arab, anti-Muslim outbursts. The more recent conflicts in Lebanon and disputes with Libya and Iran have created a further climate of negative opinion in the country. Some leaders complain of FBI and CIA investigations of their activities, and claim that they are being unjustly treated. Shortly after the hijacking of a TWA airplane at the Beirut airport in June 1985, the Muslim celebration of Eid in Houston, which normally would have attracted several thousand Muslims to the Albert Thomas Convention Center, was cancelled because of threats received by telephone. The editor of a Muslim journal suggests that he would not be surprised if among new words added to dictionaries were, "Islamicfundamentalist" and "Muslimterrorist," because they are so often run together (Johnson, 1985:3). Muslims have been put in the defensive position of trying to correct what they perceive to be misinterpretations of Islam, and that has not allowed them to be as creative as they would like in the use of the mass media of the United States.

The relations of the immigrant Muslims with the larger American society have been tempered to some degree by their relationship with the Afro-American Muslims of the American Muslim Mission (see Chapter Four). As the former Black Muslims have moved closer to orthodox Islam and begun to participate in some religious functions with the immigrant Muslims, the immigrant Muslims have taken on some of the attitudes toward American society that characterize the Afro-American Muslims. The need to make accommodations with the American Blacks and to integrate them into an orthodox form of Islam has taken precedence over the need to establish associations with other groups in the larger society – it is a natural tendency to follow one's "brothers" into negotiations with the larger society.

Nevertheless, there are points where Muslims have entered actively into contact with the larger society, and where those concern religious matters, they have often led to confrontation. The establishment of Islamic identity in a new land involves the observance of Muslim personal law, and in some instances that has required Muslims to protest until their personal law is recognized. Muslim personal law seems to be the lightning rod that attracts threats to Islamic identity. The rights of Muslim prisoners to observe their dietary laws, festivals, and stated times for prayers become subjects of negotiation with prison officials. Muslims also protest the requirement of the public school system in Indiana that boys and girls engage in coeducational physical education classes. This is considered to involve immodesty contrary to Islamic law, and an exception was made on religious grounds for Muslim girls. It can be seen that many activities of the members of the larger society are thought to be antithetical to the faithful observance of Islamic law. Yet another area that leads to some tension is the missionary activity undertaken by Muslims to propagate Islam. The literature used often involves a polemic against Christian theology and Judaism and against modern American mores. The stated goal, of course, is to transform America into an Islamic country, but a subsidiary goal is simply to provide Muslims with their own defenses against assimilation; the resources prepared for mission also serve as an inoculation.

Despite conflicts among Muslims and with society at large, the community has made some advances. The most important organization for the students and later immigrants, including those from the Indian subcontinent, was the Muslim Students Association (MSA). Students had been gathering for prayers at the major colleges and universities where they were studying. In January 1963 during a meeting of student representatives at the Urbana campus of the University of Illinois, a national organization was formed to establish associations at other universities, to provide assistance in performing religious obligations (Friday prayers, giving of alms, marriages, and funerals) and to train and mobilize students for the propagation of Islam on the campuses. The association formed the Islamic Teaching Center in 1977 to provide materials and training for mission activities among students – one regular publication is the prayer schedule as calibrated for every location in the country. Foremost among the goals of the Muslim Students Association was the promotion of the unity of Muslim students from various countries, and it thus became the most important organization for the preservation of Muslim identity among the students, laying the foundation for the development of a Pan-Muslim religious community in the United States. Many of the leaders of more recently established Muslim organizations received their training through participation in the association, and these students may be even better prepared for leadership in the American context than traditional religious leaders. The association continues to be a significant force among Muslims on university campuses: A recent listing identified sixty-six active associations. At the end of 1981 the membership was 6,215 (MSA, 1981:13). As of 1985, the membership was engaged in graduate study (47%), undergraduate study (37%), or on the academic staff (16%). It appears, however, that fewer Muslim students have been coming from the Indian subcontinent, so leaders of the association are Arabs and Africans. In 1984 it was estimated in *Islamic Horizons* that 75,000 Muslim students were studying in the United States, and that sixty new chapters and thirty student mosques had been established in the preceding five years.

One of the contributions of the Muslim Students Association was to provide the first sense of community for Islamic immigrants during the late 1960s and early 1970s. The meetings centered around prayers and readings from the Quran, and "Sunday Schools" were established for the few children. Soon more immigrants than students had become members of the association – students speak of being "baby sitters" for the new immigrants – and both local and national organizations developed that are more encompassing in their outreach and programs. On the local level Islamic centers and mosques (*masjids*) developed, which in the early period attracted both Sunni and Shi'ite Muslims from many countries. Now there are more than two hundred centers in the United States, not including those of the American Muslim Mission. Separate centers exist for Shi'ites, and even though a few Shi'ites attend Sunni mosques for prayers, little interaction exists between the two groups either on the local level or nationally. Leaders profess to know little about the presence or programs of the other group; Sunni mosques are never identified as being for a particular ethnic group of immigrants – that would go against the teaching about unity and brotherhood in Islam – but in the larger urban areas it is obvious that some of the centers predominantly serve immigrants from particular regions, particularly the Arabs and the Asians (Pakistanis and Indians). The language spoken at the meetings and social occasions and the ethnic origin of the managing committee and religious teacher (imam) are the best indicators of the ethnic character of the center. In the smaller cities there are still groups of "Muslims at large," joining Muslims of many ethnic backgrounds in one center. No statistics exist concerning the number of Pakistani or Asian-Indian Muslim centers in the United States; all the centers publicly proclaim that they serve the entire Islamic community.

The programs of the mosques that serve Muslims from the Indian subcontinent are the same as those of other mosques. The prayers are in Arabic, and many centers have special classes to teach the children enough Arabic to recite the prayers. Urdu, the language common to most Muslims from Pakistan and India (many also speak Punjabi, and some speak Gujarati), is used for sermons and announcements in meetings and on social occasions. English is sometimes used; its use is increasing because not all Muslims, even those from the subcontinent, are fluent in Urdu and because the children have difficulty with the Indian languages. This causes tension between the generations. At one Quran study group an argument developed because, after the reciting of the text in Arabic, one group wished the discussion to be in Urdu "so the women can understand," but another group insisted it be in English "so the young people can understand" the intricacies of the interpretations.

Larger mosques have full-time imams who were trained in traditional

Islamic subjects in Pakistan or India, possibly at one of three major centers of Islamic education in India: the very conservative Deoband seminary in Uttar Pradesh, the more progressive seminary at Nadva in Lucknow, or Aligarh University in Uttar Pradesh, which provides a western-style curriculum. The local imam is a teacher who gives opinions on matters of doctrine and practice, and he attempts to preserve and apply Muslim personal law in the new setting. He may give the sermon at the Friday prayers in Arabic – a fusion of accents and syntax that one leader called "Arablish" – or in Urdu. More often now the sermon is in English, and the imam may designate other persons to lead the prayers and to give the sermon, although he remains in charge of special rituals for birth, marriage, and funerals. Many local centers serve as burial societies and provide for Muslim areas in local cemeteries.

Marriage is a contract in Islamic law and does not require the presence of the imam, but many states grant the imams the legal right to perform marriages. Arranged marriage is still the preferred form among Pakistanis and Asian Indians and although Islamic law permits marriage with any Muslim, most parents prefer that their children marry within the ethnic group. Marriage is a topic for many articles in the newsletters of mosques. Greater liberty is given to men in choosing wives than to the women, but the "safe" marriage of daughters to Muslim men is a major concern. Some men marry Christian or Jewish women, which is permitted in Muslim law – one small sample of marriage lists in newsletters reveals that nineteen of forty-seven marriages were of Muslim men with non-Muslim women. Marriage to an American citizen is an effective way for a student or temporary visitor to gain permanent resident status. Some men return to India or Pakistan for marriages "out" and "abroad," a custom perceived as a threat to the well-being of unmarried Muslim women in the United States; one imam expressed grave concerns about the effects of these marriage practices on the development of families.

The larger centers have regular weekend or daily religious education classes for children. In those centers where a sufficient population is present for separate mosques or satellite programs, the religious education classes often enroll children from a particular ethnic group. Murray Hogben has noted that the problem of language retention is a great problem for any immigrant community, but that it is especially acute for non-Arabic-speaking Muslims, who have a dual problem – they want to stress their native language, perhaps Urdu or Punjabi, and also have their children learn Arabic in order to recite the Quran (Hogben, 1983:119). The schools have classes in Arabic, but the instruction about Islamic doctrine and practice is in English – the preparation of instructional materials for the children and for new converts is a pressing task. One imam explained that parents return to the mosque when their children reach school age because they need help in providing a secure identity for them. Some families with older children are resentful that the community concern for religious education came so late. A Pakistani mother explained, "When I used to say that we should have programs for the children – Sunday Schools, summer camps, counseling programs – no one would listen. Now they see the confusion and pain in their children's eyes, and they are busy uniting and making programs for the kids. They did not help me raise my children." Adult classes for the study of the Quran and for training in the propagation of Islam are held in some centers and by small groups of friends.

The centers provide occasions for worship and religious education, and in a few instances for social and cultural affairs. In general, however, the mosques are not the centers of social and cultural programs that the Hindu temple and the Sikh gurdwara are. The mosques, even those with congregations that share close ethnic ties, have programs that must transcend the ethnic groups and cannot be exclusive. In fact, the exclusiveness of the American Muslim Mission has been troublesome to many immigrant Muslims. Other groups have developed to promote social participation, including the Pakistan Friendship Associations, which provide social occasions with other Pakistanis and Indians as well as maintain ties with cultural and political affairs in the Indian subcontinent. The organizations are ostensibly national, but the ethos is Islamic, so Pakistani Christian immigrants rarely participate, while Muslims from India regularly join with Muslims from Pakistan in these associations. The major stratification in these groups is between the doctors and engineers at one professional and economic level, who tend to be among the more secularized in the community, and those who arrived under the family reunification provisions, who are the more conservative in religious and cultural matters. A few Indian Muslims participate in India Cultural Associations, but several indicate that they do so primarily to establish business contacts.

Another group that was established to help preserve ethnic identity is the Pakistan Federation of America, which was formed as a national organization in March 1983 in part because Pakistanis were beginning to lose their identity as a community, merging with Indians to form a new Indo-Pak community obviously dominated by Hindu culture.

Regional associations of Sunni Muslims also join together for communal activities outside the mosques. One such subgroup of businessmen are the Memons from the Kathiawar region of Gujarat, many of whom resided in Pakistan and in Bombay. They are from a trading community that converted from Hinduism to Islam, and even though their community is small, they are prominent because of their standing as fairly wealthy businessmen and industrialists. They are orthodox Sunni Muslims who observe the Hanifa form of law; they maintain a very close community in India with associations, welfare programs, scholarships, and some mosques supported by the community. Although Memon women always marry inside the community, recently a few of the men have married outside. The Memon dialect does not have a distinct script; it is a spoken mixture of Sindhi and Kutchi (a form of Gujarati). In the larger cities of the United States the Memons participate actively in the programs of the Sunni mosques, but they have been forming their own associations and plan to obtain community rooms or buildings from which to conduct their affairs.

The Consultative Committee of Indian Muslims is an example of an organization that focuses on national as well as religious identity and exerts pressure to improve the condition of Indian Muslims. Muslims in the United States share with Muslims in India what they do not share with Muslims in Pakistan and the Middle Eastern countries, that is, they live as a minority in a non-Muslim environment. The Consultative Committee of Indian Muslims was founded in Chicago in December 1967, perhaps in the shadow of the All-India Muslim Majlis-e-Mushawarat (Consultative Council), which was organized in August 1964. The aims and objectives of the committee are to promote unity among Indian Muslims residing in North America, to provide information about the problems (i.e., communal tensions and riots) in India, and to marshal resources to help the Muslim community in India to preserve its constitutional rights and to improve its social, educational and economic condition. The committee publishes a newsletter, gathers funds, and exerts political pressure to help Indian Muslims preserve their power and identity as a minority in the United States. The primary issues involved are preservation of Islamic personal law, use of Urdu as a medium of instruction, and prevention of discrimination against Muslims in employment. The manifest function of these activities is to support Muslims in India, but the latent function is to help Indian Muslims in the United States maintain their identity both as an Indian and a Muslim minority. Dr. Abdussamad Patel made the association between the manifest and latent functions explicit and argued that the goal of the movement must be to evolve strategies for operating in a predominantly non-Muslim environment, strategies that must be distinct from those adopted in societies with Muslim majorities. These strategies will be able to provide the Indian Muslims with the experience, knowledge, ideas, and expertise which, although acquired in America, will be efficient in solving the problems of minority status "Islamically." He gives as an example new educational models for evening and weekend religious instruction developed in America for educating Muslim children who receive their primary education in secular schools (Patel, 1976:116–17).

The Muslim Students Association was the catalyst for other national organizations to take over some general activities of the larger immigrant community. The Islamic Circle of North America is one such organization; it began at the 1968 annual Muslim Students Association gatherings with meetings of Pakistanis who felt a need for "full-time Muslims" to live according to Islamic law and to be active in the propagation of Islam. The organization is a mission (*dawah*) to bring together committed Muslims who are willing live under the discipline of Islam as a complete way of life and work for the dissemination of the message of Islam. Although the constitution does not identify it as a Pakistani organization, the founders were from the Indian subcontinent and Urdu is the language used at meetings. They began to have annual meetings separate from the Muslim Students Association in 1976, and now sponsor conferences and training programs for workers for the local Islamic centers. In 1982–3 they reported 676 propagation meetings, 205 worker meetings, 56 study circles, and 6 training camps. The annual meeting of 1983 was held at Hancock, New York, with 600 participants on the theme "Islamic Dawa in North America, Why and How?" In October of the same year the group purchased a permanent headquarters in Jamaica, New York, for $150,000.

Another group to develop out of the Muslim Students Association, the Islamic Society of North America, was formed when the influx of immigrants from many countries made it necessary to revise the whole structure. At the 1981 convention of the Muslim Students Association the concept of an umbrella organization was approved, and in 1982 the constitution was formally adopted. The Islamic Society seeks to foster unity and brotherhood among Muslims from all ethnic groups and to convey the Islamic message to non-Muslims. It is made up of several constituent organizations, including the Muslim Students Association. Several Muslim professional organizations have also been formed; these promote the interests of Muslim professionals and encourage Islamic positions in their areas of research specialization: Islamic Medical Association (1981), Association of Muslim Scientists and Engineers (1969), Association of Muslim Social Scientists (1972). The Islamic Teaching Center is devoted to the propagation of Islam among non-Muslims, with programs that include the training of teachers, the preparation of pamphlets and books for distribution to non-Muslims, and an active program in prisons. Materials for the weekend religious schools are prepared, and plans are being developed for Islamic schools. Yet another organization, the North American Islamic Trust, provides legal and architectural services for the development of mosques and centers, maintaining the legal ownership of mosques to ensure their continued existence and Islamic identity. The trust also manages a program of audio-visual services and arranges for the publication and sale of books.

Islamic Society of North America headquarters in Plainfield, Indiana

In 1976 the Muslim Students Association acquired 124 acres of land in Plainfield, Indiana, for a permanent secretariat and center for Islamic activities. The first stage of the proposed comprehensive center was completed in October 1981 at a cost of 3.4 million dollars, much of which was donated by the governments of Muslim countries. The first building contains a mosque, a library, and offices for the constituent organizations, whose activities are coordinated through a system of zones and regions. Its total membership approaches 8,000, and the annual assembly in Dayton in 1985 attracted 4,000 participants. Muslims from the Indian subcontinent join in these activities with Muslims from other countries, and there is one service directly related to the Indians – the India Muslim Relief Committee, which attempts to help Muslims who are victims of communal violence.

The Islamic Conference in America is another comprehensive Islamic organization. Official representatives of 125 organizations met in Newark, New Jersey, in 1977; financial support for the meeting came from Saudi Arabia. The conference is affiliated with the Muslim World League, which maintains a headquarters at the United Nations, and with the Rabitat-alam-al-Islami, another international Islamic organization, which has its headquarters in Mecca. It provides advice and counsel about the application of Islamic law, provides imams for some mosques, and attempts to influence representatives of the communications media in the presentation of Islam. The secretary of the Consultative Committee of Indian Muslims attempted unsuccessfully in 1983 to gain observer status in the general meeting of Rabitat-alam-al-Islami, but otherwise, the conference has no distinct relationship with Muslims from the Indian subcontinent. These national Sunni organizations are representative of the attempt to marshal the resources and dedication of some immigrant Muslims in a unified effort to preserve Islamic identity among all immigrants – many of whom have only marginal connection with Islamic activities in the United States – as well as to propagate Islam among members of the larger society.

Arif Ghayur estimates that 20 percent of the Muslims in America belong to Shi'a sects (1981a:162). The majority of Shi'as are from Iran, officially a Shi'ite Muslim nation. Of the large numbers of Iranian students who came to the United States during the prerevolutionary reign of the Shah, many became permanent residents after the revolution. Other Iranians emigrated to the United States during the ensuing political and religious turmoil in Iran. Iraqi Shi'as who came in the 1970s constitute the second largest concentration of Shi'as, with smaller numbers of Shi'as represented by immigrants from other countries. In metropolitan areas the Shi'as have separate centers, usually distinct by sect and often by national origin, but in smaller cities the Shi'as participate in the activities at Sunni centers. The relatively small number of Shi'a Muslims that have emigrated from Pakistan and India are from three groups: the Ithna'Asharis, the Bohora Ismailis, and the Nizari Ismailis.

These sectarian differences are traced back to the time of the death of Muhammad, and involve primarily the political question of the designation of the successor to the Prophet. The Shi'ites claim that Muhammad chose his blood-relative, Ali, who was also the father of his grandchildren, to be the leader of the Muslim community. The Shi'ite groups have developed as the partisans of Ali and his descendants, whom they respect and obey as the designated Imams of Islam (see Figure 6.1). The Ithna'Asharis are by far the larger group of Shi'ites; they are known as Twelvers because they accept a line of twelve Imams between Muhammad and the final Imam, who is said to have gone into concealment in A.D. 873 or 878. The Ismailis, called Seveners, claim that the sixth Imam, Jafar Sadiq, chose the line of his son, Ismail, to be the Imams. The Ithna'Asharis deny this and claim that Jafar Sadiq passed over Ismail to designate his second son, Musa al Kazim, and his descendants to be the Imams. Thus the Ithna'Asharis and the Ismailis follow different successions of Imams. The Ismailis were further divided on the question of succession at the death of the eighteenth Imam in A.D. 1094, when the eldest son and original nominee, Nizar, was dispossessed of the office by the party of his brother al-Mustali. Those who accept the line of Imams that continues through Nizar and his descendants are the Nizaris; the Mustalians follow the line from al-Mustali that went into concealment after the death of the twentieth Imam. In the Indian subcontinent the Nizari Muslims are the followers of the Aga Khan. (See Chapter Six for a more complete treatment of the Nizari Ismailis.) The Mustalians in the Indian subcontinent are generally known as the Bohoras.

The Ithna'Asharis from the Indian subcontinent have several independent centers in the major metropolitan areas of the United States, and in general they keep themselves distinct from the Iranian Ithna'Asharis because of language and cultural differences. They prefer to keep free of the internal conflicts within the Ithna'Ashari community about the political and religious situation in Iran and to avoid identification with the "Shi'ite fundamentalists" of Iran, Syria, and Lebanon who have received so much adverse publicity and aroused such antagonism in the United States. Ithna'Ashari Shi'ites have been in a very precarious position because of public response to recent events in the Middle East, so the Indians and Pakistanis have been very discreet as well as discrete.

These groups are not sufficiently large or active to have weekly prayers; rather, they meet once or twice a month and for the major festivals. Most of the community assembles on the tenth day of Muharram for the observance of the martyrdom of Husain, the grandson of Muhammad and the son of Ali. The prayers are in Arabic, but Urdu is the language of all other religious and social communication. There is no professional religious leadership for the Ithna'Asharis from the Indian subcontinent in the United States, but a couple of people in each location lead the prayers and perform the necessary ceremonies for birth, marriage, and death. Occasionally scholars are invited from India to give lectures on special occasions; otherwise, the leadership is in the hands of young technocrats. One leader remarked that in India the sixty-year-old men would be taking the leadership of the community but that in the United States men in their early thirties and forties must become the leaders. The integration of these Ithna'Asharis with those from Iran and Iraq and their negotiation with the larger society has been thwarted and delayed by the conflicts raging in the Middle East and tensions between some Shi'ites and the United States.

The Mustalian Shi'ites of India are the Daudi Bohoras, which is a distinct and flourishing Gujarati trading community of Western India – the word "bohora" means "merchant." Recent estimates place the number of Bohoras in India and abroad at one million. The Bohoras have emigrated to many countries as part of a close-knit trading caste – about 60 percent are in India; the rest are in Pakistan, East Africa, the Gulf countries, Hong Kong, Singapore, Indonesia, Great Britain, and the

United States (Contractor, 1980:7). Those in the United States came as students and professionals, but they have begun to establish businesses and to engage in trade because their religious leader (*Dai*) has told them to work for themselves. The community is still small in the United States, numbering only about 2,000 families, but they have separate centers, which they call *jamat khanas*. They keep themselves separate from other Muslims in all religious activities and remain socially isolated within the larger society. They do not intermarry with other Muslims, much less with adherents of other religions, and they take little part in public affairs.

A community with some admixture of Yemenite Arab blood, the Bohoras are descended from Hindus who were converted by Mustalian missionaries sent from the Yemen. The first missionary is said to have arrived in Cambay in Gujarat in A.D. 1067. Along with other Mustalians, the Bohoras believe that the Imam for this age is in concealment, and they give allegiance to a religious leader (Dai), who is recognized as the representative of the Imam. In the sixteenth century the Dai moved from the Yemen to India, and the current Dai, the fifty-second in the line, resides in Bombay and has his official headquarters at Surat in Gujarat. The obscure religious beliefs of the Bohoras stress the esoteric meaning (*batin*) of the Quran and tradition. All Bohora young people give an oath of allegiance to the Dai that recognizes his absolute authority over the religious teaching and activities of the community, including girls at puberty and boys at about age fifteen. The Dai is an assistant of the Imam, who is the final religious head, but because the Imam is concealed, the Dai has the authority to interpret the religion and to give teaching on esoteric aspects of the faith. However, other than in their relegation of authority to the Dai, the esoteric teachings, some variation of the prayers (e.g., three times a day instead of five, and with the arms at the sides instead of crossed), the religious calendar (which is two days ahead), and some items of Muslim personal law, the Bohoras share with Sunnis the central affirmations and practices of Islam.

The Bohora community in the United States has centers in several urban areas: Chicago, Detroit, Los Angeles, San Francisco, New York, and Houston. Each center is administered by a leader (*Amil*) who is personally chosen and appointed by the Dai. The Amil is the representative of the Dai, and all ceremonies are authorized by him. He authorizes and performs marriages within the community and is responsible for presenting the funeral certificate from the Dai that is buried with the body of a member. The Amil receives the tithes, which are sent to the Dai or distributed according to his instructions. In India amils and *mullahs* are trained as religious leaders at the Ismaili institution of higher learning at Surat, the Jamia't us-Saifiyah, but the amils in the United States are persons without specialized training who perform services for the community in addition to their secular employment. In India and in East Africa the Bohoras have extensive institutions and schools, but these do not yet exist in the United States. The Bohoras are an example of a small, close-knit, isolated Shi'ite group trying to maintain its separate ethnic and religious identity. They have an advantage over other small groups due to their centralized administration and the presence of a single religious authority (the Dai came to the United States to visit his followers in September 1978), but the odds against success in the endeavor by such a small community are great. Thus, it will be interesting to discover how the community develops when the second generation becomes the majority.

A few smaller Islamic organizations have established themselves in the United States, including the Chishti Sufi order (Melton, 1985:8). Membership in most of these groups is very small, and few have any impact on the immigrant community. One group that does have an impact is the Ahmadiyya movement, an aggressive missionary sect of Shi'a Islam. The Ahmadiyya movement was founded in 1889 by Mirza Ghulam Ahmad (1835–1908) as a Muslim reform movement in the Punjab. Followers believe that Ahmad was the promised deliverer and religious leader (*Mahdi*) for Muslims and that his descendants are the continuous sources of divine revelation. The group moved en masse from India to Pakistan at the time of partition, and now have their headquarters in Pakistan. They are regarded as heretics by orthodox Muslims, and in 1974 the Ahmadis were officially excluded from Islam by the Muslim World League in Saudi Arabia and declared to be not Muslims for legal purposes by the Pakistani parliament. In April 1984 the military government of Pakistan imposed a new ordinance that curtails the freedom of the Ahmadis and forbids them from calling themselves Muslims or using Muslim words in the description of their activities.

The Ahmadiyya movement came to the United States as part of its aggressive missionary activity in a hundred countries, which has been very effective in sub-Saharan Africa. As early as 1921 an Ahmadiyya missionary settled in Chicago and began to publish a periodical, "Muslim Sunrise." In those early days most of the converts were Afro-Americans who formed the majority in the twenty centers that were established in Eastern and Central United States. In 1950 headquarters were established in Washington, D.C. Each of the centers is responsible to the Director General of the Ahmadiyya Muslim Foreign Mission in Pakistan. No statistics about membership and participation are available, but the numbers are known to be small. Ahmadis are not prominent among the immigrants from Pakistan, but they do organize to protest the repression of Ahmadis in that country. Tensions exist between the Ahmadis and the Sunni immigrants from Pakistan, so the Ahmadis do not attempt to participate in the activities of the Sunni mosques.

The Sunni Muslims emphasize the unity of Islam, and all their centers welcome all Muslims to participate in their activities, but Shi'ite Muslims tend to associate in religious and social affairs only with people of their own ethnic and religious group. The various Shi'ite groups and the Sunni groups have little knowledge of one another, even within the same metropolitan areas, so the separation is almost complete. In areas with relatively small Muslim populations, the Sunnis organize mosques and activities without respect to national or ethnic background, stressing Islamic identity – as one leader described it as creating "Muslims-in-general." Even in the larger metropolitan areas, where the Muslim centers are identified with particular national or ethnic groups – Pakistani, Asian, Arab, Yugoslavian, Black – with varying language, dress, cuisine, and leadership, the cultural markers may well disappear among members of the second and third generations; indeed, regional languages are already a significant problem for members of the second generation. It seems likely that soon the religious melting pot that Herberg observed (1960) will work its way among the Muslim immigrants just as it did among earlier immigrants, and the religious face of the United States will not be "Protestant, Catholic, Jew," but "Protestant, Catholic, Jew, Muslim . . . "

Christians

An Indian Jesuit visiting the United States was asked by a friendly, but uninformed American, "Father, when were you converted to Christianity?" He replied with a smile and a twinkle in his eye, "Oh, about four hundred years ago." Christianity in India is old. A Catholicos of the St. Thomas Christians of South India on an official visit to Rome in 1983 greeted the Pope: "We bring you greetings from a small Church, the fruit of the preaching and martyrdom of the Apostle St. Thomas – a Church as ancient as any, as faithful to the Tradition as any, and as proud of its heritage and autonomy as any. In a sense this is a meeting between the Apostle St. Thomas and the Apostles St. Peter and St. Paul in the persons of their successors" (Mathews, 1983:192). Christianity took root early in South India; the majority of Christians in India and of those who have emigrated to the United States are South Indians, primarily from Kerala, where the St. Thomas Christians have had a long and eventful history.

Christians make up a small minority (2.43%) of the total Indian population, but their distribution is such that this small minority in the

Table 3.2. *Christians in India*

	Population	% of total	% change since 1971
India	16,165,447	2.43	16.77
Kerala	5,233,865	20.56	16.46
Tamil Nadu	2,798,048	5.78	18.17
Andhra Pradesh	1,433,327	2.68	(21.39)
Goa, Daman, & Diu	318,249	29.28	16.78
Orissa	480,426	1.82	26.80
Gujarat	132,703	0.37	21.37
Nagaland	621,590	80.21	80.28
Meghalaya	702,854	52.62	47.89
Arunachal Pradesh	27,306	4.32	641.21

Adapted from the *1981 Census of India.*

country may be a significant minority in some states in the south and even a majority in some regions. The only states where the Christian population is a majority are in the troubled northeast, where Christianity has grown rapidly over the past decade. Over 60 percent of the Christians in India live in three states of the south and one union territory: Kerala, Tamil Nadu, Andhra Pradesh, and Goa (see Table 3.2). Kerala, which has the highest population density of any state in India, has the largest number of Christians, and it provides the largest number of Christian emigrants from India to the United States. Very few Indians of any religious tradition emigrate to the United States from the northeast areas of India, and although non-Hindu Gujaratis are prominent among immigrants, the number of Christians in Gujarat is very small.

When Hindus emigrate, they come from a country where they are the majority into a situation where they are a very small minority. Whereas Muslims are a minority in India and join Muslims from other countries to reconstitute a minority in the United States, the experience of Christians would seem to be quite different. Christians are a small minority in India, but they come into a situation in the United States where it would appear that they join the majority. An immigrant who flew directly from India to Chicago said that the only things in the new landscape that looked familiar and that gave him a sense of confidence were the church spires. Indeed, some immigrant Christians do find places immediately in American churches – Methodist, Episcopal, Nazarene, Lutheran, and Pentecostal – but no recent statistics exist regarding how many Indian Christians have joined existing churches in the United States. A survey of Mar Thoma Christians in Dallas in 1978, before an active congregation had been formed, revealed that over half of the Mar Thoma Christians held membership in local churches (T. J. Thomas 1978:48). Some parents take their children to the American churches so the children will become more proficient in English and more assimilated. Many Indian Christians feel, however, that they continue to be a minority in a "Christian land." If they came from a village or area where the orthodox St. Thomas Christians were a majority, they do not immediately identify with the various denominations of the United States. The ethos of American Christianity and certainly the morals of "Christian America" are an affront to many Indian Christians. They fear that their children will be drawn into the secularism and immorality of American society through the churches themselves, and so they attempt to preserve personal and group Christian identity by establishing Indian churches in the United States.

Kerala churches

The Malayalam-speaking Christians from the State of Kerala are the most active and successful in establishing churches and new denominations in the United States. Kerala has the largest population of Christians of the Indian states (5,233,865), with a great variation in the percentages of the major religions from the rest of India (Kerala: Hindus – 58.15, Muslims – 21.25, Christians – 20.56; India: Hindus – 82.6, Muslims – 11.35, Christians – 2.43). Although Christians are only one-fifth of the population of Kerala, about 85 percent of Kerala immigrants to the United States are Christians (A. Thomas, 1984:11). The history of Christianity in Kerala and its divisions can provide us with background for understanding the development of Malayalee churches in the United States.

The origin of the St. Thomas churches in India is shrouded in obscurity. The tradition is that St. Thomas arrived in India as a missionary in A.D. 52 and was martyred at Mylapore in Madras in A.D. 72, a martyrdom still remembered in the festival of St. Thomas Day. The details of scholarly debate about the origin and orthodoxy of the ancient Christians are not important here (for further information, see Neill, 1984). For centuries the St. Thomas Christians were affiliated with the Patriarch of Babylon, who provided bishops, and they used a Syriac liturgy according to the eastern Chalcedonian rite. In the fourth century and again in the ninth, Christian refugees from Persia came to Kerala. Because some of them came with Thomas of Cana, they became known as "Kanaya," and their descendants maintain their identity as an endogamous group in the St. Thomas churches. Until the sixteenth century they united Indian culture with Syrian creeds and rituals.

In A.D. 1498 Vasco de Gama visited the Malabar coast, and Portuguese influence came to Kerala. Francis Xavier arrived in Goa in A.D. 1542, and other Roman Catholic missionaries traveled into Kerala. Attempts were made to separate the Indian Christians from their "heretical" patriarchs in the Middle East and from traditional Indian practices. The Synod of Diamper in A.D. 1599, convened by Archbishop Alexio de Menezes, passed decrees calculated to bring Indian faith and practice into conformity with those of Rome. The missionaries consecrated a Catalan as bishop for the St. Thomas Christians, but they preferred that their bishops come from Babylon. In A.D. 1653 the Patriarch of Babylon sent a bishop named Ahatalla to Malabar, but the Portuguese seized him and took him to Goa, whereupon some 20,000 St. Thomas Christians gathered to protest before a stone cross at a church in Cochin. They took an oath, while they were touching ropes tied to that cross, that they were free from Roman domination and would not submit to the Jesuit missionaries. The Coonan Cross oath was a turning point in church history in Kerala. In A.D. 1665 a representative from the Patriarch of Antioch visited and consecrated a new bishop and introduced the Antiochian rite in Syriac, and what had been an undivided church became two: the St. Thomas Christians of the Roman Catholic Church (Syro-Malabar rite) and the St. Thomas Christians affiliated with the Patriarch of Antioch (Jacobites). The Jesuit missionaries later made many converts, primarily from the lower castes in South India, and they are called "Latin Christians" because they follow the Latin rite.

A further division developed among the Syrian Jacobite Christians in the nineteenth century. Anglican missionaries of the Church Missionary Society came to work with the Syrian Christians in the first part of the nineteenth century. They translated the Bible into the Malayalam language (New Testament in 1829; entire Bible in 1841), and they were influential in the "Old Seminary" at Kottayam in Kerala. Some Syrian Christians were impressed by the ideas and practices of the Anglicans, and they began to urge reform of the church through the introduction of Malayalam in the liturgy and the exclusion of some practices, such as prayers for the dead and auricular confession. The church did not adopt these reforms, so Abraham Malpan, a teacher in the "Old Seminary" introduced a revised liturgy in Malayalam in 1836, which marks the beginning of the reformed, progressive church known as the Mar Thoma Syrian Church of Malabar. The national meeting in the United States in the summer of 1986 celebrated the 150th anniversary of this reform. The Mar Thoma Church in India has over 800 parishes in 7 dioceses with 6 bishops and 435 priests. Although it still claims the tradition from St. Thomas, it introduced into India some of the ideas and practices of the Protestant reformation.

The Catholicos who met with the Pope in 1983 is the spiritual leader

of yet another branch of the St. Thomas Christians, the Malankara Orthodox Church. The Jacobite Syrian Church had continued under the
jurisdiction of the Patriarch of Antioch. A group within the church,
opposed to the Patriarch, claimed that the St. Thomas Christians had not
been in communion with the Antiocheans in Syria or the Nestorians of
Persia, but had been under the Catholicos of the East, who was independent of and equal in authority to the Patriarch of Antioch. In 1912
that position, which had often been vacant, was transferred to Malankara
in India. The leader of this autocephalous church carries the titles of
"Catholicos of the East" and "Malankara Metropolitan" and the headquarters is at Kottayam in Kerala. Other smaller churches have emerged
from the St. Thomas Christians, but, aside from those in communion
with the Roman Catholic Church, the three most important remain the
Jacobite Syrian Church under the Patriarch of Antioch, the Malankara
Orthodox Church under the Catholicos of the East in Kerala, and the
Mar Thoma Church under a Synod of Bishops in Kerala. All three have
established churches in the United States and are active in the affairs of
the World Council of Churches and in conversations with the Roman
Catholic Church.

Roman Catholics number about five million adults in India, but Kerala's Catholics are unique because they are divided into three groups,
each with a separate rite administered through a different diocese. The
Catholics of the Syro-Malabar rite are the most numerous and come from
those who remained with the Jesuits in the seventeenth century. They
were for some time administered by Latin bishops, but they have had
their own hierarchy since 1923. They preserve the ancient customs and
liturgy in Syriac. The Latin rite Catholics trace their origin to Portuguese
missionaries, and they share the Latin liturgy – now in the vernacular
languages – with Roman Catholics throughout India. The Catholics of
the Syro-Malankara rite are recent converts from the Jacobite Syrian
Church who united with the Roman church in 1930 under the leadership
of Mar Ivanios and Mar Theophilos. Pope Pius XI established a special
rite for them which uses the Malayalam along with Syriac (Pothacamury,
1958:35).

The other major church in the area that includes Kerala is the Church
of South India, which was formed in 1947 as a union of the Anglican,
Dutch Reformed, Presbyterian, Methodist, and Congregational churches
in the states of Tamil Nadu, Kerala, Andhra Pradesh, and Karnataka.
The Church of South India is administered by bishops in dioceses
throughout South India, including several in Kerala. The formation of
the church after independence was a major event in the Christian ecumenical movement, but even though the church incorporated several

denominations, the local churches were still identified by their language areas: Tamil, Malayalee and Telugu.

The church in Kerala has been plagued by social barriers erected to keep the "old Christians," those who claim descent from higher castes, separate from the more recent converts from lower castes and *Harijans* (Untouchables). Many of the old Christians had ancestors who were high-caste Brahmin converts or early Persian immigrants (Kanayan), whereas the "new Christians" are those of lower castes converted by the Jesuits – Karayar and Mukkuwar fishermen or Nayar gardeners – and the more recent converts of the nineteenth and twentieth centuries, both Protestants and Catholics, from the Nadar toddy tappers or Pulaya laborers. This division between the old Christians and the new Christians characterizes many of the denominations. Some of the churches in Kerala, including the Mar Thoma Church, built separate church buildings for the "new Christians" and in other ways organized the community life of the new converts on lines quite different from those of the older Syrian Christians. Even in the ecumenical Church of South India there were two different caste sections, the Syrians and the Harijans (Thoma, 1968:39, app. III). It was not until the early 1980s that 106 congregations of the new Christians in the Mar Thoma Church in Kerala were raised to the status of parishes and given full privileges. The question of intermarriage among the Christians from India from various denominations and castes continues to be a major issue.

A new phenomenon of the Kerala churches in this century has been the development of a Pentecostal movement. Hundreds of Pentecostal churches have emerged since the 1920s, some influenced by missionaries from abroad but most developing from indigenous leaders who left the established churches to start their own congregations. (The largest group is the Indian Pentecostal Church of God, which, however, is primarily in Andhra Pradesh.) Most Pentecostal churches are independent, so a history of the movement in Kerala is difficult to develop. Nevertheless, the Pentecostal groups have a significant influence both in Kerala and among immigrants to the United States.

Christian immigrants to the United States

All these denominations are now part of American Christianity. The most important factor in the emigration of Christians from India to the United States is that in the early 1970s a critical shortage of nurses existed in the urban hospitals in the United States. Not only was nursing one of the occupations listed in the third priority for immigration, but nurses from the Philippines and from India were actively recruited to come to the

United States to work in urban hospitals. Typically, the wife in an Asian-Indian Christian family would obtain a visa and the promise of a job as a nurse in the United States. She would bring her husband and children with her or, as was most often the case, would come, work for some time, and then send for her family. This pattern contrasts with the pattern of most other Asian-Indian groups, in which the man obtained a visa either as a student or a professional and then either called his family to join him or went back to India for a bride. The nurses from India came in the mid 1970s when the shortage was greatest; now nurses are not high in the preference category, so Christians come primarily for family reunification. Still, the concentration of Asian-Indian Christians in nursing and medical technology is striking. One official in New York is quoted as saying (perhaps in hyperbole), "During the evening shifts in the city hospitals the official language changes from English to Malayalam" (Badhwar, 1980:17).

As with other ethnic groups, no accurate figures exist for the number of Asian-Indian Christians in the United States or for the number of people from Kerala. A directory of Keralites in the United States contains references to 5,500 families (Andrews, 1983),[4] indicating that there may be as many as 10,000 families totalling about 40,000 Asian Indians from Kerala. The returns of the surveys for the directory indicate that 85 percent of these immigrants are Christians. That astounding figure results from the recruitment of nurses from Kerala and from the fact that the nursing profession is heavily populated by Christians. Of those who participated in the survey for the directory of Keralites, 40 percent were engaged in the medical field, 10 percent of whom were doctors (Andrews, 1984:103).

The Malayalee Christian community of Dallas demonstrates the growth rate and the professional concentration. In a six-year period from 1973 to 1978 the number of immigrants grew from 75 to 620. A survey of the occupations of the adults revealed a total of 170 nurses (49%), 145 technicians and office workers (41%), 20 students (6%), 10 teachers (3%), but only 5 engineers and doctors (1%); for a total of 350 adults with 270 children. The denominational backgrounds of these Christians were: Mar Thoma (230); Pentecostals and other Congregationalists (160); Syrian Orthodox (150); Catholics (40); Church of South India, 40 (Thomas, 1978:30–1).

The role reversal that took place in the emigration process of the Indian nurses, whose position in the social structure in India had not marked them for "good marriages," strengthened their negotiations for marriage once they had the prospect of getting the "green card," the alien registration card signifying permanent resident status in the United States. Most of the men who followed their wives took positions in machine shops or factories, or used the connections their wives had in the hospitals to get training as medical technicians. Many of the men were underemployed even though they had good educations – 55 percent of the Keralite immigrants had at least four years of college education (Andrews, 1983:99–101) – and were very proficient in English, having been educated in English medium Christian schools. Nevertheless, they could not find jobs in the professions in the United States. Thus, women have been the primary wage earners in the families, and even though very few divorces are reported, the change from the traditional family relationships to the new situation has created serious tensions within the families. Tensions were exacerbated during the recession of the early 1980s, when many of the recently-arrived men were laid off from their jobs. The jobs of the wives were by then more secure, and the wives have continued to support the families while the men seek training and new occupations.

The Asian-Indian Christians represent a profile different from that of other Asian-Indian immigrants. As would be expected, the majority are from South India because that is the center of Indian Christianity. The most active congregations and denominational organizations stand in the tradition of the St. Thomas Christians of Kerala, so that the language of the Asian-Indian Christians is predominantly Malayalam. Tamil and Telugu Christians are not as numerous as the Malayalees, and they tend to form churches and prayer groups on regional–linguistic grounds rather than on the basis of denominational ties.

Establishment of prayer groups and churches

The establishment of Asian-Indian Christian groups can be traced in three stages. In the early 1970s the few immigrant Christians attended churches of established American denominations. It was common to keep formal membership with the church in India, but to participate in the American congregations, although a few joined American congregations and became lay leaders. In conjunction with that participation, multilingual and interdenominational Indian prayer groups began to meet occasionally on Sunday evenings in homes and later in rented halls for worship and fellowship. Before the mid-1970s the number of Asian-Indian Christians was so small that it would have been difficult to sustain separate groups or denominations. One exception was that the Roman Catholics participated in local parishes but formed Indian Catholic Associations in the larger cities. In the second stage, separate groups were established for worship and fellowship in the regional languages: Malayalam, Tamil, Telugu, Gujarati, and Hindi. In the late 1960s the New York metropolitan area had between twenty and thirty Malayalees, and the average attendance of the only Christian worship service in Malayalam was fifteen.

There were Punjabi Christians from India and Pakistan, but they did not form separate groups; instead, they tended to join Methodist or Nazarene churches. The language groups incorporated persons from the various denominations; as one Malayalee leader remarked, "We even had Pentecostals in our meetings." The third stage, beginning in the late 1970s after the dramatic increase in immigration, brought the establishment of denominational congregations and ecclesiastical structures. The movement from national, to regional, to denominational identity has all taken place within a decade, even though congregations persist that are remnants of the first two stages. The future of Asian-Indian Christians is hard to predict, but the formation of denominational churches has been pronounced among the Christians from Kerala.

Mar Thoma churches. The first Mar Thoma congregation in the United States was recognized in New York in 1976. A priest studying at Princeton Theological Seminary was assigned as vicar, and he conducted regular services in a rented church building in Manhattan. Other groups had been meeting informally: One begun in Chicago in 1973, without a priest, was constituted as a congregation in 1977; in 1974 twelve families in Houston began to meet once a month with a priest who was a student at Perkins School of Theology at Southern Methodist University in Dallas – they were constituted as a congregation in 1978. The growth has been so rapid that in 1980 the New York congregation was divided into four parishes of Manhattan, Queens, Staten Island, and Newark, with a total of about 400 families. The first full-time pastor was sent from Kerala in 1979 to serve in New York and the second in 1980 to Houston (Thomas & Thomas, 1984:117). The congregation in Dallas and the Epiphany congregation in New York have purchased existing church buildings, the Trinity Church in Houston constructed a new building that was dedicated in 1984, and a new building was dedicated for the Des Plaines congregation in Chicago in November 1986. There are now twenty-two authorized congregations in the United States and six in Canada,[5] and it is estimated that there are 1500 Mar Thoma families in the United States.

The pattern of development of the church in Dallas is typical. In the early 1970s the Malayalee people started an interdenominational prayer group that met in homes, led by an immigrant who had been a pastor of the Church of South India. When he left Dallas, a Mar Thoma priest who was a student at Southern Methodist University took over the leadership. The interdenominational group gave way to various denominational groups that began their own congregations, and the Mar Thoma congregation grew to its present size of 140 families, even though it has been served on a part-time basis by student priests. For ten years it met in the chapel of the Cochran Methodist Church, which was also used by the smaller Church of South India congregation, but the members purchased an Episcopal Church in Grand Prairie for $190,000 when they outgrew the chapel.

Each congregation is organized locally with a pastor as president and an elected executive committee. There are only fourteen Mar Thoma pastors in North America, thirteen in the United States and one in Canada, and some of these are students, so the pastors travel across the country to minister to the various congregations.[6] A Zonal Council for North America, formed in 1982 and made up of the pastors and representatives from each of the congregations, oversees church activities. The council sponsors annual conferences for pastors, families, and youth that are significant for reinforcing identity and establishing the programs of the church – the conference in Dallas in the summer of 1984 attracted over 1,000 participants. The decisions of the Zonal Council and its activities are reviewed by the Synod of Bishops in Kerala, but preliminary discussions are underway about forming an American diocese.

A bishop of the Mar Thoma Church, Thomas Mar Athanasius (1914–1984), traveled to the United States three times to help establish the Mar Thoma congregations. Thomas Mar Athanasius was instrumental in reaching a formal agreement with the Episcopal Church, with which the Mar Thoma Church is in full communion. This agreement has great potential for facilitating the development of the Mar Thoma Church in the United States and its adaptation within American Christianity. The formal agreement was signed by the Metropolitan of the Mar Thoma Syrian Church of Malabar and by the Presiding Bishop of the Episcopal Church in February and March of 1982. It states that "When requested by the Metropolitan of the Mar Thoma Church, bishops of the Episcopal Church shall exercise episcopal oversight of clergy and laity of the Mar Thoma Church within the jurisdictions of this church [Episcopal]." In this way, Mar Thoma members are treated as members of the Episcopal Church by the bishop, with the understanding that they remain members of the Mar Thoma Church and that on matters of liturgy, marriage, and finance the discipline of the Mar Thoma Church prevails. The Metropolitan of the Mar Thoma Church or other bishops may visit within the diocese if they inform the respective local Episcopal bishops. The Synod of Bishops in Kerala assigns priests to the United States for a period of two or three years, and the Episcopal Church grants licenses and ministerial standing. Priests enter the United States as exchange visitors on J1 visas (their wives and children on J2 visas), and the Episcopal Church authorizes the formal visa request. Under supplemental guidelines approved in 1984 the diocesan medical insurance plans were opened to Mar Thoma priests and provisions were made for an annual visitation to the Mar Thoma congregations by the diocesan Episcopal bishop. The agreement thus allows for the development of the Mar Thoma Church as a separate denomination, but it provides for a significant ecumenical relationship that broadens the contacts and influence of the Mar Thoma Church.

The leaders of the Mar Thoma Church share with other Asian-Indian Christians the difficult problem of maintaining their denominational and linguistic identity, and preserving themselves and their children from the materialism and immorality they perceive as characterizing modern American society. The topics discussed at the youth conference in Dallas in 1984 reflect these issues: "Faith and Practice of the Mar Thoma Church"; "Peer Pressure: Identity and Conformity in American Society"; "Choosing a Life Partner: Traditional Indian Way or Modern Western Style?"; "The Generation Gap: Indian Version In America"; and "Drug, Alcohol Addiction: Is There a Way Out?" At the same time the parents in the family conference were discussing the issue, "Christian Understanding of Freedom in the Indian North American Cultural Context." The Mar Thoma Church is a fairly progressive church poised between two cultures. At the conference in Chicago in 1986, the young people met upstairs and sang in English a chorus common to most American Christian youth groups, while the parents met downstairs to discuss in Malayalam the problems of adaptation to the United States.

The Malankara Orthodox Church in America. Bearded priests in colorful flowing robes perform the ritual of the mass in Malayalam behind the closed curtains according to the ancient Eastern rite. The congregation stands, men on one side and women on the other, throughout the long service. The young men who assist the priest in the service read the scripture lessons in English. Many layers of church history and elements from many cultures coexist in a moving patchwork to provide continuity with the past and identity in the present.

When the Catholicos of the East, Moran Mar Baselius Mar Thoma Mathews I, on his first visit, established a bishop for the Malankara Orthodox Church in America, the Malankara Orthodox Church became the first Asian-Indian Christian group to establish a diocese in the United States. Metropolitan Thomas Mar Makarios administers the affairs of about thirty churches in North America from his headquarters at Episcopal Diocesan House in Buffalo, New York.[7] The churches are served by priests who are permanent residents in the United States. The orders of the church are Deacon, Priest, Kor Episcopa, Episcopa, Metropolitan, and Catholicos; the first three may be married, but the bishops are unmarried. Deacons need not have professional theological training, and some are relatively young. It is estimated that there are about forty Malankara priests in the United States, and some have received their professional education in American seminaries. Some churches have two priests, but many of the priests work in secular jobs as well. They have an annual diocesan conference, a summer camp (which was held in Tampa, Florida, in 1985), and a journal called *Malankara Light.*

The churches have regular Sunday Schools to meet the needs of the children, in which the medium of instruction is English. Some of the churches have the Holy Qurbana once a month in English following a service book first published in English in 1981. The Sunday Schools follow a graded curriculum with study books that are prepared in English at the Sunday School center in Kottayam, Kerala. One of the difficulties this presents is that these books were written for children in India with an Indian educational background. The language of the Christians who study in English medium schools in Kerala is only slightly different, but the culture is half a world away from that of the Asian-Indian children in American schools. A necessary project is the preparation of materials for the Sunday Schools that will both bridge the two cultures and the two generations, a challenge faced by all the Christian groups. The 1986 national conference in Chicago became an emotion-laden series of discussions as the young people requested more services and materials in English, and complained that their parents pressure them both to excel in the United States and to conform to the Kerala customs in which the parents were raised. The bishops present acted as mediators between parents and children, past and present, and between the church in Kerala and its offspring in the United States.

Jacobite Syrian Church. The liturgy and programs of the Jacobite Syrian churches are the same as those of the Malankara Orthodox churches, but the Jacobites preserve allegiance to Ignatius Zakkal, who is the Patriarch of Antioch and a member of the central committee of the World Council of Churches. A Metropolitan in Kerala has general administrative responsibilities over the churches in Kerala, and the priests and lay people who have come from Kerala maintain connections with relatives, churches, and bishops in India. The primate of the Archdiocese of the Syrian Orthodox Church in the United States is Archbishop Mar Athanasius Yeshue Samuel, whose headquarters are in Lodi, New Jersey. His background is in Jerusalem and Syria, not India, and he was appointed by the previous Patriarch of Antioch to be primate of a diocese in the United States made up largely of earlier immigrants from Syria. The Syrian immigrants are a well-established community more numerous than the more recent immigrants from India. When the new immigrants came from India, they established separate congregations that do not have much interaction with the immigrants from Syria except that both are under the bishopric of Athanasius Samuel and are loyal to the Patriarch of

Antioch. They observe the same discipline and follow the same rituals, but in separate congregations.

Some tension has resulted among the immigrants and priests from India over whether they should be under the direct control of the archbishop in the United States or under the metropolitan and bishops in Kerala. Some of the bishops from Kerala have visited their priests in the United States, received contributions for Christian institutions in Kerala, and encouraged the establishment of churches. Thus the bishops in Kerala seemed to be exercising direct control over churches in the United States. Ignatius Zakkal, who had studied for a period at General Theological Seminary in New York, sent an open letter to all the Jacobite Syrian Christians and clergy from Kerala in which he reaffirmed the ecclesiastical principle that they are now under the control of Archbishop Samuel (*Malankara Light*, Vol. 4, No. 3, Winter 1984, p. 2). The issue is not yet completely resolved; both the relationship between the Christians from Kerala and Syria and the connection of the immigrants from Kerala to the institutions in India are at stake. It seems unlikely that in the short run the groups from Syria and India will come together even though they share a common hierarchy.

Thirteen or fourteen congregations, a few with only five to ten families, serve a small community of about six hundred families. There are about twenty priests in the United States, most are well-educated in Indian and American educational institutions, and a few hold Ph.D. degrees. Several came for study in the 1960s, remained as permanent residents, and hold teaching positions or other secular jobs in addition to their voluntary service to the congregations. The services in the congregations follow the Eastern rite and the prayers are in Malayalam and Syriac. The prayer book has Syriac on one side, Malayalam on the other.

A distinct ethnic subgroup in the Jacobite church is made up of about 150 families of Kanayans, who claim descent from Persian refugees who emigrated to India in A.D. 345. They keep themselves as a separate community and in the United States have established several congregations for the small, dispersed community of some 150 families. Six Kanayan priests are permanent residents; four in the New York area, one in Boston, and one in Dallas. Of these, four came to the United States as students (three have Ph.D. degrees); two came for family reunification. St. Ignatius Kanaya Church in Yonkers, New York, is the only congregation that has been able to purchase a church building. These Kanayan Orthodox Christians do not intermarry with other Jacobite Christians, but they do intermarry with the Kanayan families who are affiliated with the Roman Catholic Church, which consists of some 400 families in the United States by one rough estimate. Even in Kerala, the Orthodox Kanayans are a relatively small number (approximately 100,000) with forty-five parishes and forty priests. The number of well-educated priests abroad constitutes a significant "brain drain" that is troublesome to the priests. Although these St. Thomas Christian groups are small, they are growing both through immigration and natural birth, and will eventually become a more significant feature of American Christianity.

The Church of South India. The Church of South India has twenty-one dioceses in India, including four in Kerala; many of the immigrants, however, have come from a single diocese, the central diocese in Kerala (Madhya Kerala). No exact count exists for the numbers from the various South Indian linguistic groups. Because the Church of South India has an official policy of not establishing foreign jurisdictions, no official designation of affiliated churches in the United States exists, nor is there a national organization of congregations, although congregations do exist that are led by priests ordained in the Church of South India. These priests are either permanent residents in the United States or are temporarily in the United States for graduate study. The congregations tend to be fairly small, and some groups have split to support different priests or to maintain the distinction between "old Christians" and "new Christians." Some members of the Church of South India participate in Mar Thoma congregations in the United States, because both groups have close relationships with the Anglican Church: Church of South India congregations in the United States use the English liturgy of the Church of South India or the liturgy of the Episcopal Church. Some priests in the United States discuss the possibility of formal affiliation with the Episcopal Church and hope it will regularize the ecclesiastical order of the immigrant church. The Episcopal Church is in a position to play a significant role in the cooperation of the Mar Thoma churches and the Churches of South India in the United States. It is more difficult to estimate the potential of the Eastern Orthodox churches to affect the adaptation of the Indian Jacobite churches.

The Roman Catholic Church. The Asian-Indian Catholics are integrated into the local parishes of the Roman Catholic Church, but several strategies are used to provide for their special needs. Most dioceses have offices of ethnic ministries that arrange for special services and social occasions for Catholics from India. The first such group was the India Catholic Association of Chicago, which celebrated its twenty-fifth anniversary on September 22, 1985, at Loyola University. It began as a student organization, and now has its own officers and affiliated priest to serve Asian Indian Catholics. The India Catholic Association in New York has a membership of 1,000 from an Indian Catholic population of about 3,000, and more than 400 persons celebrated mass with John Cardinal O'Connor at St. Patrick's Cathedral on St. Thomas' Day, June 29, 1986 (IA, 1986:14). In some dioceses, as in Houston, it has been possible to keep the three rites – Latin, Syro-Malabar and Malankara – together in the same group. Some of the Keralite Catholics, who in India attended church daily, have become irregular in their observance in the United States because they do not feel at home in the worship language and rituals of the American churches. They prefer the Syrian rite and Syrian priests to the Latin rite and white priests, and they do not like to contribute to the Latin churches unless their children attend the parochial schools (Andrews, 1983:111).

The Syro-Malabar rite Catholics of Dallas asked the bishop in Dallas to provide the opportunity to have the mass according to the Eastern rite in Malayalam (the first rite in Malayalam in India was in 1962 at the time of the Second Vatican Council). The result of their conversations was an agreement to have a priest assigned by the bishop of Kerala to serve under the bishop of Dallas. The promised priest arrived in Dallas in 1984 to be an assistant priest of Pius X Catholic Church and to be pastor for the 100 families of the Syro-Malabar Catholic community in the Dallas diocese. He performs the mass in the Syro-Malabar rite for about seventy-five communicants on the first Sunday of the month in a centrally located church; on the festival days, between 200 and 300 people attend. He also performs all the sacraments for the community, primarily christenings and first communions. An indication of the ages of the members is that in his first two years in Dallas he did not perform a wedding or a funeral. He will stay in Dallas for three or four years and then return to Kerala. Another priest from India, a Gujarati, is in Dallas as one of several Indian curates who serve as regular diocesan priests in the United States, but he has no special assignment in the Asian-Indian community. On August 25, 1985, a Syro-Malabar Catholic ministry was established in Chicago when Bishop Pallickaparampil of Kerala joined Joseph Cardinal Bernardine in establishing a priest from Kerala. Such cooperative arrangements will probably continue and expand as the number of Asian-Indian Catholics increases.

A significant development in the larger metropolitan area is an ecumenical movement among Malayalam Christians that finds expression in joint services, in pre-Easter retreats, in Kerala Clergy Associations, and in joint funeral services. A union Christmas carol service started in Dallas in 1984 in which the priests, choirs, and over 700 members of the various denominations participate. The movement has come full circle as Malayalee groups in the United States, which first met together in small prayer groups and then split into the denominational congregations as the community grew larger, draw together in ecumenical meetings based on language, culture, and a tradition going back to St. Thomas.

Pentecostal churches. Pentecostal churches are difficult to describe even though they are omnipresent. Priests and Pentecostal leaders generally say that twelve to fifteen Pentecostal groups meet in the metropolitan areas, but no one has an accurate count. A typical group is made up of five to ten families gathered by a person who was a Pentecostal pastor in India or one who has received the "call" in the United States. Most of these groups are not affiliated with any organized denomination, and their small size is due to frequent divisions as new local charismatic leaders attract personal followings. Individual Pentecostals participate in congregations of American Pentecostal groups. The largest single group of Pentecostal churches that maintain some sense of joint identity is the India Pentecostal Church, which has as many as fifty churches in the United States. It is planning a national conference for all the Malayalee Pentecostal churches.

One suspects that the term "Pentecostal" is used by many Asian-Indian Christians to refer to all groups that have a local congregational polity and to pastors who are not under episcopal orders. All the Pentecostal pastors and leaders identified in this study work in secular jobs to support their families. These small, intense groups provide substitutes for the extended families in India and are important for the maintenance of personal and group identity, while their individual charisma provides a basis for negotiation with the well-established American Pentecostal groups. Although not as formal in organizational structure, they are just as effective as the St. Thomas groups in providing continuity with the traditions in India as well as contacts for entry and adaptation to American society through the use of a recognized idiom.

National ecumenical fellowships. Many of the local groups were first organized as prayer groups on a national ecumenical basis, and some of the Indian Christian Fellowships continue to exist, albeit generally in very small groups. The development of the denominational and regional groups sapped the strength of the ecumenical fellowships, which are marginal because they are interdenominational, because they do not provide a clear identity, and because they fail to emphasize regional culture and language. They may in the future reach children of the second generation, but they do not attract the active participation of their now well-established parents.

The only attempt to form a national organization of Asian-Indian Christians came as a response to the perceived threat to Christianity posed by the so-called Freedom of Religion Bill that was debated in the Indian parliament (Lok Sabha) in 1978. The proposed bill was a response to mass conversions to Christianity in the northeastern areas of India (see Table 3.2), primarily of persons from the lower scheduled castes and tribes, and it provided for "prohibition of conversion from one religion to another by the use of force or inducement or by fraudulent means and for matters incidental thereto." Asian-Indian Christians in the United States believed the bill would be used to prohibit the preaching of the Christian message in India, and a Federation of Indo-American Christians was formed to protest the bill. The leaders of the movement were participants in the Indian Christian Fellowship in Chicago, and they were successful in marshaling the energies of the community to oppose the bill through rallies, protests, and political lobbying. The bill failed to pass, and after the election defeat of the government of Prime Minister Desai, the enthusiasm and united efforts of the Federation flagged. No other issue has arisen to call forth a united effort.

Regional ecumenical churches. Most cities have Christian groups for persons from specific linguistic regions of India. The Malayalam-speaking groups have formed distinct denominational groups because so many came to the United States, but other regional groups are smaller and meet in ecumenical groups. The backgrounds of the groups are quite different, and their modes of relationship with established American churches are diverse. The Christian Worship Fellowship in New York, for example, is totally independent and attracts Telugu Christians. The dominant ethos of the group is shaped by the indigenous Hebron Church in Hyderabad, Andhra Pradesh, which was founded by a Hindu convert, but other Telugu Christians also participate. It was founded in 1980 and now has weekly services for about twenty families.

Two Tamil Christian Fellowships meet in Queens, New York, and they represent two patterns for what one leader described as a "fellowship of language and country." Members of both groups come primarily from the Church of South India, but the two groups also include other denominations. Neither claims any affiliation with the Church of South India even though the prayer book and order of worship comes from that tradition. The two groups began as one in 1976, but divided over the question of what type of relationship to establish with American denominations. One group meets in the Reformed Church of Newtown in Corona – "A Reformed Church serving the community since 1731" according to the sign board – in which three congregations meet: white American, Tamil, and Taiwanese. The Tamil congregation of about seventy-five adults began to meet there in 1982 with a pastor who received his theological degree from Bangalore Theological Seminary in India in 1964. This group is moving toward affiliation with the Reformed congregation and denomination. The other group, about seventy families, meets in a Methodist Church in Astoria, and plans to remain an independent Tamil congregation because persons from several different denominations participate. The pastor is a hospital administrator.

A unique pattern of relationships has developed in the Gujarati Christian Fellowship and the Hindi Christian Fellowship, which have been incorporated into the Emmanuel United Methodist Church in Evanston (see Chapter Seven). The incorporation of these two immigrant groups with white Americans in one congregation brings to the fore both the problems and the potential associated with the preservation of religious identity, as well as the negotiation of cultural differences that is necessary for members of both the first and second generations to adapt to American religious culture and society. No example of a congregation affiliated with the Church of North India was discovered, but that will certainly develop as the number of Asian-Indian Christians grows.

Asian-Indian priests, pastors, and seminaries in America

One way in which the Christian community differs from other Asian-Indian religious groups is that the educational institutions for the preparation of religious leaders were already in place when the immigrants arrived. Indeed, many of the leading pastors of Indian denominations received part of their education in seminaries in the United States during the 1950s and 1960s, and some continued to enter for graduate study. Those who first came with scholarships were the elite from the Indian seminaries. In the 1984–5 academic year 1,130 students from Asia were studying in North American seminaries associated with the American Association of Theological Seminaries; unfortunately, no statistics are kept for individual countries. Some of these students are permanent residents who serve Asian-Indian congregations; others are appointed to regular charges in American denominations and have no official responsibility for the Asian-Indian community. Many take secular jobs or become hospital chaplains and serve as part-time pastors of Asian-Indian congregations. Perhaps it is due to the hospital connections of Indian Christians that several Indian pastors have completed Clinical Pastoral Education programs in American seminaries and hospitals. Most of the nascent prayer groups and congregations were begun by these pastors. Several Asian-Indian Christians responded to a "call" to the ministry after they arrived, and are now studying in American seminaries.

Another group of pastors came as immigrants after they had completed seminary training in India and had served as ministers of congregations when either their wives responded to the opportunity to emigrate as nurses or relatives in the United States gave them the opportunity to emigrate for family reunification. Many of the immigrant Christian pastors with permanent resident status – as distinguished from the temporarily assigned pastors – entered the country as husbands of nurses. A steady stream of Indian pastors enters the community each year, some of whom establish new congregations, whereas others become assistant pastors in established Asian-Indian congregations. There are Roman Catholic priests who have been sponsored by relatives to come and serve as diocesan priests, and some divisions among Asian-Indian Protestant Christians have even resulted from personal or denominational loyalty to pastors who emigrate from India.

The priests who come under episcopal orders for specified tours as exchange visitors with J1 visas are required by ecclesiastical discipline and federal law to return to India. They are among the elite of the priests in India, and they typically are enrolled in doctoral programs in American seminaries during the period they serve the immigrant churches. Seminaries in New York, Boston, Chicago, and Dallas have provided significant scholarship resources, secure housing, and support groups for several of these priests and, thereby, have indirectly supported these growing congregations over the past decade. This support has been a very important, but perhaps an unintended and hidden factor in the development of Asian-Indian congregations. Some of the most overworked pastors in the country are those priests who are engaged in demanding doctoral programs while they are ministering to growing congregations of immigrants. In private conversations some of the temporary visitors have expressed reservations about some of the pastors who are permanent residents, suggesting that they may be "using the congregations" to establish their families in the United States.

There are various ways in which Christian leadership is different from that of other Asian-Indian groups. Muslim, Jain, Sikh, and Zoroastrian religious organizations in the United States are generally established and led by lay people who would not have become religious leaders in India. They are of a different age and educational background from the traditional religious specialists, and it is. the very fact of lay leadership that has shaped the development of these religious organizations in their first decade. On the other hand, Christian groups have been established by members of the clergy and in most instances they are under direct control of clergymen from India. The theological and doctrinal leadership is more sophisticated, but the programs are less concerned with general Indian cultural activities and less effective and pragmatic in constructing buildings and institutions than the larger religious communities led by secular professionals.

Seminaries are very important in the professional training and support of pastors for the Asian-Indian churches, but as a group the Asian-Indian pastors and congregations have been virtually ignored by the American denominations and church leaders. More attention has been paid to Hispanic, Korean, and Taiwanese Christians among the new immigrants. Most denominations have ethnic ministry programs, but as the numbers of Asian-Indian Christians are relatively small they do not receive much attention. Two programs for the study of the impact of Asian-Christian immigrants on American Christianity and for planning assistance to the new congregations are underway at the Pacific and Asian American Center for Theology and Strategies in Berkeley and in the Program for Asian American Theology and Ministry at Princeton. These programs have great potential for assisting the Asian-Indian Christians in maintaining their distinct identities within the fabric of American Christianity, in training leaders for the future generations, and in facilitating the negotiation between Asian-Indian Christians and American religious and secular culture.

Zoroastrians (Parsis)

The world's Zoroastrians are a tiny, shrinking, economically prosperous, religious group of Iranians (approximately 25,700 persons in Iran in 1977 before the Shi'ite revolution; 12,500 concentrated in Tehran), Indians (71,630 in the 1981 census, down from 91,266 in the 1971 census), and a few Parsis who went to Karachi to engage in business (estimated at 4,500 in 1977). Parsis are the Indian followers of the ancient Persian Zoroastrian religion, which involves the worship of Ahura Mazda through rituals in which fire is the sacred symbol. In India the Parsis are concentrated in Maharashtra (56,866) and in Gujarat (11,732). In every location the Zoroastrians are threatened with extinction because they have a tradition of not accepting converts and because, in common with other elite professional groups, they experience a low birthrate.

The history of the Zoroastrians goes back to the ancient Persian past where, until the seventh-century conquest by the Muslim Arabs, it was the dominant religion. At the time of the Arab conquests, a group of refugees fled to India and landed in Gujarat, where a Hindu prince gave them permission to settle. They were known as Parsis because they came from the province of Pars in Persia. Over the centuries, and especially during the period of British control, the Parsis became a very prosperous community of businessmen and industrialists both in Gujarat and within the large Gujarati community that developed in Bombay, the city with the greatest Zoroastrian concentration. Zoroastrians continued to exist as a small minority in Muslim Persia; something of a revival seemed possible in modern Iran under the Shah, but that hope was dashed by the recent Shi'ite revolution. The Zoroastrians in Iran and India are known for acumen and honesty in business, support of charitable foundations to assist members of the community, the "Towers of Silence" where the dead are exposed, and the Fire Temples, closed to outsiders, where rituals are performed before sacred fires that are never extinguished. The modern danger is that the fires will go out.

Zoroastrians from Iran and Parsis from India and Pakistan have emigrated to the United States. The best estimate is that 7,000 Zoroastrians (the designation used in the United States for both national groups) live in widely scattered groups in North America. Three major problems are faced by the tiny community. The first is that they must forge a unity for immigrants from Iran and India who share a religion but who speak different languages and have different cultural backgrounds. Unity is essential because the group is too small to survive if it divides. As it is, members of the Zoroastrian association in the New York area live 200 miles apart. Despite the geographical separation, unity is possible because in both Iran and India the Zoroastrian community is highly educated and westernized, and because immigration regulations led to the entry of the most professionally advanced portion of the community. Some of the rituals are in the dead sacred language of Avestan, but the prayer books are in Gujarati and English. There are some problems, however. Leaders insist on a sensitivity to the tension between the Iranians and Indians, holding that the Zoroastrians do not constitute an ethnic group and that Zoroastrianism is not "a religion of India." A second problem is that of reestablishing the high social standing and positive identification they previously held. As one leader expressed it: "Here [in North America] we are recognized only as immigrants from a poor developing country. Zoroastrians have not only lost the advantage of being known as members of a highly respected community, but must struggle to remove the image of belonging to a poorly educated, impoverished part of the world. The old identity is no longer with us and the new identity of immigrants from a poor country is false" (Mavalwala, 1977:67–8). The question of identity for the young people is critical, and one leader explained the need to build Zoroastrian centers: "Our children need this identity so they can be proud of what they are. . . . At school they are sometimes ashamed to say they are Zoroastrians because people just stare at them as if they are from another planet." The third problem involves tensions over the issue of continuing the prohibition of conversion. Zoroastrians traditionally do not accept converts. Mixed marriages are allowed, but marriage partners are not admitted and traditionally the children of Zoroastrian women in mixed marriages are not admitted, although there seems to be a developing argument for admitting children of mixed marriages. There is also a movement, called the Mazda Yasnians, to agitate for admission of converts, but the community remains deeply divided on that issue. A survey of some members showed that the elders were generally opposed, the young people in favor.

The initiation ceremony (*Navjote*) is regularly performed for both boys and girls born into the community at the age of eleven or twelve. In the spring of 1983 Joseph Peterson, an American chemical engineer, presented himself for initiation as a Zoroastrian. Impressed by his sincerity, his knowledge of the Zoroastrian scriptures, and his ability in the now dead language of Avestan, a priest who settled in the United States agreed to perform the ceremony in New Rochelle, New York. The event created a furor among leaders of the community in Bombay and tensions within the community in the United States, where some favor the admission of sincere converts while others are strongly opposed. The issue remains undecided. However, posing an extreme case such as this one, the admission of a convert with no previous connection to the community, may make it easier to reform the current practice and admit the children of mixed marriages born to Zoroastrian mothers, rather than only those with Zoroastrian fathers.

The Zoroastrian immigrants have established a biennial North American Symposium that is associated with the World Zoroastrian Organization in London. The first meeting was held in Toronto in 1975 and the second in Chicago in 1977. Zoroastrians from twenty communities attended the symposium in Chicago, but the community is so small and spread out that many of those communities do not have their own formal organizations. Zoroastrian centers, called Derbe Mehers (Path of Compassion), have been established in four cities – New York, Chicago, Los Angeles, and Montreal – with the financial assistance of the late Arbab Rustam Guiv and other wealthy Zoroastrian philanthropists. These centers are not traditional Fire Temples, which require the permanent attendance of a priest and the exclusion of non-Zoroastrians, but they do have domestic-style fire altars for the rituals. Prayer meetings with the fire ritual are conducted at least once a month, and some centers hold religious education classes and social events on other occasions.

The priests (*Mobeds*) of the Zoroastrians come from a hereditary group, some of whom are trained for professional activity as priests and for the role of religious teacher in the community. The Zoroastrian centers in the United States do not have professionally trained priests to serve the community, which is one of the reasons why they cannot have the traditional Fire Temple. Occasionally scholars and religious specialists come from India to deliver lectures and give instructions in the rituals. The men who regularly perform the rituals are from the hereditary group from which priests are trained and they know enough of the sacred language and rituals to serve the community. They are businessmen and professionals, however, who have not been trained in the intricacies of either the doctrines or rituals. Some have suggested that the hereditary requirement be dropped so that any knowledgeable person may serve as a priest, but the education and support for a professional priesthood is difficult for a community as small as the Zoroastrians in the United States. A problem exists, however, in relying on priests invited from India, as one leader explained: "... as we and our children become acculturated into North American ways, we widen the gap between ourselves and those coming from India" (Mavalwala, 1977:68).

The theme of the Second North American Zoroastrian Symposium was "Survival and Perpetuation of Zoroastrianism." The small community in the United States struggles against the threat of extinction, but their hopes for the future are tied with the Zoroastrians in India, Pakistan, and Iran and with their success in unifying several ethnic groups in the United States into a single religion.

Jews

It is not uncommon to hear the leaders of several Asian-Indian groups (Gujaratis, Parsis, Sindhis, or Swaminarayan Hindus, for example) refer to themselves as "the Jews of India," by which they mean that they have become migrants, that they are successful businessmen, that they are urban dwellers, that they have high moral standards, or that they hope for equal success in preserving their religious and cultural traditions. They are not, however, the true Jews of India, who emigrated to India in several waves and lived there for centuries as a small minority. Three distinct groups of Jews were in India at the time of independence: the Malayalam-speaking Cochin Jews of Kerala, the Marathi-speaking Bene Israel of Bombay, and the Baghdadi Jews who emigrated from Iraq more recently and resided in Bombay and Calcutta. The total Jewish population in India at the time of independence was about 30,000, but it has diminished greatly since then. The establishment of the State of Israel and its policy of receiving Jews from every country led to the emigration of Jews to Israel in the 1950s and 1960s, where they were declared full Jews by the Israeli rabbinate in 1964. A smaller number emigrated to the United States, some in a second migration from Israel. According to the 1981 census only 5,618 Jews remain in India: 4,354 in Maharashtra, only 90 in Kerala, and a few scattered in other states. It appears that Indian Judaism will disappear except as it is preserved among Indian immigrants in Israel and as it is remembered by Indian Jews in the United States.

The question is if the Indian Jews can "sing the songs of Zion" in the Indian mode in the United States. A small group of Bene Israel Jews have joined together in New York to try. The Congregation BINA was founded in March 1981 by about a hundred families "to preserve and foster the ancient traditions, customs, liturgy, music, melodies, and folklore of the Jews of India." Most of the families participate in regular synagogue programs, but they also meet together once a month for prayers and programs that celebrate and preserve the Sephardic rituals and the cantillation of the service as developed in India. The Jewish Museum in New York mounted an exhibit on the Jews of India from November 1985 to February 1986 as a part of the Festival of India, but for American Jewry the living testimony of the form of Judaism that survived in India for centuries without outside assistance are the Bene Israel. Leaders of the group give presentations on their history, participate in Jewish arts and cultural festivals, and attempt to preserve the traditional songs and literature. They hope to foster academic research on the history of the Jews in India and to preserve in archives the oral histories, documents, and artifacts of their tradition.

Members speak about their desire to have a synagogue, but it seems unlikely that the small number in New York will be able to sustain one. The Bene Israel assemble in rented halls to observe the high holy days according to the Indian tradition, and they publish a bulletin, "Kol Bina," that contains information about their history and programs. They gather in homes for a special ritual (*malida*), which is performed on auspicious occasions such as a house warming. The restrictions regarding intermarriage between different subgroups among the Jews from India are being ignored. On some occasions they join with the American-Iraqi Jewish Community, many of whom were formerly in Bombay and Calcutta, for religious ceremonies. Of the very few Cochin Jews in the United States only two families are on the BINA mailing list. The Bene Israel does not stress the preservation of their native language of Marathi, except in some of the songs and the style of singing, and, as one leader remarked, "The children will not have a sense of being Bene Israel; they will think of themselves as American Jews."

The Indian Jews of the Baghdadi branch have been instrumental in the establishment of two synagogues in Los Angeles that follow the Sephardic tradition. The Kahal Joseph (Assembly of Joseph) was founded in 1959 with twenty Indian families; the Od Joseph Chai (named for a Baghdad Rabbi, Joseph Chaim) was founded in 1977. These and other Indian Jewish institutions that are founded keep alive for members of the immigrant generation the memory of how the songs of Zion were sung and a way of life preserved in India. The small community is now a living museum for liturgy, folklore, and artifacts that, if properly preserved and treasured, will enrich the larger American Jewish community. Participation in the Indian Jewish activities provides a respected locus from which these new immigrants can build bridges into the established community. In turn, the American Jewish community provides a religious home for the Indian Jews and an established identity and future for the children.

PART II

Studies of adaptive strategies

The process of adaptation for immigrants is complex, involving relations with already existing religious groups and the formation of strategies for maintaining identity as each religious group spreads across the country and establishes a national organization. The three groups studied in Chapter Four – one Hindu, one Muslim, and one Sikh – represent different strategies of adaptation to already existing, similar religious groups. Chapters Five and Six trace the spread across the country of two other groups – one Hindu and the other Muslim – that represent distinct strategies of adaptation, both of which have been very successful in maintaining group cohesion and rapid growth. Swaminarayan Hindus (Chapter Five) attempt to preserve the close association of this form of Hinduism with Gujarati ethnic identity through the use of the Gujarati language, arts, and cuisine and by maintaining close ties with the leaders and institutions in Gujarat. Nizari Ismaili Muslims (Chapter Six), on the other hand, transcend ethnic identification to stress their Islamic religious identity and allegiance to an Imam. Their goal is to make possible both the successful assimilation into American society and the preservation of an international religious identity that will provide a bridge between the Third World and Western societies. The past experience of the group as a small, sometimes oppressed minority helps shape the current adaptive strategy. Their respective chapters show how these distinct strategies have developed from the histories, theologies, and commitments of these immigrants and how they have influenced their adaptation in the United States.

CHAPTER 4

Their American cousins
Adaptation of cultural groups

The immigrant from India in the 1970s may have been surprised to be greeted at the airport by a group of white-American Hindus, dressed in saffron robes, dancing, selling books, and chanting "Hare Krishna Hare Krishna / Krishna Krishna Hare Hare / Hare Rama Hare Rama / Rama Rama Hare Hare." A few years later on a flight to India, these devotees, members of the International Society for Krishna Consciousness, would be traveling on a pilgrimage to the sacred shrines of India, while in the same section a large number of Asian Indians, loaded down with electronic appliances, gadgets, and gifts, were returning to family and friends to display the trophies of their success in the United States. The two groups were going in different directions on the same plane.

At the same time as the immigrants from India have been adjusting to secular society in the United States and to the mores of the dominant Judeo-Christian religious tradition, they have had to relate to groups of Americans who have converted to the religions of India – Hinduism, Islam, and Sikhism. Generally, the American converts differ from their Indian counterparts in several ways beyond their ethnic diversity: They have an economic and professional standing different from the immigrants, they have recently adopted their new religious identity, are fervently attached to the doctrine and practice, and they are energetic in the propagation of the religion to the American public. Between the members of the International Society for Krishna Consciousness, the American Muslim Mission, and the American Sikhs of the Sikh Dharma (Happy, Healthy, Holy Organization) on the one hand, and the Indian Hindus, Muslims, and Sikhs on the other, a complex dynamic of attraction and repulsion exists, like that often found between cousins.

The interaction between the religious cousins – white or black Americans and Asian Indians or Pakistanis – is important for both because it changes the religious practices of both. The introduction of the traditional

129

– some would say authentic – forms of religion that came with the immigrants from India and Pakistan has resulted in changes in the forms of the three religions that developed among white and black Americans, changes that have moved them toward more traditional forms of their religions. At the same time, the adaptation of the immigrants to American society and their formation of religious identities are influenced by their interaction with their religious cousins. This chapter focuses on this interaction, although no attempt is made to trace in detail the development and impact of these groups on American society in general, because that has been accomplished elsewhere.[1]

International Society for Krishna Consciousness

Mr. Abhay Charan De (1896–1977), the founder of the International Society for Krishna Consciousness (ISKCON), came to the United States in 1965 as an atypical immigrant from India. He arrived by boat, not by plane; he was old at sixty-nine; and he was retired from his position in a chemical firm, having "renounced the world" as in the traditional Hindu fourth stage of life. Moreover, he came to preach the spirituality and religious devotion of India, not to learn and profit from Western scientific technology, as was the case for so many young professional immigrants. He came to the United States when relatively few immigrants from India had become permanent residents, at about the time President Johnson signed the new immigration act and the stage was just being set for a rapid increase in the numbers of Asian-Indian Hindus in the United States.

A. C. Bhaktivedanta Swami Prabhupada, as he came to be known by devotees, began in New York to attract followers to devotion to Krishna. Along with many North-Indian Vaishnavas, he taught that Krishna is the original form of god, and Vishnu is a form of Krishna. In 1966 he established ISKCON, planning to unite the materially lame man of India with the spiritually blind man of America, thus creating a new religious community. By the time of his death in 1977, he was the chief religious figure for thousands of followers, his pictures or images were in temples in most of the major cities of the country, he had personally initiated some 5,000 disciples into Krishna consciousness (Rochford, 1985:10) – although all but about 1,000 of those have now defected from the organization – and he had established a growing and well-organized movement. After his death in 1977, the Governing Body Commission, which he had established in 1970, became important in the administration. A group of gurus from among his American followers, each with responsibility for a geographical area, took over the mantle of religious leadership after his death.

The full-time members, some who have taken vows of celibacy, and others who are married and have children, live in the temples and ashrams of the organization. ISKCON claims a core membership in the United States of 5,000, but a recent study concludes that the total adult membership is near 2,000 (Rochford, 1985:287 n2). These members are supported by the organization and perform the daily cycle of rituals in the temples and shrines. Life Members of ISKCON are a group of people, mostly Asian Indians, who pay a membership fee of $1111 and give financial support to the programs of the organization. In addition, the rituals, restaurants, and festivals of ISKCON attract large numbers of casual participants and pilgrims, as, for example, to the large ISKCON center in West Virginia. Life members and casual participants are sometimes referred to as "congregational members" to distinguish them from the full-time members who live in the temples and ashrams.

Some of the Hindu immigrants are attracted to the temples and festivals of ISKCON Hindus in India received generally positive reports about the activities of ISKCON in spreading Hindu teaching among disaffected American young people. This was taken as proof that the ancient teachings and spirituality of India represent the best hope for saving Western society from materialism, addiction to drugs and alcohol, and the reckless pleasures thought to destroy life. Hindu immigrants see in the success of ISKCON an affirmation of the value of their tradition, and, hence, its programs provide a valuable support for the preservation and affirmation of their Hindu identity. ISKCON has its feet in both eastern and western cultures, and Angela Burr's comment about ISKCON in Britain is also applicable in America: "It provides the Asian community with a link and a means of reconciling incompatibilities between their own religion and values and those of the west. Asians are not only flattered by western devotees' conversion to their religion but their confidence in their own religious beliefs and values is reinforced and legitimised by it. If westerners believe in it then it must have value" (Burr, 1984:246). Hindu immigrants comment favorably on the asceticism of the members of ISKCON, which reminds them of the holy men of India, and on the knowledge some of the devotees display of Sanskrit, rituals, Indian music, the devotional songs, and literature. ISKCON promotes vegetarianism, and their restaurants were the only place outside the home where Indian vegetarian meals could be obtained in some cities, in this case from food that had been ritually sanctified by being offered to the deities.

A powerful dynamic in Hinduism is the relationship between the "world renouncers" and the householders, who conduct the affairs of the world. In this context the young Americans, who renounced the world of American culture and security to follow the Hindu path, are admired for their religious devotion by Hindu immigrants, who are themselves, nonetheless, seeking the "good life" of householders in the United States. "They are more religious than we are, and they know more about our religion," is a common remark. Most immigrants did not receive a traditional Hindu education in India, and are not conversant with the details of doctrine and ritual, so they were impressed by the study and publications of members of ISKCON, which, to a large extent, focus on the stories about Krishna – the most popular deity of North India – and on the *Bhagavad Gita* – the most popular religious text of Hindus.

During the period before the Hindu immigrants began to build their own temples, ISKCON temples were already in place in most of the cities where the immigrants resided. The images of Radha-Krishna and the daily rituals were similar to those in India, and some immigrants began to visit the temples for worship (*darshan*) and to participate in the devotional songs. Some families went to the temples to fulfill religious vows and to perform the life-cycle rituals. During the 1970s, the numbers of Asian Indians in most congregations grew to outnumber the American converts, even though very few immigrants became full members of ISKCON. The major festivals sponsored by ISKCON, such as the Krishna Jayanti to celebrate the birth of Krishna, attracted many immigrants, up to several thousand in the major cities. However, participation by the immigrants was generally limited to attendance in the temple and at the festivals.

On the other hand, a major problem for the Hindu immigrants was that ISKCON had "given Hinduism a bad name" among the American public. The negative publicity ISKCON received during the 1970s made it difficult for the immigrant Hindus to gain understanding and a positive response from neighbors when they attempted to establish other Hindu groups and centers. The attacks against Hinduism tended in some instances to create an alliance of the persecuted, but the immigrants also distanced themselves from some of the activities of ISKCON that they also found offensive. Some immigrants criticized the public fund-raising activities of the members, and they rejected the drop-out and counter-culture mentality that in the early days separated young initiates from members of their families.

Furthermore, some of the practices in the ISKCON temples were found to be at variance with practices in some areas of India. The presence of married couples in the temple precincts, albeit identified as Brahmins, caused problems with some immigrants. During one worship ritual (*arti*), persons are permitted to approach the images who would not be allowed to do so in South India, where only the priest (pujari) enters the shrine area to perform the rituals. Some immigrants were offended when they were asked to pay to eat the sanctified food in the temple restaurants after the rituals, because that is not the custom in India. ISKCON leaders have responded that only designated pujaris can approach the images, and that there is never a charge for "mahaprasadam" (sanctified food), so that there must have been some misunderstanding. In response to the criticism, however, the temple in Dallas instituted a separate meal without charge, earlier in the afternoon, for the Asian-Indian Hindus. Yet another difficulty was that little opportunity existed for leadership by Asian-Indian immigrants in the affairs of the temples and centers because that leadership was exercised by the white American converts. The result has been that even though Hindu immigrants participate in the rituals and festivals of the temple and have become financial supporters of its programs, they are not attached to the ISKCON organization, and only a few have become initiated disciples of the gurus who became the religious leaders after the death of the founder.

The changes that have taken place in ISKCON following the death of Bhaktivedanta in November 1977 have been well-documented (Gelberg, 1985:7–14; Rochford, 1985). A relativizing of authority resulted from the plurality of gurus, who now have regional responsibilities, and from the interactions between the temple presidents and the Governing Body Commission. Oddly enough, North America is the only region where the movement has not shown growth since 1977 (Gelberg, 1985:11), and there has been a general decline both in membership and in the financial income from the activities of the full-time members that remain. There have been many defections, as well as some divisions in the temples. News reports of a two-million-dollar civil suit in California, a physical attack on one of the gurus in West Virginia, and murder charges against two former members have been published in Asian-Indian papers (IA, 1986:1,8). The stabilizing influence of the immigrant Hindus may have prevented more deviations. Even though the number of communities and preaching centers in the United States had reached fifty by 1983, the number of new full-time members in 1982 was only 151, and in 1983 it was 157 (Rochford, 1985:277–8). Several changes, described as "mellowness" inside the organization, have taken place in an attempt to make ISKCON less objectionable to the American public and to the Hindu immigrants. These include less emphasis on fund-raising in the streets, encouraging contacts between initiates and their families, and inclusion of part-time members who work at secular jobs.

The most dramatic change that has taken place has been in the clientele of ISKCON, from antiestablishment young people to the Asian-Indian immigrant professional, which promises greatly to affect the future development of the organization. Burr indicates that in Britain the influx of Hindu immigrants provided the movement with the means of "transcending its original function as an essentially youth social-protest group" (1984:255). In the United States the ISKCON devotees are also being reintegrated into the mainstream of conventional society – at least in identifiable roles as religious specialists – through their association with the immigrant Hindu community.

The source of new members and of financial support from members of the counterculture of American society dried up in the late 1970s and 1980s, at the same time that the number of Asian-Indian Hindus in the United States was growing dramatically. The emphasis naturally developed on the formation of a new laity from the immigrant group. These congregational members participate in the programs and give financial support. Some are major financial contributors to ISKCON: Asian-Indian Hindus in Detroit, for example, contributed $100,000 to the Bhaktivedanta Book Trust Fund in 1982, and in Philadelphia they contributed about $1,000 each month during 1982 for temple activities (Rochford, 1985:267–8).

A program was begun in Britain as early as 1971 to enlist Asian Indians to become Life Members by donating $1111. The program was developed as a means whereby the worldwide Indian community could mobilize its resources in the cause of spreading Krishna consciousness. By January 1984 there were 30,000 Life Members, over half in India. The number in the United States at that time was 1,684, almost all Asian Indians, including 63 members in Chicago and 84 in Houston. Membership dues do not constitute the total support for ISKCON activities; the prosperous professionals among Asian-Indian Hindus provide an important additional financial resource as well as the majority of congregational members.

The concerted efforts now made to attract Asian-Indian Hindus to ISKCON activities include a call on Indian supporters to vouch for the authenticity of ISKCON within the Hindu religion, thus protecting it against identification as a cult and from various kinds of discrimination by authorities. ISKCON sponsored the formation in 1984 of the Hindu Alliance in Washington, DC, to organize protests against reports in the news media, television programs, and movies they consider to be biased against Hinduism. To establish their status as authentic Hindus, ISKCON members also participate in the activities of the Vishwa Hindu Parishad and in other Asian-Indian Hindu gatherings. They advertise widely in newspapers that are directed at Asian Indians, with invitations to participate in festivals and celebrations at the ISKCON temples. Gurus and members visit the homes of the immigrants to spread Krishna consciousness and gain support. Thus it now seems that the most important outreach activity of the group is to reach Hindu immigrants and to incorporate them as congregational members. At least two of the temples have brought Indian members, one from Fiji, to help communicate with the immigrants. In Dallas the ISKCON leaders approached leaders of the

Hindu groups with the suggestion that the immigrant Hindus join in building their new temple at the ISKCON site, but that suggestion is not being followed.

Temples in different locations have had varying degrees of success in gaining the participation of immigrants. Estimates from several temples lead to the conclusion that at a regular Sunday program approximately 75 to 80 percent of the participants are Asian Indians; for the major festivals, such as celebration of Krishna's birth, the percentage may go well over 90. Several fund-raising projects are advertised in Asian-Indian newspapers, including an "adopt a cow" program, which permits Hindus who are interested in "cow protection" to provide for the upkeep of a cow at one of the rural ashrams and receive certain benefits, including a photograph of the adopted cow (IT, 1985:15).

In some cities, the Asian Indians associated with ISKCON are forming Hare Krishna Satsang Mandals, groups that meet together in homes on Friday or Saturday evenings for the singing of devotional songs. These meetings, scattered across the metropolitan areas, involve families who may not attend the regular Sunday meetings at the temple. They constitute a major form of outreach into the Asian-Indian community, but they are led by Asian Indians. Thus, they may represent a first step in the transfer of leadership into the hands of the Asian-Indian followers.

The major success of ISKCON in turning to reach the Asian-Indian community is seen at New Vrindaban – or Krishnaland, as it is called – which has 200 members on a 4,000 acre site in rural West Virginia. The Palace of Gold, which was opened in 1980, has become a major tourist attraction in the state, in part because it has been included on the pilgrimages of many Asian Indians to the Venkateswara Temple in Pittsburgh. Immigrants are encouraged to purchase a time-sharing portion of vacation cottages at New Vrindaban, and the summer programs include educational and devotional programs for adults and children. Camp Gopal runs four sessions each summer for Asian-Indian children.

On May 31, 1985, the groundbreaking ceremony was held in New Vrindaban for a Radha-Krishna Temple of Understanding, which is advertised as "the largest Radha-Krishna temple ever built." It is estimated that the temple will cost between ten and fifteen million dollars, and major support is being solicited from wealthy individuals of the Asian-Indian community. The temple will contain the images of several Hindu deities in the primary altars: Radha-Krishna, Gaura-Nitai, Venkateswara Balaji, and Nathaji. Already, ISKCON centers are conducting bus tours and pilgrimages to New Vrindaban, and it may well be that the new temple will become one stop on a new Hindu tourism–pilgrimage cycle in the United States.

The end result of these changes is that the future of ISKCON in the

United States may well rest with the success of American converts in gaining acceptance as religious specialists and in providing services for the growing and prosperous Asian-Indian Hindu community. Fewer white Americans are participating in ISKCON activities, and only a small number are becoming full-time members. The drop-out rate is high, as it always was. Growth is taking place only from participation of the Hindu immigrants. So, the aging dropouts from the young-American counterculture of the 1960s and early 1970s are now becoming the religious specialists for prosperous Asian-Indian technocrats and their children. Some children of the immigrants have stated that they are able to establish better rapport with the ISKCON priests, who are able to explain the rituals in colloquial English, than with what are to them foreign priests, who do not speak English well and who do not know the context of American young people. The ISKCON priests are "approachable." Because the American converts stand in two cultures, east and west, they are able to help bridge the chasm for children of immigrants, who also occupy a precarious position between the two. Rochford reports a conversation with a member in Philadelphia who looks for a Vaishnava revival among the Asian Indians from which ISKCON will get many new supporters (1985:262). He reports that a conscious, stated goal of the Governing Body Commission in 1980 is that ISKCON become recognized as "a denomination of the Hindu church" (Rochford, 1985:271). The use of the terms "denomination" and "church" as sociological terms of Christian origin indicates an amalgamation of cultures. Leaders see the group as moving away from sectarianism to denominationalism.

Tensions exist, however, between the full members of ISKCON and immigrant Hindus, and between the immigrants and other participants in ISKCON activities. Some members criticize the immigrants for having left their tradition and for being lukewarm towards their religion because, it is said, they are captivated by the allure of American materialism. This may be only a reflection of the ancient tension in Hinduism itself between the world renouncers and the householders, but it develops with different themes in the United States because of the backgrounds of the American world renouncers and the Indian householders. A significant educational and social difference exists between the members, few of whom completed college, and the highly educated immigrants. An even greater social distance separates the immigrants from what one leader in an ISKCON temple referred to as "the punks and street people," who show up for the Sunday programs and meals. The institution by the Dallas temple of two Sunday programs effectively separates these two groups.

Thus, association with the Asian-Indian immigrants has led ISKCON to the mellowing that has made the group less objectionable to many Americans and is moving it toward identification as a Hindu denomination. It is impossible to predict the future, but as presently constituted the success or failure of ISKCON may rest with its attraction to the Asian Indians, who may continue to be the major participants and supporters of ISKCON activities. One Asian Indian who has become very active in ISKCON in Houston predicts that the leadership of ISKCON in the United States will inevitably shift into the hands of the immigrants. The major threat, however, to the continued association is the construction and promotion of other Hindu temples by groups of Asian Indians. These temples will draw away some of the support that heretofore has gone by default to the ISKCON temples. A struggle for the allegiance of the Asian-Indian professionals and their children will certainly influence further changes in ISKCON and in the programs of the Asian-Indian Hindu temples and centers.

The American Muslim Mission

Malcolm X undertook a pilgrimage to Mecca in 1964, and he changed his name to El Hajj Malik El-Shabazz. His wife is reported to have said, "He went to Mecca as a Black Muslim and there he became only a Muslim. He felt all men were human beings; we must judge a man on his deeds" (PC, 1965:4). His personal transformation is prototypical of the remarkable change that has taken place within the Black Muslim community as a majority have accepted a more orthodox form of Sunni Islam and are in the process of being incorporated into the House of Islam. The American Muslim Mission, once known as the Nation of Islam, under the leadership of Wallace Muhammad continues to be the organizational home for that religious transformation.

The standard interpretation of the dynamics of the change has been threefold. One line of interpretation emphasizes the dominant influence of El Hajj Malik El-Shabazz after his return from Mecca, which led many Black Muslims, including Wallace Muhammad, to follow him in the direction of orthodox Islam. Wallace Muhammad, who became the Imam of the Nation of Islam following the death of his father, Elijah Muhammad, implemented the reforms that were intimated by his good friend. A second interpretation notes the contacts that were developed with orthodox Sunni religious and political leaders in the Middle East and Africa, evident during Malcolm X's tour following his pilgrimage to Mecca; these have been expanded to include financial support and religious leadership. These contacts encourage and facilitate the adoption of orthodox doctrine and practice. A sociological analysis suggests that the relative success of the economic self-reliance promoted by the Nation of Islam caused some followers to enter the Black middle class, so that the religion would naturally, in terms of sociological analysis, be transformed from a religion of the disadvantaged to a religion of the more secure. Moreover, the group under Wallace Muhammad's leadership has attempted to attract members of the growing Black middle class. The result is that the group has discarded many of the "peculiar" doctrines and practices, and has accepted a form of Islam more amenable to the members of the middle class.

This standard interpretation is not incorrect; it is only incomplete. Generally overlooked is the role of the immigrant Muslim population, which has grown rapidly both just before and during the period of transition of the American Black Muslims. Mosques and schools of the Nation of Islam were in place in large American cities at the time when the large body of immigrant Muslims began to establish their own mosques and religious centers. The transformation of the religion of the Black Muslims has taken place in the context of their associations on the local level with the immigrant Muslims, which has been more vital and influential than distant contact, however financially rewarding, with foreign governments and religious leaders. The immigrant Muslims provide models of orthodox Islam that are copied with great zeal and fervor by members of the American Muslim Mission, which is thus revealed as an example of an idiosyncratic religion of the disadvantaged in the process of being transformed by contacts with the more traditional religious doctrines and practices of recent immigrants. Yet at the same time, it provides the primary religious contacts for the immigrant Muslim community.

The doctrines and practices of the Nation of Islam, as they developed under the leadership of Elijah Muhammad in Detroit and Chicago in the 1930s, deviated enough from the dictates of orthodox Islam that most orthodox Muslims considered the Nation to be outside the House of Islam. The basic confession of Islam is that there is no god but Allah, and that Muhammad is the prophet of Allah. Hence, the final prophet appeared in the seventh century. The teachings of the Nation of Islam about divinity and prophethood were heretical: Wali Fard Muhammad, the predecessor of Elijah Muhammad and founder of the Nation of Islam, was revered as "God in person," and Elijah Muhammad was described as "the prophet of Allah." Most Islamic organizations would not acknowledge the followers of Elijah Muhammad as true Muslims because he claimed to have been personally appointed to be Allah's messenger in a dream visit by Allah. The celebration of Fard's birthday on February 26 as Savior's Day was offensive to orthodox Muslims, because the attribution of divinity to Fard and prophethood to Elijah Muhammad involved the negation of the primary confession of Islam. Nevertheless, in 1972 the Libyan government of Muammar el-Qaddafi made an interest-free loan of three million dollars to Elijah Muhammad to purchase a building for a mosque on Stony Island Avenue on the south side of Chicago (Gans & Lowe, 1980:130).

The explicit racism of the Nation of Islam and its teaching that the "white man is the devil" was another point of controversy; that notion runs contrary to the universalism of Islam, as Malcolm X discovered on his pilgrimage to Mecca. The Nation of Islam's myth of Yacub recounted the creation of the white race as a punishment inflicted on Blacks by Yacub, who had been expelled from paradise. This myth of creation and the race hatred it justified are not found in the references to creation or the teachings of the Quran.

Nor are the virulent anti-Americanism of the Nation of Islam and the refusal of members to participate in any civic or political activities a part of Islamic social philosophy. These views were certainly antithetical to the aspirations of the professional class of Muslim immigrants from India and Pakistan, who enjoyed great success in their associations with the majority population, and who rapidly made progress in establishing both civic and political identity in the United States. The negative stance toward American society and government that had proved itself appropriate and effective in mobilizing the American Blacks from the inner cities certainly could not be appropriate or effective in the immigrants' context, neither as political strategy nor for the formation of the group identity of these upwardly-mobile immigrants living in the suburbs.

The followers of the Nation of Islam referred to themselves as Muslims, but in the early days they were generally ignorant of the traditions and practices of orthodox Islam. The meetings of the Black Muslims, the architecture and decoration of the meeting halls, the calendar of celebrations – none showed much Islamic influence. Moreover, knowledge of the Quran, of the traditions (*Hadith*), and of orthodox rituals was minimal. The schools established by the Nation of Islam taught the myths and traditions of the Black Muslims, but did not include important aspects of orthodox Islam. As a result, when the immigrant Muslims arrived they could not accommodate themselves to the heterodox elements in the mosques and schools of the Nation of Islam. Instead, they began to establish orthodox mosques and centers in great numbers – oddly enough, at about the same time Wallace Muhammad became leader of the Nation of Islam and instituted sweeping changes in the organization.

The changes were begun by El Hajj Malik El-Shabazz (Malcolm X) upon his return from Mecca and North Africa through his new organization, Muslim Mosque, Inc., which he had established at the Hotel Theresa in Mecca (NYAN, 1964:14). His assassination on February 21, 1965, brought his reformations to a halt. His friend Wallace Muhammad was excommunicated from the Nation of Islam, and Elijah Muhammad remained as the leader of the Nation until his death on February 25, 1975. To the great surprise of most observers, Wallace Muhammad was selected to be his father's successor, and on Savior's Day, February 26, 1975, he became the spiritual and administrative leader of the Nation of Islam. He wasted little time in leading the group toward a more orthodox form of Islam. His initiatives were opposed by some, including Abdul Haleem Farrakan (Eugene Wolcott), who broke away, and in 1978 emerged to reinstitute the religion of the Nation of Islam as it had been practiced during the leadership of Elijah Muhammad and to act as its new leader. Farrakan gained public notoriety in 1984, when he aligned himself and his organization with Jesse Jackson. Wallace Muhammad, meanwhile, remains the Chief Imam of the major organization, and he continues the movement toward orthodox Islam.

The transformation has been dramatic, as reflected by the progressive changes in the name of the organization. In 1976 Wallace Muhammad changed its name from the Nation of Islam to The World Community of Al-Islam in the West, and four years later he changed it to The American Muslim Mission. He adopted the name "Bilalian" for the American Black Muslims, in honor of Bilal Ibn Rabah, an Ethiopian slave convert to Islam during the time of Muhammad whose responsibility it was to call the faithful to prayer in Medina. This provided an important historical association of the Blacks with orthodox Islam during the period of the Prophet. The national magazine of the Nation of Islam, "Muhammad Speaks," was renamed "Bilalian News." Wallace Muhammad also redefined the relationships of Wallace Fard and Elijah Muhammad to the movement in such a way that they are treated as "wise men," but not as "god in person" or "the prophet of Allah." Lawrence Mamiya concludes that Wallace Muhammad "demythologized the semidivine status his father had acquired in the Nation" (1982:140). The doctrine of racism of Elijah Muhammad has been replaced with the universalism of orthodox Islam, and the myth of creation and other elements of the "world history" of the Nation of Islam have been replaced by doctrines and stories from the Quran and by a mission to spread orthodox Islam in America.

Such dramatic changes instituted from the top of the hierarchy seep slowly throughout the membership. Professor John Cato cautions that "on the street" it will take a long time for these changes to be incorporated into the indigenous Black tradition that extends back prior to Farb and Elijah Muhammad. It will be difficult to expunge many elements of the tradition of the Nation of Islam, as, for example, the myth of Yacub. It is a process of incorporation rather than replacement, and the process is proceeding at different speeds within the various social strata in the Black community.[2]

In the summer of 1979 the American Muslim Mission sponsored a

Fourth of July parade down Michigan Avenue in Chicago (Whitehurst, 1980:229). Marchers carried American flags and signs that proclaimed the unity of all races. As part of the reforms he has made, Wallace Muhammad has discarded the demand for a separate state for Black Muslims, and encourages his followers to honor the American constitution and to participate actively in political affairs. One of the subsidiary businesses of the American Muslim Mission was awarded a twenty-two-million-dollars contract to provide food for the U.S. Department of Defense as a minority contractor.

The mosques of the American Muslim Mission are now called "masjids," and their decor has been changed to reflect orthodox patterns. Instead of anti-American and anti-Christian slogans, there are Arabic symbols. The congregation prays in the standard Arabic pattern, facing in the direction of Mecca. Members are encouraged to participate in the pilgrimage to Mecca, and Wallace Muhammad as Chief Imam has authorization from the World Muslim Organization in Saudi Arabia to certify those people who are permitted as Muslims to enter its sacred precincts. The strict discipline of the Nation of Islam is now replaced with elements of Muslim personal law. These moves toward orthodoxy have overcome the alienation of the Black Muslims from the international Islamic community, and some financial and other support has been given by Islamic countries. There are now 161 masjids in the United States that are affiliated with the American Muslim Mission. Recent membership figures are not available, but in an interview in 1979 Wallace Muhammad indicated, "We estimated that 70,000 people have really declared their faith, but over one million live Muslim lives" (Marsh, 1984:119).

Even though the masjids are formally associated with the American Muslim Mission, and Wallace Muhammad remains the Chief Imam and administrative leader, it is difficult to estimate the number of Muslims among American Blacks. Some Muslim immigrants, especially those from African countries, participate in the activities of the masjids of the American Muslim Mission. Moreover, some American Blacks participate in the activities of the mosques established by the immigrant community. Thus, the distinction between Bilalians and immigrant Muslims is being slowly muted. In an interview in 1979, Wallace Muhammad was asked, "If you could look into the future, where do you see the World Community of al-Islam in the West in the year 2000?" He responded, "I hope in the year 2000 the World Community of al-Islam in the West will be called American Muslims. I hope Muslims will be so comfortable in America that we won't have to introduce any structure or anything, just be American Muslims" (Marsh, 1984:121). More recently, the president of the Islamic Society of North America, the major organization of immigrant Muslims, welcomed Wallace Muhammad's decision to bring the

American Muslim Mission to the membership of the "worldwide Muslim community . . . not to be identified in geographical terms or political terms or racial terms" (*Islamic Horizons*, June 1985:11). The transformation is well underway.

Overtures between the Bilalians and the immigrant Muslims have increased as the Bilalians become more orthodox and as the mosques of the immigrants are established and begin to reach out to members of the host society. Bilalians are increasingly accepted as "brothers" in the faith, and the two groups participate together in religious activities. The immigrants provide examples and instruction for the Bilalians in the traditional practices of Islam, while the Bilalians provide enthusiasm and zeal in the practice of the religion. Immigrants often comment that the Bilalians are more faithful to their religion than the immigrants, and that "Islam means more to them." The secularized orthodox Muslims of the immigrant community, in seeking to reestablish their religious and cultural identity with Muslims from many countries, come into contact with these fervent Muslims from a somewhat heterodox background, who are becoming more traditional. Thus, both groups are transforming their own religion, and in the process they are moving closer together.

Immigrant Muslims attract religious leaders from abroad to serve in the United States, and they help the American Muslim Mission to train its own. Various means are available for this training and study. Organizations of the immigrant community help in the training and education of imams and religious teachers. The American Islamic College, which was established in Chicago in 1983, developed a summer institute for about 120 leaders of the masjids and schools associated with the American Muslim Mission. The institute provided the opportunity for some of those leaders to receive scholarships for study in Islamic schools in the Middle East, and other scholarships and training, provided by the World Muslim Organization, are also available to American Blacks. The Islamic Society of North America attracts participation in some of its programs from members of the American Muslim Mission. Among the results of these continuing contacts, which are the primary avenues of communication, have been the reinforcement of orthodox beliefs and practices and the incorporation of the American Blacks into the House of Islam.

These associations also influence the adaptation of the immigrant Muslims in the United States, not always constructively. Many immigrant Muslims develop a negative opinion of American society and culture, partly because they view them "through the eyes of their brothers." Muslims criticize the materialism, immorality, racism, and idolatry in American society. Furthermore, they are somewhat isolated from the majority population because world tensions and news reports have produced a negative opinion of Islam and of Muslim groups among members of the general public. While the racism of the earlier Black Muslim period has been muted, the suspicion of "white America" still remains within the American Muslim Mission, and this is transmitted to the immigrants. The criticisms have been transmuted from the racist attacks – which are no longer deemed appropriate – into religious denunciation of the "immoral society," denunciations that are in an acceptable idiom; indeed, the denunciations are similar to those heard from pulpits and temples of several other religions.

The programs and services of the immigrant Muslim organizations are also influenced by the history of Black Islam. A major program for the propagation of Islam in the United States is in the prisons. Muslims visit the prisons to make converts, further supporting their action by petitioning the authorities to allow Muslim prayers and to make provisions for the observance of Muslim personal and dietary law in prisons. Pamphlets and correspondence courses are prepared specifically for use in the prisons. Recently, a certifying board was created to provide credentials for Muslims to become prison chaplains. These activities can be viewed as an extension of the very successful prison activities that were carried out by the Nation of Islam and later by the American Muslim Mission. It is unlikely that the immigrant Muslims would have focused on prisons had it not been for the influence of the Bilalians.

Wallace Muhammad now leads his followers in the orthodox form of Muslim prayers in Arabic according to the prescriptions of Islamic law, and worship by American Blacks takes on an Arabic cast in common with that of Muslims from other countries. However, there are some changes in the services in the orthodox mosques in which Bilalians participate. The preaching of the American converts takes on the style and rhythm of the Black pulpit. Even a unison "Amen" in the prayers is not uncommon. The forms of Islam developed as "American Islam" thus have grown to incorporate elements from the traditions of both the Bilalians and the immigrant Muslims from various countries.

The associations formed are not without tensions, which exist in part because of the attraction of ethnic identity and religious identity. Most mosques and masjids attract participants from more than one ethnic group, and thereby witness to the universality of Islam. Nevertheless, the majority of participants in any single mosque founded by immigrants or masjid of the American Muslim Mission are from one ethnic group – Arab, Asian, African, European, or Black – indicating the attraction to one's own ethnic identity. The consensus seems to be that ideally the ethnic groups should worship together and have some religious celebrations together, but in most social and cultural affairs the immigrants and the Bilalians do not interact. An Eid celebration, planned to unite Muslims from the various ethnic groups in one city, failed miserably because of differences in food, manner of expressing emotions, and types of music. The establishment of a Pakistan Friendship Association, which would inevitably sponsor some religious celebrations, was vehemently opposed by the local Bilalians, because they saw it as an attempt by the immigrant Muslims to exclude them from participation. In another case, the construction of a Pakistani Cultural Center was opposed because, the Bilalians argued, the attachment to Indo-Pakistani culture represents a dilution of pure Islam. They often cite the flashy Punjabi dresses and saris worn by women as bordering on immodesty. Some of the immigrants are embarrassed by this accusation, but prefer to preserve these aspects of their culture, although a small segment of the community has altered its dress code and other aspects of its lifestyle in order to meet the strict standards of Islam as interpreted by the Bilalians.

The socioeconomic differences between the two groups are so vast that mutual understanding is difficult. The Bilalians are emerging from a religious movement of the disinherited, and thus manifest the zeal and conviction of such movements. On the other hand the immigrants from India and Pakistan were born Muslims, and are well-educated and economically prosperous; they are more secularized and less enthusiastic. The majority of the early immigrants from India and Pakistan are professionals with graduate education; the majority of the Bilalians have a high school education or less. It may well be, as Lawrence Mamiya suggests, that the Nation of Islam under Farrakan continues to be a lower-class movement, and hence has the marks of a disinherited religious movement, while the American Muslim Mission under Wallace Muhammad is becoming increasingly middle class (1982:145). At the same time, the change in the educational background and economic prospects of more recent immigrants from India and Pakistan, who arrive under the family reunification provisions of the immigration law, results in a Muslim population that is moving from two directions toward a common socioeconomic status. These conditions encourage and reinforce the major changes in Bilalian doctrine and practice, making Bilalians full partners in the House of Islam and thus bringing about the construction of an American Islam that will result from the cooperative efforts of the Bilalians and the immigrant Muslims.

Sikh Dharma Brotherhood (Healthy, Happy, Holy Organization)

"Straight-Freak-Yogi-Sikh" is the title of a master's dissertation on the recruitment of young white Americans into an organization that was originally a yoga educational institution but developed into a Sikh religious movement (Dusenbery, 1975). As with the other "American cousins" in this study, the future of the white-American Sikhs of the Healthy, Happy, Holy Organization and the Sikh Dharma Brotherhood has become intimately tied to that of the religion of the immigrants,[3] although in a very different way. The American Sikhs are virtually isolated from the immigrant Punjabi Sikh community, in part because of the traumatic events in the Punjab, but also because of differences in the appropriation of Punjabi cultural identity and Sikh religious identity. The white-American Sikhs vary from the other "American cousins" in that they are a very small group, declining in membership and influence. During the early stages of negotiation between the Sikh Dharma and Punjabi Sikhs, they were caught up in events both in the Punjab and in the United States that caused a separation, with the result that the American converts do not draw strength from the Punjabi Sikhs, and the immigrants are now little affected by their American cousins.

The yoga movement that eventually was transformed into a Sikh organization was begun by a Punjabi Sikh who came first to Canada, and then to the United States. Harbhajan Singh Puri left his job as a customs official at the Delhi airport in 1968 to travel to Toronto on the basis of a promise of a job as yoga instructor. Discovering that the job was not available in Toronto, he traveled on to Los Angeles, where he began to teach yoga at the East-West Cultural Center and then at the West San Gabriel Valley YMCA. Within a short time he attracted a group of students to his form of yoga, and he moved into his own center. His first students were recruited as students from the counterculture, young people who had left their middle-class families; hence, the movement "Straight-Freak-Yogi."

In 1969 Harbhajan Singh Puri, now known as Yogi Bhajan, established the Healthy, Happy, Holy Organization as a tax-exempt educational institution. He taught a form of Kundalini yoga, which he called "the yoga of awareness," and he introduced into the yoga some Tantric elements. The yoga involved early morning meditation in front of the picture of Yogi Bhajan – their spiritual teacher – and the recitation of the verse of the "True Name" of God in conjunction with hyperventilation in a breathing exercise. Some of his advanced students received training and permission to establish yoga institutes in other cities; the yoga instruction was the way of attracting a following. From this perspective the development of the organization resembles many yoga schools, institutes, or ashrams that were established during the late 1960s, especially in California. The students began to live in communal dwellings and to start some businesses related to the health-food movement. Hundreds of such organizations were formed and attracted a following; most disappeared in the 1970s.

The "yogi-Sikh" movement is what sets this group apart from the others, placing it in contact with the growing Punjabi Sikh community. In the early 1970s, Yogi Bhajan led his followers to become identified with the Sikh religion. In 1971 he took a group of eighty-four disciples on a visit to the Golden Temple in Amritsar, where he was received and honored for his "missionary work" by the Shiromani Gurdwara Parbandhak Committee at the Akal Takht. He began to use the title "Siri Singh Sahib," which he said was given to him on that occasion, to designate the chief administrative and religious authority for the Sikh Dharma in the Western Hemisphere. In 1973 he founded the Sikh Dharma Brotherhood, which was officially registered as a tax-exempt religious organization, and many of his American disciples were initiated into Sikhism. Dusenbery indicates that the acceptance of Sikh discipline by those previously in the counterculture is a "negation of the negation" that involves a hyperbolic return to fundamental American cultural values (1975:v,68).

The ethos of the group developed as a combination of yogic and Sikh doctrine and practice. Followers continued the practice of Kundalini yoga and the chanting, meditation, and breathing exercises. Yogi Bhajan created a mystical symbol (*yantra*) that has two side swords, representing the protection of God, and a central wheel (*chakra*), representing the law of cause and effect (*karma*); the whole represents the relationship of cause and effect to universal consciousness, or cosmic energy (*shakti*). Meditation on this mystical symbol is supposed to cause the disciple to experience Infinity (*kundalini* rising). He also promoted vegetarianism among his followers. A Sikh Dharma pamphlet describes his work: "Teaching Kundalini Yoga and meditation, he first enabled people to experience their own potential as a part of the life force of the universe, and with this technology to live healthy, happy and holy lives." A fundamental tension exists between the yogic discipline, which is individualistic and world-renouncing, and the Sikh teachings, which are communal and world-affirming (Dusenbery, 1975:11).

Another pamphlet indicates his importance as religious teacher, and quotes from his speech of May 20, 1979: "There are three in me. One is Harbhajan Singh. One is Yogi Bhajan. One is Siri Singh Sahib. Siri Singh Sahib is a very direct hassler who'll nail you on the spot. He will find everything wrong with you, analyze you like anything, shattering you like you are nobody. Yogi Bhajan is that compassionate, analytical, intelligent man who tells you this is this because of that; but it is up to you, son or daughter, do whatever you want. Then there is one Harbhajan Singh who will say, 'Well, let us freak out. Don't worry, there is no problem in the world. Everything is all right, God and me, me and God are one.'"

He also praised the teachings of the Sikh Gurus and began to set up a structure for Sikh Dharma of the West. The American converts adopted the outward symbols of full Sikh identity – their "trademark" is white Punjabi dress and white turbans for both males and females. The men wear the beards and symbols worn by keshdhari Sikhs. The adoption of "Khalsa" as a last name becomes the identification of an American convert. As Sikh Dharma Brotherhood spread to other cities, an administrative structure developed, which has Siri Singh Sahib at the top as the chief administrative and religious authority. Under him is a Khalsa Council made up of leaders of zones called "Mukhia Singh Sahibs" and "Mukhia Sardarni Sahibas." The ministers of the Sikh Dharma are called "Singh Sahibs" and "Sardarni Sahibas." In the decade of the 1970s the organization was successful in establishing centers in over 100 cities, and a publication of the group claims that over 250,000 people embraced Sikh Dharma and the practice of its various aspects or technologies.[4] That number seems totally unrealistic, unless it is meant to imply all those who were attracted to some form of yoga. The total number of white American Sikhs may reach two or three thousand.[5] No formal membership list exists, and people "come and go according to their spiritual development." The largest ashram is at the international headquarters in Los Angeles, where approximately 250 people live. The other ashrams with more than a few members are in New Mexico, Boston, Virginia, and Arizona. In the cities outside of California covered by this research in the summers of 1984 and 1985, the organization was very small. Typically, a house serves as an ashram and place for yoga instruction, and four or five persons live in the ashram, not all of them Sikhs. The impression is that the number of participants has declined significantly in the 1980s, but it is difficult to get a complete picture.

Early contacts between the white-American Sikhs and the Punjabi Sikhs were positive. When the converts began to participate in the services of the gurdwara in Los Angeles, they were welcomed, but soon tensions developed that caused them to establish their own ashram and cease participation in the gurdwara (Fleuret, 1974:32). The reception that Yogi Bhajan and the pilgrims received at the Golden Temple in Amritsar, however, indicated the attraction the Punjabis felt to the idea of making converts to Sikhism in the West, especially in the United States. Some Sikhs viewed it as a new mission field and were proud that their religion was being observed.

The main source of the tension created by American converts was their criticism of the immigrant Punjabi Sikhs. They criticized the "Westernization" of the descendants of the immigrants who came early in this century and of the newer secularized immigrants. The accommodations immigrants made by discarding the outward symbols of the religion and by ignoring the ceremonies of initiation into the Khalsa were seen as apostasy by the new converts, who wore the full beard and turban. In some ways it appeared that the new converts were more religious than those born into the religion – they seemed to consider themselves the "true Sikhs"; one leader of the Sikh Dharma remarked, "We were teaching them." Moreover, the converts rejected the continuation of some caste distinctions and aspects of subordination of women, which they claimed were only a part of Punjabi culture and not part of Sikh religion. Indeed, they claimed that such practices were antithetical to a correct understanding of Sikh religion.

Fleuret suggests that the primary source of early tension was that the immigrants strongly identified Sikhism with Punjabi culture and language. The American converts accepted the religion and exemplified many of its ideals, but they were not able to adapt to the Punjabi cultural practices (Fleuret, 1974:32). The converts insisted that the women as well as men wear turbans. Young married women wore garments of white, which in the Punjab is reserved for widows and religious leaders. They learned to chant the songs, but they did not know the Punjabi language or read Gurmukhi script. The converts were Sikhs, but not Punjabis.

Some basic differences in the religious interpretation of Sikhism also created tensions (Dusenbery, 1980:8). The followers of Yogi Bhajan and of his Kundalini yoga incorporated the yoga practices of chanting mantras and breath discipline into the daily prayers, contrary to traditional Sikh practice. Punjabi immigrant Sikhs have been critical of the devotion given to Yogi Bhajan as religious teacher (guru) and administrative head of the organization, a devotion normally reserved for the traditional ten Gurus and the *Adi Granth*. A part of the yoga tradition followed by members of the Sikh Dharma Brotherhood is the insistence on vegetarianism, which is not practiced by Punjabi Sikhs. A further reason for the division has been the formation of the Sikh Dharma's elaborate organizational structure, separate from the gurdwaras and from the developing national organizations of the immigrant Sikhs. Thus, many differences, religious and cultural, have led to the isolation of the American converts.

Political differences in the midst of the turmoil of the 1980s have led to an even further isolation. Leaders of the Punjabi Sikh community insist that Yogi Bhajan adopted a progovernment policy and made statements sympathetic to the government's position during a visit of the Sikh President of India to the United States. Moreover, the converts have not joined in the protests against the government's attack on the Golden Temple and arrests of Sikh leaders. The activities of the white-American Sikhs had previously been of some assistance in attempts to establish Sikh identity and rights in the United States, as, for example, in seeking government approval for Sikhs to wear the turban in the military, but they are viewed as being counterproductive in the attempt to marshal public support for the agitation in the Punjab. The strategy of the converts, to stress the religious aspects of Sikhism and avoid involvement in the cultural and political affairs of the Punjab, has been interpreted as betrayal of true Sikh identity and solidarity in the face of threats to destroy Sikhism. Scorn is poured on the followers of Yogi Bhajan as "dupes of the government" and "traitors." In short, they have been caught in the emotions of the "Khalistan syndrome." The boundaries and internal cohesiveness of the immigrant Sikh community, which emphasize the unity of Punjabi and Sikh demands and the strengthening of both cultural and religious identity as a bulwark against the seductions of American society, have become barriers to cooperation between the Punjabi immigrant Sikhs and the white-American Sikhs.

The converts indicate that they are trying to build a spiritual nation of Sikhs that is not based on national or cultural boundaries. Indeed, they stress that they are working with various religions to establish a spiritual nation of peace, that Khalistan is a spiritual state. They view the emphasis in the Punjabi gurdwaras on the call for political sovereignty based on geography and culture as creating a division among Sikhs, whose religion should unite them.

The white-American Sikhs are concerned about the acts against Sikhs in India, however; for one thing, they have 150 children in school in Mussoori, in North India outside the Punjab. There are some attempts to maintain contacts between converts and the Punjabi Sikhs. A joint program was held in 1986 to mark the anniversary of the attack by the Indian Army on the Golden Temple. In cities where few Punjabi Sikhs live, cooperative activities are not uncommon. It is where larger numbers of both groups reside that the political and cultural differences lead to the formation of separate gurdwaras. Questions of power, authority and control of the finances of the gurdwaras create divisions. Sikh Dharma gurdwaras attract the participation by some Sindhis, who worship Guru Nanak and perform some Hindu rituals, but the number seems not to have increased since the Amritsar incident.

It seems as though the Sikh Dharma Brotherhood will continue for some time as a small, declining movement, primarily in California, separate from the larger group of Punjabi Sikhs. One sign of this is that the number of persons presenting themselves for the baptism ceremony is very small. Three formal ceremonies are held each year – in Los Angeles, New Mexico, and Florida – where between 30 and 40 people are baptized in each ceremony. Punjabi immigrant Sikhs who might have been partial to the Sikh Dharma have been distracted by the events in the Punjab and by intramural conflict and the negotiations about appropriate responses to actions by the Government of India. Whatever the tensions within the Punjabi Sikh community, the result has been the reunion of Punjabi politics and culture with the Sikh religion as a major part of the individual and group identity of many immigrant Sikhs. For them, the reinforcement of "Sikh identity" means teaching the children Punjabi, involvement with the politics of the Punjab, some return to traditional dress by women, and concern with friends and relatives in India, as well as attention to the religious requirements of Sikhism. White-American Sikhs are extraneous to this process, and since 1980 the immigrant Sikhs have been too preoccupied to be much concerned with the success or failure of the organization founded by Yogi Bhajan.

Hindus, Muslims, and Sikhs from India and Pakistan have found it necessary to work out relationships with their American cousins as part of their adaptation to the United States. In each case, the religion of the American cousin developed peculiarities as it grew in this foreign soil prior to the immigration of large numbers of its co-religionists. The relationship is developing differently in each case. Whereas Hindu immigrants are transforming a small sect of American converts to Hinduism into leaders for a new denomination within the developing American Hinduism, Muslim immigrants are absorbing a fairly large sect into an American Islam where denominational or sectarian divisions are not on ethnic lines. Sikh immigrants, on the other hand, have virtually isolated the small sect, which is now relatively insignificant for the development of Sikhism in America. Bhaktivedanta instructed his disciples in a traditional form of Hindu devotion that was his by birth and training, whereas Yogi Bhajan converted to Sikhism and alienated some Sikhs by his deviations from traditional patterns. The differences are due to the nature of the religions, to the balance of ethnic and religious elements in the tradition and to historical events that have affected negotiations in unexpected ways.

Hinduism is loosely defined, so it was easy for members of a small sect to claim Hindu identity and to establish themselves as authentic leaders for a large number of immigrants. Nevertheless, it was necessary in the process to give up practices that had brought disrepute to Hinduism, the designation by public opinion as a cult, and embarrassment to some Hindu immigrants when they arrived. Because Hinduism is so closely bound to elements of Indian culture, it was necessary for the American cousins to adopt vegetarianism, Indian cuisine, language (Sanskrit), dress, music, and arts. In the process, the new converts became "more Indian than the Hindus." Thus, full members of the International Society for Krishna Consciousness are becoming the religious specialists for a large number of immigrants and are molding them into a new denomination. A sect provides the leadership for a denomination.

Islam has rigid standards of doctrine and practice by which loyalty to Islam can be judged apart from ethnic and cultural traits. In 1965 the

Nation of Islam was a fairly large sect, clearly outside the boundaries of orthodox Islam. The immigrant Muslims have been successful in transforming this group of American outsiders into cousins. The demands for orthodoxy and orthopraxy have led to dramatic changes in the move from the Nation of Islam under Elijah Muhammad to the American Muslim Mission under Wallace Muhammad. It is too early to predict how the ethnic groups within Islam in the United States – the Asians, Arabs, Europeans, Africans, and American Blacks – will develop, but it appears that the separate organization of the American Muslim Mission will continue to attenuate so that the American Blacks will eventually be absorbed into the mosques and organizations of that room within the House of Islam called American Islam. A sect is incorporated into a religion.

Sikhism as a religion is inextricably bound with Punjabi culture. The Punjabi Sikhs in the United States increasingly are distinguishing Sikhism from Hinduism because they feel that Sikhism is under threat by Hindus in India. The small sect of American-Sikh converts developed a form of Sikhism that is divorced from the Punjab but incorporates yogic elements of Hinduism. Perhaps some accommodation could have been reached despite these differences, but the unexpected political events in the Punjab in the 1980s made that impossible, at least for the foreseeable future. The Sikh Dharma will continue to be an isolated, small sect that will have little influence on the shape of American Sikhism. A sect remains a sect.

CHAPTER 5

Swaminarayan Hinduism

An ethnic religion

"Folks fear losing their Independence to Hindu group" (CT) and "Independence fears tax burden of $100 million temple complex" (*Star Ledger*, November 3, 1985:I, 89) and "Sect's Building Plans Jolt Jersey Town" (The *New York Times*, February 3, 1986:15) scream the headlines. They refer to the turmoil resulting from the purchase of 162 acres in Independence Township, New Jersey, about sixty miles west of New York City, by the Bochasanwasi Swaminarayan Sanstha as the site for a new religious and educational complex. The Hindu group purchased the farmland in rural New Jersey in August 1985 for $292,500, and soon rumors were circulating among the 3,000 residents of the township about tentative plans for a ten-year $100-million project to build a temple, a residential school, and a housing complex that will contribute to rapid changes in that part of New Jersey.

A red marble temple in the Gujarati style of Indian architecture is planned as the centerpiece of the complex to be built on two hills overlooking the township. It would be constructed with materials from India and by workmen from India skilled in the traditional architectural designs. The cost is projected at around six million dollars. The group already has three temples in the United States, several in England and East Africa, and many in India, but the proposed temple in Independence Township would be the first traditional marble temple of the group in the United States. A similar temple is planned for London. The images in the temple would be of the deities and religious leaders of the Bochasanwasi Swaminarayan Sanstha – Swaminarayan, Gunatitanand Swami, Radha-Krishna, and the gurus of the group – the rituals, those performed in the temples in Gujarat. Undoubtedly, the temple will draw the support and participation of Swaminarayan Hindus from across the country because it would be a national statement of their Gujarati identity and religion.

The residential school is planned to begin with elementary school children and within ten years grow to house 200 students through the eighth grade. Classrooms, dormitories, an administration building, a clinic, and a community building will provide an educational center where students can study Indian culture and Swaminarayan religion along with an American curriculum. The proposed educational program for academically elite Hindu children is modeled in part on St. James School in London. Visionaries in the group speak about the possibility of a high school and a Hindu university as part of the complex. The emphasis is upon preserving Hindu and Gujarati culture and Swaminarayan religion as protection for the children against the perceived evils of American society.

Building lots for thirty private homes are included in the master plan. Members plan to build on these lots and move out from New York to be near the new temple. Thus, Swaminarayan Hindus will join other professionals as part of the exodus to the rural and secluded area. The small town currently has a bank, a volunteer fire station, and a convenience store, but more residents are moving into the area, who will contribute significantly to the cultural and religious diversity of the township and to the problems of creeping suburbia.

The township is caught up in strong currents of change because rapid development is already taking place in the area. Several housing developments are already planned that will add more than a thousand houses. The influx of high tech industries and housing developments in adjacent townships will certainly be duplicated in Independence Township. The building plans of Swaminarayan Hindus are the catalyst for the opposition to the changes that are breaking upon the quiet small town because, in this case, added to the disruption of many construction projects is the threat to relatively homogeneous cultural patterns. The new residents will be "new ethnics" within a community of "old ethnics."

The current residents of Independence Township see visions of another Rajneeshpuram, the notorious commune of Bhagwan Rajneesh in Antelope, Oregon, and they fear that the new residents will create a sect like the Rajneeshis or like the devotees of the International Society for Krishna Consciousness, and that it will take over the town. Little is known in the community about the theology, ethics, or practices of Swaminarayan Hinduism, so some people judge it on the basis of what they have heard about the others. Town meetings were held to discuss the proposed complex. A video-cassette tape, "Gods of the New Age," circulated in the township, and although it does not deal at all with Swaminarayan Hinduism, it displays what are thought to be objectionable aspects of Hinduism, its "missionary activity," yoga as mind-control, Tantrism, and many scenes of activities at Rajneeshpuram. Mahatma Gandhi is criticized as a "sexual pervert." Finally, the tape associates devotion to a guru with Nazism. The thesis of the script seems to be, "The religion that has all but destroyed India has now infiltrated every area of Western society." Prejudice against Hinduism and Hindus seems to contribute to the emotion of the opposition by some, although the pastor of a traditional white-frame Methodist church says, "It's fear of the unknown" (CT, 1986:I,28).

Cultural and religious change are marked by discussions of zoning regulations, tax exemption, and land use. The zoning law in effect when the property in Independence Township was purchased allows churches and schools in residential areas, so the construction of a temple, a school, and new homes required minimal official action. However, a zoning amendment was proposed to members of the town council that would restrict the building of churches and schools in residential areas and require developers to meet a number of standards on traffic safety, compatibility with the neighborhood, and preservation of property values. The amendment failed to carry, in part because the lawyer for the Swaminarayan Hindus threatened to bring a civil rights suit in Federal court if the amendment passed. They argue that they are American citizens, albeit recent immigrants, and demand their First Amendment rights. They are also a minority, and claim their civil rights as such are being denied. They affirm that they are authentic Hindus, with elevated moral standards, and covet the respect and support that are given to other religious bodies. Plans are being presented to the officials, and the public discussion now concerns building codes, narrow country roads and services of fire and police departments.

Victory is important for the new immigrants, because the ambitious plans represent the remarkable success of Swaminarayan Hindus, individually and as a group, in their attempt to preserve an ethnic regional–linguistic form of Hinduism in the United States. These are immigrants who came within the past two decades with good skills and prospects, but with very little money, and have already reached a level of economic security such that they can "make their mark" with an imposing architectural statement of Gujarati identity. Some of those whose first American homes were the old apartments and houses in Queens that earlier immigrants from other ethnic groups had left to move to the suburbs are now planning to join the exodus and build in what will be an upper middle class development. Even though the grandiose plans will be scaled down – the $100-million figure now seems unrealistic, and is rarely mentioned – the project is the result of an organizational skill and religious devotion that was able to reach many Gujarati Hindus across the country and attract their support for this and other developmental projects of the Bochasanwasi Swaminarayan Sanstha.

Swaminarayan Hindus have adopted a strategy of creating an ethnic regional–linguistic form of Hinduism in the United States. Whereas ecumenical Hinduism is an amalgamation of deities, rituals, and texts from many sects and linguistic groups, purely sectarian forms of Hinduism attract people from the same regions and linguistic groups to follow a religious leader or worship a specific deity. This ethnic form of Hinduism attracts Gujaratis to a religious tradition that began in Gujarat 200 years ago and that, in spite of claims to universality, is intimately tied to its language, mores, texts, leaders, and tradition. The various branches of Swaminarayan Hinduism have developed national organizations in the United States, closely linked with religious leaders and centers in Gujarat. Several temples have been built or are planned across the country, and regular meetings are held in which Gujarati language, music, cuisine, and rituals predominate. The national and international organizations are committed to the linking of religious (Swaminarayan) and cultural (Gujarati) identities in the United States as they are in India. Their experience illustrates the success of a national ethnic religion among recent immigrants.

Religious groups new to the United States invariably begin locally, but some spread across the country and develop national organizations and strategies. Swaminarayan Hindus (and the Nizari Ismailis of the next chapter) illustrate the process of developing a national organization with lay leaders and the success in establishing centers, programs, and mechanisms for the assistance of followers in many cities. Although relatively small in numbers, they are growing rapidly, and their theology and rituals influence the direction of their growth and the shape of their adaptation in the United States. Their past provides, they assert, a springboard into their current success. Among the several angles from which immigrant religions can be viewed, an important one is the development of sects or subsects as they spread across the country. The focus in this chapter and the next is upon the elements of doctrine, practice, and administration that led from local groups to national organizations, and an attempt is made to trace that development.

A Gujarati form of Hinduism in India

Swaminarayan Hinduism is a modern form of Hinduism that took shape in the early nineteenth century in Gujarat. (For a more complete description of Swaminarayan Hinduism in India, see Williams, 1984). Sahajanand Swami (1781–1830) traveled to Gujarat from the Hindi-speaking area in what is now Uttar Pradesh in 1802, at the time British were gaining control of that portion of India transforming it from medieval to modern and from small princely states to a unified administration. The religious and social reforms instituted by Sahajanand Swami attracted both a large following among Gujaratis and the attention of the British, who provided land for the first temple in Ahmedabad. By the time of the celebration of the bicentenary of the founder's birth in Ahmedabad in 1981, Sahajanand Swami's group had hundreds of temples in India and abroad, several hundred ascetics – men and women who have "renounced the world" to become religious specialists – many schools and hostels, publications, and perhaps as many as 5,000,000 followers.

Sahajanand Swami inspired in his followers an intense devotion to manifestations of the god Vishnu in the devotional tradition (bhakti) of North-Indian Vaishnavism. He received initiation from a teacher in the line of acharyas from Ramanuja, the Vaishnava theologian of the twelfth century, so his philosophical teaching was a revision of the modified nondualism of Ramanuja, which provides the theoretical basis for devotion and for the complex metaphysics of his followers. The major deities in the first temple built in Ahmedabad are the forms of NarNarayana, and all the temples have images of Radha-Krishna. Even during his lifetime, devotion was also directed towards Sahajanand Swami himself; he was given the name "Swaminarayan" to indicate that he was the manifestation of god (*avatara*) for the modern age, and the human form of the highest divine reality (*purushottam*). Images of Swaminarayan are in the shrines of the temples, and even though the images of Radha-Krishna are prominent, Swaminarayan himself is now the major focus of devotion. His teachings prescribed acts of public and private devotion for his followers that include singing devotional songs, serving the images in the temple, prostrating before the images of god, listening to religious discourses, and the mental worship of remembering god.

Bhakitmata and Dharmadeva are the names given to the mother and father of Swaminarayan in hagiography and iconography, and they represent the union of devotion and worship (bhakti), which is the heart of the religion, with the discipline of moral conduct (*dharma*), which gives it shape. The moral code is status specific: Some rules are applicable broadly to all members of the fellowship, but many duties differ according to place, time, age, and social and economic position. Thus, the *Shikshapatri*, the basic statement of duties written by Sahajanand Swami, contains rules for conduct for the various classes of persons – householders and ascetics, men and women, Brahmins and Harijans, married women and widows – according to their station, with adaptation to the circumstances of each group. The basic distinction is made between the lay people, who live as householders involved in secular activities, and the ascetics (sadhus), who renounce the world to devote themselves to a spiritual path, becoming religious specialists. These ascetics exemplify ideal devotion and discipline for the lay people, and they are called "saints." Louis Dumont catches a fundamental dynamic of Swaminarayan Hinduism with his comment, " . . . the secret of Hinduism may be found

in the dialogue between the renouncer and the man in the world"
(1970:37).

Initiation as a lay member does not require renunciation of the world.
The ritual of initiation is simple. One chants the formula, "I give over
to Swaminarayan my mind, body, wealth, and the sins of previous
births." Then water is poured over the right hand and the Swaminarayan
mantra is repeated. Five vows are taken. The first vow begins with a
prohibition of eating meat and leads to the active practice of nonviolence
(ahimsa). Along with the Jains and most other Vaishnavas of Gujarat,
Swaminarayan devotees view the practice of vegetarianism as essential for
a peaceful way of life. The second vow of the householder is to avoid all
intoxicating drinks and drugs; a common activity even for ascetics and
youths of the movement is to conduct antiaddiction drives. Strict regulations regarding the relationships between men and women are involved
in the third vow: not to commit adultery. Men and women are separated
in meetings and in temples. Both men and women are expected to dress
and conduct themselves modestly so as not to attract the attention of
members of the opposite sex. Various further regulations exist concerning
contacts between men and women, both within and outside the family.
The fourth vow – not to steal – is elaborated to include the prohibition
of dishonesty in personal and business affairs. The last vow seems most
time-bound; it is a vow not to receive food or water from any person
from a lower caste. These days, the wording of the vow is often broadened
to say that the devotee will never defile himself or others. An elaborate
structure of personal and social duties has its origin in these five basic
vows.

Women initiate other women and conduct the programs for women,
and in some places in India separate temples and centers exist for the
activities of women. In the early nineteenth century the separation of
women and the opportunities for female leadership were viewed as progressive and as contributing to the elevation of women from a rather low
status. Followers point with pride to the teachings of Sahajanand Swami
that helped to eradicate the practices of the immolation of widows on
the funeral pyres of their husbands, the discrimination against widows,
and the practice of female infanticide. Leaders find it difficult, however,
to explain the separation of women and the restrictions placed on their
leadership in religious activities in contemporary settings in Western
countries.

Another act of reform that followers claim for Sahajanand Swami is in
the institution of asceticism, which in his time had fallen into some disrepute. He described the path of renunciation in the section of the *Satsangijivan* known as the *Dharmamrit* under five vows of the ascetic
(sadhu). The first vow requires absolute celibacy and the avoidance of

women. Strict physical and mental separation from women has the goal of removing women from the conscious world of the ascetics so that they will not have any sexual desire. The second vow is to renounce all family ties. The sadhu receives a new name at the time of initiation, which signifies his new status completely separate from his previous social, familial, and caste associations. Family ties are highly valued by the Gujarati householders, so they are considered to be the strongest attachment to the world. Various forms of fasting and control of the intake of food are part of the third vow to renounce attachment to objects of the senses. Lay people undertake regular fasts on two Ekadashi days of the month, but the ascetics have additional fasts. The ascetics also take a vow of holy poverty. The only legitimate personal possessions for an ascetic are those necessary to dress modestly, to eat, to worship, and to study. Acetics are not supposed to have any other possessions or even to touch money. (An anomaly exists in the combination of the power of some ascetics to control the assets of large institutions with the ideal of personal poverty.) The fifth vow, the most difficult to fulfill, is to avoid the pride of ego. Humility is lauded as a virtue, and ascetics are assigned to many menial tasks such as cooking and cleaning along with the more exalted tasks of the temple priest, preacher, scholar, and administrator.

Paradoxically, the sadhus of Swaminarayan Hinduism are praised by the Gujaratis for renouncing things highly valued in Gujarati society. In a way they provide the mirror image of that society. Couples yearn for children, and family ties in Gujarat are strong and deep. Yet even young men renounce family responsibilities both to their parents and to possible future generations. Gujarati cuisine is a point of pride, and guests are served a variety of tasty dishes even in the temples. Justified pride is demonstrated by the care with which the food offered to the deities is prepared, even on days when the ascetics who prepared it are on a total fast. Yet ascetics destroy the taste by mixing their food with water before they eat. Likewise, industry and success in business and financial affairs are praised by the householders, but the ascetics renounce all possessions. Despite their separation from society, the Swaminarayan sadhus act as examples, advisors, and teachers, and they are highly respected and honored by the lay people.

Swaminarayan Hinduism is basically a Gujarati form of Vaishnavism, and even where it exists outside of Gujarat, it is the religion of Gujaratis. It claims the universalism of Hinduism and shares the sacred texts of the *Vedas, Bhagavad Gita, Bhagavata Purana*, and the *Vedanta Sutras*, as well as devotion to Krishna and other forms of Vishnu and rituals and regulations with other Hindus. Nevertheless, the language, architecture, iconography, calendar, cuisine, and dress common in the group are those of Gujarat. The sacred places associated with the sacred stories are in Gujarat, many of them now locations of important temples and shrines. The *Shikshapatri* and the *Satsangijivan* are in Sanskrit, but the other sacred texts written by or about Sahajanand Swami are in Gujarati: *Vachanamritam, Bhakta Chintamani, Shri Hari Lilamrit,* and *Swamini Vato.* The language of the rituals in the temples and of the meetings and singing is Gujarati; the growth of the movement is intimately tied to the development of modern Gujarat, and virtually all of the followers of the religion are Gujaratis. In Gujarat that is unremarkable, but outside of Gujarat the convergence of religious identity with cultural and linguistic associations is a most important aspect of the transmission of the tradition.

The dioceses of Ahmedabad and Vadtal

Over the past two centuries, several sectarian divisions have occurred in Gujarat that have influenced organizational developments and are in evidence in the United States. Sahajanand Swami adopted two nephews and through them established two lines of acharyas (preceptors) for the rapidly growing organization (Williams, 1982:61–97). In 1826 he installed one as the acharya of Ahmedabad and the other as acharya in Vadtal, dividing the territory of India between the two dioceses (*gadi*). Thus, each temple and each follower in India, sadhu or householder, resides in the diocese of one of the acharyas, who are the chief administrators of the oldest, largest, and wealthiest of the subgroups in Swaminarayan Hinduism. These acharyas are Brahmin householders who have authority by hereditary office. Their wives are also religious specialists for women, and their eldest sons receive the office after them. The acharyas are primary officers for large religious institutions and trusts, and receive honor from influential ascetics, but they have little legal power to control the activities of individual ascetics, which leads to some divisions and administrative problems. Some ascetics of the Ahmedabad and Vadtal dioceses have established their own religious and educational trusts. Ajendraprasad (b. 1949) occupies the gadi of the Vadtal diocese, but he has been acharya only since 1985, so he has not yet been active in establishment of centers abroad. Tejendraprasad (b. 1944) is the current acharya of the Ahmedabad diocese. Since he became acharya in 1969, he has been active in the establishment of Swaminarayan centers in East Africa, England, and more recently in the United States. In 1984 he was a leader in the formation of the International Swaminarayan Satsang Organization in the United States, which provides an umbrella organization for Swaminarayan Hindus who are loyal to the Ahmedabad and Vadtal dioceses but who live outside India.

Swaminarayan procession in New Jersey across the Hudson River from mid-Manhattan.

The Bochasanwasi Swaminarayan Sanstha

The Bochasanwasi Swaminarayan Sanstha, also called the Akshar Purushottam Sanstha, is a sect that developed in this century in a major doctrinal and administrative split from the Vadtal diocese. It established a line of ascetics as religious and administrative leaders separate from the acharyas of Ahmedabad and Vadtal. The split came when Swami Yagnapurushdas (1865–1951) left the Vadtal temple in 1906 with a few sadhus to form a new organization. The headquarters was first established at Bochasan, hence the name, but now the administrative offices are in Ahmedabad. Yagnapurushdas taught that Sahajanand Swami had appointed one of his close followers, Gunatitanand Swami (1785–1867), to be his spiritual successor. Moreover, he taught that Swaminarayan is always manifest in the world through a line of perfect disciples who have continued in a line of succession from Gunatitanand. Swaminarayan is believed to be the manifestation of the supreme person, the first eternal principle (purushottam); the second eternal principle is the abode of god (*akshar*), which has an impersonal form as an eternal state of being and also a personal form as the most perfect devotee of god. The current successor of Gunatitanand Swami as the abode of god is Narayanswa-rupdas Swami (b. 1921), commonly called Pramukh Swami, who is thereby also the president and administrative leader. Under his leadership this branch of Swaminarayan Hinduism has grown dramatically, and even though it is younger, smaller and less well-established in Gujarat, the group is more active and prosperous abroad. The growth of this group represents the popularity and influence of the religious ascetic in modern Hinduism in relation to the authority of the Brahmin householders.

Periods of transition from one leader to another in the Bochasanwasi Swaminarayan Sanstha are fraught with danger of division as loyalty is bestowed upon or withheld from the designated successor. This led to a minor split at the time of the death of Jnanjivandas Swami (1891–1971), also called Yogiji Maharaj, when a group left to form the Yogi Divine Society. Tension developed in 1966 when Dadubhai Patel, a renowned preacher and leader of the group, made a controversial tour in East Africa to raise money to establish a temple and an order of female ascetics at Vidyanagar in Gujarat. When Pramukh Swami was designated leader in 1971, those associated with the Yogi Divine Society refused to accept his authority, and a new subsect was established with temples, ascetics (both male and female) and followers in India and abroad. Dadubhai Patel and some ascetics traveled to the United States before his death in 1985, and a group of ascetics toured following his death.. The Yogi Divine Society is very small compared with the older groups, but there are some followers in the United States.

Thus, several organizations of Swaminarayan Hinduism exist in India, each with its own legal status, variation of Swaminarayan theology and ritual, hierarchy of religious leaders, temples, institutions, and followers. The oldest and strongest organizations, which are the trusts of the Ahmedabad and Vadtal dioceses, are also the least centrally organized. There are two dioceses, each with its acharya, strong temples, and influential sadhus who exercise authority apart from the acharyas, and diverse groups of followers. The Bochasanwasi Swaminarayan Sanstha has a centralized religious and administrative authority in Pramukh Swami, who is accepted as the abode of god by devout followers. That has permitted rapid adjustment to the demands of the modern period and to the needs of Gujaratis living abroad. The religious authority of the "world renouncer" has been powerful among well-educated, upwardly mobile technocrats among Gujarati immigrants in the United States. The old dioceses of Ahmedabad and Vadtal and the new Bochasanwasi Swaminarayan Sanstha, with their different organizational structures and forms of religious leadership, are the most successful in establishing their religious centers abroad. The other groups have some influence, but they seem to lag behind in establishing their influence abroad.

Gujaratis have long been prominent in migrations both within India and abroad. Large communities reside in major cities of India; in Delhi, Calcutta, Madras, and especially in Bombay where Gujaratis constitute a significant percentage of the population.[1] They emigrated to East Africa under British protection in the late eighteenth and early nineteenth centuries to work on the Ugandan Railway and to trade into the interior. Flourishing Swaminarayan temples were established in British East Africa – now Kenya, Uganda, and Tanzania – and Swaminarayan Hinduism prospered as the Asian population grew. After independence and after the expulsion of Asians from Uganda by Idi Amin in 1972–3, many Swaminarayan Hindus emigrated to England, where they have established Swaminarayan temples and centers in most of the large cities, making them the most active and fastest growing Hindu group in that country. In the summer of 1985 Swaminarayan Hindus of the Bochasanwasi branch organized a month-long Cultural Festival of India at Alexandra Palace in London. Several hundred thousand Asian Indians and English people visited the fair-like exhibits and cultural performances, which constituted a presentation of the Swaminarayan form of Hinduism and of Gujarati culture. A Gujarati poet, Ardeshar Khabardar, wrote a popular line, "Wherever a Gujarati resides, there forever is Gujarat." The line could with truth be revised, "Wherever a Gujarati resides, soon a Swaminarayan temple appears."

The beginnings in the United States

Swaminarayan Hindus came to the United States as individuals among the new immigrants after 1965 – a student for graduate study, a physician for residency in an inner city hospital, an engineer or scientist in a company. Some continued their disciplines of daily worship, vegetarianism, and regular fasting, and as the numbers grew many participated with other Gujaratis in cultural and religious programs. Although a few maintained contacts with religious leaders in Gujarat, they were unknown to each other. One of these individuals, Dr. K. C. Patel, came to the United States in 1969 from England to study chemistry. When Jnanjivandas went to London to install images in a temple, Dr. Patel returned to England for the ceremony. While he was there, Jnanjivandas told him to establish a group in New York. The president of the group in London gave him the names of twenty-eight Swaminarayan followers, mostly students, who were in the United States. In addition, he wrote a letter to each one asking them to contact Dr. K. C. Patel. Before he returned to India, Jnanjivandas instructed four sadhus, who were in England with him, to travel to the United States to assist in establishing a group. Mr. A. P. Patel, a leader of Swaminarayan Hindus in Nairobi, Kenya, traveled with the sadhus.

They arrived in August 1970 and toured parts of the country for forty-five days – New York City, Buffalo, and Webster, New York; Newark and Hoboken, New Jersey; Cleveland, Youngstown, and Cincinnati, Ohio; Chicago; and Boston – to contact those twenty-eight persons and any other devotees or potential followers they could locate. They conducted public meetings in New York, Boston, and Cincinnati to which the contact persons invited their friends and acquaintances. Sufficient interest was generated to warrant the establishment in February 1971 of the Bochasanwasi Swaminarayan Sanstha as a nonprofit religious organization in New York. Jnanjivandas sent a letter to appoint the trustees of the new organization, and he appointed Dr. K. C. Patel as president, an office he still holds as of 1988.

The first major gathering of followers from various parts of the country was on July 4, 1971, for a memorial to Jnanjivandas Swami, who had been cremated in India earlier in the year.[2] Leaders in India decided to send portions of his ashes to be immersed in rivers in countries where there were devotees: at Murcheson Falls in Uganda, the Thames in London, the Mississippi in the United States. Approximately fifty followers from New York, Ohio, and Illinois gathered in Chicago and traveled to Davenport, Iowa, to place ashes in the river. That event is marked each year by a trip from the temple, now established in Chicago, to conduct a memorial service on the river at Davenport. Now the group in Chicago is too large for everyone to go, so only the most active followers make the pilgrimage. Men who participated in these early meetings are now leaders of the Swaminarayan groups in cities across the country.

The strategy for growth was to establish weekly or monthly meetings in the homes of any followers who would take leadership. Regular meetings, to which Swaminarayan followers in the vicinity and other Asian Indians were invited, began in several cities. Advertisement in those early days was by word of mouth and by makeshift announcements placed in Indian grocery stores and shops. Meetings were generally held on Saturday or Sunday evenings, and the programs were fairly simple. The small home shrine with pictures of the deities and religious leaders became the worship center and the rituals were conducted by any layman who knew the appropriate form. Devotional songs sung in Gujarati were a major feature of the meeting, and these were followed by readings from the sacred texts, perhaps the *Shikshapatri*, *Vachanamritam*, or the *Swamini Vato*. Occasionally a layman gave a lecture on some aspect of the religion or an interpretation of one of the texts that was read. The meeting ended with the formal ritual of waving a flame in front of the images in the shrine (arti). Women were separated from the men in different rooms or areas, just as in meetings in Gujarat. Usually the program was followed by a good Gujarati meal, which was provided by the host family. These were important social gatherings as well as religious meetings, at which Gujarati families gathered from across the city. These became the primary occasions outside their homes when Gujarati immigrants formed the majority and when Gujarati was the language of conversation. Members of the various Swaminarayan subsects joined together for these meetings because they were too few to have separate meetings. Indeed, many Vaishnavas of other sects participated regularly in these meetings.

New York was the point of entry for most immigrants. Thus, more Swaminarayan Hindus lived there – mainly in Queens – and they were the first to have regular meetings and to form an official organization. In June 1971 Dr. K. C. Patel purchased property on Robinson Street in Flushing as headquarters. In September 1973 Mr. Mahendra Patel, a lawyer and leader of the group in Nairobi, visited New York to assess the prospects. (The young immigrants in the United States, who had little experience in religious leadership, used the experience of those who led well-established and successful organizations in East Africa.) The visitor attended meetings in New York and Chicago at which donations were made to purchase property for a temple in New York. A site on Bowne Street in Flushing was purchased in February 1974 for $95,000. The street is named for John Bowne, a proponent of religious freedom and toleration in the American colonies, and the first Swaminarayan temple in the country was thus established a few blocks from the site of the current Ganesh temple.

Tours of religious leaders

In India the acharyas and sadhus of Swaminarayan Hinduism travel constantly (*padhramani*) to visit the temples, centers, and homes of their followers. Now the practice of padhramani has taken wings as the leaders include the United States, along with East Africa and England, on their regular schedule of tours. The number and frequency of visits by sadhus, swamis, acharyas, and other Hindu leaders of all sects have increased, so that every summer scores of visiting leaders are crisscrossing the country. For the Swaminarayan Hindus, the visits of leaders are important in the process of identifying and attracting potential followers, establishing the infrastructures of the institutions, inspiring commitment of followers, raising money for building projects, and providing administrative direction. All these are in addition to the manifest function of the visits to provide teaching, counsel, and spiritual guidance to followers. Because Swaminarayan acharyas and sadhus do not reside outside of India, the leadership of the group abroad rests with laymen. Therefore, the regular visits of the religious specialists are essential for spiritual and administrative direction. The growth of the centers and the establishment of temples and organizations can be traced through the visits of the leaders of the Bochasanwasi Swaminarayan Sanstha, the International Swaminarayan Satsang Organization and the other, smaller groups.

Bochasanwasi Swaminarayan Sanstha sadhus

Jnanjivandas died shortly after he sent the group of sadhus to the United States in 1970, and Pramukh Swami was designated as his successor. He had been previously the administrative president (Pramukh Swami is the title) of the organization, so he was intimately involved in the plans for establishing centers in the United States. When he came to the United States with a group of sadhus for the first time in 1974, it was to install the images of the deities in a temporary shrine. The images in pictorial form were those brought from Jinja following the expulsion of Indians from Uganda. A Brahmin priest had come from India to perform the required daily rituals in the temple, which was in the basement of a house on the property purchased for a new temple.[3] Pramukh Swami and the sadhus who were with him stayed for five weeks. They gave instruction to the leaders, visited homes throughout the metropolitan area, and conducted public meetings in rented halls. After the installation of the images, they traveled to other cities to meet followers and to attempt to establish groups, visiting eighty-five places and stopping in 300 homes. Some lay people used their vacations to travel from place to place with the sadhus. Pramukh Swami returned in 1977 to reinstall the images in the new temple that had been constructed on the site in Flushing at a cost of $200,000. The rather plain building has a large meeting hall (5,000 square feet) on the ground floor and a kitchen and dining hall in the basement for the meals (prasada) that accompany the large meetings. The images were installed under a silver canopy in the meeting hall. Again on this visit Pramukh Swami undertook an extended tour to other cities, spending a few days in larger cities and a few hours in places where only a few followers live.[4]

The next tour, in 1980, was part of the year-long celebration of the bicentenary of the birth of Sahajanand Swami, culminating in a huge festival in Ahmedabad in April 1981. The religious enthusiasm generated by the visit of a religious leader revered as the "perfect devotee" and the "abode of god" at a time when the Gujarati community in the major cities had reached a substantial size led to the marshalling of financial and personal resources both for the celebration of the bicentenary in India and for the building of temples and centers in the United States. Plans were begun during this visit for temples in Chicago and Los Angeles, and groups were formed that began regular meetings in several other cities.

The visit in 1984 was part of another year-long celebration, this time for the bicentenary of the birth of Gunatitanand Swami, the first of the line of spiritual leaders specific to the Bochasanwasi Swaminarayan Sanstha. The festival of his birth was held in Ahmedabad in October 1985. Pramukh Swami's visit in 1984 was a grand tour to install new images in the temple in Flushing and to perform the installation ceremonies in the new temples in Chicago and Los Angeles. The tour lasted from May 6 until September 8 and covered the entire country.[5] On June 30 new marble images for the temple in Flushing and Pramukh Swami himself were carried on two of seven floats in a rain-drenched parade of 1,000 Swaminarayan Hindus down Seventh Avenue through Times Square to Madison Square Garden, where a religious meeting was held for several thousand people. Such public processions, common in India, disseminate information about the sect's theology and practices, arouse public interest – especially among Gujaratis – reinforce the loyalty of those who participate, and provide impressive copy for publications. At the meeting Dr. K. C. Patel spoke about the remarkable growth of Swaminarayan Hinduism in the United States in less than fifteen years from the time when four sadhus had arrived with twenty-eight addresses until the time of celebration of the establishment of temples in New York, Chicago, and Los Angeles. He gave the number of members and participants in the United States as 35,000. That success provided the base and enthusiasm for the plans inaugurated during that visit for the new marble temple, school, and housing complex; the land was purchased the next year in Independence Township, New Jersey.

The development of the group in Chicago was just as impressive. The sadhus who came in 1970 visited six families in Chicago, and these families began to meet each week in homes. They also began to have larger meetings on the major festival days of the Gujarati religious calendar: Ramanavami, Gurupurnima, Janmastami, Holi, and Diwali. In 1974 Pramukh Swami visited Chicago for three days, visiting sixty homes and holding two general meetings in a rented hall with an attendance of about 300. After that visit the group in Chicago began to hold a general meeting (samaiyo) once a month on a Saturday evening, generally in River Park District Hall, in addition to their Sunday meetings in homes. People in Chicago were among those who contributed money toward the purchase of land for a temple in Flushing. In 1977 Pramukh Swami visited for four days, visited 100 homes, and conducted general meetings every evening attended by 600 to 700 people. He appointed officers for the Chicago group; the man appointed as secretary, an engineer by profession, now serves as priest and business manager of the temple in Chicago. During Pramukh Swami's 1980 visit, the emphasis was upon plans for another temple in Los Angeles (Pramukh Swami raised support from across the country for each of the temple projects). In Chicago for five days, he conducted morning prayers (puja) in Helen Keller High School and evening meetings at River Park District Hall. On each of his visits, larger groups gathered, and many people accepted initiation as Swaminarayan followers (*satsangis*).

Plans for the temple in Chicago were begun in the fall of 1982 when Pramukh Swami sent a leading sadhu of the group, Sastri Swayamprakasdas (commonly known as Doctor Swami because he completed medical school), with seven other sadhus to tour the United States.[6] Over 900 people attended the large public meetings during his visit. A youth camp was held in Chicago for 83 young men from nine states. The Chicago group received permission from Pramukh Swami to buy property for a temple, and in April 1983 they purchased for $250,000 the Veterans of Foreign Wars Hall in a residential neighborhood of Glen Ellyn, a western suburb of Chicago.[7] They spent $100,000 for renovation of the temple in preparation for the installation of the marble images when Pramukh Swami returned in 1984. Part of the installation festivities included a procession down Michigan Avenue in Chicago, with the lay leaders marching in front, floats carrying the marble images and the religious leaders from India, signs announcing the opening of the temple, and the followers marching and singing Gujarati devotional songs and chants. The women marched at the rear, dressed in traditional Gujarati costumes, carrying brass pots and coconuts on their heads as auspicious symbols, and occasionally performing the Gujarati stick dance. The crowds along the sidewalk were separated from the marchers by half a world of space and culture, but they could understand the public statement that was being made. Boundaries were being established not only for those who were observing, but also for those in the procession. The meanings of "inside" and "outside," "friend" and "stranger," were being expressed in a religious idiom consonant with the host society even though the verbal language, gesture and ritual language, and the theological affirmations were largely incomprehensible to those who watched from the sidewalk. The marchers moved to McCormick Place for a program of devotional songs and lectures attended by 3,000 people.

The enthusiasm of the procession and the installation of the images continued in a leadership training conference at a school near the temple. Four seminars held for men, women, young men, and young girls were attended by 650 people from centers and temples across the country. The seminars provided instruction in Swaminarayan theology, rituals, sacred texts, and discipline. Those trained in the seminars become leaders of the centers. During the time of the Chicago visit, some of the sadhus traveled to other cities in the midwest to visit Gujaratis and to try to establish groups in St. Louis, Centralia, Bloomington, Racine, Kenosha, St. Paul, and Indianapolis.

The preliminary dedication of another major temple in Whittier, California, was performed by Doctor Swami on his visit in 1982. In 1981, the members in California, with the help of others across the country, had purchased a building on two and one-half acres of land for $340,000 that would be converted into a temple.[8] The pattern of development and growth was similar to those in New York and Chicago. Pramukh Swami formally installed the marble images during his visit in 1984, and he brought a Brahmin priest from India to serve the temple. The temple is open for worship throughout the week, with special times of worship (arti) every morning and evening. As in each location, the presence of a temple and regular services has caused participation in the Sunday services and the monthly general meetings (samaiyos) to increase dramatically. The major festivals of the Hindu calendar are also celebrated in the temples.

The next temple is planned for Houston. Pramukh Swami made a brief, unplanned visit to Houston during his tour in 1977 to visit a few followers. The rapid growth of the Gujarati community in Houston in the next few years made it fertile ground for the growth of the Swaminarayan group. Pramukh Swami visited again in 1980 and 1984, making visits to homes, holding public meetings widely advertised within the Gujarati community, providing the opportunity for many people to receive initiation, confirming leaders and making plans for a temple. In 1985 the group purchased a five-acre tract in southwest Houston for $292,000. Eighty percent of the members live within ten miles of the site, and 50 percent live within five miles. Plans for a new temple complex that will cost about $700,000 were submitted to Pramukh Swami for his approval, and groundbreaking for a new temple was performed on October 19, 1986.

The theology of the Bochasanwasi Swaminarayan Sanstha establishes Pramukh Swami as chief spiritual and administrative leader. Members attribute the success of the movement to his guidance because they revere him as the personal manifestation of the abode of god (akshar). The doctrine holds that a personal relation with a spiritual teacher (guru) – they refer to him as a "god-realized saint" – is essential to spiritual development and salvation. They believe that he knows the future and gives advice on personal and organizational matters with divine inspiration. He is the president of the organization in the United States as well as in India, and no major decision about building, program, or personnel is made without his approval. That provides a centralized administration that has been very effective in developing and implementing a strategy for growth and in marshalling the personal and financial resources to support building projects and programs, and his experience in establishing Swaminarayan groups and temples among Gujarati immigrants in East Africa and England is undoubtedly valuable in the new context. Devout followers give themselves and their resources, seemingly without question, to support the projects that he approves. Thus, a sadhu, who has taken vows of poverty so that he will not touch money or enjoy the "things of the world," controls and allocates the abundant resources of an international religious organization. This union of theology, administrative structure, and devotion provides a foundation for effective program development that few groups can duplicate.

The visits of Pramukh Swami are important for the individuals and families because as guru he is their counselor and advisor (Williams, 1986b). A constant stream of people approach him to ask his advice about personal problems or decisions. He gives individual advice on the naming of children, marriage and divorce, career decisions, and business and financial decisions, as well as on "spiritual" matters with answers to questions of theology and discipline. If they cannot approach him for a brief conversation, followers reach him by telephone or write letters. He now receives thirty to fifty letters each day, more than 125,000 since 1971, and several sadhu–secretaries respond to the letters under his direction. Followers say that they trust his advice because as a world-renouncer he is impartial and gains no personal advantage, save their respect, from helping them with their decision.

An important function of the advice for immigrants is that it gives them the ability to make decisions with confidence in circumstances where the outcomes of any possible decision are unclear. One aspect of the process is to aid the individual to think through the situation as clearly as possible. He has only a few minutes to present the problem to Pramukh Swami, so he is required by the process to prepare a clear, concise, reasoned statement of the situation and the alternatives. Moreover, the reception of advice from the religious authority results in a reduction of anxiety in the individual facing a decision or a problem. A physician requests advice about which city he should choose for his practice, a young man has five marriage offers and asks which he should accept, an infant daughter is in a coma and the parents want to know what they should do about life-support systems, a college student asks if he should become a sadhu, and all receive a response. The immigrant followers are generally very competent businessmen and professionals, but the social and economic milieu in which they must make decisions and pursue religious goals is sufficiently different to introduce additional elements of uncertainty and risk in all their affairs. In the absence of other established and trusted advisors, the accessibility of an impartial authority – either through personal visits, letters, or telephone calls – who can aid the individual in facing difficulties and in making decisions in uncertain situations is greatly valued. The process places the immigrant in touch with "home" and with an authority figure who can facilitate the adaptation of traditions and practices from India to the new situation in the United States. Thus, seeking advice from the guru is part of a valuable religious mechanism for adaptation and adjustment for members of the first generation of immigrants.

Leaders of the Ahmedabad and Vadtal dioceses

The International Swaminarayan Satsang Organization of those associated with the Ahmedabad and Vadtal dioceses has been slower in developing as a national organization. In the early days when the Gujarati community was small in most cities, members of all the subsects met together. All worshipped Swaminarayan and shared most of the sacred texts and rituals. Moreover, the elements of Gujarati culture associated with the meetings were attractive to all, both those who were formal members of the various subsects and other Gujaratis. As the numbers grew, however, differences between the subsects led to division. Members of the Bochasanwasi Swaminarayan Sanstha can participate without difficulty in all the activities of the Ahmedabad and Vadtal dioceses, but members of the International Swaminarayan Satsang Organization object to the inclusion of images of Gunatitanand Swami in the shrine with Swaminarayan, to readings from the *Swamini vato* (which has stories from Gunatitanand's life) and to the reverence given to Pramukh Swami as the abode of god. In the early 1980s these differences led to a division into two distinct groups in most cities and to two different national organizations.

Acharya Tejendraprasad Pande of the Ahmedabad diocese has visited the United States several times, but the acharya of the Vadtal diocese has not. Tejendraprasad was educated in St. Xavier's School and St. Xavier's College in Ahmedabad, and he received his office from his father in 1969. He went to East Africa and England in 1971, and returned to England in 1976 and 1978 to give his blessings to temples and disciples. In 1978, 1981, 1984, and 1985 he toured the United States and discussed plans for a new organization associated with the dioceses of Ahmedabad and Vadtal. Tejendraprasad is proficient in English as well as in Gujarati and Hindi, so he communicates well with both the immigrants and their children. On his visit in 1984, he took the new constitution of the International Swaminarayan Satsang Organization to groups in the various cities and asked that they accept it, and he established a central board of directors to administer affairs in the United States. His visit included public meetings in rented halls, as, for example, in the Des Plaines Park District Hall in a Chicago suburb, and a formal procession – the traditional method of greeting an acharya – in Garland, Texas. His wife and son accompanied him, and she engaged in formal visits (padhramani) in homes with female devotees. He returned for a brief visit in 1985 to attend a meeting of the Board of Directors in Houston and again in 1987 to dedicate their first temple.

Gujarat is divided into two dioceses, and immigrants have traditional loyalty to one of them, but that division is not effective in the United States. Thus, even though Tejendraprasad is the only acharya to travel to the United States, the organization is associated with both dioceses and tries to take advice from both acharyas. Now that a new acharya is established in Vadtal, leaders are trying to arrange for both acharyas to visit as a symbol of the unity of the group. Even so, the acharyas do not have the absolute authority that Pramukh Swami exercises over the other group.

The International Swaminarayan Satsang Organization has groups meeting in several cities, but only recently obtained a temple in the United States. Members bought three and a half acres for a temple in Pine Brook, New Jersey, for $265,000, but they were unable to get approval of a zoning variance of the requirement of five acres for the construction of a church or temple. While without a temple, the group met each month in a rented hall in Guttenburg, New Jersey. They were fortunate to be able to make a considerable profit on their first property, so they were able to purchase a Christian Science Church building in Weehawken, New Jersey, just across the Hudson River from Manhattan. Acharya Tejendraprasad dedicated the building and installed the images on May 23–25, 1987. Already leaders are discussing the possibility of building temples in Los Angeles and Houston. They admit, however, that they are behind the followers of Pramukh Swami in building temples and developing an infrastructure.

One reason given for this delay is the tension and distraction caused by visits of influential sadhus from the Ahmedabad and Vadtal dioceses, who travel without the authorization of the acharyas to raise money for religious and educational projects in India. The Swaminarayan Gurukul is a separate trust in the Vadtal diocese established in 1947 by a prominent sadhu, Dharmajivandas Swami, who has his own group of sadhus and disciples. He and fifteen of his sadhus toured East Africa, England, and the United States to visit former students and other devotees. He and other sadhus independent of the acharyas have toured the country more recently. The constitution of the International Swaminarayan Satsang Organization now stipulates that any contributions given to the acharyas or sadhus during their tours will remain in the United States to support temples and programs. Further, the regulations of the *Sikshapatri* require that sadhus have the authorization from an acharya for their travels. Officers are attempting to enforce these regulations, but without total success.

Some divisions are being caused by the attempt. The primary loyalty of some members is to one of the sadhus or even to the educational or religious activities they sponsor in Gujarat. Those individuals sponsor the visits of the sadhus and arrange for programs in the major cities. For example, a famous sadhu orator from the Vadtal diocese was sponsored by an individual in Washington and by the group in Dallas without the support of the national board. Almost every summer groups of sadhus from one of the dioceses tour the country. The group in Chicago did not adopt the national constitution and incorporated themselves locally as the International Swaminarayan Satsang Organization of Chicago. It is difficult to establish the unity of the group across the two dioceses and through the various religious leaders, sadhus and acharyas, who all have some claim to authority in this branch of Swaminarayan Hinduism. Divisions may result, and the lack of unity impedes growth in numbers and programs.

The Bochasanwasi Swaminarayan Sanstha has also been troubled by some division, and the leaders of the schismatic Yogi Divine Society have visited families in various cities on several occasions. That group does not have a formal national organization or any regular meetings, but families invite their friends among the Gujaratis and from all the Swaminarayan groups when the leaders visit. Indeed, it is still the case that many persons participate in the activities of more than one Swaminarayan group, and when the acharya or Pramukh Swami or some other prominent leader visits, persons from many groups participate in the general meetings. The boundaries between the groups are not yet firmly fixed, but they are more in evidence each year.

The relationship between the laymen in the United States and the acharyas and sadhus who live in India is unique to Swaminarayan Hindus. The growth of the organizations has been traced through the visits of these leaders from India, and they have been important, even essential. One should not overlook, however, the contributions of the laymen who make their homes into shrines and meeting places, learn to perform the rituals and give the lectures, serve as officers in fledgling organizations, and perform administrative tasks, all of which would be performed by professional religious specialists in India. These young laymen recognize that few of them would be given such responsibilities or honor in India, where most often it is the retired layman who serve as lay leaders of groups. The administrative skills and modern organizational techniques that these young professionals learn and display in their secular occupations are used effectively to advance their religious commitments. Religious leadership also provides an avenue for gaining prestige and honor within the Gujarati community, and these are often withheld from the larger society. Until now, no Swaminarayan sadhus have come to reside permanently in the United States. They provide only temporary leadership, inspiration, guidance, and assistance; the day-to-day leadership and work are done by the laymen.

Laywomen are also active in the Swaminarayan groups. At the meeting in Madison Square Garden in 1984, the president pointed out that more women were in the hall than men, which he used to illustrate the point that Swaminarayan women are "more religious" than the men. In most of the meetings, where women sit on one side and men on the other, at least as many women are present as men. Even though the women regularly perform rituals in the homes, they are not permitted to perform the worship rituals (arti) in meetings where men are present. The regulations that restrict access of women to the sadhus and prohibit them from exercising authority over men in the religious gatherings result in the formation of ancillary organizations (Mahila Mandals) for women with laywomen as leaders. The wife of the acharya is a religious specialist for women, and she initiates women and gives religious lectures for those associated with Ahmedabad and Vadtal dioceses. For the rest of the groups, laywomen are leaders, perform initiations, oversee the work of women, and organize special programs for women in conjunction with the general meetings. Many women from other Hindu traditions, and some who grew up in the Swaminarayan tradition, object to the restrictive regulations, which form a barrier to active participation for many women.

Going home

Ease of travel between the United States and India and the professional and economic status of the Gujarati immigrants facilitate frequent visits home. Immigrants return to India primarily for three reasons: to arrange marriages, to visit families, and to participate in religious festivals. For whatever reason active Swaminarayan devotees visit Gujarat, they visit also their acharya, the prominent temples, and pay their respects to eminent sadhus in addition to participating in the local rituals with their families. Tourism and pilgrimage in India are intimately interrelated, and visits to the sacred places in Gujarat have become a sort of religious pilgrimage. The temple in New York is a starting point, the temple at Dadar in Bombay receives Swaminarayan followers of Pramukh Swami, and the leaders in Gujarat welcome their followers from abroad.

Major festivals in Gujarat are occasions for group pilgrimage. In April 1981 both the International Swaminarayan Satsang Organization and the Bochasanwasi Swaminarayan Sanstha organized huge celebrations in Ahmedabad on the occasion of the bicentenary of the birth of Sahajanand Swami. Special group travel was arranged, and several hundred persons from the United States joined the hundreds of thousands of Gujaratis who participated in the celebration. Each group constructed a huge, temporary park in Ahmedabad, one on the grounds of Gujarat University and the other near the Sabarmarti River, where for several days the festival was observed. The Swaminarayan Nagars, or parks, were like American state fairs with tent cities, amusement rides, food and display stalls, exhibitions, and entertainment. Nevertheless, the festival was primarily religious, and the basic purpose was to transmit the message of the religion. A second, larger celebration was held by the Bochasanwasi Swaminarayan Sanstha in October 1985 on the bicentenary of the birth of Gunatitanand Swami, and again several hundred followers traveled from the United States to participate. Many young men gave their summer as volunteers to help prepare for the event.

These festivals serve as religious revivals. The financial support that followers in the United States send, and in some cases the contribution of labor in preparation, gives them a sense of participation. Those who regularly worship in Sunday meetings with twenty or thirty people are caught up in huge gatherings with a hundred thousand participants. Devotional songs are sung by professional singers accompanied by accomplished musicians, and relatively inexperienced lay people learn how the programs and rituals are properly done. Extended meetings, sometimes lasting a month, give ample opportunity for leaders from abroad to meet with the acharya or Pramukh Swami and with each other. Many decisions about programs and projects to be undertaken in the United States are made at these major festivals. Leaders from centers across the United States reestablish contacts with each other and with the leaders in India. Special programs for women are conducted by female leaders. Some of the young men of high school and college age live, work, and travel with the sadhus, which provides them with the opportunity for inspiration and instruction as future leaders of the group. Four young men from the United States have taken initiation as sadhus at the festivals, one in 1981 (an engineer from New York) and three in 1985 (from Alabama, Texas, and New York), and that establishes a firm contact with American centers. The pilgrims bring back publications, video-cassette tapes, and audio cassettes with which they preserve their experience and share it with others. The Bochasanwasi Swaminarayan Sanstha has distributed over 20,000 audio cassettes of devotional songs and religious lectures, many recorded at these celebrations. Thus, in addition to the annual calendar of religious celebrations observed in each temple and center, individuals and the groups in the United States mark events on a longer calendar by the visits of the acharya or Pramukh Swami to the United States and by trips to attend major festivals.

Not all of these events are in India. Swaminarayan Hinduism is international – the assistance given by leaders from Kenya and England in establishing Swaminarayan Hinduism in the United States has been noted – and festivals are also held in East Africa, England, India, and the United States. Active members use their vacations from school or work to attend these religious events. In the summer of 1985 the Cultural Festival of India sponsored by the Bochasanwasi Swaminarayan Sanstha at Alexandra Palace in London attracted a large attendance. A traditional gold-weighing ceremony was held at Ranger Park Soccer Stadium in London at which Pramukh Swami was weighed in gold, contributed to support projects chosen by him. Approximately 17,000 people attended. Many who attend such festivals refer to them as "once-in-a-lifetime" experiences.

Followers in the United States have friends and relatives among Swaminarayan Hindus in England, East Africa, and, of course, in India. The festivals thus serve a dual purpose, providing the opportunity for international social and business contacts along with the religious ones. Marriage negotiations between families are conducted across national boundaries at these festivals, often with the assistance of the acharya, Pramukh Swami, or some other religious leader. Weddings are not part of the religious festivals, and sadhus do not take part in them, but arrangements are made, and some weddings follow soon after. Thus, many followers in the United States maintain strong social, economic and religious ties with the Gujarati and Swaminarayan communities in many countries. The international character of the group can be seen in symbolic acts: The ashes of Jnanjivandas Swami were immersed in the major rivers, including the Mississippi, in countries where Swaminarayan Hindus reside; water used in a major ritual associated with the bicentenary celebration in Ahmedabad in 1981 had been brought from 200 rivers around the world. Despite these ritualistic affirmations, the group also attempts to preserve its regional–linguistic character.

A profile of Swaminarayan Hindus in the United States

A profile of Swaminarayan Hindus from data on questionnaires completed by 224 persons at meetings of the Bochasanwasi Swaminarayan Sanstha confirms that they are primarily Gujarati immigrants.[9] Most of those who completed the questionnaire (83.5%) are first-generation immigrants not born in the United States, most of whom (84%) emigrated directly from India. A few emigrated from England (5.8%), Canada (1.8%) or Africa (4%).[10] The native place in India of most respondents is in Gujarat (88%), and a larger number (95.5%) indicated that Gujarati is their native language. An even larger number of those who identify themselves as Swaminarayan satsangis give Gujarati as their native language (96.4%). The strategy of the formation of a Gujarati regional–linguistic group in the United States is successful in attracting the attention and allegiance of Gujaratis. A few persons from other regional–linguistic groups attend regular Swaminarayan meetings, but very few consider themselves to be satsangis (at most, 9 persons from the sample). No white Americans other than the author and his wife were present at the meetings where the questionnaires were completed.

The persons studied are recent immigrants under the provisions of the 1965 Immigration Law. Many (27.7%) have lived in the United States for less than five years; the majority (62%) between five and fifteen years; and all who are permanent residents (98.7% of the total) became residents after 1965. Only four people (1.8%) were visitors on temporary visas; the rest are citizens (42%) or have "green cards," indicating permanent resident status (53.6%). The uncertainty among Asian Indians about the permanence of their stay in the United States is reflected in responses to the question, "Do you expect to remain in the U.S. permanently?" A larger number (47.8%) failed to answer than failed to answer any other question. Only a few (7.6%) answered in the negative, and the remainder (44.6%) indicated their intention to remain permanently. The respondents occupy the high educational, professional and economic status common among Asian-Indian immigrants. They are young; only 7 respondents were over fifty years of age. Exactly half indicate that they have at least one graduate degree, and others have a college degree (23.2%), or at least some college (9.4%). Very few (12.5%) completed only high school. There was significant variation between men and women in the possession of graduate degrees (55.8% for men and 37% for women) and in those who only completed high school (7.8% for men and 22.9% for women). The respondents have primary occupations that reflect their educational background: health services and sciences (12.5%), practical/applied sciences (23.7%), business, other than listed above (16%), education (5.4%), legal services (2.7%), student (10.3%), retired (0.5%). The only significant gender variation here was in the category for practical/applied sciences where many more men (32.5%) than women (4.3%) are represented. Only a few (16.5%) neglected to respond to the question about "current total annual family income". Some (21.9%) have a family income of less than $20,000, but most have larger incomes: $20,000 to 30,000 (18.3%), $30,000 to 40,000 (19.6%), $40,000 to 50,000 (10.3%), $50,000 to 75,000 (7.6%) and over $75,000 (5.8%). The conclusion that can be drawn is that Swaminarayan Hindus are young, well-educated, professional, affluent people who have the skills and resources to administer and support their growing religious organization.

Almost all of the respondents (91%) indicated that they are Swaminarayan satsangis. A significant number (33.3%) indicated, however, that they were not Swaminarayan satsangis prior to arrival in the United States, which is an indication of the success of the Bochasanwasi Swaminarayan Sanstha in reaching Gujarati immigrants who were not associated with them in India. Only two of those who identified their previous religious affiliation – one Jain and one Radhasoami – had been affiliated with a religion other than Hinduism. Some Swaminarayan members follow a religious tradition not participated in by members of their family in India (24.5%) or in the United States (14.2%). A surprising majority (80.4%) indicate that they are more active in religious affairs than before they came to the United States, and only a small number (14.7%) indicate that they are less active. In conversation some explain that in India they were in the student generation, which is relaxed about religious observance, but in the United States they are of an age and have family responsibilities that lead to increased participation. Moreover, whereas in India religious specialists and older people take care of religious affairs, here they have to do it all themselves. Members take pride in close relatives who have become sadhus, even though sadhus renounce family ties, and several satsangis in the United States (17.7%) indicate that they have close relatives who are sadhus.

Swaminarayan satsangis report a very high level of religious devotion. Most (84.8%) report that their family has a shrine or a place reserved for religious observance, and almost as many (80.4%) indicate that they perform the morning puja each day. Slightly more women (87.1%) than men (78.6%) perform the morning puja. Over half (58.3%) indicate that they visit the temple at least once a week, and an additional number (17.2%) at least once a month. Regular fasts are a part of Swaminarayan religious discipline, and many (36.8%) fast at least once a week. The most common fast that members observe is on two Ekadeshi days each month, and an equal number (36.3%) indicate that they fast at least once a month. A few (13.2%) report, however, that they never fast. Travel to India for religious festivals is common, and a large number of the respondents (31.9%) attended the bicentenary celebrations in Ahmedabad in 1981, and just over half (50.5%) indicated during the summer of 1985 that they planned to attend the celebration in Ahmedabad that October. Central to religious devotion in this branch of Swaminarayan Hinduism is a personal relationship with Pramukh Swami as a spiritual guide, but that is hard to gauge through a questionnaire. Over half of the satsangis (52.5%) say that they have communicated with Pramukh Swami about a personal decision or problem, most in person (57.9% of those who reported communication) and the rest by mail or through another person. (No woman can approach Pramukh Swami directly, so all of their communications must be though intermediaries.)

The family and the transmission of religious devotion to the children of the second generation are very important among the satsangis. Most of those who responded (78.6%) indicated that they are married, and only one was divorced and two widowed. Most (73.7%) report having at least one child. Because the strategy of the group is to preserve regional-linguistic identity, the preservation of the Gujarati language among members of the second generation is crucial to the future of the group. That now seems problematic. Remember that most satsangis (96.4%) claim Gujarati as their native language. While all these indicate that Gujarati is spoken at home, fewer (64.2%) responded that Gujarati was the only language used. Parents are torn between the desire to use Gujarati at home so their children will be fluent in it and the need to help their children learn English so they will do well in school and among their peers. The proficiency of the children in Gujarati is low; only about two-thirds (67.7%) speak Gujarati, and only about a third (30.4%) read and write the language. Over half (54.9%) report, however, that they have given their children formal instruction in Gujarati.

The profile is of a group with very close regional–linguistic identification whose major problems are those of preserving that form of religious identity for future generations. Other Hindus in the United States, and indeed members of the other Asian-Indian immigrant communities, face the same problem, but it is accentuated for those who follow a strategy of preserving regional–linguistic ethnic identity in any more than its purely symbolic forms.

Organization, growth, and future prospects

The Bochasanwasi Swaminarayan Sanstha has been more successful than other groups in developing a unified national organization. It is a religious corporation chartered in New York and administered by a Board of Trustees with six members. All of the temple properties and the site in Independence Township, together now estimated to be worth five million dollars, are legally held by the corporation. The trustees are responsible for the programs and projects of all the temples and centers across the country. They meet quarterly to review the activities, budgets, and plans for the centers. Each of the centers is supposed to be self-sufficient, and any income over local expenditure goes to the national office, located at the temple in Flushing, to be used for capital expenditures. Each month the local centers send a financial report to the main office for review and audit. Local organizations arrange for loans from the central budget if necessary for building projects. The annual income of the national organization fluctuates from year to year depending on the special projects, such as tours of sadhus or major festivals, that are to be funded. In the summer of 1986 the Bochasanwasi Swaminarayan Sanstha coordinated efforts of the Gujarati community to raise funds for draught relief in Gujarat (IN, 1986).

North America is divided into six zones – Northeast, Southeast, Midwest, Southwest, West, and Canada. Each zone has a volunteer coordinator who oversees the work of all the centers and acts as the contact between the national headquarters and the local centers, reporting to a national coordinator. As of 1987, thirty-seven centers are active; many have very small meetings once a month with only a handful of people, but the three established temples draw hundreds of people to their meetings.

It is impossible to be certain of estimates of the number of people who are associated with the Bochasanwasi Swaminarayan Sanstha because some Swaminarayan Hindus participate in more than one religious group. A core of very active families provides the leadership and financial support for the programs, and this group may be identified as the 2,600 families on the national mailing list. Each local center has its own mailing list that contains additional names. For example, Houston has 120 families on the national mailing list, but the local mailing list is over 1500. The number of Life Members, those who enroll with a donation of $151 – the amount was raised to $1051 in the fall of 1986 – is 1,400. Many more worship in the temples and attend the meetings of the group. The best estimate of those who participate in the meetings and who have some form of association with the Bochasanwasi Swaminarayan Sanstha in the United States is around 10,000 families or 35,000 people.

The center and temple in New York was the first established, and it has the largest participation and most active program. Approximately 1,500 families in New York and New Jersey are associated with the temple in Flushing. The programs, both local and national, are administered by volunteers, but the rituals in the temple are performed by a full-time Brahmin priest. The temple is open daily for worship, and the standard Hindu daily cycle of rituals is performed. Weekly congregational meetings are held on Sunday evening for singing devotional songs, readings from the sacred scriptures according to a lectionary prescribed for centers in every country, lectures on religious topics, communications from Pramukh Swami and the evening ritual of arti (waving a lighted oil lamp before the images). Usually about 200 people are present each week. A larger general gathering (samaiyo) is held about once a month, usually on a Saturday near a special day in the Hindu calendar, which is followed by a Gujarati meal. Over a thousand people attend, and on the major festival days over 2500 attend. When Pramukh Swami is in New York, several thousand people attend meetings in rented halls in Manhattan or in Flushing.

The program at the Chicago temple is similar to that in New York. One of the non-Brahmin founders of the Chicago satsang serves as full-time priest and manager of the temple. He was assigned the duty by Pramukh Swami when the temple was opened, and he performs the daily rituals. Only three or four families come to the temple each day for the evening worship (arti), but the regular Sunday evening meetings attract between 50 and 150, depending on the weather and other events in the Gujarati community. Volunteers conduct classes for boys and girls on Swaminarayan teaching, on singing and playing devotional songs, and on Indian culture each Sunday afternoon, and between 25 and 50 children participate. The children lead the first half hour of the evening program, which follows at 5 o'clock. The general meetings (samaiyo) in Chicago attract between 300 and 700 people, and as many as a thousand attend the major festivals. Many Hindus from other groups come to the temple on major Hindu festival days, such as Shivaratri, when special rituals are performed. The programs are advertised through newsletters, in Asian-Indian newspapers, and on Asian-Indian television programs.

The basement of the temple is used for weddings, baby showers, and other social events. One of the volunteers decorates the room for these special occasions. A youth camp is regularly held in the summer for the children. The annual expenses for the program of the Chicago temple are about $24,000, and the income is about $27,000. Already the temple is too small for major festivals, and discussions are underway about the possibility of purchasing a new, larger property.

The man who acts as priest travels to smaller centers in other cities to conduct services and encourage regular participation. Regular meetings each month are held in private homes in Racine and St. Paul, and approximately 30 people attend in each place. Over 100 attend on festival days. Attempts are made to establish regular meetings in Joliet, St. Louis, Milwaukee, and Indianapolis. The three temples provide personal resources and volunteers to help establish other centers in their areas.

Participation has increased in Los Angeles since the temple was opened in 1982 and the images installed in 1984. The meetings and programs are similar to those in Chicago and New York, with the attendance larger than in Chicago; between 150 and 200 attend the weekly meetings. The general meetings attract 700 to 800 people, and as many a 2,500 participate in the major festivals. A Brahmin priest from India performs the rituals in the temple.

In Houston, leaders expect that the construction of a new $400,000 temple on land they have purchased will lead to a similar increase in participation, in spite of the fact that some members have left Houston because of the downturn in the economy. They have 1,500 people on their mailing list, but the attendance at weekly meetings is fairly small because they meet in a different private home each week. Between 70 and 100 people attend these meetings, but between 700 and 1,000 attend the larger festivals. The rental of a hall and the food for one of the large general meetings, which are held about nine times a year, cost about $1,000. Generally, a family provides for the expenses of a meeting. The annual administrative expenses for the group in Houston are about $15,000. The monthly contribution, most of which goes for the new temple, is about $10,000, and by June 1985 they had raised $190,000 towards the construction.

Three projects undertaken in 1986 were indicative of the strategies for growth adopted by this branch of Swaminarayan Hinduism. The first was to ask volunteers to give part of their vacations in the summer to strengthen the smaller centers and to establish new ones. Leaders in the northeast zone sent thirty persons in six groups to visit all the towns and cities in their area where Asian Indians live. They visited homes, tried to inspire leaders to have meetings, and conducted public meetings where possible. They attempted to contact directly or indirectly most of the Gujaratis in the area. These visits encouraged large attendance at several meetings held in the spring of 1987 to celebrate the tenth anniversary of the dedication of the temple in Flushing, New York. Other zones plan the same activity. This program of visitation is similar to the practice of Swaminarayan sadhus in Gujarat, who travel from village to village to visit homes and to conduct religious meetings. The second project was to strengthen the youth organization for young men between fourteen and twenty years old. Many of the children of the immigrants are reaching that age. Because the youth organization in London is very successful and exemplary, a volunteer youth leader from London attended the trustees' meeting in New York in April 1986 to provide guidance for the youth organization. The largest project, of course, is the construction of the temple, school, and housing complex in Independence Township. The temple and school represents the attempt to preserve a regional–linguistic form of Hinduism for members of the second generation.

The International Swaminarayan Satsang Organization was formed more recently and is less well-organized than that led by Pramukh Swami. Acharya Tejendraprasad from Ahmedabad has been influential in founding the organization, but he does not have complete control over both dioceses nor over all the sadhus, so no single central authority exists. A Board of Directors from centers across the country has been active for two years, and the first temple was dedicated in 1987. The money raised during the visits of the acharya, which according to the constitution must remain in the United States, is used for acquiring a temple in New Jersey. For example, $6,000 was raised for the temple fund when Tejendraprasad was in Dallas in 1984. The activities of the group were delayed because of difficulties with zoning and the need to find a new location for the temple. It is even more difficult to estimate the number of active participants in this group, which, even though it is larger in Gujarat than Pramukh Swami's group, is smaller in the United States. The best estimate is that about 3,000 families or about 10,000 people have some association with the International Swaminarayan Satsang Organization in the United States.

Chapters of the organization are in New Jersey, Philadelphia, Detroit, Chicago, Dallas, Houston, and Los Angeles. These vary in size and in loyalty to the national organization. Leaders of some chapters are committed to prominent sadhus who travel to the United States to raise funds for religious and educational activities in India. A tour by Dharmajivandas of Rajkot in the summer of 1986 was sponsored by a group named the Shree Swaminarayan Satsang Mandal of U.S.A. The chapter in New Jersey rented a hall in Guttenburg once a month for meetings, but now expects rapid growth to result from the establishment of a permanent temple, regular meetings, and observances of festivals. In Chicago between 60 to 80 people attend the meetings held on Saturdays about every three weeks at the Glenwood Park District Hall. About the same number attend meetings held in homes in Dallas. Houston has a larger chapter, with about 50 families who started to meet as a separate group in 1981. When Tejendraprasad was in Houston in 1984, he visited about 70 homes and participated in a public meeting with about 700 people. The programs of these meetings are similar to those of the Bochasanwasi Swaminarayan Sanstha: the Swaminarayan mantra, reading of the Shikshapatri, devotional songs, readings from the Vachanamritam, a lecture (optional), the ritual of waving the arti light before the image, and a dinner (prasada).

The dedication of a temple of the International Swaminarayan Satsang Organization in Weehawken, New Jersey, overlooking the Hudson River and mid-Manhattan, by Acharya Tejendraprasad was accompanied by a colorful procession and elaborate programs attended by members from India, England, and East Africa, as well as by members from other areas of the United States. It was a celebration of international unity, and it is anticipated that regular visits by the two acharyas will continue to strengthen the unity of the group. One major challenge, however, is to coordinate the visits of the independent Swaminarayan sadhus so that they will contribute to the growth of the organization and not to its division.

The preservation of ethnic identity is a major concern. A Swaminarayan

Acharya Tejendraprasad Pande installing images in the International Swaminarayan Satsang Organization Temple in Weehawken, New Jersey

sadhu lecturing at Madison Square Garden in 1984 gave a compelling call
to his Asian-Indian audience to preserve Hinduism and Gujarati culture
in a foreign land. An entertaining speaker, he used humor and an ironic
tone to capture the attitude of the Gujarati community toward American
culture, its materialism and immorality. Immigrants have committed
themselves to "the good life" in America, although they fear it. He made
them laugh at American foibles, with the irony that they were laughing
at themselves as well. He made fun of Gujarati families who place covers
over the images of the deities in the shrine room to convert it into a
multipurpose room for parties so they can entertain "like the Joneses."
"A hodgepodge of cultures," he called it. He caught their attention with
the observation that if the father changes his name from "Danesh," a
good Gujarati name, to "Donald," as many of the men did when they
first came to the United States, their sons will be known as "McDonald."
The humor of the statement is related to the dietary regulations that
require members to be vegetarians and to the common practice of many
devotees to avoid eating food prepared outside their homes or temples.
The elaborate Gujarati vegetarian meals, which accompany most large

gatherings in the temples, are for them the antithesis of the Big Mac at McDonald's. Anglicization of names is viewed as a threat to ethnic and religious identity just as is the loss of dietary standards.

The strategy for preservation of this ethnic form of Hinduism has been very successful thus far for members of the first generation. Language is for Indians the main symbol of regional and ethnic identity. Gujarati, as the medium of all the rituals and communication of the Swaminarayan groups, creates a major boundary that excludes meaningful participation by non-Gujaratis. The Swaminarayan group, the primary social group outside the family that requires and supports the use of Gujarati, maintains close ties with all aspects of Gujarati ethnicity. A requirement for significant leadership is good oratorical ability in the Gujarati language, and other symbols of ethnic identity are evident at the meetings of the group: Gujarati dress, cuisine, iconography, music, and dance. The primary ties are to religious leaders and sacred sites in Gujarat. This union of ethnic and religious elements in personal and group identity has a powerful attraction for first-generation immigrants, more powerful than that of the union of Indian national elements with either secular elements or with an ecumenical Hinduism. It certainly attracts stronger emotional attachment than a universalism unattached to either national or secular ethnic identity. It is important to note that the first generation continues to grow because no signs appear that the number of Gujarati immigrants will decrease in the future. These new immigrants provide a constant renewal of contacts with Gujarat and of commitment to Gujarati language and culture. In general, Hindu groups that stress the union of regional– linguistic identity with religious commitment, as this one does, have been more successful than other Hindu groups in maintaining the participation of their members. Those that unite these two with a centralized administration based on personal commitment to a religious leader have been most successful of all.

However, the strategies that have been very successful in the short run create problems for members of the second generation in the long run. It is obvious, of course, that if the group is not successful in attracting the allegiance, commitment, and support of the parents of the first generation, little chance exists of reaching the children of future generations. What Gujarati ethnic identity stressed by the parents will mean for the children is unclear, however, and the continuing relationship of regional– linguistic identity to religious commitment remains to be decided. The children receive their secondary socialization outside the home in contexts that make the preservation of both ethnic and religious identity difficult. Will they have to learn to be fluent in spoken and written Gujarati, and will many be able to do so? Will they respect religious leaders from Gujarat who have the characteristics that attract allegiance in Gujarat – oratorical ability in Gujarati, renunciation of the world, administrative abilities in the Indian context – but that are not immediately understood or respected in American society? The lay leaders, who generally are successful professional men, have been the role models for those who are able to move with ease in both cultures – Gujarati and American, religious and secular – but recent immigrants are generally not from the same professional class.

Tentative steps are taken to meet the problem. Some of the publications of the groups are translated into English, especially those prepared for children. The translations, usually made in Gujarat, lack some grace and style necessary for good English translation, and are in Indian English or British English, not American English. Attempts to teach Gujarati in the temples and centers is restricted to teaching transliterations of texts for chanting in the rituals, and even with great effort and success, it is unlikely that more than a handful of those learning Gujarati in the United States will develop a proficiency that will permit an understanding of the complex philosophy and theology of Swaminarayan Hinduism. Indeed, the type of Gujarati that develops among the families in the United States will surely diverge from that in Gujarat just as has been the case in East Africa and England. Even the ambitious plans for a residential school in Independence Township will result in education for only a small portion of the children. Leaders have been successful in establishing in the United States a facsimile of Swaminarayan Hinduism of Gujarat, and that form will likely continue to be attractive to new immigrants from Gujarat, but the key to future success will be if they, or perhaps their children, are able to develop an American form of Swaminarayan Hinduism.

CHAPTER 6

Nizari Ismaili Muslims
A religious minority

The President of His Highness Prince Aga Khan Shia Imami Ismailia Council for the U.S.A. said several times, "We [Nizari Ismailis in the United States] are tiny, young, still crawling, not yet walking." He was expressing surprise that someone would desire information about the emerging group, and also explaining a reason for the reticence and some difficulties in providing detailed information about the community. Nizari Ismailis are some fifteen million people who live in over twenty-five countries (Aga Khan IV, 1984:I, 2 & 43).[1] Those in the United States form one of the smallest national communities – as well as the most recently established – with a growing organization for which the situation is very fluid. Nevertheless, their experience both in other countries and now in the United States, illustrates an extraordinary union of theology and practical guidance in the process of adaptation. Throughout their history Ismailis have traveled "fast and light," developing a theological system and an administrative structure that provide a bridge between the past and the present, between the Third World and the West. This has facilitated the modern movement of Nizari Ismaili immigrants and the formation of a strong and growing community. They have recently entered the United States from several countries and are united in a religious community under the umbrella of the universalism of Islam and through allegiance to their religious leader, the Imam, Prince Karim Aga Khan. They illustrate a strategy different from that of Swaminarayan Hindus discussed in Chapter Five. Their strategy of rapid acculturation and attempts to preserve their distinct identity within the house of Islam have been very successful as they have developed a strong national organization and effective local centers.

Prior to 1965 the total number of Ismailis in North America was under six hundred and most of these were transients – students, businessmen, visitors. In 1987 the number in the United States is between twenty-five

186

and thirty thousand, and it is growing very rapidly. Forty thousand Ismailis are in Canada, members of an older and well-established community; many entered when the Canadian government welcomed sixteen thousand refugees from Uganda in 1972. Canada was a preferred location because of Commonwealth ties that made it easier to gain admission. Metropolitan Toronto has more Nizari Ismailis than any other location in Canada or the United States, some 10,000 persons meet in ten centers, but Ismailis are found in at least forty-five other cities and towns in Canada. In the United States they are scattered throughout twenty-two states, with the largest centers in New York, Chicago, Los Angeles, and Houston (Nanji, 1983:157).

A minority of a minority

Ismailis are an international community that developed from the early geographical spread of the community from Arabia and then Persia through the process of missionary activity (dawah) to call people to the faith. Ismailis took part in the large-scale emigrations in Asia and Africa – from India to Africa in the nineteenth and twentieth centuries; from India to Pakistan after partition; from Burma to India and Pakistan in the 1960s; from Uganda, Kenya, and Tanzania to the West in the 1970s. Thus, emigration has been a major part of the history of Ismailis. In the Middle East, Nizari Ismailis live in Syria, Iran, Lebanon, Iraq, and Kuwait; in Asia – in Pakistan, India, Afghanistan, Russian and Chinese Turkestan, and Indonesia; in Africa – in Kenya, Tanzania, and several other countries; and in the West – in Britain, Canada, and the United States. Even in Pakistan, where they number anywhere between 500,000 and 600,000, they are a small group among eighty-five million. The community is very diverse in cultural, linguistic, and economic matters and is everywhere a small minority in the midst of tremendous social and political change.

The majority of all Ismailis in North America trace their origins back to parts of the Indian subcontinent, primarily Sind, Punjab, Gujarat, and Kutch (Nanji, 1984:171–2). Some are from families that within this century have emigrated two or three times: from India or Pakistan to Africa, then to Britain or Canada, and now to the United States. Thus, even though Nizari Ismaili Islam is not an exclusively Asian-Indian religious phenomenon, in the United States it is the religious tradition of a small but significant group of immigrants, most of whom have roots in the Indian subcontinent.

The Ismailis world-wide are not easily categorized by nationality, language, or culture. They may be most easily divided by occupation. Thus in Syria, Iran, Northern Pakistan, and Afghanistan farming is the community's principal source of income, whereas in India, other parts of Pakistan, and East Africa the Ismailis are for the most part retail traders and industrialists, and in Britain, Canada, and the United States they are part of the more recent immigration patterns of professionals and businessmen. They have developed a remarkable strategy and ability to maintain their religious identity while adapting to new situations and restructuring their community to meet the challenges of the modern period.

The Nizari Ismailis, officially known as the Shia Imami Ismaili Muslims, are a tiny minority of a minority within the Muslim faith worldwide, as they are also in the United States. Sunni Muslims make up about 80 percent of the total world-wide, and the Shi'ites the rest. The majority of Shi'ites are Ithna'Asharis, who form majorities in Iran and some other areas of the Middle East. Although there are no censuses to ascertain numbers precisely, on the basis of internal assessments including sample surveys, it is reasonable to estimate the numbers of Nizari Ismaili as between eight to ten percent of the Shi'ites, a small minority in Islam.[2]

The Ismailis share with all Muslims the basic confession that God is one and Muhammad is his Prophet, and with other Shi'ites the confession that the designated leader, the Imam, comes from the descendants of Ali, the cousin and son-in-law of Muhammad. Shi'ite Muslims differ from Sunnis on the interpretation of the office of the Imam as a line of spiritual leaders and on the designation (nass) of the descendants of Ali as the Imams. The Shi'ites believe the designation passed to Ali's sons, Hasan and Husain, when Ali died in A.D. 661. The major division among the Shi'ites came after the death of the fifth Imam, Jafar Sadiq, in 765. At that time a disagreement developed over which of two sons had been designated to be the successor: Ismail (d. 775), the older son, or Musa Kazim (d. 796/7), the younger. The Ismailis are the Shi'ites who follow the Imams from the line of Ismail through his successor Muhammad (d. 813), and the Ithna'Asharis are those who follow the line of Musa Kazim. The Ithna'Asharis are by far the larger group of Shi'ites, known as Twelvers because they accept twelve Imams between Muhammad and final Imam, who is said to have gone into concealment in A.D. 873 or 878 and is still the "awaited Imam" or the "expected Mahdi" to appear before the Day of Judgment (see Figure 6.1).

A schism developed in the Ismaili community after the death of the eighteenth Imam in 1094 at the conclusion of the Fatimid period. Again, two sons were involved; the eldest son and original nominee, Nizar, was dispossessed of the throne by the party of his brother al-Mustali. According to the Nizari tradition, one son of Nizar was murdered in prison together with his father, but his infant son and

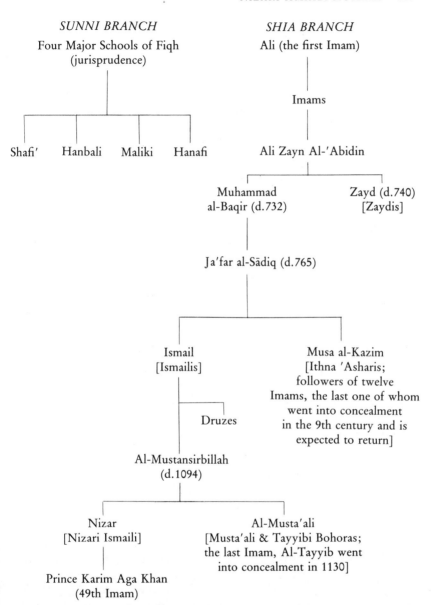

Figure 6.1. A chart of the branches of Islam. The branches of Islam are represented in outline in the chart above. It should be noted that the principles that divide the sub-branches differ between the Shi'a and the Sunni. Sunni schools differ in relation to the interpretation of *Shari'a* (law); Shi'a schools differ in relation to the designation (*Nass*) of the rightful Imam.

heir, al-Muhtadi, was taken by a trusted servant to Persia. Historian Wladimir Ivanow judges this to be substantially correct (1961:180). Those who accept the line of Imams that continues through Nizar and his descendants are the Nizaris or Eastern Ismailis; the Mustalians follow the line from al-Mustali and are called Western Ismailis. In the Indian subcontinent the Mustalians are popularly called Bohoras, and the Nizaris are called Khojas, but the designations are not precise. The word "bohora" means "merchant" and does not signify any particular school of Islam – there are Sunni Bohoras and Hindu Bohoras as well as Ismaili Bohoras. Moreover, the title "Khoja" is a term of respect that means "honorable person" and refers to a group of Hindu converts to Islam; it is not a general term for all Nizaris. According to the Mustalians, who have followers chiefly in Gujarat and Bombay in India and in Yemen, the minor son of an assassinated twentieth Imam was taken into concealment, so the line of Imams ceases with him. Thus, the Mustalians and the Ithna'Asharis both maintain a tradition of lineages of Imams that are not currently public but are represented by various religious leaders. The Nizaris are the only Ismailis who claim an Imam for this time in a line that is traced to Ali: Prince Karim Shah, Aga Khan IV, is followed as the forty-ninth Imam with the designation (nass) traced back to Muhammad.

The subgroups of Ismailis share a complex history as a minority in the Muslim world. They gained some political dominance briefly during the Fatimid dynasty in North Africa (A.D. 909 to 1094), which for a time was the greatest in the Islamic world. The Fatimid Empire at its peak included Egypt, Syria, North Africa, Sicily, the Red Sea coast of Africa, the Yemen, and the Hijaz in Arabia (Lewis, 1967:31). Ismailis continue to take pride in the fact that they established al-Azhar, the oldest university in the world.

They continued to be a force to be reckoned with in Syria as some Ismailis opposed the Crusaders there. Subsequently, the Nizaris maintained power in a fortress at Alamut in Persia for a time after the decline of the Fatimids until it fell to the Mongol conquerors in 1256. After that time practically nothing is known about the Imams and the Nizaris until the nineteenth century. The list of Imams considered official in the Nizari branch is generally accepted by scholars. These Imams had a close relationship with the Persian Sufis (Madelung, 1978:201). In the nineteenth century the focus changed to India when Hasan Ali Shah, Aga Khan I, moved from Persia to the Indian subcontinent, where many converts to Ismaili Islam lived. In the late nineteenth century and in this century Ismailis have emigrated from the Indian subcontinent and other locations to many countries in Asia, Africa, and the West. Bernard Lewis reflects on this long history, "No single, simple explanation can suffice to clarify the complex phenomenon of Ismailism. . . . The Ismaili religion evolved over a long period and a wide area, and meant different things at different times and places" (1967:138–9). Ismailism, like Islam itself, is not a monolith; it faces the problems of continuity in change.

The various Nizari communities were widely dispersed and partially separated by language barriers, and they developed largely independently of each other, but they survived under many different social, cultural, and economic systems. Sultan Muhammad Shah, Aga Khan III, commented in his *Memoirs* on the ability of the community to accommodate to these changes while maintaining their religious identity: "Ismailism has survived because it has always been fluid. Rigidity is contrary to our whole life and outlook" (1954:185).

One strategy used by Shi'a Muslims for survival in hostile and uncertain circumstances is *taqiyya* – dissimulation and secrecy. This is a practice that reflects the reality that individuals have different levels of understanding, and that a particular interpretation of a concept or practice may be misunderstood or not appreciated by others who do not share the tenets or ethos of the group. Thus the Ismailis developed an extreme caution that allows them, when faced with compulsion or menace, to be free from fulfilling certain external obligations of the religion and to conceal information about the religion and even their allegiance to it. The historical origin of the doctrine of secrecy is not clear, but it became an important element in the protection of the faith from opponents. Hodgson suggests that, "To be an Ismaili was to share in the secrets of the universe" (1960:425–6), and at times Ismailis were forbidden by oath to reveal anything about the teachings or membership of the community. Although it seems that dissimulation is no longer encouraged, the practice continues of keeping some information about the faith and details about the membership and religious activities internal to the community. Although it is very difficult to get detailed information about Ismailis in the United States, it can be seen that such caution and secrecy have been effective in protecting this small minority of a minority that is somewhat exposed in volatile areas of the world.

Asaf Fyzee indicates some difficulties that are created because the history of the Ismailis has been written by historians without access to accurate information or by Ismailis who considered taqiyya a religious duty. Students of the contemporary community may agree with his conclusion: "It is therefore not surprising that the majority of students should give up the quest as hopeless, after struggling with the subject for some time" (Fyzee, 1969:329). What was purposefully hidden has not been revealed, and the shape of it is difficult to discern.[3]

A religion, not an ethnic group

In premodern times groups of Nizari Muslims developed in different cultural traditions independent of one another, and Nizari doctrine is marked by major shifts in time and nearly completely independent local traditions (Madelung, 1979:205). Variations in interpretation of belief and in practice have developed over the centuries, but in the past century remarkable changes have taken place during which the Nizari Ismailis have moved from a scattering of isolated groups shaped by the traditional cultures in which they lived to a unified religious group with centralized organization and leadership and a program of modernization and development. Leaders openly stress that the Nizari Ismailis do not constitute an ethnic group, nor is their faith an Indian religion. Thus, they insist, it does not support Asian-Indian ethnic identity in the way Hindu or Sikh groups, for example, serve Asian-Indian immigrants. They stress that it is a religious community within Islam that has maintained its Islamic identity throughout a complex history in which Ismaili groups have been widely separated, virtually isolated, and often persecuted.

Ismaili Islam developed over the centuries in the context of three major cultural and linguistic areas: in the Middle East, Arabic; in Northeast and Central Asia, Persian; and in India, Gujarati, Sindhi, and Punjabi. The customs and traditions of the Nizari Ismailis have been shaped to some degree by the intellectual currents in these areas. Some scholars emphasize the similarities between the Ismaili esoteric cosmologies derived from allegorical interpretations and the neoplatonic philosophic tradition that was influential among Muslims in Egypt and Syria before and during the Fatimid Empire (Canard, 1965:169; Hodgson, 1960:1099). This neoplatonic tradition in Islam became very important in the development of Western philosophy and theology as well as Ismaili thought. Other scholars have tried to trace the connections between forms of Ismaili thought and the mystical tradition in Persia stemming from the Zoroastrian tradition (Corbin, 1983; Ruthven, 1984:206–7). In fact, many cultural motifs and strands of thought are in evidence in Ismaili theology and practice.

Azim Nanji suggests that the history of the adaptation that characterizes the Ismailis has led to a flexibility and ability to relate to different cultural settings that is a "historically conditioned, built-in trait" (1974:137). In their odyssey the Nizaris have gone from Arab culture to Persian, to Indian, to East African, and now the descendants of those earlier immigrants are adapting to a new cultural setting in modern Western technological societies with great success. Many of the aspects of Nizari Ismaili thought and practice that encourage such adaptation took shape in the Indian subcontinent and among Asian emigrants to Africa; the

Indian subcontinent developed a large Nizari Ismaili community, and East Africa later became the "proving ground" for the eventual movement into Western society.

Three elements of Indian Ismailism illustrate its adaptability and are important for its modern development: the conversion of large numbers of Hindus to Ismaili Islam; the move of the Aga Khan from Persia to India; and the Aga Khan Court Case.

The first missionaries mentioned in the religious literature of the Indian Nizaris cannot be dated with any degree of certainty (Madelung, 1978:205). One tradition has Ismaili preachers in India as early as the ninth century (Ivanow, 1961:180–1). Another tradition preserved among the Khojas indicates that the first major missionary to India was Nur-ud-Din, who adopted the Indian title of Nur Satgur (from Sanskrit meaning True Teacher). He was sent to India in the twelfth century by Hasan ala Dhikrihi al-Salam, the fourth Grand Master at Alamut, and preached in Gujarat. The second missionary in this tradition was Shams-ud-Din, and the third, and most important, was Sadr-ud-Din (Pir Sadruddin) who went to India from Iraq and was buried in Kutch. From the fourteenth century on many Nizari missionaries went from Persia to India and they were successful in converting Hindus to Islam in Kashmir, Punjab, Sindh, and Gujarat – in the latter many converts were from the lower castes, such as the Kanbis, Kharvas, and Koris. Later they were successful in attracting the trading caste of Lohanas and others to the Ismaili faith. The vast majority of the Ismailis in India were subsistence farmers or farm laborers, with a few engaged in business.

The preaching of the Ismaili missionaries is an example of how the message of Islam can be clothed in the language and thought patterns of the hearers. The poems and songs (*ginans*) were written in the vernacular languages of Gujarati, Kutchi, Sindhi, and Punjabi. The cosmology and theology expressed in the ginans and in a work called *Dasa Avatara*, which is attributed to Sadr-ud-Din, incorporated many local ideas and traditions. Poems and folk songs were an important vehicle for the spread of Islam by both Shi'a and Sunni teachers. As A. Schimmel notes, "There is no doubt that the Indian Sufis were inclined to take over images and forms from their Hindu neighbors" (1975:387). New converts in the later part of the nineteenth century continued to follow Hindu customs (Amiji, 1969:146).

The Ismailis maintained allegiance to the Imam in Persia, and when the Imam of that time, Hasan Ali Shah, moved from Persia to Bombay in 1843, it was a major event for Indian Ismailis. He had married the daughter of Fath Ali Shah Qajar of Persia and become governor of Kirman, but later, as a result of intrigues in Persia, he fled to India and died there in 1881 (Fyzee, 1969:323). "Aga Khan" is an honorary title given to Hasan Ali Shah (Aga Khan I) at the court of the Kadjar Shahs of Persia; it was later recognized by the British in India (Gibb, 1960:246). The presence of the Imam aided the development of the Ismaili community in British India because it gave them a readily accessible leader who was effective both in organizing the community and in representing their interests to those in power.

During the time of Aga Khan I, however, a dispute developed among the Khojas regarding the leadership of the Imam and the payment of traditional tithes. The details of the dispute are not important here, but the judgment of Sir Joseph Arnould in the case (*Advocate-General vs. Muhammad Husen Huseni*, popularly known as the Aga Khan Case) set forth the recent history of the Nizari Ismailis in a manner helpful to later historians and established a legal judgment specifying that the followers of the Aga Khan are not Sunni Muslims and as such are not required to follow Sunni legal practices. The case thus established the future direction of the administration of the Nizari Ismailis. Azim Nanji has commented on the importance of the judgment for the community: "On the one hand, it clarified the position of the Imam and his relations with his followers, giving him absolute right to all communal property, without any responsibility of trusteeship. On the other hand, it served to establish the identity of the Ismailis as a community in its own right, with an additional safeguard against dissenters or dissatisfied seceders, who could be excommunicated" (Nanji, 1974:127). So, at the end of the nineteenth century the Nizari Ismailis were established as a distinct community with a Muslim tradition that had been adapted to the languages and cultures of the converts from Hinduism, an accessible Imam with headquarters in Bombay, and a clearly stated legal status in British India.

Ismailis were among the emigrants who left the Sind, Kutch, and Gujarat at the end of the nineteenth and the first part of the twentieth centuries to find better economic prospects in East Africa, Burma, and other areas under British control. Many of those who went originally to engage in trade or to work on the construction of the Ugandan railroad became a significant factor in the respective economies as businessmen and industrialists. In Africa the Asians developed as distinct communities under the tripartite colonial policies that separated the British, the Africans, and the Asians. Some suggest that from as early as the brief Imamat of Aga Khan II (1881–1885) followers in Kutch and Gujarat were advised to migrate to East Africa; certainly as early as 1895 Sultan Muhammad Shah, Aga Khan III, advised Ismailis to leave India for better prospects in Africa (Walji, 1974:30). At its height in the 1960s the Nizari Ismaili community in East Africa numbered over 50,000 (Nanji, 1983:152), but rapid decline occurred in the Ismaili population in East Africa as both forced and voluntary migration brought persons of Indian origin to Britain and North America.

In Africa, under the astute guidance of Aga Khan III (1885–1957), major steps were taken to reform the Nizari Ismailis by encouraging the modernization of the community. Indian customs and patterns that tended to identify the religion with an ethnic group were discouraged as preventing the effective operation of Ismailis in the modern world. The advice of the Aga Khan to his followers in Africa paralleled the advice he gave to those in Burma: to identify themselves politically and culturally with the outlook, customs, aspirations, and way of life of the people among whom they lived. The Aga Khan was at home in the cultures of Asia, Africa, and the West, and his advice to followers in Africa was to adapt to the modern changes in Africa. He advised them to give up their Indian names, dress, and habits and, apart from their religion, to assimilate to the host culture as much as possible (Aga Khan III, 1954:323), directing the Ismailis in official communications (*firman*) to modify their "Asiatic habits" and become more Westernized (Walji, 1974:215). He advised them to educate both boys and girls and set up schools that would provide modern education in English and French. At the times of his highly publicized Golden and Platinum Jubilees, he established health, educational, and financial institutions that provided for the material advancement of Ismailis and other Muslims. He advised many followers to send their children for higher education in Western universities. He established a constitution for the Ismaili community and procedures that established Muslim family, marriage, and legal practices to replace some traditional customs brought by the emigrants from the Indian subcontinent.

Aga Khan IV (1957–) continued the policy of his grandfather. At the time of the independence of the African countries, he advised his followers to identify with the newly established African countries and to take citizenship in order to assist in the foundation and growth of the new nations. In these and many other ways, the community in Africa became a testing ground for the adaptation in this century of the Ismaili community outside of India. When the situation in the African countries caused mass migration, the Ismailis were the best organized Muslim community of East Africa and ready to adjust to new demands. Most of the Ismailis who had to leave have been successfully resettled in Britain and in North America; those in the United States are forming a new community along with those who emigrated directly from India, Pakistan, and other countries. The several centuries of adaptation to the Arabic, Persian, and Indian cultures where communities have existed, and especially the experience in Africa during the last century, provided the resources and training necessary for the adaptation of the Ismailis to modern Western society as represented by the United States. Only time will tell exactly how the Nizari Ismailis will adapt to this new setting, but the process is already well begun.

A theology for change

Ismaili Muslims make the central confessions of the Islamic faith that God is one and that Muhammad is the prophet of God. They accept the Quran as the basic revelation of the faith and the five pillars of Islam. They have an exoteric as well as an esoteric interpretation of the faith and its practices in which the esoteric (batin) accompanies the exoteric (zahir). A list of the fundamentals of Ismaili faith was issued by the Ismaili Association of Pakistan:

1 That God Almighty is one. He is eternal. He was neither born nor gave birth. He is the creator and maintainer of everything, and everything entirely depends on Him. Nothing from His creatures is like unto Him.
2 That the Holy Prophet Muhammad is the last and final Prophet. Before him Prophets came with books revealed to them; the Holy Quran being the last revealed book.
3 That the life hereafter is true and the Dooms-Day is certainly to come when the good will be rewarded according to their deeds and the bad will be punished according to their actions.
4 That after the demise of the Holy Prophet Muhammad the presence of the Imam is necessary in all ages to maintain the unity of faith of those who believe in him and to give them guidance befitting the changing conditions of the time and developing human society.
5 That such Imam must always be available to his followers and is responsible for their guidance always and everywhere on the surface of the earth.
6 That every such Imam must be in a genealogical line of succession right from Hazrat Aly, the first Imam, on the principle of a formal appointment of each predecessor Imam to his successor Imam.
7 That Hazrat Aly, the first Imam, according to Ismailis received his appointment as Imam from the Holy Prophet Muhammad (peace be on him) who declared openly; "O! Aly you are to me as Aaron was to Moses, except that there will be no prophet after me."
8 The Imam's guidance on matters of faith is binding on the community.[4]
9 That all Muslims are one, despite their differences on account of their respective sects.

These are the fundamentals of Ismaili Faith followed by the followers of His Royal Highness Prince Karim Aga Khan, the present Imam of the Ismailis (Makarem, 1972: 73–4).

These basic elements provide the foundation for the continuity and unity of Islam and for Ismaili claim to a special place within the house of Islam.

Three major aspects of Ismaili tradition are significant in providing the intellectual foundation for the flexibility and adaptation in new situations characteristic of the group: the belief in and obedience to the Imam of the time, the esoteric interpretation (batin) of the tradition, and the union of the mystical and rational traditions.

The Imam

The most important of these, and the primary identifying characteristic of the Nizari Ismailis, is spiritual allegiance to the Imam of the Time (*Hazar Imam*). At a recent Ismaili Heritage Exhibition in the United States there was an artistic display that stated an understanding of the position of the Imam. The Imam's portrait was at the center, confirming his importance in the faith. All the major prophets beginning from Hazarat Adam were indicated in the painting by pearls. All the manifest Imams starting from Hazrat Mowlana Ali were indicated by forty-eight diamondlike stones and the forty-ninth portrait in the center was surrounded by twenty-five large diamonds to indicate the Silver Anniversary of his Imamat. Ninety-eight names of Allah appeared on the outer circle and the ninety-ninth name was in the middle to signify that everything is from Allah and eventually returns to Allah. The diamond is seen as an appropriate symbol for the light of the Imam (*Nur*) which is thought to illuminate the way for Ismaili followers. The statement of a ten-year-old Ismaili in the United States gives a flavor of the devotion: "I am a Shi'a Imami Ismaili Nizari Muslim. To me an Imam is a guide, an ever living power that Allah has chosen Himself. An Imam is a spiritual father, a guide to the right path, a guide for a good, meaningful, and peaceful life. He is a direct descendant of Prophet Muhammad. He is the teacher who teaches the real meaning of the Quran. He has Noor [Nur] that no other person has." The Imam is the executor (*wasi*) and the vice-regent (*wali*) of the Prophet, from whom he derives his authority to guide the community.

The light (Nur) is a powerful symbol in Ismailism because it is believed to have existed before creation. It is manifest in the world by the prophets and the Imams in a cycle of eons, each of which is commenced by a prophet who has an esoteric representative, the Imam, who gives guidance to Muslims throughout that cycle of time. The elaborate metaphysics, cosmology, and spiritual anthropology is based on a celestial model with seven heavens, seven cycles of prophecy, and seven Imams. The major prophets bring the message of Allah for each eon beginning with Adam, for whom Seth was Imam, to Abraham, who had Ismail, and, of course, to Muhammad, for whom Ali was the designated Imam. The Ismailis share with all Muslims the belief that the cycle of prophecy terminated with the Prophet Muhammad, who was the Seal of Prophecy; henceforth, no new revelations will come until the Great Resurrection. In addition, Ismailis believe that the light (Nur) has always been present in the line of Imams, and that in the present age the descendants of Ali possess the Light of guidance and the designation to represent the Prophet as the sustainers and authentic interpreters of the revelation. The world can never be without an Imam, otherwise humans would be without divine guidance and the world would perish. S. H. Nasr indicates that the duties of the Imam in Ismaili thought are essentially threefold: to rule over the community of Muslims as the representative of the Prophet, to interpret the religious sciences and the Law to his followers – especially the inner meaning – and to guide them in the spiritual life (Nasr, 1966:162–3). The light comes from eternity through the Imam and is enshrined in the hearts of those who are true followers of the Imam.

The Imam is thus accepted as the only correct interpreter of beliefs and practices. He is the focus for the unity of the Ismailis across time and in the diverse social and cultural contexts where they find themselves and, at the same time, the primary agent through which adjustments in thought and practice can be implemented to aid the Ismailis to respond to changing times and circumstances. Sultan Muhammad Shah, Aga Khan III, referred to this tradition of change in a speech to his followers on November 22, 1903: "From time to time as circumstances change, some new things come up and fresh issues arise. At different times, new difficulties crop up. The world also changes. The conditions of this world prevailing thousands of years ago were different from the present times and will radically change in years to come. There have always been great transformations in the world. It is on account of this that the Imam of the Time is always present to guide you according to changing times."

A brief outline of Ismaili rites, rituals, ceremonies, and festivals that was distributed to Ismailis in the United States included a statement of the importance of the Imamat: "Imamat, according to the Ismailis is a religious necessity for the maintenance of the unity of a faith and for making the religion always possible. Without the leadership of the Imam, the unity of faith is not possible and religion becomes a subject of metaphysical controversy of and for the theologians and the men of letters. This makes the religion beyond the understanding of a large number of men, who consequently become victims of superstition which then comes into conflict with reason that leads that (*sic*) the religion loses its hold over the intelligent."

The Ismailis differ from other Shi'ites, who also have a doctrine of the Imam, in the belief that the line of Imams continues to the present in the physical person of Prince Karim Aga Khan, and part of the religious duty of Ismailis is an oath of allegiance (*bai'at*) to him. The oath promises obedience to the official guidance of the Imam and involves a recognition that the believer's person, mind, and possessions (*tan, man,* and *dhan*) are to be used in "the way of Allah" in accordance with the Imam's guidance. Implicit in the oath of allegiance is the acceptance of the Imam as the infallible authority in spiritual matters and in the direction of the affairs of the community. It is a logical contradiction to give an oath of allegiance in spiritual matters to one who is thought to be fallible, so the Imam has absolute authority in spiritual affairs. The concept of infallibility does not carry over into the personal affairs of the Imam, who, like the Prophet, is a businessman and engaged in the everyday affairs of directing his own personal business empire. When he gives official guidance to the community in matters of faith, his guidance is followed by the faithful because he conveys to Ismailis their sense of rightness. In this century formal constitutions have been prepared for the administration of the affairs of the Ismailis in various countries, but in them the Imam is granted the power to alter, amend, modify, vary, or annul at any time any part of the constitutions.

The attempt to explain the doctrine of the Imamat to potential converts from Hinduism led teachers to relate the role of Ali as the manifestation of the Nur to ideas about the incarnations of the avatara of Vishnu in Hindu thought. According to Hindu teaching, a manifestation of God comes in times of crisis to save people from the threat of evil and to lead them to righteous lives in a redeemed society. The early Ismaili missionaries in the Indian subcontinent superimposed the Shi'ite doctrine of the Imam of the Time on the Vaishnava Hindu structure. The most important example of this attempt to form a bridge between Ismaili Islam and Hinduism is the *Dasa Avatara*, which became one of the sacred texts of Indian Ismailism (Khakee, 1972). It is part of the Khoja Ismaili ginanic literature and, like many other ginans that were richly imbued with Hinduistic elements, its recitation was discontinued during the time of the previous Imam. In the text, various avatara were presented as religious teachers of previous ages whose work and teaching has been superseded by Muhammad and Ali, who is the manifestation of the Nur of Allah for the present time as the Tenth Manifestation (literally, *Dasa Avatara*). The criticism made of this interpretation demonstrates the difficulty the missionaries face in interpreting a monotheistic faith in Hindu contexts.

G. Khakee suggests that readers of her translation of *Dasa Avatara* keep in mind two guiding principles of Ismailism: Teaching should be done in terms that can be understood and assimilated by those who are taught; and Ismailism always operates at two levels, the exoteric and esoteric, but we do not know the details of the esoteric interpretation of the *Dasa Avatara* in those times (Khakee, 1972:41).

Several texts of the Imams and their representatives criticize tendencies to exalt Ali over Muhammad and to identify him with sacred figures (Ivanow, 1949:60–2; Fyzee, 1974:54–7). Considerable outrage is expressed by reports that suggest that the Imam is thought to be God, which would be contrary to the fundamental confession of Islam (Dougherty, 1983:70–80; see letter in *Life*, February 1984:15). The teachings of the *Dasa Avatara*, when correctly understood as analogies, are said to have been appropriate to the early converts in the Indian subcontinent, but are not directly appropriate in different contexts. The text is of historical interest, but is not much used today.

Also, a clear distinction is made between the Christian teaching about the divinity of Jesus, and the belief that Ali was fully a man during his presence in the material world. When he is called "Lord of the Age" the designation does not imply divinity or equality with Allah. Still, the Imam possesses the light (Nur) that has existed from the foundation of the world and he is the center of Ismaili doctrine and practice. One statement in praise of Ali suggests that during his life on earth Ali was the river separated from the Ocean of the Almighty – separated from it and running towards it – overcoming all material resistance and moving toward its origin. This analogy is expanded to view all the faithful followers as small streams starting from the earth and then joining the ocean with the river. The faithful follower will not be separated from the Imam after death.

The guidance of the Imam is credited with enabling the Nizari Ismailis to survive through the worst ravages of religious, political, social, and economic upheaval. The presence of a religious leader who can make decisions respected by the community at times of rapid change and dislocation has been the most important aspect of the transformation of the Ismaili community in the past century into the best organized and wealthiest Muslim community outside the oil territory. It gives the community confidence as they face the inevitable changes of the future. The office passes from the Imam to his descendant by designation (Nass); the community does not have the authority to nominate, elect, or appoint the Imam. Sultan Muhammad Shah, Aga Khan III, surprised everyone by giving the designation to his grandson, Prince Karim, in preference to his two sons, justifying the decision in his will: "In view of the fundamentally altered conditions in the world . . . due to the great changes which have taken place . . . I am convinced that it is in the best interests of the Shia Muslim Ismaili community that I should be succeeded by a young man who has been brought up in the midst of the new age and who brings a new outlook on life to his office of Imam."

Prince Karim Aga Khan became Imam on July 11, 1957, at the age of twenty. Born on December 13, 1936 in Geneva, he spent his childhood in Nairobi, Kenya. He attended Le Rosey School in Switzerland before he entered Harvard University, where he was an honors student in Islamic history at the time he was designated to be Imam. After taking a leave from his studies to be formally installed as Imam, he graduated with a Bachelor of Arts in 1959. He was certainly prepared as "a young man who has been brought up in the midst of the new age." His headquarters and the administrative center of the Nizari Ismailis is at Aiglemont near Chantilly, France. The first twenty-five years of his tenure as Imam has been a period rife with major political and economic changes within the sect, including the emigration of many of his followers around the world, a significant number to the United States. He has both the authority and the background to guide the community in its transition to the United States and other Western countries. In a speech at the occasion of the chartering of the Aga Khan University in March 1983 at Karachi he said, "In everything we do we must look to the future, seeking always to think creatively, to innovate and to improve."

Esoteric interpretation

A second element of Ismaili tradition that enhances the ability to adapt to new cultural and intellectual contexts is the emphasis on the esoteric aspects of the religion. According to the esoteric system, every sacred text or tradition has an apparent or literal meaning (zahir) and a hidden inner meaning of esoteric truth (batin). The zahir represents the practical creed of the Shi'ites, and the batin constitutes their religious philosophy. The emphasis on esoteric teaching has led to a distinctive allegorical interpretation of every aspect of the sacred tradition analogous to the allegorical interpretation of the Alexandrian interpreters of the Jewish and Christian scriptures. In order to derive the deeper esoteric meaning, not only the metaphorical passages, but the historical passages, moral exhortations, legal and ritual prescriptions, persons, acts, and objects were all interpreted symbolically (Hodgson, 1960:1098–2000). The function of the Quran and the traditions from Muhammad is to point to the hidden truths, which are accessible to the Imam and to those who gain the spiritual insight to understand them through his guidance, even while they are kept disguised in symbols. The Prophet's role was public, to proclaim the apparent aspects of the message, and even though he certainly understood both the zahir and the batin, he left it to the Imams to lead the following generations into an appropriate understanding of the higher truths.

This world of higher spiritual truths, which is parallel to the visible ordinary world and to the literal interpretation of sacred texts and traditions, is vast and permits many levels of interpretation. The true meaning of texts and rituals is to be found in the esoteric teaching. The result has been the creation of sophisticated intellectual systems that have often resembled and included elements from the intellectual systems of the dominant culture. Each disciple receives the esoteric interpretation according to his or her spiritual achievement from teachers ultimately dependent upon the Imam for their office and teaching – the Imam is the repository and final authority of correct esoteric doctrine. The content of the batin is secret and is not to be imparted to those who are not prepared for it, and it is in this sense that "to be an Ismaili is to share in the secrets of the universe." Many similarities are said to exist in both structure and content between the esoteric interpretation of Ismaili doctrine and the teachings and practice of some great Sufi saints.

The mystical and cosmological aspects of Ismaili teaching led to the development of mystical poetry in Persian and Arabic, much of which has been lost, and to a large body of poetic literature written in India called ginan, a term derived from the Sanskrit root *jnana*, which means "contemplative or meditative knowledge." The ginan are important hymns, poems, and texts used in the devotional services of the Khoja Nizari Ismailis. Azim Nanji's study of the ginan tradition among the Ismailis determined that some 800 sacred poems and hymns were composed by thirty teachers over six centuries before the turn of this century, when the material was incorporated into a sacred corpus for use in the prayer services (Nanji, 1975). The texts, written in a distinctive Sindhi script, Khojiki, that represents the earliest form of written Sindhi, are in several languages and dialects, including Sindhi, Kutchi, and Gujarati. The ginan are the product of the contact between Islam and Hinduism, as the Ismaili teachers sought to present their message in the poetic style of devotional Hinduism and with some of the same images and symbols. Most are poetry, but some contain treatises of moral and religious instruction that include theories of creation, time, mythology, daily behavior and life, descriptions of the last judgment, legendary histories, and miracles (Madelung, 1978:206). The material was composed in India at a time of resurgence of Hindu devotional and yogic practices, so it is no surprise that it contains concepts and practices similar to those in Hindu devotional literature. This body of devotional material is also the object of allegorical and esoteric interpretation, and the singing and interpretation of the ginan in Gujarati continues to be popular during meetings in the prayer halls, although both the current and previous Aga Khans, through reinterpretation, have gradually removed most of the Hindu doctrines and practices that had entered during the centuries in India. The restatement of the esoteric meaning of the faith in new patterns continues to be a means of explaining the appropriate interior meaning of the visible text and rituals to persons living in the United States, allowing them to maintain their religious identity even as they adapt to their new surroundings. This esoteric interpretation rejects the fundamentalism that would anchor the faith to a particular time or place. The reinterpretation is not without discipline, however, because the Imam is respected as the source of truth and acknowledged as the authorized interpreter of all esoteric knowledge.

Union of mystical and rational traditions

The third aspect that facilitates adaptation is a view of humanity which places great emphasis on speculation and intellectual activity. Esoteric Islam gives an enlarged role to the intellect in matters of faith. Paul Tillich once observed that basic structural similarities exist between inner light as stressed in mystical traditions and human reason upon which the rationalistic traditions of modern science and technology are based. Being imaginative is not antithetical to being rigorously analytical because these are the two sides of the coin of human intellectual activity: Rationalism is the daughter of mysticism (Tillich, 1967:18–23). In the same way, modern Nizari Ismailis attempt to claim both, to suggest that the mystical and the rational have always been two parts of one Ismaili intellectual tradition and that this union of the spiritual and the material provides the foundation for the bridge to modern technological culture. Great pride is taken in the fact that the oldest university in the world – at al-Azhar – was founded by Ismailis and in the contributions made during the Fatimid period to mystical and scientific thought.

The basic idea of the mystical tradition is that God is Pure Being and that man, although made in the image of God, is living in an order of reality that is separate from that Pure Being. The goal of the interpretation of the ginan and of the discipline of meditation is to regain the original state of man as Pure Being, Light, and Intelligence. The light and intelligence that will guide the follower to his or her true being comes through the Imam, whose Nur is the focus of the dedication and discipline. Thus, the Ismaili path (tariqah) has two levels: the perception of the Imam and the Imam's esoteric guidance. The goal of this quest is the inner, spiritual transformation that in the world will lead to a worthy life lived in the illumination of the Imam's Nur and after death the vision of what Sultan Muhammad Shah, Aga Khan III, called "the companionship-on-high" (Shariff, 1982:6). Thus the essence of human nature is divine, the call is for man to fulfill his destiny, in part in this world and finally in the world to come, by regaining his lost kingdom in order to play his role in the divine plan and to share in the creative life of the Maker. The goal, then, is finally dissolution in the Truth and Light.

In earlier works of the Ismaili mystical tradition some nine stages of ascent are set forth, but it does not seem that distinct orders of Ismailis are now marked according to their level of attainment. The esoteric interpretations and techniques are kept secret among Ismailis, and, of course, it is maintained that the full experience of the Truth cannot be described in words or fully represented in forms or rituals. This is an interior journey of the mind, although it develops from human speculation within a framework. That framework is constructed from the Quran, the traditions of the Prophet, and the guidance of the Imam of the time.

Ismailis stress that the mystical speculation of the inner light is never in conflict with modern scientific thinking. Indeed, just as mystical theology is human speculation within a framework, so beyond a certain point modern science is also human imagination and speculation within a framework. There is no conflict between the Ismaili faith and modern science. The Aga Khan remarked in his address at the inauguration of the Aga Khan University: "The Divine Intellect, Aql-e-Kul, both transcends and informs the human intellect. It is this intellect which enables man to strive towards two aims dictated by the Faith, that he should reflect upon the environment Allah has given him and that he should know himself." Leaders suggest that although many people perceive a conflict between faith and science, it is not so in Ismaili Islam because the teaching is that Allah's creation is continuous and limitless and science is merely one means by which an individual can perceive it. Thus, the Imam regularly urges the youth of the Ismaili community to participate fully in scientific and technological development in the West and in the Third World. He encourages the young people to seek the best educations available to them, and he provides scholarships to assist them in study in universities in the West, with the idea that the intellectual faculties of the individual should be developed to the fullest in esoteric speculation on matters of faith and in scientific studies, and at higher levels no conflict is necessary. Thus, in an address entitled "Muslims, Awake," Sultan Muhammad Shah urged his followers: "Formalism and verbal interpretation of the teachings of the Prophet are in absolute contradiction with his whole life history. We must accept his divine message as the channel of our union with the 'Absolute' and the 'Infinite' and once our spiritual faith is firmly established, fearlessly go forward by self-sacrifice, by courage and by application to raise the scientific, the economic, the political and social position of the Muslims to a place of equality with Christian Europe and America" (Aga Khan III, 1953:3).

The Ismaili community has a theological and intellectual structure that provides for the centralized leadership of the Imam in matters of faith and practice, the tradition of an esoteric level of knowledge as interpreted by the Imam, and an emphasis on human imagination and speculation that can be applied to both the esoteric truths of the faith and the natural laws of god's creation. These provide the theoretic structure for change and adaptation necessary in the community's new context as part of modern Western culture, as well as the background for the practical actions that have facilitated the move.

Practical guidance of the Imam

The guidance of the Imam is concerned with not only the spiritual development but also the material welfare of his community, with the justification that Islam is an all-encompassing religion related to the total well-being of individuals, so the leadership of the community must be involved in all aspects of life. In a speech on the occasion of the celebration of the Silver Jubilee of his Imamat, Prince Karim Shah, Aga Khan IV, made this point: "The nature of the religious office I hold neither requires nor is expected by members of my community to be an institution whose existence is restricted to spiritual leadership. On the contrary, history and the correct interpretation of the Imamat require that the Imam should also be continuously concerned with [his followers'] safety and material progress" (Aga Khan IV, 1984:18). This guidance reaches throughout the world wherever followers reside, across their variety of cultural and economic contexts and their spectrum of spiritual and material concerns. It involves advice about major trends in the worldwide economic situation as well as support for an individual in times of trouble. This union of spiritual direction and assistance with provisions for material welfare is characteristic of the Ismaili community around the world. The Imam's guidance provides the entire community with social and religious unity in spite of the cultural diversity of the five continents where it exists.

The official communications (firman) of the Imam to the community, through which development and the modernization of every aspect of the life of Ismailis has been encouraged, are internal and a matter of privilege between the Imam and the community, so the exact nature of the guidance is not revealed to those outside. However, in them the Imam speaks to his "spiritual children," and some of the firman have been quoted in the published speeches or memoirs of the Aga Khans or in other publications. Current and earlier communications are regularly read in the Jamat Khanas. The Aga Khan directs the Ismailis toward effective action in many areas – resettlement, education, health, or the adoption of what is useful from Western customs. In addition, the Imam gives advice to particular individuals through personal correspondence to answer questions ranging from matters of health, career choices, and business to spiritual development. The regular weekly or biweekly communications from the Imam are in response to reports by the various committees and councils and also include blessings to various people (Walji, 1974:100). The communication between the Imam and his followers is thus continuous, specific, and effective.

The written communications are supplemented by personal visits of the Imam, which become occasions of celebration by his followers. At the time of his accession to the Imamat in 1957, Prince Karim Aga Khan undertook a world tour to meet with his followers and to receive their oaths of allegiance. Twenty-five years later he undertook a triumphal Silver Jubilee tour, and the speeches he gave on those occasions have been published (Aga Khan IV, 1984). In the intervening years he traveled extensively, giving guidance to the individuals and institutions of the Ismaili community, for whom he is the visible public spokesman, and representing in places of power the interests of the Muslims of the Third World, which he has taken as a special concern.

Much of the Imam's guidance concerns spiritual development, but in other matters, such as community strategy and development, four areas are exemplary: citizenship and cultural adaptation; women's rights; education; and economic development. Both of the Imams of this century have advised their followers to take citizenship in and give full secular loyalty to the countries where they live. Aga Khan III gave the direction: "You Ismailis know perfectly well that it is a fundamental point in your religion that wherever you be, whatever the state where life and honour are protected, you must give your entire loyalty and devotion to the welfare and service of that country.... Do remember that in democracy, voting and the rights of citizenship should be used with care and attention with serious thought however humble with the full realisation to the best of your ability that not personal, parochial or provincial interests are to be served but the greater good and the welfare of the population as a whole and the security of the state as such" (1953:43–4). Following his advice, Ismailis took citizenship in Burma, Uganda, and Kenya, and now in Britain, Canada, and the United States. Aga Khan IV continues that advice and emphasizes the nonpolitical character of the Ismaili Imamat (1984:43). As long as the freedom of worship and the protection of life and property are provided, the Imam does not interfere in national politics.

The Aga Khan's family exhibits exemplary involvement in international affairs. The current Imam's grandfather, Sultan Muhammad Shah, Aga Khan III, was President of the League of Nations, and his father, Prince

Aly, was Pakistan's Ambassador to the United Nations. His uncle, Prince Sadruddin Aga Khan, was United Nations High Commissioner for Refugees from 1965 to 1977, at a time when Ismailis and other persons of Indian origin were being resettled from African countries, and his brother, Prince Amyn, served from 1965 to 1968 with the United Nations Secretariat. These positions have given the Imam's family international visibility and important contacts for cooperation in aiding the development of the Ismaili community and the people in Third World countries.

The Imam guided the community in British East Africa to live their lives along British lines and in general to adopt British and European customs where these are not in conflict with Islam. Referring to the fact that the Ismaili community arrived in Africa with Asiatic habits and an Asiatic pattern of existence, the Imam said that to have retained an Asiatic outlook in matters of language, habits, and clothing would have been to live socially under a "dead weight of archaism" (Aga Khan III 1954:190, 323). One example of a specific directive comes from a 1952 conference in Switzerland called to discuss various economic and social problems confronting Ismailis in which leaders urged all Ismaili women of East Africa to adopt Western dress for "political and economic reasons" (Walji, 1974:218). The result of the advice on assimilation was to play down the Asiatic and Hindu cultural traits that the emigrants had carried from the Indian subcontinent. At the same time as social customs became more Western, some religious practices were also reformed. Until 1956, the Khoja Ismaili daily prayer was said in Gujarati, but in that year a new prayer book with the Arabic text was issued that had the transliteration of the Arabic into Roman and Gujarati characters and translations into English and Gujarati (Amiji, 1969:153). The Hindu inheritance laws that had governed the community in India and in the early days in East Africa were changed to those of the Shi'a, along with the Indian rituals for marriage, birth, and death (Nanji, 1974:134). Many of these matters received attention in the formal constitution adopted by the community, which dealt with personal law as well as administrative structure. Thereby the effectiveness of Ismailis in Western society and their identification with other Muslims was strengthened, as the guidance of the Imam during the period in East Africa provided the foundation and pattern for the immigrants to the United States.

Even though Ismailis may lose touch with the ethnic cultures, such as Gujarati or Punjabi, from which they have come, their hope is that they will not lose touch with the religion. The guidance for assimilation in cultural and economic affairs is intended to enable the members of the Ismaili community to be successful in their new homeland while preserving their religion. Undoubtedly tensions exist between the generations – the parents were socialized in India or East Africa under one pattern and the children are growing up in the United States – but one result of the Ismaili principle is that any preservation of ethnic customs, such as language, cuisine, and dress, becomes a private matter in the home and not a source of conflict between the young people and religious leaders; that aspect has been removed from the religious prayer halls.

One part of the transformation has been the change in the position of women, who have an active part in the activities of Ismailis. Aga Khan III emphasized the education of women, and it is reported that he said that if he had a son and a daughter but only enough money to educate one, he would provide the education for the daughter. The Aga Khan schools and scholarships created in East Africa made provision for girls as well as boys. The Imam's injunctions to women were revolutionary for the time; his message to the women was: "Organize yourselves, resist and fight for your rights" (Aga Khan III, 1953:55–6). In a more direct statement, he said: "Oh my sisters, agitate. Leave no peace to men till they give you religious freedom . . . so that the habit of praying in public and self-respect and self-confidence become general amongst women. On that foundation of religious equality, you can then build social, economic, patriotic and political equality with men. I pray Allah Almighty to open the eyes of our benighted men and some of our still more benighted women" (1953:59). The result is that the women of the Ismaili community in East Africa and now in the United States are encouraged to engage in religious activities in the prayer halls, albeit in an area reserved for women, and to advance in education and the professions as far as they are able.

Ismaili commitment to education is seen in the 300 educational institutions they have established, which span the spectrum from preprimary schools to the Aga Khan University, which was opened in 1983 at a cost of 300 million dollars. At any given time, over 5,000 students are pursuing higher educational courses on Aga Khan scholarships (Aga Khan IV, 1983b:6). It is said that no Ismaili student fails to gain a good education for lack of finances. Aga Khan IV stresses that for both men and women two things are important, the soul and education, and he urges the young people of the community to get the best professional education available to them because that is something that can never be taken away from them. The young people are urged to seek to become the best students in the school or university they attend. The Ismailis do not establish separate secular schools in the United States or in other developed countries because that would tend to isolate Ismailis from the rest of society. Indeed, it is suggested that even the religious leaders of the community should not receive their education in isolation from other students lest they become parochial and isolated. The guidance and practical assistance available to Ismailis for professional education has long-term implications for the adaptation and success of the community in the United States.

Guidance is also given in economic affairs. The Imam and his grandfather before him have been astute businessmen, and no conflict is felt between spiritual authority and business activity because, as it is often observed, the Prophet himself was a businessman and emphasized both the spiritual and material aspects of an all-encompassing faith. A distinction must be made, however, between the personal wealth and business affairs of the Imam on the one hand and the guidance he gives to his followers in economic affairs and the financial and industrial institutions established to facilitate the economic development of the community on the other. The advice to emigrate itself has significant economic implications. The Imam has encouraged his followers to enter industrial and professional activities other than trade. In the various countries of the Third World the Imam stresses the need for an "enabling environment" that will permit creative economic activity to overcome the difficulties of the past and the problems of the world recession (Aga Khan IV, 1976:3–8; 1983b:5–8). The collective wisdom of a World Leaders' Forum meeting at Aiglemont resulted in a warning that the first few years of the 1980s would see continued recession, so the advice to the Ismailis was that they and their institutions should exercise discipline with regards to personal and business debt, and should avoid financial speculation. Thus, the guidance is specific, practical, and directed at the situation in each of the locations where members reside.

The economic advice is backed up by a sophisticated set of financial, health, and educational institutions that provide information and assistance aimed at the self-sufficiency of the Ismaili community. After the Golden Jubilee celebrations of 1937 the Aga Khan III undertook a program for economic growth and material well-being that continued with voluntary support following the Diamond Jubilee. The establishment of the Diamond Jubilee Investment Trust and the Jubilee Insurance Companies was an important development in providing resources for the Ismaili community in East Africa. Housing schemes supported by these investments enabled many families to purchase their own homes, and loans were given to enable Ismailis and others to enter business. Trusts and foundations now operate in a number of countries to provide technical expertise and financial assistance in such diverse areas as farming, agricultural industries, industrial and commercial real estate, and cooperative housing financing. The current Imam has taken steps to develop within the community a modern economic infrastructure that harnesses skills and expertise in order to diversify Ismaili ventures. In 1963 he established the Industrial Promotion Services group of companies, which operates in a number of countries and has launched over 100 enterprises, ranging from building materials and textiles to mining and tourism, which altogether employ some 10,000 people. The Industrial Promotion Services was established in Canada in 1974–5 to help Ismaili immigrants get into business and establish themselves in North America. The program was designed to provide information the person needs to establish a new business, to make him or her "bankable" in a new location, and – on occasion – to provide loans. It is administered from Canada, but it is available to Ismailis in the United States as well.

Other educational and social institutions are directed more specifically to developing countries, but Ismailis in the United States are related to them by their voluntary support. In 1982 the Aga Khan Health Services in Pakistan, India, Syria, Kenya, Tanzania, and Bangladesh consisted of some 200 health care units, including maternity homes, primary care centers, diagnostic clinics, dispensaries, and four general hospitals. The Aga Khan University, which was chartered in Karachi, Pakistan, is now a medical school for doctors and nurses associated with the Aga Khan Hospital of 721 beds in Karachi. Plans are underway to expand the work of the Aga Khan University into other areas, perhaps in other countries.

Much of the welfare work is supported through the Aga Khan Foundation, established in Geneva in 1967 with Aga Khan IV as chairman of the Board of Directors and his brother as the second of three members. The annual budget for the foundation rose from twenty million dollars in 1980 to seventy-five million in 1984, which puts it among the largest foundations worldwide in terms of annual expenditures. The foundation has branch offices in Pakistan (established in 1969), Britain (1973), Kenya (1974), India (1978), Bangladesh (1980), and Portugal (1983), and has independent affiliates in Canada (1980) and the United States (1981). Part of the welfare activities includes the advice to Ismailis in the United States that – if they can do so without jeopardizing their careers and futures in the United States – they should give of their time, professional expertise, and resources to help those in the Third World. The Aga Khan Foundation in the United States raised $1.6 million in 1984 for programs that were primarily in the Third World.

One result of the guidance of the Imam in these matters has been the remarkable transformation of the occupational profile and demography of the Ismaili community over the past fifty years. Rural Ismailis in Afghanistan, Iran, and Syria are at the early stages of the transformation, but the immigrants to the United States represent a relatively advanced stage of the modernization, urbanization, professionalization, and upward mobility. The rural support programs in Pakistan have made some impact on farm incomes, but it is easier to help a doctor from East Africa establish his family in the United States than to change the prospects for a farmer in the Northern Areas of Pakistan.

Growth in the United States

The growth of the Nizari Ismaili community in the United States from 600 in all of North America in 1965 to some 2500 in the United States in 1975 to between 25,000 and 30,000 in 1986 is astounding. One report indicates that the community grew by twenty-five percent in one year alone – 1985 (*The American Ismaili* Special Edition, January 1986:10). The early immigrants and students preserved their religious identity through their prayers and rituals at home and through contacts with the local councils in the regions from which they had come. In the early 1970s a few families began to meet in homes and apartments for Friday prayers and for special celebrations. Now, in most cities where significant numbers of Ismailis live, one or more centers have been formed, and each year sees more being established. The size of the groups varies greatly; the group in Chicago has about 4,000 people, the one in Houston has about 4,500. The center in Atlanta has grown in the past three years from about 150 persons to over 1,000, in part because of resettlement of people from Texas. In 1979 only eight centers had a population of over a hundred, but by 1981 twice that number had more than a hundred members.

Ismailis meet in jamat khanas, not called mosques, which are the focal points for the religious and social activities. The term "jamat khana," meaning a place of meeting or a prayer hall, is derived from the Sufi background in India. In 1975 Ismailis met in twenty local jamats, and by 1986 the number had grown to about 75.[5] The practice in the early years of settlement had been to lease properties for jamat khanas instead of owning them because of the flexibility that allows. The only center specially built and owned in the United States is the national council headquarters and jamat khana in New York. A new policy for five-year development adopted in 1986 changes that policy and proposes the construction of buildings in each of the other three regions – Chicago, Houston, and Los Angeles – and in a few other centers, perhaps in Dallas and Miami. The Aga Khan matches dollar for dollar the amounts raised for these buildings. A showcase jamat khana in North America, which cost ten million dollars, was dedicated in Burnaby, British Columbia, in August 1985; the buildings planned for the United States will not be so spectacular.

The prayer meetings in the jamat khana are the primary means of maintaining the specific Ismaili way of practicing Islamic observances (tariqa). The prayer halls in the larger centers are open every morning at about 3:45 and every evening at about 7:30, with the smaller centers open on a reduced schedule of only evenings or on two or three days a week. The Ismailis follow the five pillars of Islam, adding distinct esoteric interpretations of the pillars, which, however, do not replace the exoteric observances. They confess the unity of God and the prophethood of Muhammad, to which they add obedience to the Imam. They engage in obligatory prayers three times a day, and, like other Shi'a Muslims, they combine their congregational prayers, which they offer before sunrise, immediately after sunset, and between sunset and midnight. The standard prayers are now in Arabic. Some Ismailis also participate in early morning meditation and personal prayers (*du'a*), which are observed only in the jamat khanas before the recitation of the morning prayers. In the prayer halls a portrait of the Aga Khan is in a prominent place as a symbol of the authority of the present living Imam and of the community's reverence and affection for him. The order of the program varies, but may contain: the prayers – which are universally the same – reading of firman of the Imam (either one just received or earlier ones appropriate to the current situation), chanting of ginan, individual prayers, recitation of the Quran – especially on important days – and perhaps a lecture by a learned person. Generally, few people are able to attend morning prayers and meditation in the jamat khana. Evening prayers are held in the jamat khana every day, with higher attendance on Friday evenings and on the anniversaries of the birth of Muhammad, Ali, and the Imam and of the accession of the Imam. The prayer ends with the recitation of the names of the Imams one by one, celebrating a historical link between Muhammad and the Imam of the present time. A special service of forgiveness is occasionally held. At the end of the prayers, participants share in a sacred ceremony of sipping water blessed by the Imam. A traditional practice of donating food to the Imam is continued with the food then sold to those in the jamat so others can share in it, and the money donated to the Imam's treasury. The important languages of communication in the jamat khanas in the United States are English and Gujarati.

The Ismailis pay *zakat* and give other voluntary contributions, with the Iman as sole administrator. These include the obligatory tithes – called *dashond* from the Gujarati, originally set at one-tenth of one's income and now at one-eighth – voluntary offerings given at the time of special occasions, and contributions from estates of the deceased (Makarem, 1972:63). These offerings support the work of the jamats, regional councils, and institutions that serve a wide range of social welfare and development needs of the Ismailis in the United States.

The person in charge of the activities of the jamat khana is the *mukhi* (chief or leader), who is neither a priest nor a professional religious specialist. He is an active Ismaili who is chosen by the community and confirmed by the Imam to be leader of the local Ismaili jamat for a specified period on a voluntary basis; he is not a paid employee even at larger centers, where the mukhi gives full-time service. He decides the content of the prayer meetings and authorizes persons to lead in parts of the service. He does not interpret matters of faith – that is not his job – but he does act as the representative of the Imam to listen to the problems of members and to arrange for assistance as needed. The mukhi is "the most honorable person" and is the chief guest at social and religious occasions. He gives the prayer for blessing at weddings and other occasions, visits the sick, and performs ceremonies at birth and death. Beyond the local jamat, he serves as a member of the regional council. A female associate, called the *mukhiani*, usually but not always the wife of the mukhi, is responsible for women's activities and is a representative of the women. Her responsibilities are similar to those of the mukhi, but she does not lead the ceremonies. These two are assisted in overseeing the jamat khana by another official called the *kamadia* (deputy chief). The first national mukhi/kamadia conference in the United States was held in Dallas, Texas, on May 24–6, 1980, and 96 persons appear in the photograph of the occasion. Other training conferences for these volunteer officials are held regularly.

The role of the mukhi has undergone some changes in contemporary Western countries (Bhaloo, 1980:33–4). The traditional role of the mukhi was that of a wise advisor and father figure who could bring maturity and wisdom to the solution of the social problems of individuals in the community. The American scene, however, is very complex and places a greater emphasis on technology, which makes it difficult for those with responsibility for leading the local communities to be well-versed in the various fields and services where only the very specialized can speak with authority. The new leaders oversee an organization that can bring specialized resources to bear on the various problems people experience. It is a different type of religious leadership, with a tendency in the United States for these leaders to come from the younger, professionally trained group in the jamat khana, and much of the success of the community results from the volunteer service of these leaders. The Aga Khan gave direction in Pakistan in 1976: "During the years ahead, much work remains to be done. By far the most effective way for us to do this work is to continue to rely on the goodwill, the intelligence, the capability of spiritual children to do honorary work.... Those who are working in my Jamat and who are giving time for service to the Jamat and to the Imam, have my highest praise and my highest esteem."

A constitution for the Ismailis in the United States, approved by the Imam in 1977, established the administrative structure and the administrative procedures for the national and regional councils, associations, and institutions. The programs of the local jamats are administered through four regional councils: East (New York), Midwest (Chicago), Southwest (Houston), and West (Los Angeles). Members of the councils have responsibility for economics, youth, women, social, education, and health portfolios. Because the jamats are so widely separated, some of the large and rapidly growing centers are administered through administrative or liaison committees. Under the Regional Council East, there is a Miami Administrative Committee and the Atlanta Liaison Committee; under the Regional Council Southwest is the Dallas Administrative Committee; and under the Regional Council West there are the San Francisco and Seattle Liaison Committees. Jamats in Australia and New Zealand have an administrative committee that is affiliated with the Regional Council West.

The regional councils meet every two weeks to oversee the programs. Each region develops its objectives and strategies for the next year and presents them to the national council for approval along with a proposed budget of what is needed to accomplish the objectives. A quarterly review of the success of the programs in meeting their objectives provides the opportunity for evaluation and revision.

The national council for the United States has its headquarters in New York, but the president is a physician from Chicago. The council is made up of ten members, and the majority of members meet once a month as the Executive Committee. The full committee has a formal meeting twice a year. It is responsible for formulating long-term goals and strategies to be implemented for the next five years. At an Executive Committee meeting in New York on October 25–7, 1985, five long-term goals were established: (1) "A Jamat that understands, practices and can sustain and uphold our tariqa, and Islam:" with strategies suggesting staff and facilities for religious education, provision of teaching materials, the organization of parents, development of summer camp programs for young people, and adult education. (2) "A Jamat that is self sufficient with an emphasis on economic strength and excellence in their field;" the strategies are to provide financial assistance, counseling, job placement assistance, formation of self-help co-ops, and development of networks and business associations. (3) "A Jamat that is united, mutually supportive and provides skills and resources to the Jamat in the developing world." The perceived need to promote unity among the various regions and the jamats in the regions would be filled by an International Youth Exchange Program as well as a program for professional service abroad that would strengthen ties with the jamat in other countries. (4) A Jamat that produces "well-integrated contributing American citizens while maintaining our value system and pursuing healthy life styles." The strategies are to help immigrants know their rights and how to get assistance, to encourage participation of members as individuals in outside associations, clubs, and political groups, to counsel parents in parenting, and to help members understand Ismaili values and culture as these relate to Western society. (5) "Efficient high calibre Councils that relate to jamati needs." The national council approves the work of all the councils as they relate to these goals, and presents their budgets to the Supreme Council for approval. A journal of the national and regional councils, the *American Ismaili*, records their proceedings and is widely distributed within the community, but not outside.[6]

Associated with the national council is a Grants Council made up of seven persons who review all the budgets of the local centers and the regional councils and give advice about all the financial affairs of the institutions. The president of the Grants Council is second in authority to the national president. The Ismailia Association president is also on the national council and is responsible for the religious education of the community. The Aga Khan Aid Fund is administered by two committees, one in the East and the other for the West – these committees were active in the resettlement of immigrants from East Africa; now they are responsible for emergency financial assistance to members.

The jamat in the United States is under the Supreme Council, which is located in Nairobi and oversees activities in Europe, England, Canada, and the United States (including also Australia and New Zealand) – basically all the areas to which modern Ismaili immigration has taken place. Ismailis in Pakistan, India, Syria, and other traditional locations are administered through their own federal councils. Recently, a Leadership Conference has been instituted, made up of the presidents of all the national and federal councils, which meets with the Aga Khan. It has no constitutional authority, but it is a powerful body because it meets with the Imam, who appoints all the officers of the various councils and who has ultimate authority in all matters of the jamat.

All of these global activities require the sophisticated and efficient centralized organization that has developed in this century, centered in the international secretariat at Aiglemont in France. The secretariat oversees the programs of the institutions of the jamat, some of which are not directly related to the council structure. Prince Karim Aga Khan has made the point that the Ismaili Imamat has no single home country and so its activities are international and institutional as opposed to governmental (Aga Khan IV, 1982:4–5). The institutional system involves a combination of elements of modern mass communication with the traditional elements of personal communication that have maintained the relationship between the Imam and the individual member, so the Imam is in possession of a great deal of grass-roots information from many countries. The reorganization of the institutions in this century is both a cause and result in the transition of the Ismaili community from a number of relatively isolated and independent regional groups to a highly structured, unified, and successful religious community under the guidance of one individual. He has assembled a multinational staff, including Mr. Robert H. Edwards, who left the presidency of Carleton College in 1986 to join his secretariat in the area of health and education in the Third World. Through this network of administration, the Nizari Ismailis in the United States are linked with other Nizari Ismailis around the world.

The regional councils are organized with volunteers who have portfolios that mirror those of the volunteers in the local jamat khanas. The problems for the community are different in the West from those of Third World countries, so the programs and work of the councils have to be adapted to the new setting. They report to the Imam and to the president and secretariat of the Supreme Council now based at Nairobi. In any case of serious wrongdoing, proceedings for expulsion may be initiated by a local council, with provision for appeals to councils of superior jurisdiction, the final appeal being to the Imam. The local council of each jamat khana has unpaid volunteers in a hierarchy that oversees portfolios including health, education, the economy, and women's affairs. Questionnaires are circulated to give members the opportunity to identify their academic and professional backgrounds and to offer service in various areas.

Health

In Third World countries the health concerns are addressed by the establishment of clinics, hospitals, and medical schools; in the United States they are addressed by marshalling the resources of information and personnel of Ismailis to serve the community. In 1980 about 200 Ismaili health professionals were in the United States. National Health Fairs have been instituted in the larger jamat khanas, and at the first fair in Houston on February 13–18, 1981, an eighteen-member team performed 759 specialized medical examinations on 309 members of the jamat khana. At the second fair in Chicago on November 26–9 a total of 1,300 examinations were performed, and it was so successful that plans were announced to hold such medical fairs at regular intervals. A profile of the medical needs, health problems, and medical insurance was prepared from surveys, and a basic five-year plan was developed for implementation between 1982 and 1986 for education about diseases and basic health care. A burial scheme was developed to provide for funeral expenses, as was the custom in other countries, but now a life insurance program through an outside company has been provided. The concern for the material well-being of the community thus reaches from birth to the grave.

Education

It is estimated that over half of the current Ismailis are of school or university age. The educational portfolio is concerned with the secular educational opportunities of Ismailis. Excellence in education is stressed in the jamat khanas, and although it is not necessary to establish separate schools, finances are made available to students for college and professional school through the Aga Khan Aid scholarships. The local jamat khanas provide encouragement, information about opportunities, and financial support for their young people. A rough estimate is that as of 1983 one thousand Ismailis were studying in the colleges and universities in Canada and the United States, mostly in the professional programs of accounting, business, engineering, medicine, and the sciences (Nanji, 1983:159). One leader summarized the importance of education for a community whose members have moved across the continents: "Education is the international passport."

Economy

It has been noted that the guidance of the Imam covers both spiritual and material aspects; the economic portfolio is concerned directly with the economic development of the Ismailis. One instance of this concern is that the Imam advised members in Texas during the early 1980s that the oil boom would be temporary so they should not put all their financial resources there. Many practical applications of the concern can also be cited: An employer exchange program was developed to help people find jobs when the recession hit the area and unemployment rose; an Ismaili Businessmen's Association was formed to provide a forum for exchange of information about development trends and to promote more business within the community; local councils also organized seminars on immigration policy where members could get answers from experts to their questions about immigration. The major agency for economic development is the Industrial Promotion Services (IPS), which sends representatives to visit local communities and give information about their services, which include professional advice about business ventures and financial backing. Under the business program members can borrow with 100% IPS guarantee for projects up to $20,000, they can gain assistance in applying for financing under Small Business Administration programs for projects up to $250,000, and the IPS Venture Capital Investment Program will participate directly in larger business projects as an equity investor. Guidance in economic matters coming through the agencies of the Imam is substantial and practical.

Further examples of the support services can be seen in the economics committee of the southwest region, with an active program that includes a legal information center to provide data on business, immigration, financial, and other personal matters; the business information center, which directs members to appropriate agencies for management advice and loans; and the employment information center, which directs members towards potential jobs. When the recent downturn in the oil business caused many members in Texas to lose their jobs, a special resettlement program helped them relocate and find jobs, many in Atlanta. A cottage industries program helps persons develop small-scale home businesses. These centers are staffed by volunteers and meet at the jamat khanas, usually following the evening prayers.

Women

Women have a distinct organization as well as a specified leader in the mukhiani. Part of the work under the women's portfolio is to help the Ismaili parents to bring up children in the new setting. Mothers from the Third World, even well-educated professional women, do not bring up children the same way as in the United States. The task is to make a good transition to the new context without losing the values of the tradition or the religious identity of the family. Women are active in the administrative structure, with at least one position reserved on regional councils and at least one-third of the positions on the Supreme Council. Women also serve as officers of the councils.

Ismailia Association

The Ismailia Association is a separate international organization, parallel to the council structure, charged by the Imam with responsibility for the religious education and nurture of Ismailis. The associations in other countries train, authorize, and oversee persons who are capable of teaching about the Ismaili religion in a professional manner because they have been trained in religious education (*waezeen*). The resident, professional teachers travel to the various jamat khanas to give lectures or sermons (*waezes*). They have the equivalent of a Master of Arts degree in education. No professional waezeen have been trained and appointed for the United States, in part because the community is so young, but ten honorary waezeen were listed for the United States in 1983, three of whom are women. In addition, thirteen people – including three women – hold certificates to preach in the United States. In September 1984 a Waezeen Conference was held in Houston to review the qualifications status of the waezeen and to consider the implementation of a training program in the United States that would provide waezeen who can deliver the lectures both in English and in other languages.

The association also conducts daily religious education classes at the larger jamat khanas and publishes a journal, called *Roshni*. Growth in the program has been impressive. In 1979 only seventeen centers had facilities for a total of 290 students, but two years later thirty-one centers accommodated a total of 779 students, who represented a large majority of the 950 school-age Ismaili children in the United States. At a World Ismaili Association meeting in Paris in 1975, the Imam indicated that religious education should be interesting, entertaining, and a source of happiness. He also instructed that the Ismaili Association should have the goal of excellence: excellence in language, excellence in research, and excellence in documents produced for Muslims. He said, "There should be no second-rate work coming out of the Ismaili Association in the future." The various centers have volunteer teachers in the religious education program, and the association provides teacher-training programs and materials for them, such as the lending library of 1500 English and Gujarati books that opened in the New York center in 1983.

The resources and education for some of the teachers are provided at the Institute of Ismaili Studies, a separate institution founded in London in 1977. It offers a course of study for the Master of Arts degree in Islamic Studies in cooperation with McGill University, and some students go on to participate in the doctoral program in Islamic Studies at McGill. It also provides resources for degree programs in the University of London Institute of Education for training waezeen, as well as specialists in curriculum development and research and educational materials. In 1983 ten teachers from several countries were sent to the University of London for eighteen months to study curriculum development and textbook writing in preparation for a program to prepare a full graded curriculum and textbooks for their religious education program by the 1990s. The first textbooks for preschool children were published in 1986. A page on "The Holy Kaaba" provides an illustration of the content of the material:

> The Kaaba is a building in the city of Makkah.
> Makka is a famous city.
> Our Holy Prophet and
> Mawlana Ali were born there.
> Mawlana Ali was born inside
> The Kaaba itself.
> . . . .
> Prophet Ibrahim and Prophet Ismail are
> the ancestors of Prophet Muhammad,
> Mawlana Ali and our Imams.

Another duty of the Ismailia Association is the nurturing of new converts to the Ismaili faith. Only about two dozen Western converts are present in the jamat khanas, consisting primarily of those who have married into the community. The strong tendency is to marry inside the community, but Aga Khan III indicated that "As a good Muslim I have never asked a Christian to change her religion to marry me. For the Islamic belief is that Christian and Jew and, according to some, Zoroastrians and reformed Hindu Unitarians may marry Muslims and retain their own religion" (1954:274). A conversion kit has been prepared by the Ismailia Association to help those who decide to become Ismailis to understand the essentials of the religion. Leaders insist, however, that conversion of persons from other religions in the United States is not one of their goals.

A survey conducted by the national council in November 1981, which had a total of 518 respondents from across the country, reveals some basic information about members of the community. The largest percentage of members (40%) lived in Pakistan before they settled in the United States; the percentages for other countries are: Tanzania (13%), Uganda (13%), Canada (11%), Kenya (8%), India (6%), United Kingdom (5%), and Bangladesh (3%). Most (86%) had lived in the United States less than ten years, and many (44%) less than five years. Only 13% of the members had not changed their place of residence in the previous five years. Nevertheless, 74% reported a family income of more than $15,000. A third of the respondents indicated that they were self-employed, the most prominent occupations being: business management (20%), accounting (19%), engineering (16%), data processing (6%), and medicine/dentistry (4%). Persons between the ages of 25 and 54 constituted 84% of the respondents, and 72% had at least some college background. They reported a high level of satisfaction with their life and work and with the achievements and prospects of their children. A large number (74%) of those who responded indicated that regular attendance at jamat khana was very important for them, and 63% indicated that participating in other jamati activities was very important. Respondents were generally less positive about the quality of the service they received from the committees of jamati institutions (health, education, economic, marriage, youth, etc.). Responses to the questionnaire indicate that the Ismailis are young, well-educated, relatively prosperous, and concerned about the religious education of their children.

The Ismailis will continue to be a small minority of a minority in the United States, but the prospects for the community seem bright. The United States provides both the religious toleration and the economic opportunity needed for the type of "enabling environment" that the Imam encourages. The age demography of the recent immigrants leads to a prediction of growth through births, and it is certain that Ismailis will continue to be among the immigrants on quotas from India, Pakistan, Africa, and other countries. The guidance of the Imam combined with the educational and economic programs in Third World countries promote the skills are essential for the community's development. In times of the recent crises that have resulted in emigration, these same skills have helped to minimize the problems of resettlement in the United States. Through the community and its organizations, support for religious identity and for material welfare is available to Ismaili immigrants from many cultural settings. Hence, the emphasis in the group is upon its specific identity as a religious minority within the Muslim community. Its unity and focus, centered in obedience to the Imam's guidance and not upon regional–linguistic identity, has resulted in the muting of the signals of ethnicity among members, and the religious organization's modern resources thus provide support and services for members in a most efficient way not seen among immigrants who are provided for by ethnic organizations. The unity of this religious group is maintained by the Imam and his institutions, which form a "kind of religious multinational corporation" with a secretariat in Aiglemont and councils and associations around the world. The Aga Khan, with his wealth, sophistication, and personal contacts, serves as a world spokesman and Ismaili bridge to Muslim and non-Muslim leaders (Segal, 1983:22).

The Aga Khan, as the spiritual leader for a community mainly concentrated in the developing countries, but now growing in the West, has as a stated goal of many of his programs to develop a bridge between the developed and the developing worlds. The difficulty is to find and hold a "path of stability between democracy and totalitarianism, between Islamic belief and secularism, between the pressures of poverty and of wealth" (Aga Khan IV, 1985). The recent large-scale emigration to the United States and other Western countries is one result of that bridge-building, which through the development of intellectual underpinning and an effective social superstructure has facilitated this movement. Movement also takes place across the bridge in the other direction as the Aga Khan marshals the resources of the immigrant community through financial contributions and volunteer service to provide for social and economic projects in the developing countries where Ismailis live. The Ismaili community is a multinational and multiethnic religious minority that has developed an effective strategy for personal and group identity and progress in the midst of modern technology and the religious pluralism of the United States.

PART III

Profiles of religious organizations in metropolitan areas

In Chicago and Houston, immigrants from India and Pakistan – the doctors, engineers, and professionals of the "brain drain" – quickly join the other urban professionals of their economic status in the better neighborhoods and affluent suburbs. Their residential patterns more nearly coincide with the professional and economic distribution of the urban areas than with any ethnic or religious distribution. However, the networks that are established are not residential, but cut across the geographic boundaries on the basis of language, religion, or a newly created ethnic identity. The urban centers, as nuclei of their respective communities, also attract those who live in surrounding areas for special cultural and religious events – they come to Chicago from Milwaukee and northern Indiana, to Houston from Austin and even from New Orleans and Dallas. People travel long distances within the urban area for regular religious gatherings, and they travel from outlying cities to attend the special festivals.

The profiles of the Asian-Indian religious organizations in Chicago and Houston provide illustrations of the distribution of the religions and types of organizations, and they show how the various religious organizations develop and serve the immigrant community. Chicago and Houston have large populations of immigrants from India and Pakistan, but the urban areas are sufficiently discrete to permit an analysis of most of the relevant organizations. In Chicago, the second most populous city in the United States, 2.9 percent of the population is Asian Indian, but the city has lost nearly 11 percent of its overall population since 1970 (Bogue, 1985:373; Marlin, 1983:326). Houston, the fourth most populous city, has a 3.5-percent Asian-Indian population, and was the only one of the most populous cities to register a significant increase in overall population during the 1970s. Its growth has been due primarily to immigration, since its birthrate ranks very low among the cities (Bogue, 1985:372; Marlin,

1983:334). The Asian Indians in both of these cities suffered some dislocation during the recession of the early 1980s: Many from Chicago took part in the southern migration, and Houston is so dependent on the fortunes of the oil industry that the boom time of the late 1970s was followed by the bust of the 1980s. Thus, the two cities can be seen as representative, Chicago as an older, northern industrial city, and Houston as a rapidly growing, brash, high-tech city in the Sun Belt.

The profiles drawn in this study of Chicago by religion and of Houston through periods of development provide two ways of seeing the development of Asian-Indian religious groups. These two metropolitan areas were chosen to demonstrate both similarities and differences of adaptation because they are sufficiently unified that every significant religious group could be contacted and studied. It was not possible in the scope of this study to do a complete analysis of relevant groups in dispersed metropolitan areas such as New York or Los Angeles. Chicago and Houston are not idiosyncratic in their development, however, and they illustrate well the symbiotic development of religious groups in metropolitan areas.

CHAPTER 7

Asian-Indian and Pakistani religions in Chicago

Elderly grandparents come directly from villages or urban neighborhoods of India to Chicago or Houston for visits to their sons, who originally left that village or neighborhood in India for study in the university. They come to substantial apartments or suburban homes with all the comforts and conveniences modern technology provides, and they are given the respect – at least from their sons and daughters-in-law – traditional in Indian families. They rarely stay for long, however, because they miss the regular contacts with their extended family, the daily visits in homes of friends, the regular trips to the temple or mosque down the street, the entire network of associations that make a community in a village or neighborhood in India. They notice, more than their sons, and certainly more than their grandchildren, how shallow are the contacts within the Asian-Indian community. When one speaks about an urban community in the United States – the Asian-Indian Christians in Chicago or the Sikhs of Houston, for example – the use of the term "community" is merely metaphorical because, as Anne Fleuret suggests, the group of individuals spread throughout a major metropolitan center does not constitute a community similar to an African or Indian village (1974:28–35). The development of religious organizations with their regular meetings, the use of Indian languages and symbols, and the reinforcement of the Indian hierarchies of power and values are important efforts to create a true community among the dispersed immigrant groups.

In the late 1960s and early 1970s the cultural gatherings were simply extensions of Indian film series for university student groups. The monthly showings of Indian-language films were the major social gatherings for immigrants from India and Pakistan, a phenomenon that ceased when many families purchased video cassette players and Indian stores began to stock the films. The Indian grocery stores, which provided spices and foodstuffs from South Asia, were themselves important centers of

225

communication. Social and religious groups used the bulletin boards of the food stores to advertise their meetings and to communicate with potential participants. As the number of immigrants grew, the informal social gatherings expanded into All-India Cultural Associations, into regional–linguistic groups such as the Gujarati Samaj, the Bengali Association, or the Telugu Association, and into religious groups meeting first in homes and then finally in newly constructed temples or churches. Many streets with Indian grocery stores developed into shopping areas, such as Devon Street in north Chicago, to which South Asians come for its Indian restaurants, sari shops, Indian food stores, and appliance outlets. The bulletin boards of the food stores have mostly been replaced by Indian and Pakistani programs on local radio and television stations and by newspapers published for Asian Indians in English, Urdu, and Gujarati. The film showings have been replaced by extravaganzas in theaters, sponsored by cultural associations or commercial promoters and featuring film stars, musicians, and comedians. All of these programs and organizations help to provide the networks that establish the sense of community common in the Indian villages and neighborhoods of the immigrants' memory, but lost when they arrived in Chicago and Houston. The religious groups that develop and grow in the urban areas are important parts of the development of these networks; they meet basic religious needs and at the same time help to create and preserve personal and group identity in these new urban settings (See Figure 7.1).

The 1980 census numbered 32,567 Asian Indians in the Chicago area (USCen5::389).[1] At the time of the census, leaders of the Asian-Indian community in Chicago were estimating that the number was about 50,000. It is safe to say that by the middle of the 1980s the number of Indians and Pakistanis in the Chicago area was between 50,000 and 75,000.[2] Almost half of those immigrants born in India came to the United States between 1975 and 1980 (USCen6:Table 342), so it is remarkable that they have been able so quickly to establish religious organizations and to purchase or construct temples, mosques, gurdwaras, and churches. Although the splintering of old groups on the basis of personality conflicts, religious controversy, regional–linguistic differences, and sectarian distinctions continues apace, the professional level and economic success of the immigrants are the foundations for the formation of successful religious organizations of the various religious traditions.

Hindus

Two large Hindu temples in the South Indian style are being completed in the Chicago area, and it appears like a contest to see which will be

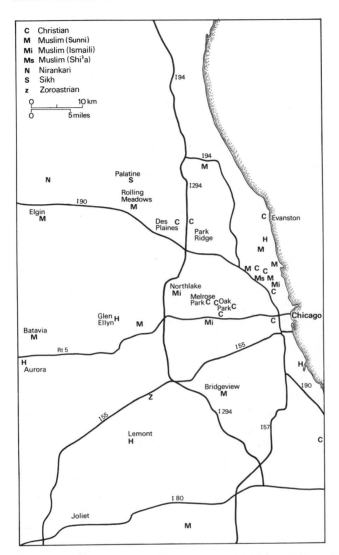

C   Christian
M   Muslim (Sunni)
Mi Muslim (Ismaili)
Ms Muslim (Shi'a)
N   Nirankari
S   Sikh
z   Zoroastrian

0   10 km
0   5 miles

I 94

Palatine
S
N
Rolling
Meadows
M
I 90
I 294
I 94
M
Elgin
M
Des   C   C
Plaines
Park
Ridge
C   Evanston
H
M
M C C   M
Ms M
Mi
C
Northlake
Mi
Melrose
Park C   C Oak
Park C
C
Glen H
Ellyn   M
Mi
C
Chicago
Batavia
M
Rt 5
I 55
H
Aurora
H
Bridgeview
M
I 90
Z
I 294
I 55
I 57
Lemont
H
C
I 80
Joliet
M

Figure 7.1. Locations of Asian-Indian and Pakistani religious centers in the Chicago area.

larger and more ornate. The general consensus is that the South Indians are the temple builders, and their style is typified by large complexes whose intricately carved temple towers stretch into the South Indian sky. The two temples in Lemont and Aurora, Illinois, at some distance from the main Asian-Indian population centers in the western and northern suburbs, duplicate the style of architecture as well as the rituals of the

South Indian temples. Some Asian-Indian observers complain about the building of temples because it has distracted the Hindu community from other important activities in the early stages of their settlement in Chicago, and they suggest that the Hindu community cannot support two temples of the same type. The fund-raising for their construction has been very successful, however, and it remains to be seen how successful the temples themselves will be in attracting the allegiance and participation of the Hindus. Even though both temples are being constructed by South Indians in the South Indian style, leaders urge all Hindus to visit the temples and to support them. Moreover, they hope that they will become pilgrimage sites for Hindus of the midwest.

The highest spot in Lemont is occupied by a church built by immigrants of an earlier time, with a spire that reaches into the sky. Just north of it, across the river on the opposite hill, the Hindu temple tower stands over the large complex being built by new immigrants. The Hindu Temple of Greater Chicago began as an organization in 1977 for the purpose of constructing an authentic Hindu temple and community center in the Chicago area, which in turn developed from a meeting of the leaders of various regional, cultural, and religious groups in that area. The original idea was that the temple and community center would encompass all the religious and linguistic groups and become a unifying force for all Hindus. It was decided that the main shrine in the temple would be for Rama because, as the hero of the epic *Ramayana*, he is known and worshipped all over India. There was as yet no major temple for Rama in the United States, so a temple to him would not be in competition with the temples to Ganesh (New York), Venkateswara (Pittsburgh), and Meenakshi (Houston). Plans, fund-raising, and search for property for a temple were undertaken, but no unified center existed for religious ceremonies; religious rituals and instruction were provided through the various associations and sects. Organizers in Chicago developed a mailing list of 8,000 people to contact for support for the temple, stressing the need to provide a religious center for the children of the second generation.

The project progressed slowly, and it was not until 1981 that a location was selected for the temple, on a twenty-acre hilly site north of Lemont that cost $300,000, and plans were approved by a general meeting in December. Construction was then delayed by difficulties encountered in getting permission from the DuPage County authorities for construction on the site. In the meantime, a center was needed for religious ceremonies. For a period during 1982–3 the Hindu Temple of Greater Chicago rented a hall from a Hindu businessman in Downers Grove and installed a shrine to Ganesh for worship (darshan) on the weekends for several months. A few major festivals were celebrated there, but local officials protested that the location had not been approved for religious services, so the Ganesh shrine was moved to a hall in Romeoville, not far from the temple site, for several months in 1983.

Funds for the temple project came from various sources. The Tirumala Tirupati Devasthanam assisted with plans for the temple and gave an interest-free loan for professional services and the supply of images (murtis) from India. The loan, in the amount of approximately $150,000, was divided between the Rama temple in Lemont and the Venkateswara temple in Aurora when the decision was made to build two temples in the Chicago area. Further support was supplied by banquets, a major fund-raising technique; some 600 people attended in April 1985 and about 800 in April 1986 to make contributions and pledges. Another loan was granted by the National Republic Bank of Chicago, an Asian-Indian minority bank, a millon dollars to finance the construction.

Groundbreaking for first phase of the complex at Lemont, a temple to Ganesh, was held on June 17, 1984, with N. T. Rama Rao, the Chief Minister of Andhra Pradesh, as the chief guest, and the dedication was held on January 25, 1985, when the paraphernalia were moved from Romeoville to the new temple. Some 3,000 people attended the ceremony. The full schedule of temple services with resident priests was begun. In April 1985 the contract for the principal temple, the one to Rama, was awarded, and the dedication (*Kumbhabhishekam*) was held on July 4, 1986, even though the temple building was not complete.

The Rama temple honors the three major Vaishnava deities, with the image of Rama in the central shrine and those of Venkateswara and Radha-Krishna in the side shrines. The great care that has gone into this building is evidenced by the facts that the architect is the chief temple architect for the Tamil Nadu state government, and twenty-one craftsmen from the government school at Mahabalipuram worked for four months to prepare the temple towers. One of the Ganesh images from the first temple was moved to the Rama temple, and the Ganesh temple itself was converted into a Shiva temple housing a Shiva *lingam*, with one of the images of Ganesh remaining in that temple. Thus, the complex contains both a Vaishnava and a Shaiva temple as an indication that it is intended for all Hindus.

Despite the attempt to include people from all areas in the planning and support of the temple, the leadership has come primarily from South Indians. Of the twenty-five board members and chairpersons listed for the 1986–7 year, ten, including all but one of the officers, are originally from Andhra Pradesh, and eight more are from Tamil Nadu, Mysore, or Kerala. The difficulties encountered in developing the plans and in raising the funds for the temple indicate how hard it is to unite people from the various regions and sects in support of one project.

The temple employs Brahmin priests (pujari) to conduct the rituals, and for a time two priests with very different backgrounds were active

Dedication of the tower of the Rama Temple in Lemont, Illinois

there. Neither had formal association with the Tirupati temple, and both were appointed because of their acquaintance with members of the governing body. The younger priest, forty-three years old, came to the United States from Kerala as a student in 1961, completing a Ph.D. in metallurgy at the University of Minnesota in 1971. While working in Indianapolis and serving as president of the Gita Mandal there, he developed a deep interest in religious matters that led him to affiliation with the International Society for Krishna Consciousness. Pursuing this interest, he returned to India for a study of the sacred texts and spent some time at the ISKCON temple in West Virginia. He is fluent in Malayalam, Tamil, and English. In addition to the basic rituals at the Rama temple, he conducted Friday evening classes for the children and lectured on Vedic scriptures for the adults on Sunday. He is one of the very few immigrants who has changed careers to become a temple priest in the United States, but after a few months he left the temple to return to work with ISKCON.

The older Brahmin had served as a priest in Varanasi in India for forty years before he came to the United States; he then worked as an independent priest for several years before being invited by a member of the committee to come to Chicago to serve the temple. He is fluent in Tamil, Telugu, and Kannada, but not in English. A Punjabi Brahmin served the temple for a few months after the first priest left for West Virginia. It is becoming more difficult to get visas for priests from India, so the selection of priests who know all the temple rituals (agamas) and who can explain them in English to the young people is also increasingly difficult.

The temple is now open for individual worship every day; the majority of visitors are South Indians. The priest performs the regular rituals for those who come as well as for those who arrange for the rituals by paying a fee. The temple publication, *Ramalaya Samachar*, lists the fees for the various rituals, beginning with a simple ritual (arti) for five dollars. The more elaborate rituals are performed in the temple or in private homes, to which the priest will travel. The fee for a Satyanarayan puja at the home on a weekend is $125; the fee for a wedding at the temple, including the facilities and the priest, is $300. Approximately 300 to 400 people visit the temple on an average weekend, and when a major festival is observed, over 1,000 attend. In addition to religious ceremonies, the temple provides for numerous activities. Some of the devotional and study groups meet at the temple, and the temple hosts a series of visiting lecturers; classes in Hindi and Sanskrit are conducted each week at the temple by a former professor of Agra University; a Hindu Heritage Children's Day Camp was conducted in June 1985 at McCormac Junior College in Elmhurst for over a hundred children. After a relatively slow start, the construction of the temple and the development of programs have proceeded rapidly. Plans for the future include a community center and guest houses.

The delays caused by internal dissension over the location and plans for the temple combined with external problems related to governmental approval led to a division and to the construction of a second South-Indian temple in Aurora. In the fall of 1983 a meeting with about thirty-five persons present was held to discuss the problems that were delaying the construction of the Rama temple. A group of Telugu professionals wanted to select another location and move with more dispatch. The result of that meeting and of a subsequent one in June 1984 was that a group was formed that decided to build separate a Sri Venkateswara (Balaji) temple on a twenty-acre site at the edge of Aurora. The site, valued at $240,000, was donated by twelve individuals on October 12, 1984. The same group pledged fifty additional adjacent acres as collateral for a bank loan to finance the construction of the temple. They mailed 35,000 brochures to raise money and hosted fund-raising banquets, and as a result obtained a construction loan from the State Bank of India (Chicago Branch) and donations that together totalled 1.95 million dollars toward the projected cost of more than 2.5 million dollars for the completed project. The board and chairpersons of the new group are made up of fifteen persons from Andhra Pradesh, six from Tamil Nadu, Kerala, and Mysore, and three from Maharashtra and Uttar Pradesh in the north.

A house on the property was converted into a temporary temple and the rituals were begun on October 13, 1984. About twenty-five people regularly visited the temporary shrines installed in the house on the property before construction had begun on the new temple. Considerable opposition to the construction of a Hindu temple near Aurora was overcome, and the appropriate approval was granted by the council. The groundbreaking for the temple was held on May 11, 1985, with 100 families present and Moraji Desai, the former Prime Minister of India, as the chief guest. The completed building, housing nine separate shrines, is one of the largest Hindu temples in the United States. The image of Sri Venkateswara (Balaji), the manifestation of Vishnu for the age of decline (Kali yuga), is in the main shrine; other shrines house the images of Lakshmi, Brudevi and Sridevi, Shiva, Parvati, Ganesh, Andal, Subramanya, Satyanarayana Swami, and Hanuman. The loan from the Tirumala Tirupati Devasthanam provided the services of eighteen artisans (*silpis*) from India to work on the construction. The dedication ceremony was held on June 22, 1986. Future plans call for the construction of visitors' cottages as a part of the temple complex, similar to those at the Sri Venkateswara temple at Tirupati.

The rituals and programs of the Balaji temple are similar to those of the Rama temple. The business manager of the temple is a widower who retired in 1981 after twelve years in an electric company in Boston and he accepted the invitation to come to Chicago to assist with the foundation of the temple. Two brothers from Andhra Pradesh were hired as priests with the assistance of the business manager of the Ganesh temple in New York, where the younger brother had worked for several months as priest. They receive a small stipend and living expenses. The temple arranges for daily rituals in the temple and for special rituals (Satyanarayan pujas, sacred thread ceremonies, marriages) in the temple and in homes, and an astrologer is associated with the temple to provide horoscopes for devotees. A center for Hindu dharma and a library are included in the temple plans for the future. A regular publication, *Sri Venkatesa Nivedika*, carries news, religious articles, and announcements for the Hindu community. The temple's income for the year ending September 30, 1986, was $887,387.

These two temples are close neighbors in location, design, regional identification, and programs. The success of the fund-raising activities of both may indicate that the community is sufficiently large to support two such temples and some Hindus actually generously support both. While they are South Indian in style and basic support, each group claims to have an authentic temple for all Hindus of the midwest. Although the Rama temple now seems to claim a broader support, the future of both temples is uncertain; they have great potential but also serious difficulties.

The Akshar Purushottam Swaminarayan temple in Glen Ellyn, in a converted Veterans of Foreign Wars building, was the first Asian-Indian Hindu temple in Chicago. The Swaminarayan organization has opted for a strategy of group formation and primary personal identity based on the affirmation of regional, linguistic, and sectarian ties. (For a more complete description of Swaminarayan Hindus, see Chapter Five.) In 1974 and 1977 Narayanswarupdas Swami, popularly called "Pramukh Swami," visited Chicago and gathered a group of followers who began to meet monthly in homes. He visited again in 1980, and the devotees began to rent halls for monthly meetings. During this period a temple was constructed in Flushing, New York, with the assistance of members from across the country. In May 1983 the Chicago group purchased the VFW hall and began to have regular weekly meetings in the redecorated temple. Several thousand people were present for the formal installation of images of Swaminarayan and Gunatitanand Swami in June 1984. A non-Brahmin immigrant has been assigned by Pramukh Swami to be caretaker and priest for the temple. The temple is open daily for visits and special services and regular daily rituals are performed for the images, but the major gatherings for worship in this tradition are on weekends. On a regular Sunday evening approximately 175 people attend. Once a month a special convocation attracts between 400 and 500 people; the major festivals attract 700 to 1,000. Each Sunday afternoon language, music, and religious education classes are conducted for boys and girls. Most of those who attend are Gujaratis, and the meetings are conducted in that language.

The temple has a shrine of Radha-Krishna, however, so some non-Gujaratis come to the temple for their family and life-cycle rituals. The basement of the temple is especially decorated for marriages and baby showers for members of the Hindu community. Some Hindus from

northern India are attracted to the services of the temple and become
followers of Swaminarayan, even though the langauge difficulties remain.
Participation in the temple has grown steadily since the temple was dedicated, and a proposal is being discussed for the purchase of a larger
property.

A much smaller group of the International Swaminarayan Satsang Organization meets once a month in homes. (For a description of the different groups in Swaminarayan Hinduism, see Chapter Five.) The group,
which is loyal to the acharyas in Ahmedabad and Vadtal, arranges for
large gatherings in one of the park district halls when Acharya Tejendraprasad and the sadhus visit from Ahmedabad. Another group that
gathers periodically is affiliated with the Yogi Divine Mission and has
meetings when the leaders of that group visit Chicago.

The International Society for Krishna Consciousness already had a
temple in the Chicago area when most of the immigrants arrived. (For a
discussion of the International Society for Krishna Consciousness, see
Chapter Four.) The Hare Krishna center was then in Evanston, but
difficulties with the local authorities made it necessary for them to move.
In 1980 the group purchased a three story Masonic Temple in north
Chicago near the lake and converted it into a Hindu temple. During the
period before other Hindu temples were constructed, the Hare Krishna
temple attracted many Asian-Indian immigrants. Approximately twenty-
five devotees live in the temple – all but one are Americans. About 1980,
a Gujarati devotee came to Chicago to assist in making contacts with the
Asian-Indian community. The national magazine is mailed to 8,000 people in the Chicago area. The mailing list of the Chicago temple is 5,000,
and some 500 people are members. ISKCON advertises heavily in the
Asian-Indian newspapers, and perhaps eighty percent of the participants
in the temple programs are Asian Indians. Navayogendra Swami, the
leader of the ISKCON group in Chicago, visits the homes of many Asian
Indians, and they actively support the programs of the temple – all twenty-
eight sponsors of a Gita Yagna, a special ritual associated with the reading
of the *Bhagavad Gita*, in September 1985 were Asian Indians. The regular
Sunday meetings attract between 300 and 500 people, and the celebration
of Krishna's birthday in September 1985 attracted an estimated 8,000
people, mostly Asian Indians. The street in front of the temple was
blocked off and filled with worshippers so that, as one Indian woman
remarked, "It seemed just like in India." The temple arranges regular bus
tours to their center in West Virginia to enlist the support of the Asian
Indians in that building project. However, the construction of authentic
Hindu temples in Chicago may well cause a decrease in the participation
of Asian Indians in the activities of the Hare Krishna temple.

The oldest Hindu tradition in Chicago, however, did not begin with either ISKCON or the new immigrants. Those who bring Hinduism to Chicago follow in the footsteps of Swami Vivekananda, who came to the World Parliament of Religions held in conjunction with the Chicago World's Fair in 1893. His legacy is the Vivekananda Vedanta Society of Chicago, which was founded by a Ramakrishna monk from India in 1930 in a Masonic Temple downtown. The current home of the society is in Hyde Park in a mansion purchased in 1966. Leaders stress the fact that their mission is to present Vedantic philosophy for Westerners; therefore, their appeal is very limited. Fewer than half of the fifty people who attend the Sunday meetings, conducted in English, are Asian Indians. The society's emphasis on meditation and philosophy has not been as attractive to recent immigrants as has the emphasis on ritual in other centers. Previously the swamis of the center wore Western-style suits similar to those of Catholic priests, but now they wear the saffron robes more familiar to Asian Indians. Even though few Asian Indians visit the center, its influence is significant because Swami Bhashyananda, who was assigned by the leaders of the Ramakrishna Math and Mission in Calcutta to be the person in charge of the Chicago society, is a prominent lecturer and spokesman for Hindu philosophy. He regularly lectures for Vedanta Societies as well as for other Hindu groups across the country. In addition, one of the Western monks teaches classes once a month for a Hindu group that meets in Vernon Hills.

Swami Bhashyananda established a monastery and retreat center in 1971 in Ganges Township, Fennville, Michigan, on a farm that in 1987 consisted of 101 acres. The private buildings are residences for Swami Bhashyananda, monks, aspirants, and visitors, and the public buildings contain a shrine room and auditorium, a library, a bookstore, and a museum. The museum contains memorabilia associated with Swami Vivekananda and exhibitions of Indian art and religious artifacts. Even though few Asian Indians in Chicago are actually affiliated with the Vivekananda Vedanta Society, some groups plan tours for adults and children to Ganges Township.

In addition to these large organizations, many small Hindu groups meet for study, singing of devotional songs, and religious education classes for children. They meet in homes, rented halls, and now in the newly constructed temples, with programs generally conducted in the regional Indian languages. As one leader commented, "If there is a language, there will be a group," and he estimated that fifteen or twenty small devotional groups meet in Chicago. The groups are transitory because they move from place to place, leadership changes, and some are short-lived. Nevertheless, they keep the religious activities close to the people – in the homes and neighborhoods and in the Indian languages (although religious education classes for children are generally conducted in English).

The two Sat Kala Mandirs are groups that meet once a month for two hours to sing devotional songs (bhajans) in Tamil. One group meets the third Saturday of each month in the Rama Temple at Lemont with between thirty and fifty people participating. A second group of about the same size meets in homes because they live too far from the temple. These two Tamil groups have met together in Bolingbrook and in Buffalo Grove for singing and fellowship.

The Gita Mandal is a stable group which has met over several years for a sustained study of the *Bhagavad Gita*. It was established in 1979 following the visit of a famous lecturer from India, who suggested that the Hindus form a Gita study group. Twenty to twenty-five families, mostly Gujaratis, have been meeting in private homes on the second Friday of the month since that time. The programs last for three hours and include meditation, chanting of verses from the Gita, an interpretation of a few verses, and a period of social fellowship. As of 1986, the group had finished one round of study of the text. The leader of the group is a Brahmin who also conducts classes in a local community college. He is one of the few independent Brahmins in the Chicago area who also performs marriages, Satyanarayan pujas, funerals, and other rituals for the Hindu community, although temple priests now perform most of these rituals.

Many of those who participate in the Gita Mandal also support the Hindu Culture Center, which has conducted a Hindu Sunday School for ten years. The Sunday School now meets every other Sunday morning at the Lakewood School in Park Forest. The curriculum is in English, and it follows the major festivals of the Hindu calendar. Classes are also offered in classical Indian music and dance. A subscription pays for the rent of the hall. The mailing list of the Hindu Culture Center serves 400 families, and its membership is about 100, but only about twenty-five children and thirty adults participate in the Sunday School.

Another Geeta Mandal serves a Malayalee group that meets on the fourth Sunday of each month. They have met in the Hollywood Community House in Brookfield, but members are spread throughout the western suburbs. The programs of this group are in English because, they explain, the purpose of their getting together is to provide some training and background for their children, who are not fluent in Malayalam. Approximately fifty families are members of the Geeta Mandal, but on occasions of special festivals about 400 people attend.

The Hindu Satsang Mandal is a Hindi group that meets on the last Sunday of the month in the Lombard District Park Hall in order to sing devotional songs (bhajans) and have religious education. One leader remarked, "You can get a good education only in your mother tongue." Approximately fifty people attend. Additionally, the Hindu Society of Metropolitan Chicago (to be distinguished from the Hindu Society of Greater Chicago that is constructing the Rama temple) meets in a religious gathering on the second Sunday of the month, and also sponsors an annual social program. These devotional and study groups are locally organized and, even though some were formed at the urging of leaders from India, they are not affiliated with organizations or sects in India, so their programs, successes, and failures depend upon local leadership.

Other Hindu organizations have formal affiliation with religious organizations and leaders in India. The Manav Seva Mandir (Human Services Temple) of Chicago is a Gujarati organization formed at the urging of Devendra Viyaj, who is the founder of the Manav Mandir Trust at the temple of the goddess Ambalji in Ahmedabad. He visited Chicago for the first time in 1975, and on his next visit in 1983 the organization was formed. The goal of the organization is to stop the process of division among Gujaratis by profession, caste, and sect and to build a temple and community center in which all relevant images of Sanatan Hinduism will be worshipped. Leaders of fifteen Gujarati cultural and religious organizations attended a meeting in 1983 to discuss the possibility of an ecumenical temple, and a fund-raising drive was begun.

Each year the group sponsors a seminar for several days given by a famous religious speaker from Gujarat: In 1984 Krishnashankar Shastri lectured on the *Sri Bhagavata* for seven days in a high school auditorium in Skokie; in 1985 Goswami Indirabetiji, a renowned woman lecturer, conducted a ten-day seminar at the Lawrencewood Theater in Niles; in 1986 Morari Bapu conducted a seminar on the *Ramayana*. Over a thousand people attend these lectures. Goswami Indirabetiji is a leader of the Vallabhacharya branch of Vaishnavism (Pushti Marg), and following her visit in 1985 one group of the Manav Seva Mandir began to meet in the Park District Hall in Glenview for worship and singing according to the Vallabhacharya tradition.

Approximately a hundred people participate in the Vallabh Priti Seva Samaj, which meets on the first Sunday of the month. A second group meets on the second Friday of the month in homes under the title of the Jay Bhagavan Bhakti Mandal, with approximately seventy-five people attending. The Manav Seva Mandir is a Gujarati regional–linguistic group. Although Gujaratis make up a large percentage of the Asian-Indian population in Chicago – perhaps as much as forty percent – the failure of the Manav Seva Mandir to gain broad support from many groups indicates how difficult it is to unite even persons from the same regional–linguistic group into an ecumenical Hindu organization.

The Shakti Mandir was established in 1983 to build a temple for the goddess. The leadership is Gujarati, but participants include those from other language areas. They meet each week in a high school in Findley Park, and at the times of the festivals of the goddess have large gatherings to which they attract four to five hundred persons.

The Devotional Associates of Yogeswara (Swadhyah) is an organization of followers of a religious teacher from Bombay, P. P. Pandurang Adhavale. His Bhagavan Institute in Bombay carries out extensive religious and social activities in villages in India. He visited followers in Chicago for the first time in 1978 and formed the organization, and in the 1980s has visited almost every year. The group has been successful in attracting the participation of immigrants who were not followers of Adhavale in India. Six groups meet in Chicago, all in rented park district halls. The meetings are in Gujarati before a shrine of Krishna, and they consist of videotaped lectures by Adhavale, a presentation by a leader, some songs (kirtans), announcements, and perhaps a presentation by the children in English. The group that meets at the Lombard Park District Hall on Saturday nights has usual attendance of about thirty-five adults and twenty-five children. They conduct a Children's Cultural Center for about forty children on Sunday mornings at the Lombard Park District Hall. Another, larger group meets in Des Plaines, which joins with the Lombard Park group to sponsor a summer camp in northern Indiana for the children. A large international meeting was held at Allahabad, India, in March 1986, and many of the leaders attended the meeting. Very few of the Hindu groups sponsored by immigrants have tried to attract Westerners, but this group is beginning to make an effort to propagate the teachings of Adhavale. They regularly invite American Christians to celebrate the birth of Jesus Christ with them as part of their universal religious commitment.

Other small groups loyal to various religious teachers meet in Chicago. The Satya Sai Baba group has about sixty members, most of whom are Asian Indians, and they meet every Sunday for devotional songs in English. An attempt was made to establish a branch of the Sri Aurobindo Society in July 1984, when the general secretary of the society from Pondicherry visited Chicago on his tour of American cities, but the group is very small. The Chinmaya Mission, on the other hand, is more active because of the leadership of Chinmayananda, who has become a leader among Hindus. He was a featured lecturer at the dedications of both the Sri Venkateswara Temple and the Rama Temple.

The various branches of Hinduism are not exclusive, so some Hindus participate in more than one organization. An individual may be a member of a bhajan group, teach in a Sunday School, attend the monthly meetings of a sectarian group, and go to the temple for special annual festivals or life-cycle rituals. Some of the regional groups join with the religious groups in sponsoring activities. The Federation of Gujarati Associations in North America, for example, sponsored the lecture tour of Morari Bapu. When a group plans a festival, members expect and receive both support and attendance of Hindus of other religious and linguistic groups. One small local group that encourages cooperation among the various Hindu groups is the Vishwa Hindu Parishad in Chicago. Its membership is only 150, and its primary activities are to arrange for religious lectures and festivals in conjunction with other groups and to publish an annual directory of Asian-Indian religious groups. During the 1970s when the Hindu community was small, the Vishwa Hindu Parishad was active in planning religious and cultural events, such as a major concert by Ravi Shankar in 1976, but in the 1980s the initiatives have been toward the development of temples and sectarian and regional–linguistic groups. It remains to be seen whether the emphasis will return to cooperative activity among the Hindu groups, and, if so, what forms it will take.

Jains

The Jain Society of Chicago was established in 1972 with only three families, but it now has 350 registered family members from a community of over 1000. The sectarian differences within Jainism have been ignored, so the group remains united. The Jains were originally concentrated on the north side of Chicago, but since 1980 they have moved to the suburbs,[3] with the heaviest concentrations in Des Plaines and Mount Prospect. Monthly meetings are held in homes, with between 50 and 100 persons in attendance. The programs are in Gujarati, native language of ninety percent of the Jain community in Chicago. Only Asian Indians attend the meetings, even though two or three Jains have married Americans. The Jains meet for special home festivals on auspicious occasions, such as when a family moves into a new house. They rent halls for the major festivals at which several hundred Jains will gather. In August 1985 the Jains sponsored a Paryusan Parva at the Arndt Park Hall in Des Plaines, at Devonshire Hall in Skokie, at a Veterans of Foreign Wars hall in Bensenville, and at Lynn Tech High School in Chicago. The rituals and meetings are conducted by laymen because no Jain religious specialists live in Chicago. They have a fund to purchase land or a building for a Jain temple, but they have not located an appropriate site. In 1984 a Chicago chapter of the Jain Social Group was formed by fifty-five member families to provide free medical services for Jains who have no insurance, to fund scholarships for Jain students, and to support welfare projects in India. The Jain community is growing steadily, and so far it has been able to avoid division.

Sikhs

The Chicago Sikhs are one of the few Sikh groups that have remained united through the turmoil created by the Amritsar incident. Good lay leadership, a respected Granthi and a beautiful facility have enabled the Sikh society to make progress at a time when other Sikh groups have been divided and distracted. Even in this gurdwara, however, dissention has appeared, as some Sikhs boycotted an election in the spring of 1986 over the issue of whether a person who does not wear a turban and beard should be elected as a president and represent Sikhs in an official capacity.

The first Sikh meetings in Chicago took place in 1958 at the University of Chicago, and a society was formed in 1961 under the name Sikh Study Circle. For the first few years the meetings were held in the basements of members' homes, and later in the Lombard Park District Hall. The newly reorganized Sikh Religious Society of Chicago purchased a four-acre site in Palatine in 1974 and started construction of a new building for a gurdwara in 1976. At that time 200 members were active; by 1986 the number of members grew to over 500. The annual membership fee of twenty-five dollars gives members the right to vote for officers and in the business meetings. It is estimated that 1,000 Sikh families live in Illinois, northern Indiana, and Wisconsin.

A small Sikh Dharma (3HO) group has a residence in north Chicago, but only three or four American Sikhs are in residence, and it has no impact on the Asian-Indian Sikh community in Chicago. (For a discussion of Sikh Dharma, see Chapter Four.)

The Sikhs were the first Asian-Indian religious group in Chicago to construct their own building – the gurdwara in Palatine, which the community occupied in 1981. The Sikh architect who designed it said that he incorporated elements of Sikh tradition in the 82-foot-square building: It has doors in all four directions to indicate that it is open to all; the clear windows open out on a pastoral setting to emphasize openness and harmony with nature; the construction of concrete and plain wood is symbolic of the simplicity of the religion. The ground floor houses offices, meeting rooms, a kitchen, and an open hall for meals. The upper floor is the carpeted prayer hall. In 1985 the society acquired additional land to be used for parking, classrooms for children, and a community hall.

A full-time religious specialist (Granthi), whom the people refer to as their priest (even though Sikhism does not have priests), came from India in July 1980 to serve the gurdwara. He had been a Granthi in India for twelve years and is married with three children. Because of difficulties that delayed his obtaining permanent resident status until 1986, his wife and children remained in India and he was unable to visit them. He enrolled in a program at Harper College to study English as a second language when he arrived from India. He leads the regular Sunday services at which approximately 400 people are present; three or four times that number attend on major festival days. Following the service of hymns, readings and lectures, a common meal is served to all the worshippers by a volunteer family. Classes are conducted in the gurdwara for twenty or thirty children. The Granthi also goes into homes where he is invited to sing hymns (kirtans) and teach the children. He also performs the life-cycle rituals, but, because of the relatively young age of families in the Sikh community, he has been called on to conduct only ten marriages and seven funerals in five years. Special services are held on Saturday evenings in homes at a distance from the gurdwara, and the Granthi has a set schedule to attend these services. A summer school is conducted to teach the Punjabi language to about thirty children, and a summer camp was held at Palatine in 1985. Other children attend summer camps in Michigan and Pennsylvania.

The crisis in the Punjab has led to an increased attendance and activity in the Chicago gurdwara. The Granthi and the Chicago members actively participated in protests in Washington and New York, and members of the society established a fund to support victims of the violence in India. The leaders have contacted representatives of the news media and academic institutions in an attempt to overcome the negative publicity Sikhs received following the rioting and the assassination of Prime Minister Indira Gandhi. They were offended by the announcement of a lecture at a Big Ten university in 1986 entitled "Sikh Terror and World Peace," and they attended to protest. They have been frustrated in the attempt to gain the sympathy and support of the American public. In October 1984 the society held a large reception for Senator Percy to inform him of their interpretation of events in the Punjab.

At meetings in the gurdwara, it appears to a visitor that about forty percent of the men wear the traditional beard and turban, but now the community as a whole has distanced itself from the Hindu community in attitude and also in the dress of the women and through the use of turbans by more men and boys. A few Sindhis continue to worship at the gurdwara, but most no longer attend. People at the gurdwara are anxious about relatives and friends in Punjab and troubled about the future of the Sikhs in India, but the activities of the Sikhs in Chicago seem to be flourishing.

Chicago is the national headquarters for the Nirankari Universal Brotherhood Mission, a religious group that rejected the standard conventions and rituals of the Sikhs and separated in 1929. It is now a religious organization completely separate from the Sikhs and claims 2,000 members in twenty centers in the United States (Melton, 1985:82 Supp.). The group was established in Chicago in 1973 and attracts a small following, primarily of people from the Punjab. For several years they met in a house in Des Plaines that had been converted to a meeting hall, and in May 1986 they moved to a renovated church building in Carpentersville, which will be the new national headquarters. Only about sixty people attend the weekly Sunday meetings.

Muslims

A 1987 listing of locations for Sunni Muslim Friday prayers in Chicago listed twenty-five places.[4] Estimates of the number of Muslims in Chicago vary widely; one leader suggested 100,000, excluding the Black Muslims, but another set the number at about 250,000 Muslims. Estimates of the number of Indo-Pakistani Muslims also vary widely, from 15,000 to 150,000.[5] Arif Ghayur estimated the number of people of Pakistani origin in the United States at 96,537 in 1984, which would suggest a number closer to the lower range of estimates for Chicago (1984:114). The mosques are open to all, but individual mosques can be identified by the ethnic group of the leaders and the majority of the participants as Arab, Indo-Pakistani, Albanian, European, American Black, or Yugoslavian. For example, the Northbrook Islamic Cultural Center serves the Yugoslavian Muslims, whereas the Mosque Foundation on the southside serves the Arabs. Several of the centers serve primarily the Indo-Pakistani Muslims.

The Muslim Community Center is the largest Muslim organization in Chicago, and it has been the parent organization for several neighborhood centers that serve Indo-Pakistanis. It was established in 1969 and purchased its first building, on North Kedzie Avenue in Chicago, in 1972. Arson in a nearby building in 1981 led to the purchase and conversion of a second building, in north Chicago, for use as a mosque and educational center. Several new groups have been generated from this center, but the paid membership as of 1986 was over 900, including 410 families and 62 individuals. It is estimated that the center actually serves a community of 10,000. There is a resident Islamic scholar who was trained at Deoband in India as well as a business manager and other officers. The building is open five times a day for prayer, and between 500 and 600 people, primarily men, attend the Friday noon prayers. The prayers are conducted only in Arabic, but meetings and lectures are conducted in Urdu and English as well.

Islamic education for the children and youth is a priority for all the Muslim groups, and one leader commented that Muslims become active in the center when their children become adolescents because they want to reinforce their Muslim identity. The Sunday School of the Muslim Community Center operates in two shifts, accommodating about 400 students whose parents pay a tuition. An evening school that meets four days a week enrolls 50 students. During the summer, a full-time summer school is conducted for about 75 students, and a youth camp is held in Wisconsin for 130 campers by 20 adult teachers. One of the camp leaders was on the staff of the Boy Scouts both in India and in the United States. The classes for the children and young people are conducted in English. Quranic lectures for adults are conducted in both English and Urdu – the Urdu program attracts the larger audience. A Sunday class for the study of Arabic has about forty adult students. The leader of the mosque gives the sermons and lectures in the mosque and performs marriages and funerals, and also administers Muslim personal law and adjudicates disputes.

Thirty committees administer the program of the center, which includes religious education, outreach to people in prisons, financial assistance to Muslims through a rehabilitation and welfare committee, neighborhood study circles, and programs to reach non-Muslims with the message of Islam. The officers of the Muslim Community Center and of the other Muslim centers are elected each year. The Consultative Committee of Indian Muslims, organized in December 1967, now operates out of an office in the Muslim Community Center. The Memon Association of Chicago was founded in 1982 as a social group of Memon Sunni Muslims, and they participate fully in the activities of the center. They also meet every two months for a social gathering, and they have their own officers. They have only 150 enrolled members, but they estimate that there are between 2,500 and 3,000 Memons in the Chicago area. The programs of the other centers duplicate the programs of the Muslim Community Center, but each is an independent organization.

Indo-Pakistani Muslims first settled in the northside of Chicago – the Ravenswood area contains the largest number – but they gradually have moved to the suburbs, and mosques have been established where they live to cut down on the distance required to travel for prayers and special services. The Islamic Foundation, one of the suburban organizations, was established by a former president of the Muslim Community Center and by about twenty families who had moved to the western suburbs during the early 1970s. It was formed in 1974 and purchased an eight-acre site on which to build a mosque, but local opposition made it impossible to get the appropriate approval. After purchasing a school building in Villa Park in 1980, they still had difficulty in getting a permit, so they filed a court case, which they won. In the meantime another school in Villa Park had become available, and in 1983 the Islamic Foundation purchased that school and adjacent property for $550,000; it is now used as a mosque and religious school on the weekends. Approximately 200 people, mostly Hyderabadis, attend the Friday noon prayers. The educational programs in Urdu and Arabic are conducted on Saturday and in English on Sundays. When the Eid festival is celebrated in Villa Park, about 2,000 participate. Leaders of this group say that the religious education of the children and new converts is the most pressing task, the second most important task being to counter the negative publicity about Muslims in order to gain the respect of neighbors and of the general public. The Islamic Foundation also conducts a summer school and joins with the Muslim Community Center in organizing the youth camp.

Several centers have developed in the 1980s. In the middle of the decade the Islamic Center of Northwest Chicago purchased a building in Rolling Meadows. Previously the group met in a public school in Schaumburg. The Islamic Society of Illinois has been meeting in three different houses in Bensenville, where they have begun a fund-raising drive to purchase a building for a mosque. The American Islamic Association has purchased a large site in Frankfort, and they use a small house on the property as a mosque while they make plans and raise money for a large Islamic center. In Chicago, the Elmdale mosque is in a large building, the first floor of which was donated by the owner for use as a mosque. The Tablighi Jamaat on West Roscoe is the center for an orthodox brotherhood that purchased and converted a church building; the majority of participants are Indo-Pakistanis. The Jamaat emphasizes spirituality and ethics, and prohibits the introduction of politics into its programs. These centers welcome all Muslims, but their programs serve primarily the Indo-Pakistani Muslims. Each indicates a steady growth and predicts the development of more elaborate programs and the development of additional centers as the Muslim population expands and spreads throughout the Chicago area. A mosque has already been established in Elgin, and Muslims in Batavia meet in a rented hall in a church.

Many Muslims in the Chicago area join together for some activities. The Eid celebration at the end of Ramadan, the month of fasting, is the largest celebration in the Muslim calendar, and that event has been celebrated in some years at gatherings of some 15,000 people in McCormick Place. There are radio and television programs for the Muslim community and English and Urdu newspapers for Pakistani immigrants. Two cemeteries now have areas reserved for Muslim burials. The American Islamic College was established in a national landmark building on the North Shore in 1983, and it grants a bachelor's degree in Islamic and Arabic studies and in education. It was granted candidacy status by the North Central Association of Colleges and Schools in 1985. An attempt was made to establish an Islamic parochial school in Chicago, but the attempt was unsuccessful because zoning approval could not be obtained. Other initiatives are being made in that direction because parents desire education for their children outside the public schools so they can receive religious instruction. Some families currently send their children to Catholic parochial schools, but they are also planning for an Islamic parochial school.

Four Indo-Pakistani Shi'ite groups have regular meetings in Chicago. The Ithna'Asharis from India, which may number between 700 and 1,000 in Chicago, have two groups. Formerly they met together, but now they have separate buildings. The Midwest Association of Shi'a Muslims, made up of Shi'ites who came primarily from Pakistan and East Africa, was formed in 1977 and met in homes until it purchased a building in what proved to be an undesirable area. Women were afraid to go to the meetings wearing their jewelry. In 1985 the group, which has seventy paid members, purchased another building, on West Addison, for their meetings. They meet approximately twenty times a year for prayers and special occasions. Regular meetings are small, even when they have visiting lecturers from India or Pakistan, but approximately 300 people attend the commemoration of the death of Husain (the president said, "Everyone I know shows up then"). The association conducts Sunday School classes for about twenty children every Sunday. A couple of men in the association perform marriages and funerals for members, and they have purchased twenty plots in a cemetery for Muslim burials. The Hussaini Association of Greater Chicago was established in 1972, serving primarily Muslims from Hyderabad. Their meetings, conducted in Urdu, take place two times a month, and approximately forty people attend; for festivals 300 people attend. The association purchased a building on Washtenaw Avenue in Chicago in 1982.

Two groups of Ismaili Muslims meet regularly in Chicago. (For a detailed discussion of the Ismailis in the United States, see Chapter Six.) The Dawoodi Bohora Jamat of Chicago, formed in 1972, is affiliated with the Dai, whose headquarters are in Bombay. He appoints a local leader (Amil), a businessman who donates his service to the almost 200 Bohora families that are in the Chicago area. The group purchased a former Eagles Club in Forest Park as their religious center (*markus*), and although they are supposed to meet every Friday for prayer, they actually meet only two times a month for services in Arabic and Gujarati. Approximately a hundred people attend the regular meetings, and 500 attend the special festival meetings. They used to have Saturday classes for the children, but those have been suspended because of lack of volunteers. The other group, the Nizari Ismailis, have rented a hall in north Chicago for one of the largest Nizari communities in the United States – about 4,000 persons – although the jamat in Houston may have overtaken it in size. They originally met in private homes and then in a hall at the University of Illinois before moving into the leased property. The ground floor contains offices and meeting rooms; the upper floor is the prayer hall. The center is not identified by signs or external designation as an Ismaili jamat khana, and few other Muslims seem to be aware of the Ismaili community – the Nizari Ismailis keep a low profile – but the full range of activities described in Chapter Six is conducted there. A second jamat khana was opened in 1984 in Northlake to serve the Ismailis who had moved to the suburbs. They had been meeting in Lombard, but some members purchased the school building in Northlake and made it available to the jamat. Although the president of the Nizari Ismailis in the United States is a physician in Chicago with a home in Evanston, the regional headquarters is in New York.

Christians

The early history of Asian-Indian Christianity in Chicago traces an ecumenical beginning through the development of separate churches based on denominational and linguistic differences. The first Christian group was formed in November 1969, when a small group of people met in a Chinese church on the near north side to hear the Reverend Bhakta Singh, a visiting evangelist from India. The Asian Indians at the meeting responded to his encouragement and began to meet regularly for prayer and fellowship in members' homes, often in the apartment of a doctor who worked at the Cook County Medical Center on South Ashland. In 1973 they registered their church as the India Christian Fellowship Church and were sponsored by the United Church (Presbyterian and Methodist) at the Medical Center, where they began to have Sunday evening services. The church is by design interdenominational and multilinguistic, and it attempts to serve Christians from every part of India, although members are primarily from South India.

The organizing pastor came to Chicago in 1969 as a student at Trinity Evangelical Seminary, where he received a master's degree in 1971. He had been a missionary pastor outside of Kerala in the evangelical branch of the Mar Thoma Church even before he came to the United States. After completing his studies, he remained as pastor of the congregation for several years. The church grew during the period of immigration in the early 1970s to a size of about seventy families, but in 1976 tensions resulted in groups leaving the congregation to form other churches. The organizing pastor resigned and formed a new Telugu congregation in Oak Park. Another pastor, called in 1976, continues as the pastor of the original congregation. In 1982 an Indian student at Northern Baptist Seminary was appointed as assistant pastor. He came as an immigrant in 1972 with his mother, who is a nurse. He had been a Roman Catholic in India and worked as an engineer in the United States, but he became active in this church and left his job to prepare for the Christian ministry.

The membership of the congregation consists of seventy-five people, and they continue to meet on Sunday evenings at the United Church at the Medical Center on South Ashland. Attendance for regular services is about fifty, but 150 attend on Christmas and Easter. Ninety-nine people are pictured in the tenth anniversary picture of the congregation. Some of the members are active in churches of American denominations in the morning and attend the Asian-Indian service in the evening. The services are in English and follow a liturgy prepared for the church based on the worship services of several denominations. Most of the members speak Tamil, Telugu, or Malayalam, but a few are from northern India. Many are employed in the medical field as nurses or medical technicians. The programs of the church are those familiar in American denominations: Sunday worship, Bible study, summer vacation Bible school, and youth programs.

The prayer group in Oak Park has grown into a regular congregation, and in 1984 it was organized as the Indo-Christian Fellowship Church, which now meets on Sunday evenings in the Free Methodist Church in Melrose Park. Seventeen families are members, and about sixty-five people attend the Sunday services. The pastor who organized the India Fellowship Church is the organizing pastor of the new congregation, which continues the interdenominational and multilinguistic character of the original church. Both congregations support evangelistic work in India.

A Telugu congregation separated from the India Fellowship Church in 1976 to conduct services in their native language and it has now become three small congregations. Two meet in Oak Park, and one meets in the afternoons at the United Church at the Medical Center. The attraction of services in the regional Indian languages is strong, even though it means that the congregations are very small, with some prayer groups being held in homes.

A unique experiment is being conducted at the Emmanuel United Methodist Church in Evanston, where the senior pastor is a Gujarati immigrant who established a Gujarati Christian Fellowship, the associate pastor is a white-American Methodist, and the assistant pastor ministers to a Hindi fellowship. The old Emmanuel Church, which was a union of Swedish and Norwegian immigrants in the early part of the century, is now attempting to incorporate the recent Asian-Indian immigrants by having one congregation with two linguistic fellowships as part of the congregation. The membership of the united congregation is 155. They meet together for communion each month, but the fellowship groups conduct a Hindi service and a Gujarati service each Sunday. The adult classes are separate for the Gujaratis and the Hindi-speakers, but some of the children attend the Sunday School classes conducted in English because that is the language the children prefer. The Gujarati fellowship was begun in 1977 by a Gujarati student who is now the senior pastor of the church. He came to the United States in 1976 with his Methodist bishop to attend a church conference and stayed on with his sister, attending Kendall College and North Park Seminary. He received a Master of Divinity degree in 1984. The Methodist Church is relatively strong in Gujarat, and the Gujarati Methodists and some members of churches now a part of the Church of North India began to attend the Gujarati services held bimonthly at the church. In 1982 they began to have services every week, and now the Gujarati fellowship has twenty-five families with twenty-nine full members and ten affiliate members. About half of the group are young people; on one Sunday in 1986 only two of the twenty-five adults in attendance at the Gujarati service were over fifty years of age. The leader was ordained a deacon in the Methodist Church when he graduated from seminary, and he was appointed as full-time associate minister of the congregation in June 1984 and senior pastor in 1985. His wife, who is a nurse, and his children came from India to join him in 1984. The church receives grants from the Methodist conference and the national board to support the salaries of the ministers. They conduct a Gujarati and Hindi radio ministry on a Chicago station. A division developed in the fellowship, however, and a group of several families left and meet in Chicago at the Granville Methodist Church.

The Hindi fellowship was started by an Indian pastor who came to the United States in 1977 to join his wife, who had gained entry as a nurse. His father had been a Methodist pastor in India, but he was ordained in the Reformed Presbyterian Church and had served for twenty-five years as a pastor and evangelist in India. The Hindi fellowship met in homes and at an Assembly of God Church for three years and began to rent space for meetings in 1980. A chance meeting with the Gujarati pastor in a K-Mart led to the invitation to meet in the Methodist church in Evanston in 1981. The Hindi group is smaller than the Gujarati fellowship; approximately twenty people attend the Sunday services. The pastor, who worked full-time in a factory and served the congregation on Sundays, died in 1985, and a relative of the senior pastor now serves the Hindi fellowship as assistant pastor while he attends North Park Theological Seminary. A second Hindi fellowship split off and meets at the Ravenswood Methodist Church in Chicago. It appears that the Christian immigrants from India are receiving some support from Methodist churches, and several Asian Indians are members of the local Methodist conference, but no separate Asian-Indian Methodist Church has been established in Chicago.

A First Indian Church of the Nazarene was established in June 1982 with twenty-six members, and it meets at the First Nazarene Church of Oak Park. The organizing pastor is from a town in Kerala near Meramon, where the Mar Thoma Church holds its annual convention. His father was an evangelist of the Mar Thoma Church, but he was influenced by E. Stanley Jones to live in an ashram near Jabalpur to undertake evangelistic work in the villages. While there, he received a scholarship from the International Gospel League to come to the United States for study at Fuller Theological Seminary from 1967 to 1970. After a period in India, he returned to the United States and completed the Master of Divinity degree at the Nazarene Seminary in Kansas City in 1978. The district superintendent of the Nazarene Church appointed him to be assistant pastor of the church in Oak Park and gave him the charge to minister to the Asian-Indian Christians. He began to contact families and gathered a group that was chartered as a congregation in 1982. Now the congregation has sixty members, and on Easter 1986 seventy-five people attended the worship service. The Nazarenes do not have churches in Kerala, so those who participate have come from other denominations, primarily Syrian Christian. The worship services are in Malayalam, but the pastor says that he switches to Hindi or English if people come who cannot understand Malayalam. He is the only Asian-Indian Nazarene pastor in the United States.

The Church of South India of Greater Chicago was formed in May 1983 with a membership of fifteen families. Two Church of South India pastors, who are doctoral students at McCormick Theological Seminary, serve the congregation, but they plan to return to India when they complete their studies. The congregation meets on Sunday evenings at the Lakeview Presbyterian Church on West Addison, and members conduct cottage prayer meetings once a month in homes. Many of the members of the Church of South India had become active in other churches before a congregation of their own denomination was formed.

The Malayalee St. Thomas Christians have the largest Asian-Indian congregations. On one Sunday in May of 1985 the Mar Thoma Church of Chicago had more people at its Malayalee service in the chapel of the First Methodist Church of Evanston (325 people) than there were Methodists meeting in the main sanctuary (295). The average attendance in 1986 was approximately 350, and over 500 attended on Easter. The Mar Thoma congregation was started as a prayer group without a pastor in 1973. The first priest was assigned to serve the congregation when he was sent for graduate study at McCormick Theological Seminary. That started a pattern of the assignment of a student as pastor of one of the fastest growing churches in Chicago. When the first pastor completed his studies and was reassigned to India, another pastor entered McCormick Theological Seminary to complete a doctoral program in New Testament studies. The congregation now has a membership of 150 families, and it conducts a full program of Sunday worship, Sunday School, prayer meetings, evangelistic meetings, women's programs, and an annual retreat. Two services a month are conducted in Malayalam and two in English; the Sunday School for children is in English, the one for adults, in Malayalam. In January 1985 the congregation purchased property on Porter Road in Des Plaines, and dedicated a new church building in November 1986. The pastor also travels to Des Moines to serve a new fellowship group of seven families who meet in a Lutheran Church. The national zonal conference for the Mar Thoma Christians and the annual clergy conference were held on a college campus in Chicago in July 1986 (Williams, 1986a). The pastor returned to Kerala at the end of 1986 to become director of the St. Augustine Retreat Center.

Three Malankara Orthodox Churches are also in the Chicago area. The oldest is St. Thomas Orthodox Church, which was started by a priest who has since become an immigrant. When he arrived in 1971, he did not know any Malayalee Christians, so he began to perform the mass in the Eastern rite for a few Syrian immigrants. That same year, they formed a congregation named St. John the Divine Orthodox Church. The priest gathered a few Malayalee Christians, and in 1972 they began to meet in St. Peter's Episcopal Church at Belmont and Broadway in north Chicago. They were recognized as a Malankara Orthodox congregation in 1973, named the St. Thomas Orthodox Church, by which time they had grown to approximately fifteen families. In 1976 there was a great influx of nurses and their families, and that brought changes in the congregation. A number of the members left in 1978 to form St. Gregorios Orthodox Church, which met in a rented church hall in Evanston. St. Gregorios is now the largest Malankara Church in Chicago, with about eighty families, or about 150 people, in attendance. In May 1984 they purchased a church building in Oak Park, which was consecrated in October 1984. The diocesan conference of the Malankara churches was held at St. Gregorios in 1985.

St. Thomas Orthodox Church continued to meet for a while at St. Peter's Episcopal Church. The organizing pastor left the congregation to complete a doctoral degree at Loyola University. The current pastor came for a visit in 1980, and the congregation arranged to get a visa so he could stay on as their pastor. He works in a bank and serves the congregation part-time, and his younger brother, recently ordained as a deacon, serves as assistant pastor. The congregation of forty-five families now meets in a Presbyterian church on North Greenview in Chicago for services in Malayalam.

St. Mary's Orthodox Church in Park Ridge was organized in 1982 by the pastor who founded St. Thomas, and, with thirty families, it is the youngest and smallest of the three Malankara churches. They meet in the chapel of St. Mary's Episcopal Church in Park Ridge, with about sixty persons attending Sunday services. All of the services of these churches are in Malayalam, except that St. Mary's, whose priest translated the service book into English (it is being printed in Kerala), has one service a month in English.

St. Peter's Syrian Orthodox Church is the only Malayalam church in Chicago that is affiliated with the Patriarch of Antioch through the archbishop in New Jersey. The congregation was founded in 1979 and purchased a house on North Spaulding near North Park Theological Seminary. The ground floor and basement were converted for use as a sanctuary and Sunday School classrooms; the upper floor is used as a residence for the priest. The founding priest returned to Kerala to become a bishop, and another priest was appointed in March 1982. His family accompanied him to the United States under the sponsorship of the archbishop in New Jersey, and he works in a hospital to support his family and serves the church on the weekends. Another St. Peter's church is affiliated with the Patriarch of Antioch, but it serves Syrian Christians from Iraq and Lebanon.

Several Pentecostal groups also meet in the Chicago area, but it is impossible to make an accounting because many are "house churches" with two or three families and because the groups rapidly form, multiply, and expire. The first Indian Pentecostal group in Chicago started in 1969, when some Pentecostals came to study at a Bible institute. They formed a prayer group that developed into a congregation that now has its own building on West Fullerton. The largest Indian Pentecostal church, with twenty member families, meets in its own building on Courtland Avenue. Its pastor was ordained by the American Assemblies of God; the other pastors were ordained by the Indian Pentecostal Church of God in Kerala. One small congregation meets in the YMCA in Des Plaines, and another meets in a classroom of a Lutheran school in Country Club Hills on the far south side. On the third Saturday evening of every month the Pentecostal pastors hold a joint service at the Fullerton church that approximately 100 people attend.

The Roman Catholics from India worship in the parish churches, and they participate in the India Catholic Association, which began in 1960 and is thus one of the oldest Asian-Indian associations in Chicago. They sponsor social occasions and special masses under the direction of the coordinator of ethnic ministries of the diocese. In 1985 a priest of the Syro-Malabar rite was installed by the bishop in the diocese to minister to the Asian Indians. (See the discussion of the Syro-Malabar Catholics in Chapter Three.)

The Asian-Indian Christian churches have developed independently, with little ecumenical cooperation either among the Asian Indians or between them and the American denominations. Most of the cooperation has been to provide meeting places for the Indian Christians. Some interesting attempts at cooperation have begun, but the complex administrative structure of the Emmanuel United Methodist Church in Evanston indicates how difficult that cooperation is. The denominational and ecumenical executives in the Chicago area have taken little notice of these Christian groups, and it has been the various seminaries that have done more to assist the Indian-Christian groups by providing education, housing, and some support for the pastors. The Indian churches are thus establishing their own denominational structures in the United States that can nurture and support the work of their congregations. Some Indian pastors have begun meeting once a month since late in 1985 for prayer and fellowship, but only about a dozen participate. They meet on the last Friday evening of the month at the United Church at the Medical Center. The Federation of Indo-American Christians was founded in Chicago in 1978, and it has a mailing list of 500 Christian families in the Chicago area, but it has not been able to develop cooperative work. In this second stage of development of congregations, many leaders fear that other Christian pastors and groups will "steal their sheep." Perhaps a third stage of greater cooperation will follow as the congregations grow and together face the challenges of ministering to the members of the second generation.

Zoroastrians

The Zoroastrian Association of Metropolitan Chicago has the distinction of having the first building specifically built in the United States for a center (*derbe mehr*). The group was the beneficiary of the philanthropy of Arbab Rustam Guiv, who provided the funds for a beautiful brick-and-cedar building in a residential area of Hinsdale that looks like a suburban church. The Zoroastrians had begun to meet in 1974, and beginning in 1978 they had used the Unitarian Church of Hinsdale. Mr. Guiv purchased a twenty-acre property in Mettawa in 1978 as the future site for a center, but it was not possible to build there. However, in September 1983 the Zoroastrians were able to dedicate the $250,000 center in Hinsdale, with 400 people present. Zubin Mehta, the most prominent Parsi in the United States, was the chief guest at the fund-raising dinner for the center. The building has a large hall with a stage on one side and a kitchen on the other. A smaller, simple prayer hall with the ritual fire urn is a separate room – it is not a "fire temple" because it has only a domestic fire that does not require continual priestly attendance.

Approximately 200 Zoroastrian families in the Chicago area are on the mailing list, and 100 families are members of the association. The attendance at the regular meetings on the second Sunday of each month is only about fifty, but the attendance for festivals such as New Year's is about 150. On the fourth Sunday of each month a Sunday School is conducted for the children. Approximately ninety percent of those who participate in the activities of the center are Parsis from India and Pakistan, and the rituals and some of the lectures are in Gujarati. The business meetings, newsletters, and educational programs are in English.

The priestly duties are conducted by part-time priests (mobeds) who work at other occupations and perform the rituals in the center and in the homes as volunteers. One of the priests participated in the initiation of an American chemical engineer into the Zoroastrian community (see Chapter Three). That act has brought a great deal of criticism and provoked considerable discussion within the community. The major issue of how far to adapt to American society and to the practices of American religious groups also involves whether to accept outsiders and the children of mixed marriages as members. The Parsis from India tend to be more conservative on the matter, and the Zoroastrians from Iran more liberal. A major task for the leaders has become to maintain the unity of the Zoroastrian immigrants from India, Pakistan, and Iran as one religious group that does not split into ethnic groups. For the Zoroastrians, as for all the Asian-Indian religious groups, the most pressing problem is to preserve their traditions and pass them on to the children in ways that will preserve their cultural identities and also prepare them to be successful in American society.

CHAPTER 8

Asian-Indian and Pakistani religions in Houston

An Asian-Indian immigrant remembers that in the late 1960s he stopped his car and ran across the street to greet a person he thought to be an Asian Indian because so few were in Houston that they tried to make contact however they could. The numbers have changed dramatically, but not the need to gather in community, as Houston became the fastest-growing metropolitan area in the United States. The growth was fueled by the high-tech developments in space research and allied areas and by the increase in oil prices and exploration. At a time of recession in the northeast and midwest, many highly skilled professionals moved to Houston to take advantage of the opportunities. The movement to the Sun Belt took place at the same time that many Asian-Indian students were finishing their graduate studies and when other professionals were emigrating from India and Pakistan. Houston is attractive because the climate resembles that of parts of India more than does the climate of Chicago, Detroit, or New York, but the Asian Indians, some of whom had lost their jobs in the industrial northeast, were actually drawn to Houston by the promise of job opportunities.

It is impossible to capture in print the excitement of the Asian Indians as they arrived in Houston during the time of great prosperity. The first few came as students, and they were soon joined by scientists and engineers; then the momentum developed: easy jobs, high pay, business opportunities, rapid growth of the Asian-Indian population, formation of social and religious networks, rapid growth of religious groups, plans for new buildings. This kind of prosperity could not continue at the same pace, and the recession came in 1982 when, on the principle of "last hired, first fired," many of the recent immigrants lost their jobs, scrambled to find other, less well-paid jobs, and thought about a reverse migration to other parts of the United States. Some became what has been described as "the educated poor," but very few returned to India or Pakistan, although a number of Muslims did leave for greener pastures in the Middle East. A period of retrenchment began for families and for religious organizations: slower growth, less money, less ambitious plans for the future.

A profile of the religious organizations that have served the Asian Indians and Pakistanis as they passed through these periods shows how, in the social and economic climate of Houston, the various religious groups developed, grew, subdivided, and built centers, mosques, churches, and permanent homes. In this study the development of the religious organizations by Asian Indians and Pakistanis is traced through three periods: arrival – the period between 1970 and 1979 when the Asian-Indian population grew from a few families to a significant size; boom time – the period between 1980 and 1982 when the population was increasing steadily, the community was fully employed at high salaries, and religious groups were prospering; hard times – the period between 1983 and 1987, when the economic recession has restricted both the growth of the population and the development of religious organizations (see Table 8.1).

Arrival (1970–1979)

The calm of this early period is hidden away in the minds of the students and first immigrants who were in Houston during the early 1970s. The students gathered in the India Students' Association or the Muslim Students' Association, which had been formed in the 1960s and provided the social and religious contacts for students and some early immigrants. These students and immigrants were primarily single men, and little is known of their private religious activity. When the large influx of immigrants began in the early 1970s and the students brought brides to join them, worship with the family in homes or the gathering of a few friends was the primary religious activity. Indeed, in the early period, religious gatherings provided an excuse for visiting other homes, which is so much a part of Indian tradition, but which in the United States is not done without a specific occasion. When leaders speak about that period and the formation of religious groups that now may have hundreds of participants, they tell of two or three families gathering in an apartment or home, or of Muslim immigrants who joined with students at the universities for Friday prayers.

The early 1970s was the time for the gathering of a few people of each tradition to establish a group for worship and fellowship. The Nizari Ismaili Muslims were among the first groups to form in 1970 when three or four families began to gather on Friday evenings for prayers. Also in 1970, the Hindu Worship Society began to meet once a month in homes

Table 8.1. *Chronology of Asian Indians and Pakistanis in Houston*

1960s	India Student Association
1970	Hindu Worship Society started Nizari Ismaili group started
1972	First Muslim mosque opened
1973	First Indian grocery opened India Pentecostal Church formed Sikh group purchased land St. Thomas Orthodox Church formed Mar Thoma bishop visit (December)
1974	Mar Thoma group formed India Culture Center formed
1975	Durga Puja Society formed Zoroastrian group formed
1976	Vivekananda Vedanta group formed Hindu Worship Society first building Hindu Ashram & Temple Society formed International Society of Krishna Consciousness rents house
1977	Swaminarayan Hindu group formed Mar Thoma congregation incorporated India Pentecostal Church registered Sri Meenakshi Society formed (October)
1978	St. Gregorios Orthodox Church formed (January) Sri Meenakshi Temple site purchased (May) Satya Sai Baba group formed Church of South India formed
1979	Mar Thoma Sunday School started Masjid al-Islam founded Kerala Hindu Society formed Ganesh Shrine (Meenakshi) dedicated U.S. Census Houston shows population of 1,595,138
1980	Asian-Indian Roman Catholic priest assigned Chinmaya Mission formed India Culture Center reorganization begun Unemployment rate at 3.5% (October)
1981	Ismaili National Health Fair (February) St. Johns Orthodox Church formed Jain Society incorporated (April) Dharmajjivandas Swami visit International Swaminarayan Satsang Organization formed Devotional Associations of Yogeswara established Ismaili Association Center opened (December) Unemployment rate at 3.9% (December)

Table 8.1. (*continued*)

1982	Islamic Society new mosque opened (January)
	Mar Thoma church purchased site
	Masjid Dar us-Salaam formed
	Hindu Worship Society temple opened
	Sanatan Samskara Kendra formed
	Indo-American News begins publication
	Houston population (July) 1,725,617
	Sri Meenakshi Temple opened
	Chinmaya Mission formed in southwest
	Sikh protest of military dress code (December)
	First Ecumenical Malayalee Christmas program (December)
	International Society of Krishna Consciousness purchases house
	Unemployment rate at 8.1% (December)
1983	India Pentecostal Church purchased building
	Madan Mohan Lalji Haveli formed
	AsiAmerica Digest begins publication
	Kerala Hindu Society registered
	Unemployment rate at 10.1% (September)
	St. Gregorios Church site purchased (November)
1984	Second Sikh gurdwara established
	Morari Bapu visits (June)
	Chief Minister Rama Rao visits
	[Army enters Golden Temple (June)]
	Trinity Mar Thoma building dedicated (July)
	Sushil Muni visits Jains (August)
	Ismaili waezeen Conference (September)
	[Prime Minister Indira Gandhi assassinated (October 31)]
	St. Thomas Evangelical Church of India formed
	Unemployment rate at 5.9% (December)
1985	Swaminarayan group land purchased
	Vallabh Priti Seva Samaj formed
	Disturbance at Sikh gurdwara (March 10)
	Goswami Indirabetiji visits
	Rajiv Gandhi visits (June 15)
	Gujarat Samaj site purchased
	[Bombing of Air India flight (June)]
	Eid Celebration cancelled
	Asian-Indian population of Houston at 40,000
	Unemployment rate at 6.7% (December)
1986	Ismaili centers expanded
	ISKCON purchases school
	[Second attack on Golden Temple in Amritsar (May 1)]
	International Society for Krishna Consciousness purchases church building (July)

for worship (puja) and for the singing of sacred songs (kirtans). The songs were sung in various languages – Gujarati, Punjabi and Hindi. At that time it was the only Asian-Indian Hindu group in town, and an attempt was made to provide a place for all Hindus to worship. They met at times in a chapel of the University of Houston and for a period in the Rothko Chapel at Rice University, which was a first meeting place for several groups. Several rituals included fires, which would be a threat to the chapel, and for these the Rothko Chapel provided a nearby house. The Islamic Society of Greater Houston grew out of Islamic services in the Rothko Chapel sponsored by the Muslim Students Association, and in 1972 the Muslims renovated a house in the Montrose area that became the first official mosque in the southern United States. It is estimated that the number of Muslims in Houston grew from a small number to a thousand in a period of five years.

The first Indian grocery store opened in 1973, which is a good indication of the stage of development of the Asian-Indian community. As the Asian-Indian population grew, other groups began to form. Four or five Sikhs met and planned for a gurdwara. They were able to purchase property in northwest Houston and established the Sikh Center of the Gulf Coast, where a small frame building on the property served as a meeting place until it was destroyed by lightning. In 1975, with the assistance of the Richmond Hill Society in New York and other Sikh societies, they began construction of the building currently used as a gurdwara.

Malayalee nurses came to the medical centers in Houston and brought their families, and, because of the movement of these nurses, it is estimated that eighty percent of the Malayalees who came are Christians. Several Christian groups began to meet. The Indian Pentecostal Church, which has grown into the largest Malayalee Pentecostal church in Houston, and the only one with its own building, began to meet in homes. St. Thomas Malankara Orthodox was established by a few families meeting in homes. In December of 1973 a bishop of the Mar Thoma Church came to Houston as part of a tour of the United States, and he gathered a few families who began to meet in homes. A Mar Thoma priest who was a graduate student in Dallas came to Houston to conduct the eucharist services in the chapel of St. Mark's Episcopal Church, and later at Holy Cross Episcopal Church. In 1978 the congregation was officially named Mar Thoma Syrian Church of India, Houston, and it was formally accepted as a church by the synod.

Conversations about the need for an Asian-Indian cultural and social group broader in scope than the India Students' Association led to the incorporation of the India Culture Center in 1975. The center continued for several years without a building, sponsoring cultural programs – music, dance, movies, festivals – and national celebrations such as Indian Independence Day. These programs were held in facilities of the University of Houston or in other rented halls. The India Culture Center is by constitution a secular organization, but it has been important for the development of religious organizations because it provided occasions for members of the Asian-Indian community to become acquainted with each other and to pursue common interests, because it provided a small meeting place when the center obtained a building in 1979, and because it became an umbrella organization when the center was reorganized in 1980. However, some of the religious organizations resist becoming a constituent group of the center because of its nature as a secular organization and because of its concern with Indian national and political identity.

A small group of the International Society for Krishna Consciousness moved to Houston early in the 1970s and began meetings in a rented house in about 1976. Immigrants began to participate in their activities in the middle of the decade, largely through the influence of an American geological engineer who invited some of the immigrant engineers with whom he worked. Some took the first level of vows: not to eat meat or eggs, not to drink intoxicants, not to engage in illicit sex, not to gamble, and to chant sixteen rounds of the Hare Krishna chant each day. None, however, took full initiation to become full-time members or to live in the house.

The second half of the decade was a period that saw the establishment of several new organizations, the division of some, and acceleration in the purchase of sites and dedication of buildings. The Durga Puja Society was established by the Bengalis to sponsor the major religious festivals of Bengal. Generally the Bengalis do not have regular weekly rituals; they say, "We are not religious like the Gujaratis or the Tamils." Nevertheless, the society grew in number until it had 300 families in 1980. Two Bengali Brahmins, a doctor and an accountant, perform the life-cycle rituals for the community. The Durga Puja Society provides the religious rituals; the Bengali Cultural Association and the Tagore Society sponsor cultural programs.

The Vivekananda Vedanta Society in Houston began in January 1976 with meetings in homes on the second Sunday of each month. The programs included readings from sacred texts, study of Vedanta philosophy, meditation, and hymns. The participants in Houston are Asian Indians, not Westerners as seen in other centers. The success of the educational programs is the result of the work of an Asian-Indian child psychologist who became a follower of Vedanta in Chicago. She began a Vedanta Sunday School with seven children in her home, and, when the school outgrew her home, moved it to a Jewish Community Center for two years and then to the India Culture Center building after it had been purchased. At its height the Sunday School had seventy students and three teachers in graded classes that studied Indian religion and philosophy for one hour and Indian culture the second hour. Swami Bhashananda now visits from Chicago once a year, but the group is smaller.

The Hindu Worship Society purchased an old building in northeast Houston, which they remodeled for use as a Hindu temple. That proved not to be a wise move; the property was in an unsafe neighborhood, the Asian-Indian women were afraid to wear their good clothing and jewelry to the temple, and the inside of the temple was destroyed by vandalism, so the building was abandoned. The Hindu group was then given refuge by the Unitarian Church on Wirt Road in northwest Houston, where they met until they were able to build a new temple nearby. When the first building was purchased, a division occurred with the separation of the Hindu Ashram and Temple Society, which continued to meet in the house that had been provided by Rothko Chapel. The Hindu Ashram and Temple Society later obtained a three-acre property for an ashram at San Leon, but because no buildings have been constructed, the small group now meets in private homes.

In 1977 the leader of the Akshar Purushottam Swaminarayan Sanstha, Narayanswarupdas Swami, visited Houston briefly on his tour of the United States. Only a few followers of the Swaminarayan religion were in Houston by that time, but the visit inspired regular meetings in which members of various Swaminarayan groups began to participate. This is one characteristic mode of the establishment of religious organizations of all types in the early days, except Muslims (for whom the congregational Friday prayer is fundamental): A family would sponsor the visit of a religious leader (guru) or famous lecturer, and that visit would provide the occasion and the impetus for the formation of a group with both regular meetings and outreach to attract more participants. The Swaminarayan group was able to prepare a major celebration when Narayanswarupdas Swami returned in 1980 for a second, longer visit.

Also in 1977, a group of thirty Hindu families from South India organized the Sri Meenakshi Society with the goal of building a temple to the goddess Meenakshi, a consort of Shiva. It is estimated that twenty percent of the Asian Indians in Houston are from South India. They chose to build a temple to Meenakshi because temples already existed in the United States to Ganesh (New York) and Venkateswara, a form of Vishnu (Pittsburgh). No temple to the goddess nor of Shiva had yet been built, so it was hoped that the Shaivites from across the country would support a Shiva temple. Moreover, most South Indians were familiar with the famous pilgrimage temple of Sri Meenakshi-Sundareshwara at Madurai in Tamil Nadu. They began a vigorous program to raise funds, making it possible to purchase a five-acre site in Pearland for the construction of

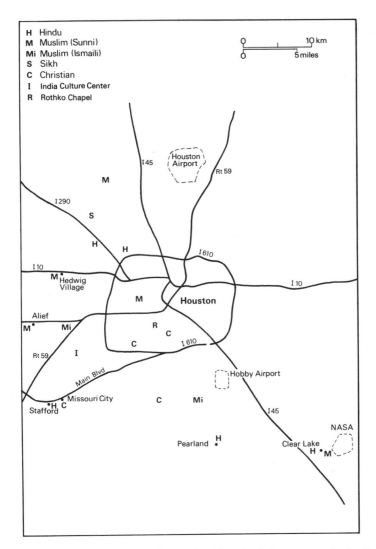

Figure 8.1. Locations of Asian-Indian and Pakistani religious centers in the Houston area.

a temple. Their meetings were held in homes, a store, and then a bank while they planned for a temple. The high cost of property in Houston proper and the requirements of traditional Hindu temple construction made it necessary for its location to be in a relatively remote area. In 1979 they dedicated a small, temporary Ganesh shrine on the property, which made possible regular worship at the site (see Figure 8.1):

Several Christian groups began to meet in 1978. Members of several denominations had participated in the early years of the Mar Thoma congregation, including several families of the Church of South India who participated because the two denominations are "in full communion." One family of the Church of South India invited a priest from New York to perform the baptism of their child, and the other families attended. Seven families decided to meet together and encouraged a son of a Church of South India pastor, who had received a theological degree from Dallas Theological Seminary, to lead the group. He went to India to be ordained as a deacon and returned to be pastor of the church. The congregation began to have regular services in St. Luke's Presbyterian Church in 1980, and the bishop visited in 1981 to ordain the pastor as a presbyter. The congregation continues to use the facilities of St. Luke's, and does not feel the necessity to construct a new building.

An ecumenical Malayalee Christian group of three or four families had begun to meet in the apartment of the young man before he organized local members of the Church of South India. When a leader from Dallas came to encourage them to establish a nondenominational, charismatic prayer group, one of the recently arrived families who had been members of such a group in Ann Arbor, Michigan (not an Asian-Indian group), also wanted to establish one in Houston. A Sunday evening, ecumenical prayer group began that still meets each week, with an emphasis on healing, prayers, singing, and occasional speaking in tongues. The group is led by lay people – they have no pastor – and most of the participants attend other congregations in the morning. They are "born-again Indian Christians," and approximately seventy-five people attend the meetings each week. They have a Sunday School during the hour before the prayer meeting.

A difference of opinion in the St. Thomas Orthodox Church caused seventeen families to leave the church and request the permission of the bishop in Buffalo to organize a new congregation. They organized St. Gregorios Malankara Church in 1978 with twenty families, meeting two times a month for holy communion service in a rented hall of an office building. One of the former presidents of St. Thomas, who received his theological education at Holy Cross Seminary in Boston and his pastoral counseling degree from Christian Theological Seminary in Indianapolis, was ordained by the bishop in 1978. His regular position is as supervising chaplain in one of the hospitals, and he was also assigned to be pastor of St. Gregorios in 1981.

A group of five Hindu families from Kerala began to meet in homes for worship. The great majority of immigrants from Kerala are Christians, but some are Kerala Hindus, and in Houston they decided to follow the example of the Christians and organize. They began an organization that was officially registered in 1983 as the Kerala Hindu Society, with a membership of about forty families. Most of the members are from the Nair caste of Kerala; no Kerala Brahmins participate. They meet once a month in homes and plan one large Onnam festival each year to celebrate the victory of Vishnu, in the form of Vamana, over the demon king. The Kerala Hindus also go to the Meenakshi Temple, but they preserve the Malayalee rituals and songs in the meetings of the society.

The common refrain from most of these religious groups is "We began meeting with four or five families in homes." That is also the report of the Satya Sai Baba group, which began in 1978. In many American centers the majority of participants in this group are Westerners – indeed, all the zonal leaders are Westerners – but in Houston the majority of participants are Asian Indian. The native languages of the participants are given as Gujarati (60%), Hindi (15%), and Tamil (15%). Many of these, however, have emigrated from Central Africa, Fiji, Canada, and not directly from India. Not all are from a Hindu background. It seems that the Satya Sai Baba group attracts those immigrants without direct ties to India and immigrants from other places (Philippines and Iran) who find a religious home and support group in the intense devotion to a personal guru without the need for elaborate ritual or intricate philosophy. The group of about seventy-five people meets one Sunday a month in the India Culture Center and on other Sundays in homes.

The Asian Indians participated in the steady growth of the population of Houston in the 1970s. By 1980 it was the fifth largest city in the United States, with an internal population of 1,595,138 and 2,905,350 in the six-county metropolitan area. The Asian-Indian population of Houston was 11,107 (USCen5:389), and it was young, with 3,997 persons under twenty years of age and only 187 over sixty-five. There were 3.56 persons per family (USCen7:138). Seven-eighths of those who were foreign born had emigrated to the United States between 1970 and 1979;[1] it was rare to find a person who had been in the country more than ten years. Asian Indians were professionals, heavily employed in the hospitals, aerospace industry, and in oil exploration and construction; they had secured a firm foothold and had begun to form religious organizations.

Boom time (1980–1982)

Asian Indians refer to this as the best of times. The population grew at a rapid rate so that by July 1982 Houston had gained 8.2% over the 1980 base and, with a population of 1,725,617, replaced Philadelphia as the nation's fourth largest city. It was the fastest growing major metropolis. Those who came found high-paying jobs easily. The unemployment rate was traditionally low in Houston – at 5.2% in October 1976 – but by October 1980 it had dropped to 3.5% and was still at 3.9% in December

1981. Many Asian Indians who were underemployed or had lost their jobs in the northeast and midwest joined friends or relatives in Houston. Everything seemed possible, as new religious groups formed and old groups undertook ambitious building programs. Activity, donations, enthusiasm, and participation all reached a "high water mark" during this period.

Two major Hindu temples were consecrated, one North Indian and the other South Indian in style, and they represent two ways of maintaining Hindu identity and transmitting the tradition to the second generation. In 1982 several hundred people gathered to dedicate "the only Hindu temple in Houston." It was a new 70' by 45' building of the Hindu Worship Society that cost $125,000, constructed on 1.3 acres in northwest Houston that cost an additional $48,000. In 1982 the society had 700 registered members, mainly Gujaratis, Punjabis, and a few Kashmiris. The temple, with its images of Radha-Krishna, is open on Friday evenings whenever a family arranges to do the puja and provide the food items the visitors require, and each Sunday a different worship service is held in an attempt to include all Hindus. On one Sunday a traditional fire ritual without an image of the deity (murti) is performed for those in the Arya Samaj and others who reject the worship of images. Another Sunday observes a traditional ritual performed for the images of Radha-Krishna. The next Sunday may be "the puja of the book," when the emphasis is upon the *Bhagavad Gita* or some other religious text. On the open Sunday the rituals to various deities are performed. No professional Brahmin priest serves the temple, so the rituals are informal and performed by a member of the society, although independent Brahmin priests are invited for weddings and other special rituals. At each meeting there is the singing of religious songs (kirtan), lectures, and education classes. Lessons on the *Bhagavad Gita* and language lessons in Hindi and Sanskrit supplement the lectures. The regular attendance on Sundays is about 100; on the days of major Hindu festivals 500 to 600 will attend. In addition, the Hindu Worship Society has started a monthly meeting in Clear Lake for those who live a great distance from the temple.

The emphasis of the Hindu Worship Society is on the explanation of the meaning of Hinduism through books, lectures, and classes so that the children will have an intellectual understanding of the philosophy of Hinduism and of Indian culture. Even though rituals are performed, the emphasis remains on the written word and education. A leader explained: "Our children are American citizens, and even though they are Hindus, one cannot alienate them from the mainstream. You cannot worship here like you do in a small village in India."

The need for the other major Hindu temple was presented when a leader of the Sri Meenakshi Society quoted a Tamil saying, "Do not live in a village where there is no temple" – so the group built a beautiful temple in the South-Indian style in Pearland. The architect for the temple, the chief architect of the Government of Andhra Pradesh, was also the architect for the Ganesh temple in New York and the Venkateswara temple in Pittsburgh. The Tirumala Tirupati Devasthanam gave some assistance and donated the image of Venkateswara, but the major assistance came from the Sri Meenakshi-Sundareswara temple in Madurai through the Hindu Temples and Religious Endowments Board of the Tamil Nadu state government. The newly formed Bharatiya International Trust of Madras also gave some assistance. The cost of the land and temple was about $500,000, which includes the work of ten Indian craftsmen who finished the decoration. The images of the deities were installed in June 1982 in the presence of 3,000 people. The goddess Meenakshi is in the central shrine; her consort Sundeswara (Shiva) is on one side, and Venkateswara (Vishnu) on the other. Smaller shrines on a side wall contain images of Lakshmi, Rama, Radha-Krishna, and Ayyuppa – their presence represents an attempt to be somewhat ecumenical. The guardian figures of Nandi (the companion bull of Shiva) and Garuda (the winged companion of Vishnu) are present in front of the respective shrines. Plans for expansion call for the construction of a library, a cultural hall, and a kitchen, but the recession slowed the process of fund-raising.

The emphasis in this temple is on rituals, which are performed according to the *kamaga agama* just as they are in the Sri Meenakshi temple in Madurai. The services of the Brahmin priests are obtained through the temple in Madurai, so the rituals are authentic. One of the priests comes from a line of priests that has been associated with the Madurai temple for seven generations. When the temple was first built, large numbers came on Sunday morning, perhaps because they had become used to assemblies, but gradually they adopted the typical South-Indian pattern of visiting the temple as families for individual worship rituals and for the circumambulation of the shrines. A full range of rituals is provided in the temple, and the priests perform the life-cycle or special rituals in homes. The temple has an average of 250 visitors a week, but on special days several hundred will visit. The annual budget for the temple in 1984 was $322,000.

"Authentic" is the word that describes both the building and the rituals. Immigrants are attracted to the temple because it preserves tradition and reinforces their Indian Hindu identity by providing the services and rituals they remember from India. The children of the second generation are taught by participating in the rituals, in the same way, one leader observed, that he learned Hinduism by going to the temple with his parents and grandmother. In India one could absorb the meaning of the rituals because they were a part of the Hindu fabric of calendar, duties, rituals, and hierarchies of life in a South Indian village or city. Parents raise the question whether children can learn Hinduism in the United States primarily through rituals as they did in India. One parent was pessimistic, "Unless we change the way we educate the children, they will not be interested; a two-hour abhishekam does not mean anything to them." The problem is compounded because the priests do not have sufficient facility in colloquial English to explain the rituals to the children. Perhaps under the influence of the problems of the economic recession, one person reflected pessimistically on what will happen in twenty-five years: "Hindus moved to Southeast Asia in large numbers and built temples which are now in ruins. They went to East Africa and have been thrown out. Now they are in Houston and have built an impressive temple, but the future is uncertain." When the temple was dedicated during the boom time, however, the dark clouds seemed far away.

In 1982 a group of independent Brahmin priests who perform rituals for the Hindus formed the Sanatan Samskara Kendra. The first priority was to arrange the funerals for Hindus. That seems incongruous given the age of the Asian-Indian population, but a special feature of Houston is the medical center, which attracts many heart patients and others for treatment. Many come from India and Pakistan for major operations, so the various religious organizations provide these services. Six independent Brahmin priests also provide the full range of life-cycle rituals (samskaras) and special pujas for the Hindu community. Eight funerals were performed by the independent Brahmins in May 1985. The priests advertise their services in newspapers and on the Indian radio programs. They travel to San Antonio, Austin, Dallas, New Orleans, and other cities to perform weddings and pujas. The Brahmins have different backgrounds: One is retired and came to stay with his son; another worked in a company and was laid off from his job; a third is employed as an engineer. Income from work as an independent priest will not support a family, and one of the Brahmins has started a Gujarati religious magazine; another casts horoscopes and gives advice about traditional herbal medicines. Generally these Brahmins provide the services for North Indians that the priests of the Sri Meenakshi temple provide for South Indians.

In 1982, the International Society for Krishna Consciousness finally purchased for $80,000 the house they had been renting. Members of the Asian-Indian Hindu community provided much of the financing for the purchase through an annual contribution of $12,000. The immigrants became the primary participants in ISKCON activities.

New Hindu groups were formed and spread through the city during this period. The Chinmaya Mission was formed in north Houston in 1980 and began to meet in homes. That group expanded into two groups that meet in the northwest. In 1982 a third group was formed in southwest

Houston after Purushottamananda visited the groups in the northern part of the city and inspired one follower to start a group in the southwest, which is now the largest of the three. The contact list includes thirty-five families, and approximately seventy-five people hold prayer meetings in an office building. The Swaminarayan group divided in 1981 after a visit of Dharmajivandas, who encouraged the members loyal to the religious leaders (acharyas) of Ahmedabad and Vadtal to meet separately. (For a full discussion of the Swaminarayan groups, see Chapter Five.) Tejendraprasad Pande, the acharya of Ahmedabad, visited in 1984, when some 700 people attended a meeting, and 1985, when the Board of Directors of the International Swaminarayan Satsang Organization met in Houston. The Houston group meets every other Sunday in homes with between fifty and seventy people present and they sponsor four large gatherings a year. The Devotional Associates of Yogeswara was started by five people in 1981 when one of its original members was inspired by the success of the group in Chicago on a visit there. The five went door-to-door among the Indian community and developed a list of some 200 people, primarily Gujaratis, who were interested. Approximately forty people began to meet Sunday mornings in a rented hall in southwest Houston. Pandurang Adhavale, the founder of the group in India, visited Houston for the first time in 1982. Thereafter, three study circles were developed of ten to fifteen people each; they meet on Sunday evenings or Wednesday evenings in northwest, southwest, and southeast Houston, but they have not attempted to branch out into the Western community, as the organization in Chicago has attempted to do. Many other groups were started: Some remained private meetings of two or three families, others faded away, but the period was definitely one of religious ferment as the immigrants regrouped based on personal loyalty to religious leaders or on regional–linguistic ties.

The programs of the Islamic Society of Greater Houston also expanded at this time, with the acquisition of a larger center and the dispersal of mosques and Islamic schools throughout the metropolitan area. The great increase in numbers made it necessary to find new locations, and at the beginning of 1982 the society moved into a structure renovated by volunteers and valued at almost $500,000. By then it was estimated that 10,000 Muslims were in Houston, and the center accommodates about 500 for prayer. The Sunday School classes have 200 children in two sessions. Sermons are in English and Arabic; week-day classes are in English, Arabic, and Urdu – exclusively or mixed depending on the background of the participants. The society also divided the city for purposes of management into five zones where prayer facilities exist, either owned or rented, and the number of zones is projected to increase to nine. The society organized Friday prayers and Saturday classes in many of these zones, and purchased land in northwest Houston and in the Alief area as sites for future mosques. Students can also meet for Friday prayers at the university. Muslims negotiated with the State of Texas for a site for a cemetery of 274 plots for Muslim burials. The Masjid Dar-us-Salaam established a separate group in 1982, which follows more conservative practices regarding the position of women in the mosque and other traditional practices. The group of about twenty active families meets for Friday prayers with about sixty people, seventy percent of whom are from the Indian subcontinent.

At the end of 1981, the Ismailia Association opened an educational center with three classrooms and a library in a commercial building adjacent to the jamat khana, and 112 students were enrolled for daily classes in a graded curriculum under volunteer teachers. The Ismaili community grew to about 1,200 during this period, and it became necessary to open a second jamat khana in north Houston.

Over 1,000 Asian-Indian Christian families are in Houston, 300 of which are affiliated with the Catholic Church. In January 1980 the first Asian-Indian Catholic priest arrived in Houston. He had come on his own to visit his sister, and she talked him into staying because all his relatives are in the United States. He visited the bishop, who approved his move and assigned him to a parish. He was also given responsibility for a special ministry to Asian-Indian Christians. Thus, in addition to his parish work, he conducts a mass in Malayalam on the last Sunday of each month for Asian-Indian Catholics from the Syro-Malabar, Malankara, and Latin rites. Thus far, he has been able to keep all three together, and between 250 and 300 people attend. He conducts special services on days that are important in Kerala, such as St. Thomas Day. He divided Houston into thirteen areas and appointed a volunteer in each area who visits the Asian-Indian Catholics, encourages them to become involved in local parishes, and helps with arranging education for the children. The priest, who did his Clinical Pastoral Education at Houston Baptist University, reports that the major concern of the parents is the nurture of the young people, so he has begun a youth organization. A second Asian-Indian priest is now assigned to the Houston diocese, but he has no direct responsibility for the Asian-Indian community.

St. John's Syrian Orthodox Church (Antioch) was started by some Kanaya families from St. Mary's Church in 1981. The Kanayas claim descent from Thomas of Kana, who fled to Kerala from Persia in the fourth century, and they form a group of "old Christians" of Kerala who marry only other Kanaya Christians. Because Kanaya families are found in both Syrian Orthodox churches and Syro-Malabar Catholic churches, some intermarriage does occur among the churches. The congregation in Houston grew to about 32 families and was served by a part-time priest until 1986 when the priest moved to New York. The number has decreased to about 25 families who meet for prayers and occasionally have the holy communion when a priest travels from Dallas to lead the service.

The optimism of the period is reflected in the building plans of the Mar Thoma Church, which received its first full-time vicar in June 1981. By the end of 1981, the membership of the congregation was 180 families. They purchased five acres for a new building and laid the foundation in August 1982 for a building that would cost half a million dollars and seat 600 worshippers. It was the first Mar Thoma congregation in the country to undertake the construction of its own building, and was helped by contributions from the Mar Thomas congregations in Dallas and Chicago.

The Kerala Clergy Association of Houston began with a meeting of nine pastors from its various denominations. At Christmas 1982 the association sponsored the first ecumenical Malayalee Christmas service, which brought together members from the various congregations. Several hundred people, choirs from each congregation, and pastors gathered for what has become an annual festival of the Asian-Indian Christians in Houston.

For all the religious groups the period from 1980 to 1982 was a period of growth, expansion, optimism, and plans for building. It is estimated that between 30,000 and 40,000 Asian Indians resided in Houston, and more were arriving every day. The infrastructure of the community in the form of newspapers, magazines, stores, and cultural and religious organizations appeared to be on the threshold of continued growth and prosperity. It was a high-water mark, if not in numbers, then certainly in enthusiasm, spirit, and hope. Then the economic recession came abruptly.

Hard times (1983–1987)

The deep recession in the oil industry hit Houston suddenly in 1982. In the period between December 1981 and December 1982 the unemployment rate in Houston increased by more that 100 percent from 3.9 percent to 8.1 percent.[2] Only two other cities in the country, Wichita and Tulsa, experienced a greater percentage rise in unemployment (Marlin, 1983:142). In the year that the Mar Thoma congregation began construction of their new building, over half of the members lost their jobs. The men were typically employed as machinists with the oil exploration companies and affiliated businesses. Many of the professional people, especially the engineers, had to change careers. Some created new businesses to serve as financial advisors or real estate managers for those members of the Asian-Indian community who continued in their professional jobs. Many opened shops, real estate agencies, insurance agencies, and motels.

Disillusionment and frustration were common, and most religious leaders reported that many of the men in their congregations were unemployed and more were underemployed. By September 1983 the unemployment rate had risen to 10.1 percent, and some families were forced to leave Houston. Improvement followed for a brief period until 1985, when the drop in oil revenues and the difficulties for NASA caused by the failure of the shuttle flight led to a further downturn in Houston's economy. The unemployment rate reached 12.6 percent by June 1986 (*Employment and Earnings* 33, August 1986:115), and this caused great difficulties for the Asian-Indian community. As of 1987, growth in numbers has slowed, and personal and organizational finances are tight. Ironically, the depressed economic conditions have provided good opportunities for acquiring real estate at more reasonable prices, and active organizations are now able to purchase property.

The Christian groups had begun building programs that were completed in adverse circumstances. The Trinity Mar Thoma building was dedicated in July 1984, on the tenth anniversary of the congregation, with more than 1,500 people present. The largest Mar Thoma parish in the United States, it has 210 member families. The congregation conducts two services a month in Malayalam and two services in English. The Sunday School for almost 200 students from ages four to fourteen is taught by twenty-three teachers. A small group of seven families left Trinity in 1984, following the visit by a bishop from Kerala, to form a prayer group of the St. Thomas Evangelical Church of India. The India Pentecostal Church purchased a Baptist church building in 1983 and is the only Asian-Indian Pentecostal church in Houston with its own building. The congregation has a membership of 170 people from 42 families, and it is the largest of the several Pentecostal churches, but even so the pastor has a part-time job to help support his ministry. The program includes a Sunday School with seven classes in English for children, a Sunday morning worship service in Malayalam, with "a few minutes in English for the children," Sunday evening services held in locations away from the church building, Friday daytime prayers, and a Saturday evening meeting. St. Thomas Malankara Church began the construction of their building south of Houston in April 1983; the high cost of property during the boom forced some religious organizations to move away from the main population centers. The two priests serve a membership of 110 families, and the Sunday School of 120 students is the largest among the Malankara churches in the United States. A service book in English was published in 1981, and the service is a combination of English and Malayalam. St. Gregorios Malankara Church meets in a rented office building two times a month and purchased two acres of land in southwest Houston as a site for a new church building, although financial constraints make

St. Thomas Malankara Orthodox Church in Houston

it impossible for them to build now. A group of Tamil Christians began to meet once a month for Bible study and prayer in homes, and for larger celebrations on Christmas and Easter in rented halls.

The Akshar Purushottam Swaminarayan group made plans to build their fourth United States temple in Houston, but development of the plans and financing have been delayed. In 1985 they purchased a five-acre tract in Fort Bend County at a cost of about $300,000. In October 1986, they had a groundbreaking ceremony for a temple that will cost almost a million dollars. Approximately eighty percent of their members live within ten miles, and half within five miles, of the site. The mailing list of Gujaratis is about 1,200, but not all are members. Between 500 and 700 people participate, but the core group that meets every Sunday is of about 100 people. They attract the participation of many Gujaratis who were general Vaishnavas in India, that is, worshippers of Krishna. Members have pledged $250,000 and the group will receive some additional assistance from Dallas and from the national organization for the construction of their temple. Narayanswarupdas Swami approved the plans in 1986, and the dedication is tentatively planned for the summer or fall of 1988.

Two Gujarati Vaishnava groups were established in Houston during this period. A Vallabhacharya group, called the Madan Mohan Lalji Haveli, had been meeting for the singing of devotional songs, but it was formally constituted in 1983, with a prominent engineer as the founder and leader. In 1984, when one of the religious leaders of the Vallabhacharya sect visited Houston, he formed a new group and made Houston the central headquarters of the International Vallabhacharya Priti Seva Samaj in the United States. During his tour the leader collected the addresses of several thousand families of the Vallabhacharya sect (also known as Pushti Marg) in the United States, which included several hundred in Houston. Ninety-five families are registered members of the new association, which meets two times a month in a rented hall. In June 1985 a renowned female Vallabhacharya speaker, Goswami Indirabetiji, gave a series of lectures on the *Srimat Bhagavata* at which some 1500 people were present.

These two visits can be taken as illustrative of the many important visits by religious leaders from India. Some leaders undertake annual or semiannual tours, which are significant for attracting and identifying persons who organize and perpetuate the various religious groups. These visits are important to all the religious traditions, and include tours by Christian bishops and evangelists, Jain monks, Hindu holy men, Sikh singers, and Muslim teachers. In fact, the groups that seem to have the most unity and clearest direction form around a religious leader who can attract followers, incorporate them into the group, and give religious and administrative direction.

The Houston chapter of the International Society for Krishna Consciousness continued until 1985 in the small house in the central part of Houston where approximately thirty people lived (not Asian Indians) and where approximately 100 Asian Indians attended Sunday afternoon services. The majority of the participants and of the forty Life Members are Gujaratis. The facilities were very limited, and in July 1986 the group purchased for $300,000 a former Baptist church in northwest Houston where they have larger facilities – a 3,000-square-foot meeting hall and a separate educational building – and adequate parking. The location was chosen because the Asian Indians live in the suburbs. At least seventy percent of the funds came from Asian-Indian Hindus, with fund-raising activities that included visits to the homes of 200 families to ask for $360 from each toward the installation of images; the ceremony was performed in August 1986. The estimate is that 400 to 500 families, mostly Gujaratis, participate with some regularity in the programs.

The Jains of Houston became a formal group in 1981 and began to meet on the last Sunday of the month in the India Culture Center; before then they met in homes. The average attendance is about 40, but 250 attend if Sushil Muni, Chitrabandhu, or another famous teacher from India is scheduled to lecture. Some 170 families of the 200 Jain families in Houston are members, and approximately sixty percent of these are Gujaratis. They conduct a Sunday School in conjunction with the Sunday meeting to help the children be proud of being Jains and observe Jain customs. It is estimated that there are 1,000 Jain families in Texas, and one goal is to establish contacts with Jains who live in the smaller cities. They meet occasionally in the Hindu Worship Society temple when the India Culture Center is not available. Some discussion has taken place about building a temple, but over a quarter of the Jains have been laid off and many of these are in the process of starting private businesses, so they continue to meet in the center and temple.

The Nizari Ismailis have continued to expand in numbers during the hard times, and now number some 4,000 in Houston and between 8,000 and 10,000 throughout Texas. The group outgrew the property that had been rented for the first jamat khana, and in 1986 a new prayer hall and an educational building were rented in a four-condominium complex with an 800-car parking lot. Also in 1986, the jamat khana in north Houston was expanded to double its size. As a leader in another state remarked, "They have become Texas Ismailis, and everything has to be big."

Hard times for the Sikhs have involved both economic difficulties and the feeling that Sikhism itself is threatened by the antagonism of the government of India and by the indifference of the American public. At a time when their livelihood in the United States is in question, Sikhs feel they cannot return to India – even out of necessity. The "Khalistan syndrome" (for a discussion of the "Khalistan syndrome," see Chapter Two) in Houston is compounded by other difficulties that intensify the emotion and the tensions within the community. The results have been a division within the gurdwara, disturbances in the gurdwara that have required both police action and a court decision, and protests at the time of the visit to Houston by Prime Minister Rajiv Gandhi.

The division in the gurdwara took place at the time of the visit of the Sikh President of India to Houston for medical treatment. One group became identified with the position of the Congress Party in the Punjab in support of negotiations with the government, whereas another group supported the position of the Akali Dal Party under Mr. Brindranwale and increasingly called for the creation of a separate state, Khalistan. Those identified as supporters of the Congress Party were voted off the managing committee, and a group left the gurdwara in early 1984 to form a new group. Opponents say that they are "stooges of the government" because either they or their relatives are dependents of the government. The new group may have 200 families – it is difficult to determine how many now support each position – and 100 people meet regularly each Sunday in a school building ten miles away from the original gurdwara. Subsequent events in the Punjab have moved the two groups toward a common position, but they have not reunited.

The supporters of the Akali Dal position, also about 200 families, took control of the gurdwara. Some Houston Sikhs were active in opposition to Indira Gandhi, in support of Khalistan, and in agitation for Sikh rights. The first full-time religious specialist (Granthi) was appointed in 1983. He had a masters degree in comparative religion from the Punjab and had served as Granthi in Tanzania for about five years. A new Granthi came to the temple from Yuba City, California, in 1985, and, although the regular program continues, it has been a difficult time. The sixty Sindhi families in Houston stopped going to the gurdwara to avoid the political conflict. Financial support has diminished, because of both the recession and the conflict in the gurdwara, which has broken out in harsh words and even blows, so that special appeals have been made for funds to pay the bills. On March 10, 1985, a disturbance occurred during the Sunday religious services and the next Sunday a group of thirty Sikh men went en masse to the gurdwara, creating a confrontation with those in charge. The conflict finally was settled through court action (*The Sikh Center of the Gulf Coast Area vs. Tarsem Singh, et al.* in the District Court of Harris County, Texas, 334 Judicial District, May 31, 1985).

Prime Minister Rajiv Gandhi visited Houston and met with 2,000 invited members of the Asian-Indian community at the Albert Thomas Convention Center on June 15, 1986, one year after the Amritsar incident, in a meeting sponsored by the India Culture Center. The Sikhs organized a protest meeting of 250 Sikhs in a park across the street. Saffron-colored turbans, signs charging genocide, chants, and slogans marked the peaceful protest. (In the Punjab, followers of the Congress Party wear white turbans and followers of the Akali Dal wear blue turbans; now, saffron turbans are becoming a symbol of unity in opposition to the central government.) The juxtaposition highlighted the isolation of the Sikhs from the rest of the Asian-Indian community — not only in Houston – caused by the events in the Punjab, the riots in Delhi, and the assassination of Prime Minister Indira Gandhi. One active opponent of the government reports that he received more than 175 threatening telephone calls after he compared Indira Gandhi to Hitler (HC, 1984).

Inside the convention center, the speech of the Prime Minister and his answers to questions dealt with two issues of great importance both in India and to Asian Indians in Houston, but present in a different way among the latter: communalism and technology transfer. The communal groups in India are well established and the relationships among them formalized, but in Houston the regrouping of social and religious organizations is still in process and the structure of the networks of interrelations among them still developing. The isolation of the Sikhs, the inward character of their group development, and the growing antagonism between Sikhs and Hindus is a very visible part of the process. Other communities in Houston are also involved in the work of establishing new communal groups that have great potential for conflict but also for increased unity and cooperation among Asian Indians. The question of technology transfer raised the issue of the relation of the Asian-Indian scientists, engineers, and physicians to India. It is clear now that few will elect to return to India even though the Prime Minister said that he was taking steps to make that easier. He observed with some humor that Indians abroad display tremendous energy and competitive spirit, but when they return to India they want "a government job and solid-state security." Even those who lose their jobs in the technical fields in the United States look for positions elsewhere or enter other businesses in Houston. Mr. Gandhi stated his goal to speed India's move into areas of modern technology and economic development, and it became clear to the people who emigrated from India fifteen or twenty years ago that, as a former Foreign Minister of the Government of India said, "The India you left is not the India of today, and certainly not the India of tomorrow."

The society of a metropolitan area is a complex network of organizations and institutions – economic, political, educational, social, and religious. Religious organizations and institutions are like the blood vessels of several sizes and functions in the human body; they extend throughout the social organism and tie it together: silent, fragile, and essential. This study of Chicago and Houston demonstrates how these religious networks extend through the community and work in interrelation with each other, touching other religious groups and ethnic associations. Because metropolitan societies live through time, like organisms, it is instructive to observe how immigrant religious organizations develop through time. The Asian-Indian and Pakistani community had an early and steady growth in Chicago, and the religious organizations have reached a relatively high level of size and physical facilities. On the other hand, the immigrant community established itself a little later in Houston, but then experienced rapid growth followed by stagnation or decline. The general pattern of growth and function of religious organizations is similar in the two cities, but the peculiar economic situation in Houston since 1970 has affected the development of religious groups. Other cities have experienced similar general development, but each social location is unique in the way it shapes the Asian-Indian and Pakistani experience. It is not possible in the scope of this study to analyze the experience in every location, but local histories will be essential to preserving the religious history of immigrants from the Indian subcontinent, and they would do well to include the experience of all the "new ethnics."

Conclusion
Religious life under the Statue of Liberty

"E Pluribus Unum" and "In God We Trust" are two sides of the American coin. Implicit in a democracy of immigrants are the pluralism of cultures and the process of creating from that very pluralism a unity that can sustain a common life in spite of the inevitable strains. The other side of the coin is the religious legitimation of the unity in diversity by positing a single divine being who transcends the diversity. That synthesis allows diverse religious groups from around the world to preserve the sacralizing power of each tradition as related to individual and group identity and, at the same time, sanctions the legitimating power of the one god in whom we trust. One does not enquire too closely into the question of whether "nature's god" of the Declaration of Independence is the same as the god of Abraham because the powerful tradition of monotheism is essential in both formulations as well as to the theology of the American coin. At one level the issue of unity in diversity is theological, and peaceful communal life in any country involves skillful negotiation and the evolution of shared commitments.

To how many gods have immigrants prayed as they flew over the Statue of Liberty or came through other gates of entry? The patterns of immigration dictated by social and geographical location, modes of transportation, and legal restrictions resulted in earlier generations of immigrants who prayed – as they sailed under the Statue of Liberty – to the god of Abraham understood as nature's god in a wedding of the Hebrew, Greek, and Christian traditions – this in spite of great diversity. The phrase "Judeo-Christian tradition" came into common usage when negotiations among immigrants led to a sense of a common tradition that was constructed for a new situation (Cohen, 1970). It is curious that "Judeo-Christian tradition," as the phrase is now used, was recognized, named, and perhaps created through the contact of immigrants in the new land. The god of the Judeo-Christian tradition, loosely defined to

277

include concepts of the Greeks and of the Enlightenment, became for a
period the trusted god. Many of those immigrants who later flew over
the Statue of Liberty to Kennedy airport pray, however, to gods with
many names. That poses fundamental theological and social questions
resulting from the religious pluralism of the new ethnics. Will common
life together create out of many people one god? Will common life together create out of many gods one people?

The adaptation by immigrants to the pluralism created by their movement – even if it is only "myself as in continuity–discontinuity with the
past" or as "the other as a present alternative" – produces tensions that
make religion important in the formation and preservation of their individual and group identity. Religion is a powerful scheme for sacralizing
the elements of identity and preserving them through the identity crises
that are endemic to emigration. This is true even if religion is observed
only on the altar of the mind during the immigrant's early period in a
new location. Then, as a group is formed based on the similarity of
remembered pasts, religious affiliation becomes the creation of and the
affirmation of a peculiar, separate identity. Thus, religions are significant
both in the regrouping of immigrants and in the negotiation of identities
and new relationships both among the immigrants themselves (in this
case, Asian) and between these and other ethnic and religious groups.
Religion is a socially accepted idiom in the United States by which individuals and groups establish their identity and can demand that it be
recognized and affirmed by others.

Immigrants do not, however, establish the terms of negotiation by
themselves. The need for the unity that will lessen the anomie threatened
by social diversity leads, on the one hand, to a secular relativism under
the law and, on the other, to a theological unity of people from diverse
religions in the language of a new monotheism of the god we trust. This
is not civil religion, exactly, but it is to this one god that immigrants pray
when they affirm unity in diversity. The pressure is real. A young volunteer at the dedication of the images of nine deities in a new temple in
Chicago gave a careful description of "Hindu monotheism" for visitors.
Only recently have American presidents begun to refer in public announcements to religious traditions other than Catholic, Protestant, and
Jew, but it is certain that soon Muslim, Eastern Orthodox, Buddhist,
and Hindu will be included in presidential proclamations and on both
sides of the American coin.

The immigrants themselves will determine the theological and social
unity or diversity that will renew or change the affirmations of the American coin, but they must form religious groups and adopt strategies of
negotiation among themselves, before they are in a position to respond
to the pressure of the host society to create an effective interpretation of

"In God We Trust." This study has shown that each group selects its own strategy or combination of strategies. It is not clear which strategy will prove most effective or which will be followed by most groups, but four major patterns of adaptation are clearly in evidence.

Trajectories of adaptation

The negotiation of adaptive strategies is a long process in which the various religions function differently in the sacralization of personal and group identity. These differences are due to elements of theology, peculiar group histories, and the social and political context in new settings, and these in turn determine how religions are reappropriated by immigrants. Immigrants are not captives of the religious traditions they bring with them because, in the regrouping that accompanies emigration, they are able to choose elements of the religions in a dynamic that permits both the retention of the religious tradition and its reformulation. Choice and malleability of religion through new interpretations of the tradition, reshaping of boundaries, and reclothing basic elements empower the immigrant to create a religious future under the Statue of Liberty.

The various Asian-Indian and Pakistani religious groups illustrate the importance of four trajectories in the dynamic of adaptation: ecumenical, national, ethnic, and sectarian. These four trajectories, given in order from the most inclusive to the most restrictive, are not mutually exclusive, which means that some groups emphasize more than one element according to context, and some groups within the same general tradition – Hindu, Muslim, or Christian – emphasize different elements, so that the trajectories of adaptation vary. Trajectories are related to, but not determined by, the situation in India or Pakistan, and they take on new forms with both positive and negative aspects in the United States.

Ecumenical

Religions explicitly international in character may transcend ethnic and national boundaries to create ecumenical commitments. The ecumenical is always in tension with the national and ethnic, as most religious groups appeal to some form of universalism. On the theoretical level the claim is made that the religion is open to all or offers a truth about god or the sacred that transcends other formulations. On the practical level, the spread of a religion in more than one cultural setting indicates a transcultural appeal. Even those religions intimately connected with ethnic identity, such as Sikhism, or those closed to converts, such as Zoroastrianism in India, nonetheless contain aspects of religious universalism that are useful in establishing a new identity in the United States.

No such thing as a universal religion exists, however, one not in culture-specific dress. People are not "religious-in-general," but "religious-in-particular." They follow specific religious traditions, with texts, history, rituals, and leaders specific to a group. These are transmitted in a language, with music, persons, and gestures joined into rituals that have meaning in a specific social location and in "native dress." Every ecumenical movement must take account of the power of cultural particularity.

Muslims are creating an American Muslim minority made up of many ethnic groups. Some Christians from India and Pakistan participate in American denominations, but others form national or regional groups to preserve their cultural traditions. A difference of opinion divides Hindus. Some say that a person cannot become a convert to Hinduism, but must be born into it; missionary Hinduism stresses the universal truth of Hinduism, variously understood and available to all. Even in missionary Hinduism it is said that a person can remain a Christian or a Muslim and still follow a Hindu path – one can be a Christian Hindu but not a Hindu Christian. Hinduism is, however, deeply embedded in a culture, so that Western converts to ISKCON have adopted Indian culture – dress, language, cuisine, architecture – along with the worship of Krishna.

The ecumenical aspects of these religions provide a foundation for the negotiation of covenantal relationships with members of the same religion from other recent immigrant groups, as in the case of the Muslims, or with the majority population, as in the case of Christians. Claims of brotherhood may be more valuable to members of the second generation than to the immigrants, who find it necessary to stress the continuity of their personal and group identity through national and ethnic commitments rather than seek ecumenical unity with either other immigrants or the majority population.

Will Herberg showed that the descendants of earlier immigrants moved to ecumenical identifications within the three major religious traditions – Protestant, Catholic, and Jew – and these provided the primary boundaries for marriage and social development in the American "melting pot" (Herberg, 1960). A similar ecumenical strategy for the more recent immigrants may well lead to their primary identification as Muslim, Orthodox Christian, or Hindu, which take precedence over their original national or ethnic identification. It may well be the wave of the future, but it has not been the most effective strategy for the first generation of immigrants, most of whom have moved toward ethnic or sectarian forms of religion.

National

The nation state is a modern phenomenon, and few religions are national in origin. Shinto as the national religion of an island state is an exception, and that is the reason it is the *locus classicus* of civil religion. The power of the modern nation states, with boundaries almost as fixed a those of an island, tends to create such national forms of religion as, for example, Islam *de jure* in Pakistan and Hinduism *de facto* in India. The national form of religion, developed in India through the processes of Sanskritization and the formation of neo-Hinduism and in Pakistan by exclusion – of the Ahmadis, for example – unites in one fragile community people from many ethnic groups and sects.

The creation of new minority immigrant groups (such as Asian Indian and Pakistani) in the United States, with specific legal identification and rights as minorities based on their national origin but ignoring ethnic identities, reinforces the national element in the dynamic of adaptation. For example, all-India religious groups are formed in which English is the dominant language because it is the all-India language of the elite. Similarly, Sanskrit is the Indian language used in some Hindu rituals, even though few immigrants are familiar with it, because it is the all-India sacred language. When members of the dominant society identify immigrants as Asian Indians or Pakistanis, the immigrants – and especially their children, who do not have the same emotional attachment to a region of India or to a regional language – are encouraged to define their religion in national terms. Indian Muslims are an anomaly because they already respond to the ecumenical dynamics of Islam, which creates closer identification with Pakistani Muslims than with other Asian Indians. However, Asian Indians are in the United States, not South Asia, so the long-term process to observe will be the formation of an American Hinduism and an American Islam with a new American national character. Because of the selectivity of immigration laws and the peculiar ethos of American culture, these new national forms will be unique.

Asian-Indian and Pakistani religious groups were first formed on the basis of national identity, at least within the major religions, but as numbers grew to sufficient size in each location, the ethnic and sectarian forms of religion became prominent. National religious groups now find their future in jeopardy. During the time of the first generation, therefore, size of the immigrant population seems to be the determinative factor. The pressure of legal identification based on census designations and succeeding generations' loss of fluency in Indian or Pakistani languages may, however, lead to a return to prominence of religious organizations based on national identity.

Two national identities are involved in the development of an immigrant group: the nation of origin (India or Pakistan) and the nation of residence (United States). Tension between the two identities is often experienced as a generational gap between Indian or Pakistani parents and their American children, but the situation is more complex because elements of both national identities are found in every generation. Thus, religious organizations have the option of stressing, for example, either Indian or Pakistani national and religious holidays or American ones, or of elevating their estimation of the national administrative structures and leaders of America above the traditional ones of India or Pakistan. The national aspect of religious identification continues to exercise influence on immigrant organizations.

Ethnic

Ethnicity is intermediate between kinship and national identity, and it binds together minority populations whose members claim a common background, participate in shared activities, and value a language and culture. Ethnic identity for immigrants from India and Pakistan is formed in regional–linguistic groups, such as Gujarati, Punjabi, or Telugu, which develop within a city as soon as its immigrant population has grown to a sufficient size. Then religious groups proliferate, formed along ethnic trajectories. Thus, religious groups of Tamil Christians, Hyderabadi Muslims, or Punjabi Sikhs celebrate a union of religion and ethnic identity. Sikhism is the religion most closely identified with ethnicity, and the "Khalistan syndrome" represents an attempt to make religious and ethnic identity coterminous.

Certain conclusions can be drawn: In the first quarter century of immigrant experience, religious groups that stress ethnic identity grow rapidly and attract strong allegiance. They claim the loyalty of the most active members, who exercise leadership skills recognized and honored in India and Pakistan. They manipulate symbols tied to regions and languages of the subcontinent to which immigrants have deep emotional commitments. Religious ceremonies become occasions outside the home in which the ethnic language and arts are enjoyed and shared with members of the second generation. The administrative structures of these groups maintain ties with the traditional centers of religious authority in India or Pakistan. Even organizations that are developing ecumenical commitments can be seen to preserve their ethnic elements. Mosques are officially ecumenical and open to all Muslims, but many are unofficially ethnic in character, and as soon as the Arabic prayers are over, ethnic language, cuisine, and leadership prevail. Ethnic and sectarian trajectories often reinforce one another, moving in directions different from the ecumenical and national.

Members of the second generation are naturally less influenced by the ethnic element because few are fluent in the regional languages or maintain primary emotional ties with persons or institutions in India or Pakistan. The short-term strategy of stressing ethnic identity, which has been very successful for the first generation, may not be the most effective long-term strategy for the maintenance of religious groups unless forms of symbolic ethnicity are created in association with religious commitment.

Sectarian

"Sectarian" as used here refers to that trajectory created by allegiance to a particular religious hierarchy. It does not imply the meanings associated with sects in classic sociological typology; indeed, some forms of Roman Catholicism are sectarian as the category is used here. Generally, church-sect typology is not adequate for analysis of the religions of the Indian subcontinent. "Sectarian" does, however, imply a specific tradition and rituals transmitted and authenticated by a hierarchy. Sectarian forms may be closely associated with an ethnic identity, as in the case of Swaminarayan Hindus, or they may transcend ethnic and national boundaries, as in the case of Nizari Ismailis. The advantage of sectarian groups is that loyalty to a religious leader as the living symbol of the hierarchy and the ability of a leader to attract others and to marshal resources enhance their institutional development. An authoritative leader facilitates both personal and organizational decision-making when decisions must be made but the followers are stymied by the complexity of the situation or uncertainty about the effects of the various alternatives. Allegiance to religious leaders – gurus, metropolitans, or imams – seems easier for immigrant parents to transmit to their American children than language or ethnic identity. Indeed, authoritative religious leaders, around whom sectarian groups form, are often the mediators between past and present, between parents and children, between the forms of religion in India and Pakistan and their emerging counterparts in the United States. Such leaders ease the tensions between the generations regarding religious affiliation. Other tensions are created, however, by shifting loyalties among various religious leaders within the same traditions, especially at the time of the death of a leader and succession in the hierarchy. That has been the cause of some new sects and a source of fragmentation.

These four trajectories are present in various combinations in the dynamic of adaptation of Asian Indians and Pakistanis in the United States. A religious group might emphasize more than one aspect depending on the circumstance – ecumenical Christian in external relations, for example, and ethnic Malayalee identity internally. In Swaminarayan Hinduism, the trajectories are combined and reinforce each other in the union of ethnic and sectarian commitments. It is possible that groups will move from one emphasis to another in the process of maturation, a process that may cause some to assimilate patterns that are prominent in the host society, such as denomination or church types. Which element is dominant in a particular group depends on many things: on the tradition, history, and theology of the religion, on vagaries of the current situation in the United States, and on the conscious decision of members and leaders of the group regarding both their own future and that of their children.

Common problems

No matter what strategy they adopt, the leaders of these organizations face common problems as they prepare for an uncertain future. The leaders of earlier immigrant groups could actually be advisors to these new leaders, if they could remember the way it was, because many of their problems are similar. Nevertheless, Asian Indians and Pakistanis view their experience of immigration as unique, as do most new immigrants. Their problems of adaptation are intensified because of the variety of religions involved and because these differ significantly from the religions of earlier immigrants. The following are the problems that have surfaced earlier in the discussions of individual groups; they are not particular to any one group, but are shared by most immigrant groups, including the so-called old ethnics. Asian Indians and Pakistanis share many of their experiences both with the old ethnics and with other new ethnics.

Communalism

Communalism has become a major issue in the Indian subcontinent with India's development as a secular democracy and Pakistan's as an Islamic republic. Centrifugal force threatens to throw off various groups or to create internal friction so great as to cause conflict. Some of those tensions and conflicts have already surfaced in the United States; at the least they have made some unified efforts impossible and at the worst have caused outbreaks of violence. Tensions have been less disruptive in the United States than in Britain and Canada, in part because the educational and professional background of the first immigrants after 1965 facilitated their transition, but as the number of new immigrants admitted for family reunification increases, the problem of communalism may become more pronounced. The moderate leaders of some groups have already been replaced in annual elections or have resigned under pressure. These tensions, originating in the Indian subcontinent, could be magnified if they are absorbed into the negotiations of power among other ethnic and religious groups in the United States.

Mobility

Immigrants are moving all the time; their length of residence is short in any location in the first few years. Although their paternal native place in India or Pakistan is fixed, the present is full of movement, as immigrants become more active or less active in religious affairs, participate in one or in several religious groups, become officers or lay leaders, or convert to a different sect or religion. The religious groups themselves appear to be relatively stable, even in the immigrant community, but people inside are always on the move, changing their status, commitments, and beliefs. Another form of movement is the passage of time, which brings individuals and families to new stages of the life cycle: Students become householders and children are born who need to be socialized. The whole immigrant group is moving through life stages, and the religious activities appropriate for one stage may not be effective for another. This change is partially obscured by the arrival of new immigrants from the Indian subcontinent who constantly "renew" immigrant communities. The immigrants currently arriving from India and Pakistan for family reunification differ from earlier immigrants in education, professional certification, and job skills and prospects, and these changes in the social and economic makeup of the community affect the goals of religious and other cultural groups.

Immigration

References to America as "the land of immigrants" and spirited calls for liberal immigration laws, usually by politicians who are the chief guests at religious meetings, call forth applause. The leaders of religious groups publicly support liberalization of the laws, but privately they express concern about some of the more recent immigrants who do not have the education or skills to gain the social or economic status of the first wave of immigrants. In most organizations, tensions are just under the surface between the "doctors and engineers," who are accused of flaunting their wealth and of being worldly and insensitive, and the less successful immigrants, who are considered more religious and faithful to the traditions. The more recent immigrants have less economic power, but they have more direct contacts with leaders and practices in India. They are further removed, however, from the children of the "doctors and engineers." The assimilation of these new immigrants is a significant problem that has created strain. In addition, most religious and social groups have to deal with the presence and needs of illegal aliens in their midst – a silent sanctuary movement. In some cases this means finding jobs, housing, and – as the best solution for those with illegal status – a marriage partner who can bring a green card to the marriage contract.

Leadership

Leadership changes are common among immigrant religious groups, an understandable situation considering the great pressures. Only the Christian immigrants brought their religious specialists with them, and most of these are either students or priests who have full-time jobs outside the church. The local and national organizations of the other religions are organized and led by lay leaders. These leaders have considerable resources, administrative ability, and commitment, but they lack knowledge of the intricacies of doctrine and rituals of their religions. Immigration regulations make it difficult to import traditionally trained religious specialists without formal graduate degrees. Indeed, those with only traditional training may not be at all effective in communicating with those persons educated and assimilated in the United States. Religious specialists are generally marginal people, but the position between traditional Indian or Pakistani culture and American culture is a special type of marginality difficult to prepare for or to maintain, although many of the Christian bishops and metropolitans most closely associated with the immigrant churches have the advantage of having had part of their graduate education in American institutions.

Thus far the immigrant community has not generated its own religious specialists and would not have an appropriate infrastructure to train them if it had. A return to India or Pakistan by young people at an early age for the traditional study needed is difficult and would negate one of the main reasons given for emigration by the parents, and academic study of religion in American universities would not be adequate. This vacuum has attracted all types of self-authenticated volunteers for positions as religious specialists, and that has created problems for the religious groups. Many are attempting to control the appearance of these uninvited specialists. New religious organizations and impressive buildings appear all the time, but securing the appropriate religious specialists to serve the community continues to be a pressing problem.

Strategies of transmission

Religious traditions are transmitted through various media – rituals, teachings in oral and written form, and by attachment to a person – related to the traditional Indian categories of action (karma), knowledge (jnana) and devotion (bhakti). Leaders ponder which combination of these media will be most effective in preserving religious identity and transmitting it to their children. Each involves some symbolism that is difficult to translate across generations and cultures. Temple rituals in Sanskrit, church services in Malayalam or mosque prayers in Arabic are performed without much understanding of the verbal or gesture language – of the "words said over the things done." Some leaders place their faith in the ritual acts themselves to communicate messages that both children and adults can appropriate without being able to articulate the meaning. "That's the way we learned in India when our grandparents took us to the temples" is a frequent remark. Cultural performances and instruction in ethnic dance, music, and arts are variations of the rituals that preserve in powerful forms elements of the religious traditions. Teaching in the form of translation and interpretation is the main medium of transmission in many organizations, where lectures and discussions of sacred texts are primary and some groups, especially those associated with the Hindu philosophical traditions, stress this form of religious activity almost to the exclusion of ritual and devotion. Other groups emphasize intense personal devotion to a deity or to a religious leader who provides a point of emotional bonding between devotees of various generations, here and in India. Each of these strategies has value but also produces difficulties in adaptation in the United States, and although most religions have elements of all three, at this point it is difficult to predict which of the three or what combination will be most effective.

The children

Religious organizations are usually formed at the time when the children of immigrants reach the point of significant socialization outside the home. That is not a sufficient cause, but it is the major cause. One father reported a typical experience, "My wife began daily prayers when our first child was born, and we started attending religious meetings when she started . . . school." Parents regularly give as their reasons for participating in and supporting the construction of sacred shrines the desire "to find peace" or "to be near to god" and the need to preserve Indian or Pakistani religion and culture so the children will "know who they are." Hence, religion is a significant arena of negotiation between the generations. Parents are frightened by peer pressures on their children regarding dating, marriage, drugs, alcohol, and familial relations. "Will they still be sufficiently Indian or Pakistani to respect me when I am old?" is one unspoken question. A major issue is the custom of arranged marriages, which most parents wish to maintain in some form and against which most of their American children complain. One of the latent functions of religious organizations and other cultural groups is thus to provide "safe" contacts leading to semiarranged marriages in that the young people have a major say in the contract and which is becoming the standard compromise between the generations. Parents say that they hope their children will have "the best of both worlds," but the weight of negotiating between the two worlds and between the generations rests heavily on the shoulders of older youths who lived the first few years of their lives in India or Pakistan and are now growing up in the United States. They form the cutting edge, and there will never be another partial generation with the same challenges they face.

One generalization that can be drawn from the observation of many groups is that those who have reached the ages between fifteen and twenty-five – a relatively small group to this point – are largely absent from the temples, mosques, gurdwaras, and churches. One should note, however, that these pioneers of the second generation grew up at a time when the religious infrastructure was nascent. They are generally without children and of an age that their parents were also relatively inactive in religious affairs during their student days. It is too soon to predict whether the new infrastructures, strategies, and building projects will be effective in preserving continuity with the parents' past and in shaping new identities for the children. The children will, after all, determine what "Asian Indian" and "Pakistani" mean, other than a legal designation of minorities.

Language

Translation is essential because of the variety of languages in both India and Pakistan and because the children of immigrants are gaining only marginal ability in spoken and written forms of those languages. Bilingual education in American schools is not feasible, even though most of the fathers and some of the mothers received bilingual education in India or Pakistan. Religion is a cultural phenomenon that, along with poetry, is clothed in native language in texts, rituals, and doctrines difficult to translate with precision into another language. At the theoretical level, the question is raised as to whether basic concepts and their interrelations can be fully or adequately translated and have meaning in contexts where American English is the mode of communication. Probably not. There is always something lost and something created in translation. Translation is a conscious act, moreover, in which some things are intentionally lost or transformed. At the practical level the immigrants are generally not theologically competent to explain the details of their religion even in their native language, much less in English, and authentic religious leaders from India and Pakistan are rarely fluent in American English. The result is that translation is often done incompetently or by persons who are not full members of either the religious leadership in India or Pakistan or of the immigrant community in the United States. Language selection, the absence of adequate translation, and the use of regional Indian languages in ritual and in religious education are among the most difficult and emotionally laden problems religious groups face because they impinge directly on the transmission of tradition, identity formation, relations between generations, and most of the other problems faced by the immigrants.

Relations with India

Ambivalence of pride and anger, suspicion and fraternal feelings, fear and sympathy, mark the relations between expatriates and the people and governments of India and Pakistan. When Prime Minister Rajiv Gandhi spoke to the Asian-Indian community in Houston, he expressed pride in their accomplishments. He said, however, that they would serve India best by being successful in the United States and not by attempting to influence affairs in India. The religious and political relations of Sikhs with the government and in the Punjab are intense, and these provided the background for the prime minister's comments. The government does not want these conflicts to become the model.

Neither the government nor the immigrants themselves know if they will someday return to live in India or Pakistan. Reverse migration attracts only a few, mainly those who are so concerned that their children will become thoroughly Americanized that they take the children back to India or Pakistan for education and marriage. The rest engage in regular visits back and forth. Parents and small children first visit the extended family at the "native place." Contacts with religious leaders and institutions, communication with families, and international business contacts are part of visits to the subcontinent. Then, once the children have become teenagers busy with summer band, accelerated classes, football, and jobs, the grandparents visit the United States. But, can a person go home again? Yes, for a while! Can a person occupy the parents' native place? Not really! A young Asian Indian on his first trip to India, sitting in the heat and disarray of a small village temple, remarked, "This is not my cup of tea." For most of the children, India or Pakistan is "a great place to visit, but I wouldn't want to live there." They are constructing a place for India in their mental map of the world different from the India of their parents.

Public relations in the United States

Asian Indians enjoy good press and bad press. India and Indian immigrants have a relatively high rating in the estimation of the American public. India is an ancient culture, the world's largest democracy, the home of Mahatma Gandhi. The education and professional attainments of the immigrants have reinforced that generally positive picture. Neither are these recent immigrants openly competing for jobs with working-class Americans, either black or white. Thus, little economic or social conflict is visible. Pakistanis share in this positive opinion because they are few in number and are not recognized as a distinct group by the general public.

The religions of India and Pakistan, however, do not share in this positive evaluation. The negative reaction to aspects of the Hare Krishna movement and to some "high flying gurus" has brought Hinduism into disrepute in the public arena. Publicity about activities at Rajneeshpuram was an embarrassment to the Hindu community, and leaders attempted to make clear their judgment that this was a perversion of Hinduism. They were relieved when Rajneeshpuram was disbanded. Muslims also suffer from negative publicity, about Iranian Muslim radicals, Muslim terrorists, and protests in the Middle East. Sikhs are on the defensive because of unrestrained verbal outbursts by some leaders against Indira and Rajiv Gandhi and a few acts of terrorism. Among the negative reactions has been opposition to building projects, causing long delays in obtaining building permits. Some vandalism to buildings and homes is all too common, but leaders do not make a fuss about it lest it create further dissension. Leaders have been frustrated in their attempts to get a sympathetic hearing on matters of great importance to them, and they recognize that presenting a more positive picture of their religions and cultures has become a top priority. Little assistance is received from leaders of long-established religious groups. Even the Asian Indian-Christians are largely ignored by denominational leaders, who are concerned about refugees from Southeast Asia and Latin America but are uninformed about other immigrant groups. Urban politicians, many of whom are children of immigrant families, are more attuned to the growth, problems, and potential of these new immigrants. Tensions within the immigrant community and projection to other groups have caused them to face inward and outward at the same time.

Uncertain future

The president of a national immigrant religious organization invited a consultant to meet with his cabinet for a day's discussion of future directions. "We are now well-established," the president said, "but we must look to what will happen in the next two decades." He proposed the reading of analyses of earlier immigrant groups, especially of the experience of the Jewish immigrants, because they have been successful in maintaining their religious identity while fully participating in American economic, political, and social life. Emigration patterns vary, however, and the country "new ethnics" enter is so different from that of earlier generations that past immigration experience may not be able to provide models for the future. The general direction of development and the forks in the road may be viewed from a distance, but the exact path to be taken by individuals remains uncertain.

Asian-Indian and Pakistani communities will increase at an accelerated pace in the future. The quotas for immigration from the Indian subcontinent have been full, and people wait for years for their turn to emigrate, so it is reasonable to expect that the national quotas will remain filled in the future. Although no official refugees come from India or Pakistan, an undetermined number of illegal aliens do enter each year. Birth rates for these communities will be higher than the national average because so many immigrants are of child-bearing age. They are increasingly visible and prominent representatives of the "new ethnics" and of "new religions," even though they are small and heterogeneous groups compared to the Hispanics. It is not clear, however, if they can find a common cause, politically or religiously, with other recent immigrants. Thus far, each group has associated with other immigrants on the basis of religious affiliation – for example, with fellow Christians or Muslims. Little coordinated political action has been possible, as tension develops within the Asian-Indian and Pakistani communities between the well-established and partially assimilated immigrants of previous decades and the newer immigrants. The groups differ in social and religious needs as well as in attachments to things Indian and Pakistani. Those tensions will certainly persist.

Increased immigration, natural growth, and the resulting rapid social changes may create a backlash in American society of increased racial and religious tension and conflict. Some overt hostility has already surfaced. Temples, mosques, and gurdwaras, along with those who worship there, may become objects of hatred in a divided society. It is impossible to predict how groups would respond to such tensions, or to feel confident that religious and political leaders have the knowledge and the will to promote harmonious relationships.

The nature of relationships with other immigrants and with members of the host society will be affected by the efforts and successes of Hindu, Muslim, and Sikh groups in attracting converts from a wide spectrum of American society. Immigrant Muslims are active in the propagation of Islam in the American Black community and have had some success in reaching other Americans. Hindus and Sikhs experienced some success in previous decades in making converts, and a small number of potential converts participate in their religious activities, but no mass movement appears in the offing. Islam is an overtly missionary religion, is theologically and ritually more accessible, has strong international connections and support, and probably will have the greatest success in attracting converts. Asian-Indian and Pakistani Muslims will occupy an Asian room in the House of Islam, and will preserve elements of ethnic culture outside the mosques. By the year 2000, the religious scene may well be "Protestant, Catholic, Jew, Muslim. . . . "

Asian Indians and Pakistanis come from a divided subcontinent, and they cannot be expected to become united in the United States. They will continue into the next generation to be divided along lines of religion, nationality, and language. The ethnic identity of various regional groups will weaken because of the loss of fluency in regional languages and the constant pressures to assimilate. Religion could become an important part in the creation of a truncated "symbolic ethnicity" that conveys some political or economic advantage, while making few demands on those who move outside the ethnic group while preserving some marks of ethnic identity. The Indian subcontinent provides the resources for several forms of "symbolic ethnicity" and in spite of pressures to conform, it is unlikely that the immigrants will be totally assimilated or that they will be united into one (Indian) or even two (Hindu and Muslim) national or religious groups.

Some religious groups have developed strong national organizations, while others jealously preserve local control, and a tension between these two loci of control exists in most religious groups. More effective national umbrella organizations will surely be formed in the next decades – certainly more than will survive the weeding-out process; indeed, many have sprung up and already disappeared. Those that survive will facilitate the growth and development of the major religious groups, and will be the agents of external public relations for the immigrant communities. These national organizations will become responsible for the training and certification of professional religious leaders in the future. Moreover, they will determine the nature of the relationships that will be maintained with religious leaders and organizations in India and Pakistan.

Neither on local nor on national levels do these immigrant religious groups participate in councils of churches or ministerial associations. They have occasionally received support from the leaders of liberal denominations in gaining approval from various governmental agencies for the construction of buildings. A major question to be addressed, then, is the venue and nature of interreligious dialogue in the United States. The National Council of Churches and the National Conference of Christians and Jews, along with their local organizations, have until now remained aloof from the religious groups that are outside the Judeo-Christian tradition, even from the Asian-Indian Christian denominations now spreading throughout the country. An important next step is to develop structures for interreligious dialogue that will facilitate harmonious relationships among religious groups and provide the basis for communal harmony. Lurking in the background is the dreadful possibility that pluralism may weaken and destroy those structures that encourage harmony, with the result that the society will be rent asunder by communal and religious conflicts. It will be good fortune indeed if people of good will are able to establish harmonious relations.

Immigrants live at the margins between two cultures, and their religions are reformulated and transformed in the process of shaping and preserving their personal and group identity in that space. At the margins is the creative point for both the development of religions and the study of religions. Americans seem to be more religious than people of other Western industrialized countries. One reason may be that nearly the entire population is made up of immigrants who have had to regroup and reformulate their religions as people establishing identities at the margin of a new social world. New Americans have regularly become more religious in the process. Their identity involves both the establishment of boundaries and the means for transcending those boundaries in order to establish a common life together. That is both a sociological process – E Pluribus Unum – and a religious and theological negotiation – In God We Trust.

Notes

Introduction

1 More than 400,000 Southeast-Asian refugees came to the United States between 1975 and 1980, entering primarily under a series of parole authorizations granted by the Attorney General under the Immigration and Nationality Act (USCen2:2).

2 "Host society" has connotations that are unfortunate and seem to place the new immigrant in a subordinate place in a land made up of immigrants. The phrase is used, however, because no other phrase easily denotes the people and structures into which recent and current immigrants move.

1 A new pattern: Made in the U.S.A.

1 Between 1907 and 1920 approximately 6,400 Indians, mostly agricultural workers and mainly from the Punjab in northwest India, were admitted and made their way to California.

2 During the period between 1920 and 1974 Indians ranked second only to Canadians (9,056 to 10,519) in the numbers of non-American recipients of the Doctor of Philosophy degree from American universities (CHE, 1978:XVII,14).

3 Note that the figure 387,223 for the Asian-Indian population is the revised figure. The 100% figure is 361,531 (USCen2:6). The figure given in earlier census reports was 362,544 (USCen8:8). Some minor confusion in national, regional, and state population figures results from these revisions. The number of 15,792 for Pakistanis is based on a sample survey, and it is certainly low. The census report of persons who reported at least one specific ancestry recorded 25,963 as having Pakistani origin and 311,953 as having Asian-Indian ancestry (USCen9:21, Table 3).

4 The estimate of 525,000 is from a lecture by Peter Smith at a conference sponsored by The Asian Society on "India in America: The Immigrant Experience" in Chicago on April 20, 1986.

5 The rapid increase in the number admitted as permanent residents is reflected in the number of persons from India naturalized as citizens, which grew from

224 in 1966 to 8,298 in 1982. Persons from Pakistan registered a similar increase to 1,523 in 1982 (INS, 1982:111-12).

6   Of the 2,720 persons of Indian origin who became naturalized citizens in 1975, 1,687 were listed as professionals and technicians, and 141 as managers. Another 520 were housewives and children. These new immigrants were predominantly young. Of the arrivals in 1970, one out of seven was under ten years of age and more than three out of five were under thirty years (Hess, 1976:176). Only one in fifty was over sixty-five years of age in 1980.

7   A report of the Census Bureau records the success of the immigrants admitted under the new law (USDCN, 1984). Virtually the entire population of immigrants from India and Pakistan are new immigrants. Of those residents born in India recorded in the 1980 census, 43.7% immigrated between 1975 and 1980, 33.1% between 1970 and 1974, 19.3% between 1960 and 1969, and only 3.9% prior to 1960. A larger percentage of persons born in Pakistan came in the years 1975 to 1980, 52.3% of the residents in 1980. Almost a quarter of those from the Indian subcontinent were already naturalized citizens in 1980.

8   Note that the number 16,964 is for immigrants admitted by foreign state of chargeability under the worldwide numerical limitation of immigration. The total number of immigrants from India for 1982 was 21,738 (see INS, 1982:16, 54). More immigrants entered the United States from India in 1982 than entered in all the years prior to 1960.

9   States with the largest Asian-Indian populations in 1980 were: New York and New Jersey (97,321), Illinois (37,438); Texas (23,395); and California (59,774).

10   In the 1980 census the numbers of persons between the ages of twenty and fifty-four years born in India were 55,375 females and 64,965 males (USCen3:Table 255).

11   The number of Asian Indians under the age of twenty years was 124,075 out of a population of 387,223 in the 1980 census. The breakdown is: 42,815 under 5 years, 36,321 between 5 and 9, 25,670 between 10 and 14 years, and 19,269 between 15 and 19 years. The Asian-Indian population is very young.

2 The religions: Hinduism, Jainism, and Sikhism

1   "American Hinduism" is used in two senses in this work. One use is to designate the missionary Hinduism that attracted some American followers prior to and separate from Asian-Indian immigration. Included here are Vedanta Societies from an earlier period and ISKCON from the 1960s along with other, less successful attempts to attract Americans to embrace Hinduism. The other use of the term is for one shape that Hinduism will take in the future, on the supposition that at some future time there will be Indian Hinduism, British Hinduism, African Hinduism, and American Hinduism. The molding of American Hinduism is currently in process, but its exact shape is unclear. Part of the excitement of observation of the scene is the attempt to discern the shape of this new form of Hinduism.

2   The full order of samskaras begins with life implanting and ends with the cremation of the body. The sixteen main samskaras are: impregnation, fetus-protection, satisfying the cravings of pregnant mother, childbirth, giving the child

a name, first outing of the child from home, giving the child solid food, shaving the child's head, piercing the child's ear, investing with the sacred thread, starting the study of the Vedas, returning home after completing education, marriage, invoking ancestors, taking holy vows (2), and cremation. Only the most important of the rituals, such as birth, shaving the child's head, marriage, and cremation, are generally observed by Hindu families.

3   Careful accounts of income and expenditures are reported in the *Saptagiri Vani*, the quarterly publication of the temple. The income has been substantial over the past few years: $684,679 in 1981; $737,331 in 1982; $634,762 in 1983; $862,793 in 1984.

4   The complete list of professions is: engineering (38.1%); medical (19.8%); self-employed (12.4%); finance (9.8%); science (7.3%); management (4.1%); education (3.5%); other (3.5%); architect (0.8%); student (0.6%). These figures are from the 1986 Jain Directory with the kind permission of the Jain Study Circle of Boston.

5   The percentages in each state and province are: New York (14.7%); California (13.5%); New Jersey (11.2%); Ontario (8.7%); Michigan (7.1%); Texas (5.7%); Illinois (5.1%); Ohio (4.8%); Maryland (4.3%); and Massachusetts (4.1%). These figures are taken from the 1986 Jain Directory with the kind permission of the Jain Study Circle of Boston.

6   The percentages from each of the Indian states are: Gujarat (40.9%); Maharashtra (37.5%); Delhi (5.3%); Rajasthan (4.5%); Madhya Pradesh (3.9%); Uttar Pradesh (2.9%); West Bengal (1.9%); Punjab (1.4%); Harayana (0.5%); Karnataka (0.5%). These figures are from the 1986 Jain Directory with the kind permission of the Jain Study Circle of Boston.

7   The Jain calendar is lunar, so the festivals may fall in one of two months of the solar calendar, as Passover and Easter in March/April. The Paryusanaparva ritual is observed by the Svetambara Jains for eight days and by the Digambara Jains for ten days.

8   The identification as Asian Indian is used in this section even though it is an anachronism. The terms used earlier for immigrants from the Indian subcontinent were "East Asians," "Indians," and "Hindoos."

9   A leader of the Sikh Society of New York and of the World Sikh Organization who helped prepare the directory says that only organizations whose leaders responded to the questionnaires were included, and many failed to respond. He estimated that as of 1986 there were some two hundred societies, including the smallest, and that sixty of them owned some property. The others met in homes or rented halls.

10   The number is my conclusion from discussions with leaders of the Sikh Council of North America, the Akali Dal, a publisher of a Sikh magazine, and several leaders of gurdwaras. The Sikh Council publishes a directory of gurdwaras and of individuals (distributed from the Sikh Council of North America, 95–30 118th Street, Richmond Hill, NY 11419). The gurdwaras did not provide accurate information about membership, which even if included would only be of Sikhs who paid the annual dues, and only about seven hundred families submitted information for the directory. If a generous estimate of 500,000 Asian Indians in the United States were used as a base, an estimate of 50,000 Sikhs would mean

that they make up ten percent of the Asian Indians, and even though it is likely that they are better represented among immigrants than in the general Indian population, they are probably not much over ten percent. Punjabis may be a larger number, but they would then include Punjabi Muslims from Pakistan and some Punjabi Christians.

11   Radio and television in India is a government monopoly through All India Radio.

3 The religions: Islam, Christianity, Zoroastrianism, and Judaism

1   These estimates come from personal correspondence from Professor Ghayur, who permits use of them with the note that they are preliminary conclusions based on his data that will be further refined prior to his publication. I am grateful for his willingness to share his data.

2   These figures are working figures calculated by Professor Arif Ghayur. His earlier calculations will be found in his works of 1981 and 1983.

3   Professor Ghayur estimates the number of Asian-Indian Muslims who participate freely in Pakistani and Muslim community activities all over North America at 25,000 (1981:5). He projects a total of 135,837 Pakistanis in the United States by 1990 (1984:122).

4   Estimates vary widely, and an estimate that 15,000 nurses from Kerala came to the United States and that 7,000 families from Kerala are in New York seems very high (Badhwar, 1980).

5   The congregations in the United States are: New York (which has four), New Jersey, Rochester, Boston, Philadelphia, Baltimore, Washington, Detroit, Chicago. South Florida, Oklahoma City, Lubbock, Dallas, Houston, Los Angeles, San Francisco, St. Louis, Des Moines, and Seattle. The six in Canada are: Edmonton, Fort McMurry, Montreal, Ottawa, Toronto, and Kingston.

6   The priests in the United States are located in Houston, Dallas, Chicago, Detroit, Los Angeles, Philadelphia, and New York (where there are three).

7   A list of churches in the United States given in the Spring 1985 issue of *Malankara Light* (Vol. 5, No. 1) includes the following churches: St. Thomas' in Yonkers, St. Gregorios' in Queens, St. George's in Staten Island, St. Mary's in the Bronx, St. Basilius' in Brooklyn, St. Thomas' in Philadelphia, St. Gregorios' in Philadelphia, St. Mary's in Philadelphia, St. Thomas' in Washington, St. Thomas' in Detroit, St. Gregorios' in Evanston, St. Gregorios' in San Francisco, St. Thomas' in Syracuse, St. Thomas' in Houston, St. Gregorios' in Houston, St. Stephen's in Bergenfield, NJ, St. Mary's in Chicago, St. Mary's in Tampa, St. Thomas' in Chicago, St. Thomas' in Miami, and St. Thomas' in Oklahoma.

4 Their American cousins: Adaptation of cultural groups

1   For the International Society for Krishna Consciousness, see Rochford, 1985, Judah, 1974, Daner, 1976, Burr, 1984, Gelberg, 1983. For the American Muslim Mission, see Marsh, 1984, Lincoln, 1983 , Mamiya, 1982, Gans and Lowe, 1980. For the Happy, Healthy, Holy Organization, see Dusenbury, 1981 and Fleuret, 1974.

2 I am indebted to Professor John Cato for sharing this insight in private conversation.

3 The members of the Healthy, Happy, Holy Organization (3HO) or the Sikh Dharma Brotherhood are known as *"gora* Sikhs" or "white Sikhs" within the immigrant community. "White" is not a precise designation because some Punjabi Sikhs have as light a complexion as most Americans. "American Sikhs" is not a precise designation, because many immigrants are now citizens, and are, therefore, American Sikhs. Moreover, the Sikh Dharma has spread to other Western countries where there are non-Indian converts. Therefore, I use the phrase "white American Sikhs" to designate the non-Asian Indian converts of Yogi Bhajan. The original title of the group included the word "brotherhood," but that has been dropped.

4 This claim is found in a pamphlet "Sikh Dharma: Another Way to Live, Another Way to God," which was distributed by Sikh Dharma, 1620 Preuss Road, P.O. Box 35006, Los Angeles, California 90035. In a telephone conversation with a spokesperson, the number 250,000 was used of those who "relate in some ways to 3HO teachings." The number includes those in the West outside the United States.

5 The best estimate of the number of people living in the ashrams is about 2,000, and the estimate of the number of "white Sikhs" is 5,000. These numbers include those outside the United States.

5 Swaminarayan Hinduism: An ethnic religion

1 During the period of British rule and for the first two decades of Independence, Bombay was the capital of an area that includes Gujarat.

2 Participants do not remember the date; it was a long holiday weekend in the summer. The general agreement is that it was July 4. It was not on Good Friday (Williams, 1984:196).

3 The address of the property is 43–38 Bowne Street, Flushing, NY.

4 A list of the places visited gives an idea of the scope of the tour: New York, Hoboken, Newark, Boston, Utica, Rochester, Toronto, Erie, Cleveland, Dayton, Cincinnati, Ann Arbor, Elkhart, Chicago, Davenport (to mark the memorial to Jnanjivandas Swami), Wichita, San Francisco, Los Angeles, Dallas, Houston, Huntsville, Birmingham, Dublin, Georgia, Spartansburg, High Point, Richmond, Baltimore, Washington, Philadelphia, and back to New York. The listing of the tour is important because it gives a reliable indication of the locations of Gujaratis in 1977.

5 The tour was extensive and reached the following cities: New York, Jersey City, Philadelphia, Tampa, Jacksonville, Valdosta, GA, Atlanta, Birmingham, Huntsville, Jackson, TN, Lebanon, TN, Knoxville, Spartanburg, Salisbury, NC, Greensboro, Richmond, Sykesville, MD, Washington, Cleveland, Ann Arbor, London, ONT, Toronto, Dundas, ONT, Kitchener, ONT, Montreal, New York, Piscataway, NJ, Boston, Chicago, Dallas, Houston, Bryan, TX, New Orleans, San Francisco, and Los Angeles. Due to recent illness, Narayanswarupdas did not undertake padhramani to devotees' houses during this visit, but the several sadhus who accompanied him did visit homes. This listing is important because it indicates the location of important centers and families of the group.

6 Doctor Swami and the other sadhus toured the country in a van and visited Swaminarayan Hindus in the following cities: New York, Philadelphia, Washington, Oxford, NC, Greensboro, Salisbury, Charlotte, Spartansburg, Knoxville, Livingston, TN, Shelbyville, Manchester, Florence, AL, Huntsville, Athens, GA, Birmingham, Atlanta, Valdosta, GA, Jacksonville, Orlando, Emporia, VA, Staten Island, Boston, Rochester, NY, Toronto, Erie, Cleveland, Pittsburgh, Columbus, OH, Upsilanti, MI, St. Louis, Dallas, Henderson, TX, Bryan, Corpus Cristi, Houston, El Paso, Midland, Phoenix, Tucson, Los Angeles, Bakersfield, Fresno, Stockton, San Francisco, Salinas, and San Jose. Public meetings were held in most of these cities.

7 The address of the temple is 1 South 631 Milton Avenue, Glen Ellyn, IL.

8 The address of the temple is 12401 Pellissier Road, Whittier, CA.

9 The 224 questionnaires do not constitute a random sample. They were received from people attending meetings of the Bochasanwasi Swaminarayan Sanstha in Chicago (110 people; 49.1%), Dallas (49 people; 21.9%), Houston (45 people; 20.1%), and New York (20 people; 9%). Those in Chicago were attending a Sunday evening service in the temple in Glen Ellyn on May 18, 1985; approximately 25% of the 425 people (approximately 175 men and 250 women and small children) attending completed the questionnaire. Those in Dallas were attending a Sunday evening service in a home in north Dallas on June 9, 1985; approximately 50% of the 100 people (38 men and boys and approximately 60 women and small children) attending completed the questionnaire. Those in Houston were attending a Sunday evening service in a home in southwest Houston on June 16, 1985; approximately 75% of the 75 people (35 men and 40 women – the children were in separate rooms) attending completed the questionnaire. Those in New York were gathered to begin a trip to London to attend the Cultural Festival of India in July 1985; approximately 40% of the people (20 men and 30 women) completed the questionnaire. Women are underrepresented in the data (70 women to 154 men) compared to their attendance in the meetings. Two explanations are likely: (1) Gujarati women generally leave it to their husbands to complete official documents and questionnaires for the family and (2) some women have little facility in written English and could not easily complete a fairly complicated questionnaire with 69 items. Of those who completed the questionnaire, 204 persons (91.1%) responded in the affirmative to the question, "Are you a Swaminarayan satsangi?" Some of the tabulations used in the profile refer to all the persons who completed the questionnaire; some refer only to those who identify themselves as Swaminarayan satsangis. Percentages are rounded off to one decimal point.

10 Note that this statistic is different from that for Swaminarayan satsangis in England, the great majority of whom emigrated to England from Africa, not directly from India.

6 Nizari Ismaili Muslims: A religious minority

1 Some works give estimates of twenty million which may come from an earlier estimate by the Aga Khan IV (1969:1). He indicates, however, that the numbers

are not precise because it is impossible to get a precise community census and some governments do not have national censuses (quoted in Makarem, 1972:61). Note that Ivanow gives the total number of Khoja Nizaris as about 250,000 (1961:181), but that seems low.

2 The estimate was provided by Mr. Shams Vellani of the Institute of Ismaili Studies in London.

3 Leaders of the Nizari community in the United States were unfailingly kind and gracious throughout this research, and they provided some information about the group, but it was not possible to interview any members except a few leaders. Nonmembers are not permitted to attend the prayer services in the Jamat Khanas. Leaders have reason from recent publications to be suspicious of the motives of authors gathering information about the community. Information is available to those who are themselves Ismailis, with the result that much of the interpretation and writing about the contemporary Nizari Ismaili community is done by young Ismaili scholars who have been supported in graduate study by Aga Khan scholarships. Members of the staff of the Institute of Ismaili Studies in London were generous with information and material from their library, for which I am grateful.

4 In a statement of basic principles in *A Brief Outline of Ismaili Rites, Rituals, Ceremonies and Festivals*, reprinted by H.H. The Aga Khan Shia Imami Ismaili Association for the U.S.A., the items numbered 5 through 8 were replaced with "5. That Hazrat Ali, the first Imam, according to Ismailis, and other Shias was openly declared by the Holy Prophet Muhammad (peace be upon him) as Imam of the time. 6. That the obedience of the Imam of the time is a fundamental religious obligation on the Ismailis, and his disobedience is a paramount sin."

5 The locations of 55 jamat khana centers in the United States are: Albany, NY, Albuquerque, NM, Atlanta, GA, Austin, TX, Boston, MA, Bryan, TX, Cedar Rapids, IA, Chicago North, IL, Chicago West, IL, Cleveland, OH, Columbus, OH, Connecticut [sic], CT, Dallas, TX, Denver, CO, Detroit, MI, Edison, NJ, Fort Lauderdale, FL, Fort Wayne, IN, Houston, TX, Ithaca, NY, Kansas City, MO, Lancaster, PA, Lansing, MI, Las Vegas, NV, Miami, FL, Midland, TX, Milwaukee, WI, Minneapolis, MN, New York, NY, Normal, IL, North Houston, TX, North Miami, FL, Oakland, CA, Ocala, FL, Oklahoma City, OK, Orange County, CA, Orlando, FL, Pasadena, CA, Philadelphia, PA, Phoenix, AZ, Porterville, CA, Poughkeepsie, NY, Richmond, VA, Rochester, NY, Royersford, PA, San Antonio, TX, San Diego, CA, San Fernando, CA, Santa Monica, CA, Seattle, WA, Spartanburg, SC, Sunnyvale, CA, Tampa, FL, Torrance, CA, and Washinton, DC (*Ismaili Directory USA 1985*:xxv). About 20 other jamats meet in private homes, motels, or university halls.

6 *The American Ismaili* and *Roshni, U.S.A.*, the former magazine of the Ismailia Association, have now been combined into one magazine to be published two times a year. Each regional council publishes a newsletter.

7 Asian-Indian and Pakistani religions in Chicago

1 The SCSA number for Chicago, Gary, Kenosha, Indiana and Wisconsin is 34,073 (USCen5:385). Of the 32,357 population given for the Chicago area, 11,115 were under twenty years of age and only 647 were over sixty-five. The family size was 3.56 persons per family (USCen10:114). Those who were born in India (this number does not include Indians born in East Africa or England) number 21,740, and the periods of their immigration were: 10,202 between 1975 and 1980; 7,755 between 1970 and 1974; 2,679 between 1965 and 1970; 649 between 1960 and 1970; 354 between 1950 and 1960; 101 before 1950. By 1980, 4,310 had become citizens; 17,430 had not (USCen6:Table 342). Cook County had 23,062 Asian Indians, many in the north and northwest suburbs: Addison Village, 445; Bolinbrook, 406; Downers Grove, 448; Elk Grove, 508; Park Forest, 443; Glendale Heights, 593; Hanover Park, 453; Hoffman Estates, 497; Morton Grove, 463 (USCen10:247-48, 421).

2   No separate reliable estimate of the number of Pakistanis in Chicago exists. An editor of an Urdu newspaper estimates that there are 20,000 Urdu-speaking families in the Chicago area, which would include Pakistanis and Asian-Indian Muslims, but that estimate seems high. An estimate of 5,000 families or 20,000 persons would seem more reasonable.

3   In August 1984 a survey of 323 member families showed that residence was spread out: 72 in Chicago; 133 in western and northwestern suburbs; 34 in northern suburbs; 30 in southwestern suburbs; 54 in other locations.

4   The list includes the Muslim Student Association locations at Northeastern, Northwestern, University of Chicago, and Illinois Institute of Technology. It includes some mosques of Afro-Americans, but not all.

5   Many of the Muslims from India are from Hyderabad, which was a princely state ruled by Muslims. A rough estimate given by one leader is that 50–60% come from Hyderabad, 30% from Gujarat, and 10–20% from other parts of India.

8 Asian-Indian and Pakistani religions in Houston

1   There were 8,029 foreign born Asian Indians in Houston, and their periods of immigration were: 4,106 (1975–80); 2,729 (1970–4); 841 (1965–70); 212 (1960–4); 97 (1950–59); and 44 before 1950. 1,478 were citizens and 6,551 were not citizens.

2   The unemployment rates, in percentages, for Chicago and Houston for selected months from 1976 to 1985 are as follow (from EE for relevant months): Chicago: Sept 1976 (7.0); Oct 1976 (na); Sept 1980 (8.1); Oct 1980 (8.5); Sept 1981 (7.9); Oct 1981 (7.9); Sept 1982 (11.4); Oct 1982 (11.0); Sept 1983 (9.1); Oct 1983 (8.1); Sept 1984 (8.1); Oct 1984 (8.3); Feb 1985 (8.0); March 1985 (7.0); June 1986 (7.8). Houston: Sept 1976 (5.6); Oct 1976 (5.2); Sept 1980 (3.7); Oct 1980 (3.5); Sept 1981 (4.4); Oct 1981 (4.1); Sept 1982 (8.3); Oct 1982 (8.0); Sept 1983 (10.1); Oct 1983 (8.1); Sept 1984 (6.4); Oct 1984 (5.7); Feb 1985 (7.6); March 1985 (7.8); June 1986 (12.6). The percentages for Chicago are high, but the swings are not so great.

Glossary

acharya: a spiritual preceptor or teacher; the head of a sampradaya; the two hereditary leaders of the Ahmedabad and Vadtal dioceses of the Swaminarayan religion.

agama: theological manuals; a traditional religious text prescribing details of rituals; prescriptions for building of temples, dedication of temples and temple rituals.

ahimsa: not to injure or harm any living being; specifically, not to kill or eat animals; nonviolence; a central vow of Jainism and the Swaminarayan religion.

akshar: the abode of the supreme person; an eternal state, thought to have an impersonal form as a state of being and a personal form as an abode of god.

amil: a title in the public administration of the caliph; local leader of Bohora Ismailis appointed as representative of the Dai.

amrit parchar: ritual of initiation into the Khalsa of Sikhism; drinking sugared water.

arti: the waving of a special oil light before the deity; the ceremonies of daily worship in the temple or before the home shrines in which the lights are waved before the images.

avatara: a descent or manifestation of a deity, specifically of a human or animal form assumed by Vishnu; the *Bhagavata Purana* names twenty-two, but adds that they are numberless.

ayurveda: traditional Indian health system and medicine.

bai'at: act of swearing allegiance to the Imam or to a sovereign; the covenant entered into with the Imam by every mature Ismaili.

batin: esoteric; inner, secret meaning of a text or rite; inner meaning of the Quran, contrasted with the literal meaning.

bhajan: singing of sacred songs; communal singing of devotional hymns.

bhakti: religious devotion as a way to salvation; fervent devotion to god; participation in a devotional cult.

chakra: the image of a wheel used as a symbol of cosmic order; chief centers in the body of Hindu physiology, subject of esoteric knowledge.

Dai: missionary; propagandist; the representative of the Imam in some forms of Shi'a Islam.

darshan: a looking at or viewing; the act of looking at the image of the deity in the shrine, sometimes of seeing a holy person.

dashond: obilgatory tithes in Ismaili Islam.

dawah: missionary activity; propagation of Islam.

derbe mehr: prayer hall and assembly hall for Zoroastrians; not an official Fire Temple, but a place for rituals.

Devanagari: literally, divine script; the script in which Sanskrit, Hindi, and Marathi are written.

dhan: believers' possessions dedicated to god to be used in accordance with the Imam's guidance.

dharma: obligations incumbent upon a Hindu according to his social status or stage of life; the basis of social order; duty and custom; codes of conduct for individuals and groups.

du'a: imploring; individual, informal prayer, as distinguished from salat, the obligatory prayers in Islam.

firman: order issued from the Ottoman chancery; an official communication of the Imam to Ismaili Muslims.

gadi: a couch; a throne-like chair for the acharya of the Vallabha and Swaminarayan religions; the seat of the acharya in Ahmedabad and in Vadtal.

ginan: some 800 sacred poems and hymns composed over six centuries and used by Nizari Ismailis in their services.

gotra: exogamous group within castes among the three "twice-born" varnas, defined by its members as being descended from the same (remote, probably mythical) male ancestor through an uninterrupted patriline.

Granth Sahib: the Sikh sacred writings.

Granthi: religious specialist in Sikhism; a teacher; a singer of hymns.

Gurbani: recitations and readings of the *Adi Granth* in Sikh rituals.

gurdwara: literally, Gateway of the Guru; prayer hall and assembly room for Sikhs.

guru: a religious teacher or adviser; a preceptor, especially one who gives initiation.

Gurumukhi: the script used for writing the Sikh sacred scriptures.

Hadith: tradition of an act or saying attributed to Muhammad.

Hajj: pilgrimage to Mecca.

Harijan: literally, child of god; Mahatma Gandhi's designation for the Untouchables.

Hazar Imam: literally, Imam of the Time; title of the Imam.

Imam: leader of prayer in mosques; specifically used in Shi'a Islam for those descendants of the Prophet who carry the prophetic light.

jamat: assembly; the community.

jamat khana: place of assembly; prayer hall for Ismailis.

jnana: knowing; the path to salvation by knowledge of the ultimate reality.

kamaga agama: Hindu ritual texts in the Shaiva tradition.

kamadia: deputy of the mukhi in the leadership of local Nizari Ismaili jamats.

karma: result of actions; effects of behavior; cause and effect in moral affairs.

keshdhari: unshaven head; initiates in the Khalsa of Sikhism who wear the five symbols of a Sikh.

kirtan: a devotional song; singing of devotional songs, as in a kirtan aradhana, which is a concert of sacred songs.

Kumbhabhishekam: ceremony of dedication of a Hindu temple and the installation of images of the deities for worship.

kundalini: energy at the base of the spinal column that is awakened through the exercise of difficult yogic techniques.

langar: literally, kitchen; the communal meal that follows each service in a Sikh gurdwara, which is open to all regardless of caste or status.

lingam: one of the forms of Shiva; a phallic form.

Mahdi: the guided one; a leader to come in the future as the Deliverer; return of the concealed Imam.

malida: ritual held on auspicious occasions by Bene Israel, often in homes.

man: believer's mind dedicated to god in the oath of allegiance to be used in accordance with the Imam's guidance.

markus: religious centers for Bohora Ismaili Muslims.

masjid: a Muslim mosque; prayer hall.

Mobed: a Zoroastrian priest; person from a hereditary class with the right to perform Zoroastrian rituals.

mukhi: leader; male leader of a local jamat of Nizari Ismaili Muslims.

mukhiani: female leader; leader of women's activities in Nizari Ismaili jamats; often, but not always, the wife of the mukhi.

muni: a Jain ascetic; monk; mendicant.

murti: material form of the deity; image of the deity installed in a temple; a picture, statue or relief image of a deity.

nass: designation and authority as Imam, as the legitimate leader of the believers in Shia Islam.

Navjote: ritual of initiation for Zoroastrian young people.

Nur: light; prophetic light resident in the designated descendant of the Prophet in Shi'a Islam; light manifest by the Prophet and the Imams.

padhramani: a visit to the home or business of a devotee by a religious leader; ritual of blessing the homes and businesses of devotees.

prasada: a gift; grace; food distributed after having been offered to the deity in the temple or at the home shrine.

puja: an act of worship; daily worship in household, temple, or shrine; used especially of the morning and evening worship.

pujari: one who performs the act of worship; the priest who cares for the deities in the temple and performs the daily rituals.

purushottam: Supreme Reality; the supreme person, the highest divine reality.

sadhu: a Hindu ascetic, one who has renounced the world; one who has received initiation and taken the vows of the Swaminarayan ascetics.

sahajdhari: Sikhs who are not initiates in the Khalsa and who do not wear the five symbols of a Sikh.

samaiyo: general meetings of Swaminarayan Hindus; monthly meetings.

samskara: one of the life-cycle rituals of Hinduism, sixteen rituals prescribed in the sacred texts, including birth, sacred thread, marriage, and cremation.

satsangi: a companion of the truth; follower of a religious path; member of a religious fellowship or satsang.

sayyid: a descendant from Ali through his son, Husain.

shakti: energy; female, creative divine power; female aspect of divinity; cosmic power.

shaykh: literally, old man; a descendant from the tribe of the Prophet; a religious leader.

silpi: traditionally trained craftsman, trained in arts and crafts of Hindu temple construction.

swami: master; title of respect for a sadhu or ascetic; head of a monastery.

tan: believer's person dedicated to god in the oath of allegiance to be used in accordance with the Imam's guidance.

taqiyya: guarding oneself; religious dissimulation or secrecy; not to practice some external rituals or to make public profession when under persecution; not to make known esoteric aspects of the religion.

tariqah: literally a road, way, or path; a form of Islamic religious discipline; Sufi discipline.

umma: community; the community of Muslims founded by Muhammad.

waezeen: religious specialists trained to give religious instructions or sermons (waezes); preachers and religious educators in Nizari Ismaili Islam.

wali: one to whom a ruler delegates authority; trustee; executor of the Prophet.

wasi: vice-regent of the Prophet; saint; holy man in popular Islam.

yantra: a mystical symbol in Hinduism; a Tantric symbol.

zahir: exoteric; literal meaning of a ritual or text; contrasted to the esoteric (batin); literal meaning of the Quran.

zakat: the general religious tax stipulated in Islamic law.

Abbreviations

APSG   Andhra Pradesh State Government. Revenue [Endts. III] Department, G. O. MS. No. 827, Dated 23rd May, 1984.

CHE   *Chronicle of Higher Education*, January 15, 1986/September 5, 1984:21.

CT   *Chicago Tribune*, April 24, 1986:I, 28.

EE   *United States Department of Labor*, Bureau of Labor Statistics "Employment and Earnings."

FR   *Federal Register*, August 23, 1982, Vol. 47:36743.

HC   *Houston Chronicle*, November 12, 1984.

HE   *Harvard Encyclopedia of American Ethnic Groups*. Stephan Thernstrom, ed., Cambridge, MA: Harvard University Press, 1980.

HT   *Hinduism Today*, Vol. 8, No. 1, January 1, 1986.

IA   *India Abroad*, July 4, 1986:14.

IAMR   Institute of Applied Manpower Research. "Migration of Indian engineers, scientists and physicians to the United States." IAMR Report No 2/1968. New Delhi, March, 1968.

IN   *India News*, June 2, 1986.

INS   United States Immigration and Naturalization Service. 1982. *Statistical Yearbook of the Immigration and Naturalization Service*.

IT   *India Tribune*, November 16, 1985:15.

MSA   Muslim Students Association. 1981. "Nineteenth Annual Report of the Muslim Students Association."

NYAN   *New York Amsterdam News*, May 23, 1964:14.

PC   *Pittsburgh Courier*, March 6, 1965:4.

PL   United States Congress. Public Law 89–236, 89th Congress, H.R. 2580, October 3, 1965.

USCen1   United States Department of Commerce. *1970 Census of Population: Supplementary Report: Country of Origin, Mother Tongue, and Citizenship for the United States*, PC–S1–35:1.

USCen2   United States Department of Commerce. *1980 Census of Population: Asian and Pacific Islander, Population by State*, PC80–S1–12:2,8.

307

USCen3   United States Department of Commerce. *1980 Census of Population: United States Summary*, PC80–1–D1–A, Table 255A.

USCen4   United States Department of Commerce. *1980 Census of Population: Characteristics of the Population*, PC80–1–C1:1–391–401, Tables 106 & 248.

USCen5   United States Department of Commerce. *1980 Census of Population: Characteristics of the Population*, PC80–1–C1:389.

USCen6   United States Department of Commerce. *1980 Census of Population: United States Summary*, PC80–1–D1–C:Table 342.

USCen7   United States Department of Commerce. *1980 Census of Population*, PC80–1–B45:138.

USCen8   United States Department of Commerce. *1980 Census of Population: Race of the Population by States*, PC80–S1–3:8.

USCen9   United States Department of Commerce, *1980 Census of Population: Supplementary Report, Ancestry by State*, PC80–S1–10:21, Table 3.

USCen10   United States Department of Commerce, *1980 Census of Population*, PC80–1–B15:114.

USDCN   *United States Department of Commerce News*. 1984. "Socioeconomic Characteristics of U.S. Foreign-born Population Detailed in Census Bureau Tabulations," CB84–179, October 17.

References

Aagaard, Johannes. 1982. "Hinduism's world mission." *Update* VI, 3:4.

Abraham, P. M. 1967. "An outline for a study of brain drain from India." *Manpower journal*. III (Oct/Dec):15–44.

Abu-Laban, Baha. 1983. "Canadian Muslim community." In *The Muslim community in North America*, ed. Earle H. Waugh, et al., pp. 75–92. Edmonton: University of Alberta Press.

Aga Khan III. 1953. *Message of H.R.H. Prince Aga Khan III to nation of Pakistan and world of Islam*. Karachi: Ismailia Association Pakistan.

1954. *The memoirs of Aga Khan: world enough and time*. New York: Simon & Schuster.

Aga Khan IV. 1969. "Ismaili Community and its contribution to the Commonwealth." Speech made at Oxford University on November 2, 1960. In *Africa Ismaili* (NS) I, 8:1.

1976. "The role of private initiative in developing countries." Address to the Swiss–American Chamber of Commerce on January 14 in Zurich, Switzerland. Zurich: Swiss–American Chamber of Commerce.

1982a. "The Aga Khan social welfare and economic development institutions in Tanzania." Speech made during a visit to Dar-es-Salaam, Tanzania in November. Aiglemont: Islamic Publications.

1982b. *Speeches of the Aga Khan*. Karachi: His Highness Prince Aga Khan Shree Imami Ismailia Association for Pakistan.

1983a. "The Aga Khan social welfare and economic development institutions in India." Speech made during a visit to New Delhi, India on January 14. Aiglemont: Islamic Publications.

1983b. "Economic development and the enabling environment." Speech made during a visit to Dhaka, Bangladesh, on January 6. Aiglemont: Islamic Publications.

1984. *Silver jubilee speeches of Mowlana Hazar Iman*, Vol. I. Karachi: His Highness Prince Aga Khan Shree Imami Ismailia Association for Pakistan.

1985. "Welcome address at the opening of the Ismaili Center in London" on April 24. Quoted in *Horizon*, May 3, 1985:1–2.

Amiji, Hatim M. 1969. "The Asian communities." In *Islam in Africa*, ed. James

Kritzeck & William H. Lewis, pp. 139–84. New York: Van Nostrand-Reinhold Co.

Andhra Pradesh State Government. 1984. Revenue [Endts.III] Department, G. O. MS. No. 827, Dated 23rd May.

American Ismaili. 1986. "Special Edition," p. 10.

Andrews, K. P., ed. 1983. *Keralites in America: community reference book.* Glen Oaks, NY: Literary Market Review.

Archibald, K. A. 1971. *The supply of professional nurses and their recruitment and retention by hospitals.* New York: Rand Institute.

Ashby, Philip H. 1974. *Modern trends in Hinduism.* New York: Columbia University Press.

Badhwar, Inderjit. 1980. "Indians in America – at the crossroads." *India Tribune* 15, August 16, pp. 16–7.

Barrett, David B. 1982. *World Christian encyclopedia.* Oxford: Oxford University Press.

Barth, Fredrik, ed. 1969. *Ethnic groups and boundaries: the social organization of culture difference.* London: George Allen & Unwin.

Berger, Peter. 1969. *The sacred canopy: elements of a sociological theory of religion.* New York: Anchor Books.

Berque, Jacques. 1974. "Islam and innovation." In *Islam, Philosophy and Science,* pp. 69–98. Paris: UNESCO Press.

Bhaloo, Shams H. J. 1980. "The role and image of community leaders." *American Ismaili,* December:33–4.

Bharati, Agehananda. 1967. "Ideology and content of caste among the Indians in East Africa." In *Caste in overseas Indian communities,* ed. Barton M. Schwartz, pp. 296–311. San Francisco: Chandler Publishing Co.

Bhardwaj, S. M., & M. N. Rao. 1983. "Religious reknitting of ethnic Hindus in the 'New World'." Paper presented at the 79th Annual Meeting of the Association of American Geographers in Denver, CO, April 24–27.

Bhatt, Bharat L. 1977. "The religious geography of South Asia: some reflections." *The national geographical journal of India* XXIII, 1 & 2:26–39.

1980. "India and Indian regions: a critical overview." In *An exploration of India: geographical perspectives on society and culture,* pp. 35–61. Ithaca, NY: Cornell University Press.

Bodnar, John. 1985. *The transplanted: a history of immigrants in urban America.* Bloomington: Indiana University Press.

Bogue, Donald J. 1985. *The population of the United States: historical trends and future projections,* New York: The Free Press.

Bose, Mihir. 1984. *The Aga Khan.* Kingswood, UK: World's Work.

Braden, Charles S. 1959a. "Islam in America." *International review of missions* XLVII, 2:309–17.

1959b. "Moslem missions in America." *Religion in life* XXVIII, 3:331–43.

Brass, Paul. 1974. *Language, religion and politics in North India.* Cambridge: Cambridge University Press.

Brelvi, Mahmud. 1964. *Islam in Africa.* Lahore: Institute of Islamic Culture.

Brown, L. W. 1956. *The Indian Christians of St. Thomas,* Cambridge: Cambridge University Press.

Brown, Linda Keller, & Kay Mussell, eds. 1984. *Ethnic and regional foodways in the United States: the performance of group identity.* Knoxville: University of Tennessee Press.

Brush, John E. 1949. "The distribution of religious communities in India." *Annals of the Association of American Geographers* XXXIX, 2:81–98.

Burr, Angela. 1984. *I am not my body: a study of the International Hare Krishna Sect.* New Delhi: Vikas.

Cafferty, Pastora S.J., Barry R. Chiswick, Andrew M. Greeley, & Teresa A. Sullivan, eds. 1983. *The dilemma of American immigration: beyond the golden door.* New Brunswick, NJ: Transaction Books.

Canard, M. 1965. "Da'wa." In *Encyclopaedia of Islam*, ed. B. Lewis, Ch. Pellat, & J. Schacht, II, pp. 168–70. Leiden: E. J. Brill.

Caroli, Betty Boyd. 1979. "Recent immigration to the United States." In *Ethnic and immigration groups: the United States, Canada, and England*, pp. 49–69. New York: Institute for research in history.

Chandler, Russell, & Tyler Marshall. 1981. "Guru brings his ashram to Oregon." *Los Angeles Times*, 30 August.

Chathaparampil, Joseph. 1970. "The brain drain: a case study." *Asian forum* II:236–44.

Chen, Sheryl. 1983. "Ethnic parishes aren't catholic." *U.S. Catholic* XLVIII:12–17.

Chicago Tribune, April 24, 1986:I, 28.

Christianity in India: a critical study. Madras: Vivekananda Kendra Prakashan, 1979.

Chronicle of Higher Education. 1984. "Foreign students in U.S. institutions, 1983–84," Vol. 19, No. 2, September 5, p. 21.

Chronicle of Higher Education. 1986. "3,800 physicians failed to get U.S. residencies in 1985." Vol. 31, No. 18, January 15, p. 4.

Clothey, Fred W. 1983. *Rhythm and intent: ritual studies from South India.* Madras: Blackie & Son.

Cohen, Arthur A. 1970. *The myth of the Judaeo-Christian tradition.* New York: Harper.

Cohn, Bernard S. 1967. "Regions subjective and objective: their relation to the study of modern Indian history and society." In *Regions and regionalism in South Asian studies: an exploratory study*, ed. Robert I. Crane. Durham, NC: Duke University Program in Comparative Studies on S. Asia.

Cole, W. Owen, & Piata Singh Sambhi. 1978. *The Sikhs: their religious beliefs and practices.* London: Routledge & Kegan Paul.

Contractor, Noman [*sic*] L., et al., 1980. *The Dawoodi Bohoras.* Pune, India: New Quest Publications.

Corbin, Henry. 1983. *Cyclical time and Ismaili gnosis.* London: Kegan Paul.

Craighill, Peyton G. 1982. "The ministry of the Episcopal Church in the United States of America to immigrants and refugees: a historical outline." *Historical magazine of the Protestant Episcopal Church* LI:203–18.

Cuddy, Dennis Laurence, ed. 1982. *Contemporary American immigration.* Boston: Twayne Publishers.

Dadabhay, Yusuf. 1954. "Circuitous assimilation among rural Hindustanis in California." *Social Forces* XXXIII:138–41.

District Court of Harris County, Texas. 1985. *The Sikh Center of the Gulf Coast Area vs. Tarsem Singh, et al.*, 334 Judicial District, May 31.

D'Souza, Victor. 1983. "Religious minorities in India: a demographic analysis." *Social action* XXXIII:365–85.

Dougherty, Margot. 1983. "His Highness Prince Karim Aga Khan." In *Life* VI 12:70–80. See also the letter to the editor in Vol. 7, No. 2, February 1984, p. 15.

Dumont, Louis. 1970. *Religion/politics and history in India*. Paris: Mouton.

Dusenbery, Verne A. 1975. "Straight-freak-yogi-Sikh: a 'search for meaning' in contemporary American culture." Unpublished Master's Thesis, Department of Anthropology, University of Chicago.

1980. "Hierarchy, equality and the assertion of Sikh identity in North America." Unpublished paper presented at the Central States Anthropological Association Meeting, April 9–12.

1981. "Canadian ideology and public policy: the impact on Vancouver Sikh ethnic and religious adaptation." *Canadian ethnic studies* XIII, 3:101–19.

Dutta, Manoranjan. 1981. "Asian Indian Americans: search for an economic profile." *Population review* XXV:76–85.

Dwivedi, O. P. 1985. "Samskaras: preserving and protecting the basic Hindu values." *Hindu vishwa* XI, 5:5–10.

Dye, Lee. 1984. "California Sikhs split by bloody strife in homeland." *Los Angeles Times*, 29 May, pp. 1ff.

Employment and Earnings 33 (8), August 1986:115.

Engineer, Asghar Ali. 1980. *The Bohras*. New Delhi: Vikas Publishing House.

Erikson, Erik H. 1980. *Identity and the life cycle*. New York: W. W. Norton.

Esmail, Aziz, & Azim Nanji. 1977. "The Ismailis in history." In *Ismaili contributions to Islamic culture*, ed. Seyyed Hossein Nasr, pp. 225–65. Tehran: Imperial Iranian Academy of Philosophy.

Faruqi, Isma'il Ragi, & David E. Soper. 1974. *Historical atlas of the religions of the world*. New York: Macmillan Publishing Co.

Federal Register, August 23, 1982. Vol. 47:36743.

Fenton, John Y. 1984. "A center of history and opportunity." *Voice of India: inauguration special* IX, 4.

1985. "The Indian community in Atlanta." Unpublished paper presented at the India Cultural and Religious Center in Atlanta, August 10.

Fleuret, Anne K. 1974. "Incorporation into networks among Sikhs in Los Angeles." *Urban Anthropology* III, 1:28–33.

Fornaro, Robert J. 1984. "Asian-Indians in America: acculturation and minority status." *Migration today* XII, 3:29–31.

Fyzee, Asaf A. A. 1960. "Bohoras." In *Encyclopaedia of Islam*, ed. H. A. R. Gibb, J. H. Kramers, E. Levi-Provencal, & J. Schacht, Vol. I. pp. 1254–5. Leiden: E. J. Brill.

1964. *Outlines of Muhammadan Law*. Oxford: Oxford University Press.

1965. "The study of the literature of the Fatimid Da'wa." In *Arabic and Islamic studies in honor of Hamilton A. R. Gibb*, ed. George Makdisi, pp. 232–49. Leiden: Brill.

1969. "The Isma'ilis." In *Islam*, Vol.2, *Religion in the Middle East*, ed. A. J. Arberry, pp. 318–29. Cambridge: Cambridge University Press.

1974. "Book of Faith." From *Pillars of Islam* by al-Qadi al-Nu'man b. Muhammad al-Tamimi, translated from the Arabic. Bombay: Nachiketa.

Gans, Bruce Michael, & Walter L. Lowe. 1980. "The Islam connection." *Playboy*, May, pp. 119–204.

Gans, Herbert J. 1979. "Symbolic ethnicity: the future of ethnic groups and cultures in America." *Ethnic and racial studies* II, 1:1–20.

Gelberg, Steven J.(Subhananda Das), ed. 1983. *Hare Krishna, Hare Krishna*. New York: Grove Press.

1985. "ISKCON after Prabhupada: an update on the Hare Krishna movement." *ISKCON review* I, 1:7–14.

George, Poikail John. 1965. "The St. Thomas Christians and their eucharistic liturgy." Master of Sacred Theology Thesis, Perkins School of Theology of Southern Methodist University, Dallas.

Ghayur, M. Arif. 1980. "Pakistanis." In *Harvard encyclopedia of American ethnic groups*, ed. Stephan Thernstrom, pp. 768–70. Cambridge: Harvard University Press.

1981a. "Muslims in the United States: settlers and visitors." *The annals of the American Academy of Political and Social Sciences* CCCCLIV:150–63.

1981b. "Pakistani Immigrants in America: A Socio-demographic Study." *Pakistan Studies* Vol. 1, No. 1 (Winter 1981):3–23.

1984. "Demographic evolution of Pakistanis in America: case study of a Muslim subgroup." *American journal of Islamic studies* I, 2:113–26.

Gibb, H. A. R. 1960. "Agha Khan." In *Encyclopaedia of Islam*, ed. H. A. R. Gibb, J. H. Kramers, E. Levi-Provencal, & J. Schacht, Vol. I, p. 246. Leiden: E. J. Brill.

Gordon, Milton M. 1964. *Assimilation in American life: the role of race, religion, and national origins*. New York: Oxford University Press.

1981. "Models of pluralism: the new American dilemma." *The annals of the American Academy of Political and Social Sciences* CCCCLIV:178–88.

Haddad, Yvonne. 1983. "The impact of the Islamic revolution in Iran on the Syrian Muslims of Montreal." In *The Muslim community in North America*, ed. Earle Waugh, pp. 165–81. Edmonton: University of Alberta Press.

Haley, Alex. 1966. *The autobiography of Malcolm X*. New York: Grove Press.

Halm, Von Heinz. 1981. "Das 'Buch der Schatten'." *Der Islam* LVIII:15–86.

Haniffa, Aziz. 1984. "Census reports Indians in U.S. are prosperous." *India Abroad*, 2 November, XV, 5:1,22.

Hayes, Victor C., ed. 1986. *Identity issues and world religions*. Selected proceedings, 15th Congress of the International Association of History of Religion. Bedford Park, S. Australia: Australian Association for the Study of Religion.

Helweg, Arthur W. 1983. "East Indians in England and North America." In

Ethnic and immigration groups: the United States, Canada, and England, pp. 93–118. London: The Haworth Press, 1983 (copublished by the Institute for Research in History).

Herberg, Will. 1960. *Protestant, Catholic, Jew.* New York: Anchor Books.

Hess, G. R. 1976. "The forgotten Asian Americans: the East Indian community in the United States." In *The Asian American: the historical experience,* ed. Norris Hundley, pp. 157–88. Santa Barbara, CA: Clio Press.

Hinduism Today. 1986. Vol. 8, No. 1, January 1.

Hodgson, M. G. S. 1960. "Batiniyya." In *Encyclopaedia of Islam,* ed. H. A. R. Gibb, J. H. Kramers, E. Levi-Provencal, & J. Schacht, Vol. I, pp. 1098–2000. Leiden: E. J. Brill.

   1968. "The Isma'ili State." In *Cambridge history of Iran: the Saljuq and Mongol periods,* ed. J. A. Boyle, Vol. 5, pp. 422–82. Cambridge: Cambridge University Press.

Hofstetter, Richard R. 1984. *U.S. immigration policy.* Durham, NC: Duke University Press.

Hogben, Murray. 1983. "The socio-religious behavior of Muslims in Canada: an overview." In *The Muslim community in North America,* ed. Earle Waugh, pp. 111–23. Edmonton: University of Alberta Press.

Hollister, John N. 1953. *The Shia of India.* London: Luzac.

Houston Chronicle, November 12, 1984.

Humme, Reinhart. 1979. "Hinduistische Gurus und Gruppen im Westen." In *Reformatio* XXVIII:165–78.

Hunzai, Allamah Nasir Al-Din Nasir. 1980. *Studies in spiritualism and dreams.* Trans. F. M. Hunzai & Z. R. Qasim. Karachi: Khanah I Hikmat.

Husain, Mian Bhai Mulla Abdul. 1977. *Gulzare Daudi for the Bohras of India: a short note on the Bohras of India, their 21 Imams and 51 Dais, with their customs and tenets.* Surat: Progressive Publication (n.d. for original, 1977 for reprint).

Imam, Zafar, ed. 1975. *Muslims in India.* New Delhi: Orient Longman.

"Immigrants and religion: the persistence of ethnic diversity." *Spectrum* Vol. 2, No. 3, September 1975: 1–9.

"Inde: Les évêques de quatre Eglises de l'Inde." *Irenikon* Vol. 56, No. 1, 1983: 115–17.

India Abroad. 1986. July 4, p. 14.

India News. 1986. June 2.

India Tribune. 1985. November 16, p. 15.

Institute of Applied Manpower Research. "Migration of Indian engineers, scientists and physicians to the United States." IAMR Report No. 2/1968. New Delhi, March, 1968.

Ishi, T. K. 1982. "The political economy of international migration: Indian physicians to the United States." *South Asian bulletin* II, 1:39–58.

Institute for research in history. *Ethnic and immigration groups: the United States, Canada, and England* "Trends in history" Vol. 2, Number 4. New York: The Haworth Press, 1983.

Ismaili Directory USA. 1985. p. xxv.

Ivanow, Wladimir, ed. and trans. 1949. *Six Chapters* or *Shish Fasl*, by Nasir-i Khusraw. Leiden: Brill, The Ismaili Society Series B, No. 6.

— 1961. "Isma'iliya." In *Shorter encyclopaedia of Islam*, ed. H. A. R. Gibb & J. H. Kramers, pp. 179–83. Leiden: E. J. Brill.

Jacoby, Harold S. 1979. "Some demographic and social aspects of early East Indian life in the United States." In *Sikh Studies*, ed. Mark Juergensmeyer & N. Gerald Barrier, pp. 159–71. Berkeley: Graduate Theological Union.

Jafri, S. H. M. 1979. *The origins and early development of Shi'a Islam*. London: Longman.

Jain, Paryushana. 1984. *Essentials of Jainism*. Wellesley, MA: Jain Center of Greater Boston.

Jaina, Padmanabh S. 1979. *The Jaina path to purification*. Berkeley: University of California Press.

Jensen, Joan M. 1980. "East Indians." In *Harvard encyclopedia of American ethnic groups*, ed. Stephan Thernstrom, pp. 296–301. Cambridge: Harvard University Press.

— 1986. *Passage from India*. New Haven: Yale University Press.

Jivrai, S. H. K. n.d. "Brief history of Shia Imami Ismaili Nizari community: its contribution to the world and its future." Mimeographed paper.

Johnson, Steve. 1985. "Media sniglets." *Islamic horizons* XIV, 8:3.

Jotwani, Motilal. 1979. *Sindhi literature and society*. New Delhi: Rajesh Publications.

Judah, J. Stillson. 1974. "The Hare Krishna Movement." In *Religious movements in contemporary America*, ed. Irving I. Zaretsky & Mark P. Leone, pp. 463–78. Princeton: Princeton University Press.

Juergensmeyer, Mark. 1978. "Radhasoami as a trans-national movement." In *Understanding the new religions*, ed. Jacob Needleman & George Baker, pp. 190–200. New York: The Seabury Press.

— 1979. "The Ghadar syndrome: immigrant Sikhs and nationalist pride." In *Sikh Studies*, ed. Mark Juergensmeyer & N. Gerald Barrier, pp. 173–90. Berkeley: Graduate Theological Union.

— 1986. "The logic of religious violence." Unpublished paper presented at the Woodrow Wilson International Center for Scholars, Smithsonian Institution, July 24.

Juergensmeyer, Mark, & N. Gerald Barrier, eds. 1979. *Sikh studies: comparative perspectives on a changing tradition*. Berkeley: Graduate Theological Union.

Kamath, M. V. 1976. *The United States and India 1776–1976*. Washington: The Embassy of India.

Kannappan, S. 1984. "Construction of Hindu temples and cultural centers in foreign countries by Indian immigrants." Privately mimeographed and distributed from Knoxville, TN.

Kapoor, Coomi. 1983. "Parsis: conversion commotion." *India Today*, July 15, p. 85.

Keely, Charles B. 1979. "Immigration policy and the new immigration." In *Sourcebook on the new immigration*, ed. Roy Simon Bryce-Laporte, pp. 15–25. New Brunswick, NJ: Transaction Books.

Keshavjee, Rafique Habib. 1981. "The quest for gnosis and the call of history: modernization among the Ismailis of Iran." Thesis presented to the Committee on Middle Eastern Studies, Harvard University.

Khakee, Gulshan. 1972. *"The dasa Avatara* of the Satpanthi Ismailis and the Imam Shahis of Indo-Pakistan." Thesis presented to Department of Near Eastern Languages and Literatures, Harvard University.

King, Ursula. 1983. "A report about Hinduism in Britain." From the author's typescript translation of her article in *Zeitschrift für Missionswissenschaft und Religionswissenschaft*, July 1983/3: 220–36.

Knott, Kim. 1986. *My sweet Lord: the Hare Krishna movement.* Wellingborough: Aquarias Press.

Kolm, Richard. 1980. *The change of cultural identity: an analysis of factors conditioning the cultural integration of immigrants.* New York: Arno Press.

LaBrack, Bruce. 1979. "Sikhs real and ideal: a discussion of text and context in the description of overseas Sikh communities." In *Sikh Studies*, ed. Mark Juergensmeyer & N. Gerald Barrier, pp. 127–42. Berkeley: Graduate Theological Union.

Lee, Raymond L. M. 1982. "Sai Baba, salvation and syncretism: religious change in a Hindu movement in urban Malaysia." *Contributions to Indian Sociology* (NS) XVI, 1:125–40.

Leonardo, Michael Di. 1984. *The varieties of ethnic experience: kinship, class and gender among California Italian-Americans*, ed. Roger Sanjek. Ithaca, NY: Cornell University Press, Anthropology of Contemporary Issues.

Lewis, Bernard. 1967. *The assassins: a radical sect in Islam.* London: Weidenfeld and Nicolson.

Lincoln, C. Eric. 1983. "The American Muslim Mission in the context of American social history." In *The Muslim community in North America*, ed. Earle Waugh, pp. 215–33. Edmonton: University of Alberta Press.

Little, David. 1984. "American civil religion and the rise of pluralism." *Union Seminary Quarterly Review* XXXVIII, 3/4:401–13.

Lokhandwalla, Sh. T. 1955. "The Bohras, a Muslim community of Gujarat." *Stvdia Islamica* III, 117–35.

Lovell, Emily Kalled. 1983. "Islam in the United States: past and present." In *The Muslim community in North America*, ed. Earle Waugh, pp. 93–110. Edmonton: University of Alberta Press.

Lyon, Michael H. 1973. "Ethnicity in Britain: the Gujarati tradition." *New Community: A Journal of the Community Relations Commission* II: 1–11.

McLeod, W. H. 1976. *The evolution of the Sikh community.* Oxford: Clarendon Press.

Madelung, W. 1978. "Isma'iliyya." In *The encyclopaedia of Islam*, IV, New Edition. ed. E. van Donzel, B. Lewis, & Ch. Pellat, pp. 198–206. Leiden: E. J. Brill.

   1979. "Khodja." In *The encyclopaedia of Islam*, V, New Edition. ed. C. E. Bosworth, E. van Donzel, B. Lewis, & Ch. Pellat. pp. 25–7. Leiden: E. J. Brill.

Makarem, Sami Nasib. 1972. *The doctrine of the Ismailis.* Beirut: The Arab Institute for Research and Publishing.

Malankara Light. Vol. 5, No. 1.

Mamiya, Lawrence H. 1982. "From Black Muslim to Bilalian: the evolution of a movement." *Journal for the Scientific Study of Religion* XXI:138–52.

Mangalwadi, Vishal. 1977. *The world of the gurus.* New Delhi: Vikas Publishing House.

Marlin, John Tepper, James S. Avery, & Stephen T. Collins. 1983. *The book of American city rankings.* New York: Facts on File Publications.

Marsh, Clifton E. 1984. *From Black Muslims to Muslims: the transition from separatism to Islam, 1930–1980.* Metuchen, NJ: The Scarecrow Press.

Mathews, Moran Mar Baselius Marthoma I. 1983. "Address." *Christian Orient* IV:192–4.

Mavalwala, Jamshed. 1977. "Demography of the North American Zoroastrian community." *Proceedings of the second North American Zoroastrian symposium,* pp. 63–73. Chicago: Zoroastrian Association of Metropolitan Chicago.

Mehirnally, Akbaraly. 1982. *From Abraham to Aga Khan.* Vancouver: Akbaraly Mehirnally.

Melendy, Howard Brett. 1977. *Asians in America: Filipinos, Koreans and East Indians.* Boston: Twayne Publishers.

Melton, J. Gordon. 1978. *The encyclopedia of American religions,* 2 vols. Wilmington, NC: McGrath Publishing Co.

1985. *The encyclopedia of American religions,* First Edition Supplement. Detroit: Gale Research Company.

Michael, R. Blake. 1985. "Heaven, West Virginia: legitimation techniques of ISKCON." *ISKCON Review* I, 1:26–8.

Misra, Satish C. 1964. *Muslim communities in Gujarat: preliminary studies in their history and social organization.* New York: Asia Publishing House.

Mistree, Khojeste P. 1982. *Zoroastrianism: an ethnic perspective.* Bombay: Zoroastrian Studies.

Mol, J. J. 1977. *Identity and the sacred: a sketch for a new social-scientific theory of religion.* New York: Free Press.

Muslim Students Association. 1981. "Nineteenth Annual Report of the Muslim Students Association."

Nanji, Azim. 1972. "The Nizari Isma'ili tradition in Hind and Sind." Thesis submitted to the Faculty of Graduate Studies, McGill University.

1974. "Modernization and change in the Nizari Ismaili community in East Africa – a perspective." *Journal of Religion in Africa* VI, 2:123–39.

1975. "The Ginans tradition among the Nizari Ismailis." In *Actes du XXIXe Congress International des Orientalistes,* Paris: Etudes Arabes et Ismaliques, I:3.

1983. "The Nizari Ismaili Muslim community in North America: background and development." In *The Muslim community in North America,* ed. Earle Waugh, pp. 149–64. Edmonton: University of Alberta Press.

1984. "A Religious Minority in Transition: The case of two Isma'ili Communities." *Papers in Comparative Studies,* 1984 pp. 169–82.

Narayan, R. K. 1985. "A passage to America." *Town & Country* CXXXIX, May, pp. 168ff.

National Science Foundation. 1967. *Scientists and engineers from abroad 1962–64.* Surveys of Science Resources Series, NSF 67–3.

National Science Foundation. 1972. *Scientists, engineers, and physicians from abroad: trends through fiscal year 1970.* Surveys of Science Resources Series, NSF 72–312.

Nasr, Seyyed Hossein. 1966. "Sunnism & Shi'ism Twelve-Imam Shi'ism and Isma'ilism." In *Ideals and realities of Islam*, ed. Seyyed Hossein Nasr, pp. 147–78. Boston: Beacon Press.

Nasr, Seyyed Hossein, ed. 1977. *Ismaili contributions to Islamic culture.* Tehran: Imperial Iranian Academy of Philosophy.

Nathwani, N. P., Chairman. 1979. Dawoodi Bohra Commission (Nathwani Commission) Report [of investigation conducted by the Commission appointed by the Citizens for Democracy into the alleged infringment of human rights of reformist members of the Dawoodi Bohras in the name of the High Priest]. Bombay: Arun Naik, Akshar Pratiroop.

Neill, Stephen. 1984. *A history of Christianity in India: the beginnings to 1707.* Cambridge: Cambridge University Press.

1985. *A history of Christianity in India: 1707 to 1858.* Cambridge: Cambridge University Press.

New York Amsterdam News. 1964. May 23, p. 14.

Off, Carol. 1982. "A new battlefield for India's Sikhs." *Macleans* 95:58–60.

Papanak, Hanna. 1962. "Leadership and social change in the Khoja Ismaili community." Ph.D. dissertation submitted to the Department of Social Relations, Radcliffe College.

Patel, Abdussamad. 1976. "Role of the CCIM in India." In *Role of Muslims in changing India*, ed. Azizur Rahman, pp. 15–19. Chicago: Consultative Committee on Indian Muslims, A CCIM Newsletter Supplement.

Pittsburgh Courier. 1965. March 6, p. 4.

Pocock, David F. 1976. "Preservation of the religious life: Hindu immigrants in England." *Contributions to Indian Sociology*, New Series X:341–65.

Pope John Paul II. 1983. "Address of Pope John Paul on the occasion of the visit of the Catholicos of the Malankara Orthodox Church on June 3, 1983." *Christian Orient* IV:191–4.

Pothacamury, Thomas. 1958. *The church in independent India.* World Horizon Reports #22. New York: Maryknoll Publications.

Pthan, S. G. 1963. *The Syrian Christians of Kerala.* New York: Asia Publishing House.

Pycior, Julie Leininger. 1983. "Acculturation and pluralism in recent studies of American immigration history." In *Ethnic and immigration groups: the United States, Canada, and England*, ed. P. J. F. Rosof, W. Zeisel, J. B. Quandt, & M. Maayan, pp. 21–30. New York: Haworth Press.

Qureshi, Regula B., & Saleem M. M. Qureshi. 1983. "Pakistani Canadians: the making of a Muslim community." In *The Muslim community in North America*, ed. Earle Waugh, pp. 127–48. Edmonton: University of Alberta Press.

Rajeke, Barakat Ahmad. 1963. *Ahmadiyya movement in India.* Qadian, Pakistan: Mirza Wasim Ahmad.

Richardson, E. Allen. 1981. *Islamic cultures in North America: patterns, belief and devotion of Muslims from Asian countries in the United States and Canada.* New York: The Pilgrim Press.

Rochford, E. Burke Jr. 1985. *Hare Krishna in America.* New Brunswick, NJ: Rutgers University Press.

Roy, Shibani. 1984. *The Dawoodi Bohras: an anthropological perspective.* Delhi: B. R. Publishing Corporation.

Ruthven, Malise. 1984. *Islam in the world.* Oxford: Oxford University Press.

Rutledge, Paul James. 1982. "The role of religion in ethnic self-identity: the Vietnamese in Oklahoma City, 1975–1982." Ph.D. dissertation, University of Oklahoma. Ann Arbor, MI: University Microfilms International.

Sangave, Vilas Adinath. 1959. *Jaina community: a social survey.* Bombay: Popular Book Depot.

Sano, Roy I. 1983. "The role of Pacific and Asian Americans in theological education." *Theological Education,* Autumn 1983: 79–92.

Saran, Parmatma. 1979. "New Ethnics: The Case of the East Indians in New York City." In *Sourcebook on the new immigration,* ed. Roy Simon Bryce-Laporte, pp. 303–12. New Brunswick, NJ: Transaction Books.

 1985. *The Asian Indian experience in the United States.* Cambridge, MA: Schenkman Publishing Co.

Saran, Parmatma, & Edwin Eames, eds. 1980. *The new ethnics: Asian Indians in the United States.* New York: Praeger Publishers.

Saran, Parmatma, & Philip J. Leonhard-Spark. 1980. "Attitudinal and behavioral profile." In *The new ethnics,* ed. Parmatma Saran & Edwin Eames, pp. 163–76. New York: Praeger Publishers.

Schermerhorn, R. A. 1978. *Ethnic plurality in India.* Tucson: University of Arizona Press.

Schimmel, Annemarie. 1975. *Mystical dimensions of Islam.* Chapel Hill: University of North Carolina.

 1980. *Islam in the Indian subcontinent.* Leiden: Brill.

Segal, Aaron. 1983. "Three Moslem heterodox sects: the Alawis, Druze, and Ismailis." Unpublished paper given at the Texas Association of Middle East Scholars, Austin, October 7.

Shariff, A. R. D. 1982. "Spiritual heritage of the Ismailis." *Roshni,* October: 5–7.

Shinn, Larry D. 1985. "Changing patterns in ISKCON's membership?" *ISKCON Review,* I:24–5.

Siddiqui, Nafis Ahmad. 1973. "Religious groups in Kerala: growth (1951–61) and distribution (1961)." *The Geographer* XX:54–74.

 1976. *Population geography of Muslims of India.* New Delhi: S. Chand & Co.

Sievers, Angelika. 1964. "Christian groups in Kerala (India)." In *Abstract of Papers, Twentieth International Geographical Congress,* ed. R. E. I. Hamilton, p. 289. London: Nelson, 1964.

Singh, Gurdial. 1946. "East Indians in the United States." *Sociology and Social Research* XXX:208–16.

Singh, I. J. Bahadur, ed. 1979. *The other India: the overseas Indians and their relationship with India.* New Delhi: Arnold-Heinemann.

Singh, Rahul. 1983. "Living the American dream." *Asia*, Jan/Feb: 38–45.

Sklare, Marshall, & Joseph Greenblum. 1967. *Jewish identity on the suburban frontier*. New York: Basic Books.

Smith, Bruce L. R. 1979. "The brain drain re-emergent: foreign medical graduates in American medical schools." *Minerva* XVII:483–503.

Srinivas, M. N. 1962. "A note on sanskritization and westernization." In *Caste in modern India and other essays*, pp. 42–62. Bombay: Asia Publishing House.

Staal, J. F. 1963. "Sanskrit and sanskritization." *Journal of Asian Studies* XIII, 3:261–75.

Taylor, Colleen. 1977. "Indians in America." *The Indic Magazine*, Feb/March: 16–18.

Thernstrom, Stephan, ed. 1980. *Harvard Encyclopedia of American Ethnic Groups*. Cambridge, MA: Harvard University Press.

Thoma, Juhanon Mar. 1968. *Christianity in India and a brief history of the Mar Thoma Syrian Church*, rev. ed. Madras: K. M. Cherian.

Thomas, Annamma, & T. M. Thomas. 1984. *Kerala immigrants in America: a sociological study of the St. Thomas Christians*. Cochin, India: Simons Printers.

Thomas, T. J. 1978. "The shepherding perspective of Seward Hiltner on pastoral care and its application in the organizing of a congregation in Dallas of East Indian Immigrants from the Mar Thoma Syrian Church of India." Doctor of the Ministry Thesis, Perkins School of Theology, Southern Methodist University.

Tillich, Paul. 1967. *Perspectives on 19th and 20th century Protestant theology*. New York: Harper & Row.

Timberg, Thomas A., ed. 1986. *Jews in India*. New York: Advent Books.

Tinker, Hugh. 1977. *The banyan tree: overseas emigrants from India, Pakistan and Bangladesh*. Oxford: Oxford University Press.

Tisserant, Eugene Cardinal. 1957. *Eastern Christianity in India: a history of the Syro-Malabar Church*. Westminster, MD: The Newman Press.

Titus, Murray Thurston. 1930. *The religious quest of India: Indian Islam*. Oxford: Oxford University Press.

Tomasi, Silvano M. 1975. *Piety and power and the role of the Italian parishes in the New York metropolitan area 1880–1930*. Staten Island, NY: Center for Migration Studies.

Tully, Mark, & Satish Jacob. 1985. *Amritsar: Mrs Gandhi's last battle*. London: Jonathan Cape.

United States Congress. 1965. Public Law 89–236, 89th Congress, H.R. 2580, October 3.

United States Department of Commerce. *1970 Census of Population, Supplementary Report: Country of Origin, Mother Tongue, and Citizenship for the United States*. PC(S1)–35, April 1973.

United States Department of Commerce, *1980 Census of Population*. PC80–1–B15:114.

United States Department of Commerce. *1980 Census of Population*. PC80-1-B45:138.

United States Department of Commerce. *1980 Census of Population: Characteristics of the Population*. PC80–1–C1:1–389–401, Tables 106 & 248.

United States Department of Commerce. *1980 Census of Population: United States Summary*. PC80–1–D1–A, Table 255A.

United States Department of Commerce. *1980 Census of Population: United States Summary*. PC80–1–D1–C:Table 342.

United States Department of Commerce. *1980 Census of Population: Race of the Population by States*. PC80–S1–3:8.

United States Department of Commerce, *1980 Census of Population: Supplementary Report, Ancestry by State*. PC80–S1–10:21, Table 3.

United States Department of Commerce. *1980 Census of Population: Asian and Pacific Islander, Population by State*. PC80–S1–12:2,8.

United States Department of Commerce News. 1984. "Socioeconomic Characteristics of U.S. Foreign-born Population Detailed in Census Bureau Tabulations," CB84–179, Oct 17.

United States Department of Health, Education, and Welfare. *Immigration of graduates of foreign nursing schools: report of the conference*. Bethesda, Maryland June 23–24, 1975. DHEW Publication No. HRA 76–84.

United States Department of Labor, Bureau of Labor Statistics. "Employment and earnings," February 1986.

United States Immigration and Naturalization Service. 1982. *Statistical Yearbook of the Immigration and Naturalization Service*.

United States Supreme Court. 1923. "United States vs. Bhagat Singh," 261, U.S. 204, February 19.

Unna, Warren. 1985. *Sikhs abroad: attitudes and activities of Sikhs settled in the United States and Canada*. Calcutta: The Statesman.

Varma, V. S. 1984. *Census of India 1981, Series–1 India, Paper 3 of 1984: Household Population by Religion of Head of Household*. New Delhi: Registrar General & Census Commissioner for India.

Vatikiotis, Panayiotis. 1957. *The Fatimid theory of the state*. Lahore: Muhammad Ashraf Publisher.

Velacherry, Joseph. 1983. "Communal conflict between Christians and Muslims in Kerala." *Social Action* XXXIII:420–42.

von der Mehden, Fred R., ed. 1984. *The ethnic groups of Houston*. Houston: Rice University Studies.

Walji, Shirin Remtulla. 1974. "A history of the Ismaili community in Tanzania." Ph.D. dissertation in history, University of Wisconsin, Madison.

Walpole, Norman C., Sharon Arkin, N. Ghatate, H. J. John, A. B. Matthews, & R. Shinn. 1964. *U.S. Army handbook for India*. Washington: U.S. Government Printing Office.

Walsh, Gerard P. (compiler). 1981. *Naturalization Laws*. Washington: U.S. Government Printing Office.

Waugh, Earle H. 1983. "Muslim leadership and the shaping of the umma: classical tradition and the religious tension in the North American setting." In *The Muslim community in North American*, pp.11–33. Edmonton: University of Alberta Press.

Waugh, Earle H., Baba Aub-Laban, & Regula B. Qureshi, eds. 1983. *The Mus-

lim community in North America. Edmondton: University of Alberta Press.

Wenzel, Lawrence A. 1968. "The rural Punjabis of California: a religio-ethnic group." *Phylon* XXIX:245–56.

Whitehurst, James Emerson. 1980. "Black Muslims: healing the hate." *The Christian Century*, February 27: 225–9.

1983. "U.S. Zoroastrian center built." *The Christian Century*, October 19: 927–8.

Williams, Raymond B. 1982. "Holy man as religious specialist: the acharya tradition in Vaishnavism." *Encounter* XLIII, 1:61–97.

1984. *A new face of Hinduism: the Swaminarayan religion.* Cambridge: Cambridge University Press.

1985. "Holy man as abode of God in the Swaminarayan religion." In *Gods of flesh/ gods of stone*, ed. J. P. Waghorne & Norman Cutler, pp. 142–57. Chambersburg, PA: Anima Press.

1986a. "Translating Indian Christianity to the United States." *The Christian Century*, October 15: 989–90.

1986b. "The guru as pastoral counselor." *The Journal of Pastoral Care* XL, 4:331-40.

1987. "Hinduism in America." *The Christian Century* March 11: 247–9.

Wright, Theodore. 1972. "Question of minority identity in a pluralistic society." In *The Muslim minority in India*, ed. Syed Z. Abedin, pp. 4–9. Kalamazoo, MI: Muslim Students Association.

Yasin, Mohammad. 1958. *A social history of Islamic India 1605–1748.* Lucknow: The Upper India Publishing House.

Index